The Insurrection of Little Selves

To my father
the late Professor R.L. Nigam,
a passionate teacher and lifelong rationalist

The Insurrection of Little Selves
The Crisis of Secular-Nationalism in India

Aditya Nigam

OXFORD
UNIVERSITY PRESS

OXFORD
UNIVERSITY PRESS

YMCA Library Building, Jai Singh Road, New Delhi 110001

Oxford University Press is a department of the University of Oxford.
It furthers the University's objective of excellence in research,
scholarship, and education by publishing worldwide in

Oxford New York

Auckland Cape Town Dar es Salaam Hong Kong Karachi
Kuala Lumpur Madrid Melbourne Mexico City Nairobi
New Delhi Shanghai Taipei Toronto

With offices in

Argentina Austria Brazil Chile Czech Republic France Greece
Guatemala Hungary Italy Japan Poland Portugal Singapore
South Korea Switzerland Thailand Turkey Ukraine Vietnam

Oxford is a registered trade mark of Oxford University Press
in the UK and in certain other countries

Published in India by Oxford University Press, New Delhi

ISBN-13: 978-0-19-567606-8
ISBN-10: 0-19-567606-8

Printed in India at De-Unique, New Delhi - 110 018
Published by Manzar Khan, Oxford University Press
YMCA Library Building, Jai Singh Road, New Delhi 110 001

Contents

Acknowledgements

In these days of 'intellectual property rights' it seems necessary to reiterate, after Roland Barthes, that the author, in whose name the claim for these rights is made, is long dead! That is the ethical imperative. As authors, we merely build on what we have already received from the intellectual labour of others who came before us. We can never adequately acknowledge all the influences that form and constitute us – except by being dishonest to ourselves. Nonetheless, let me try to enumerate at least those that I can identify.

I had the privilege of growing up in the small provincial town of Dehra Dun, in the house of the legendary M.N. Roy, my father R.L. Nigam, having been his close associate. My parents were, in different ways, fired by the liberatory humanism of the Enlightenment. Humanism and rationalism and what used to be called 'women's liberation', were an integral part of my socialization.

Like many of my generation, I almost inevitably drifted into the communist movement in the turbulent early 1970s. These were formative years and I learnt a lot about life during the seventeen years I spent there, interacting with others like myself and with the people among whom I worked. All of them cannot be named but their contribution to my intellectual and political understanding can hardly be overestimated.

The massacre of Sikhs in 1984 proved to be a decisive moment, raising questions about identity and selfhood in ways that would not eventually leave intact the naïve rationalism and humanism of the young communist. Then came the 'irresistible rise' of the Hindu Right, the battles around the Mandal commission, raising ever-new questions with each passing day. To cap it all, the turn of the 1980s saw the rapid collapse of the socialist world, adding to the intellectual churning that was already beginning to take shape, at least among some people, in India. Endless discussions with hundreds of people went into forming the way I began seeing things from now on: my comrades in the CPI(M), ordinary people with whom I used to interact on a daily basis, the workers of the Municipal

Workers' Lal Jhanda Union, and, later, my colleagues at the Indira Gandhi National Open University. Subsequently, my interaction with non-governmental organizations (NGOs), especially with people involved with ecological struggles on the one hand and with those involved in the Dalit movement, have all introduced me to different ways of seeing the world. In this respect, interactions with some of my colleagues in Lokayan and Society for Participatory Research in Asia (PRIA) really opened out a whole new world for me. My involvement with citizens' initiatives like the Peoples' Movement for Secularism, Delhi Janwadi Adhikar Manch, the antinuclear and peace movements and more recently, Yamunapaar Residents' Initiative (YARI) and Aman Ekta Manch, has continued to provide me with a community of friends and a political context within which I have attempted to think the complex questions thrown up by contemporary Indian politics.

Intellectually, my coming to the Centre for the Study of Developing Societies (CSDS) in early 1996, proved to be the turning point. The heady intellectual atmosphere of the CSDS in those days was intoxicating. Everything that I had in terms of questions, could slowly begin to make sense in the course of interminable arguments. The intellectual stimulus from friends and colleagues like Ravi Vasudevan, Ravi Sundaram, Shiv Vishvanathan, D.R. Nagaraj, Yogendra Yadav, Rustam Singh, Javeed Alam, not to mention, of course senior colleagues like Ashis Nandy and D.L. Sheth, really made it possible to understand where the various questions I was grappling with were leading me to. In later years, this conversation was to continue with many of them and the influence of those conversations will be evident throughout this book.

Apart from these named and unnamed influences, there is a huge intellectual community of friends to whom I am indebted in different ways: Javeed Alam, Biswamoy Pati, Abhay Kumar Dube, Sudhir Chandra, Geetanjalishree, Harsh Sethi, Chandrabhan Prasad, Ravikant, Awadhendra Sharan, Subhash Gatade, Ranjana Padhi, Rajesh Gupta, Ranjani Mazumdar, Rishikant, Dilip Menon, Charu Gupta, Mukul Sharma, Anil Chaudhary, V. Radhika, Vijay Pratap, Rakesh Kapoor, Rajendra Ravi, Khurshid Anwar, Apoorvanand, Sohail Hashmi, Partha Chatterjee, Alok Rai, Radhika Singha, Monobina Gupta, Gopal Guru, Valerian Rodrigues, Tani Bhargava, Shuddhabrata Sengupta, Jeebesh Bagchi, Avinash Jha, Peter De Souza, Rajaram Tolpadi, Sudipta Kaviraj, Janaki Abraham, Shahana Bhattacharya, Jinee Lokaneeta, Sanjay Mishra, S. Anandhi, Arvind Ghosh, Ravindra Shukla, Rada Ivekovic, Shraddhanand Solanki, P.K. Shahi, Shivakant, and Amitabha Mukhopadhyay.

I am also indebted to my colleagues in the ongoing, shared intellectual project involving explorations of new postnational histories and politics from the south: M.S.S. Pandian, Nivedita Menon, Akbar Zaidi, Pradeep Jeganathan, Malathi de Alwis, Mary John, and Satish Deshpande.

Rajeev Bhargava has been the most accommodating and understanding supervisor for the thesis that eventually grew into this book. But he has been much more: a friend and a mentor with whom one has had the freedom to quarrel endlessly. My deepest appreciation and gratitude to him. I must also thank all my teachers at the Centre for Political Studies, Jawaharlal Nehru University for enabling my return to academics after a decade-long absence.

The other institution that made possible my return to academics and to which my debt can never be quantified, is the institution where I currently work, namely, CSDS, Delhi. Even when I was not working with CSDS, the Centre's library and other infrastructural facilities were made available to me. Without this institutional back-up, my doctoral work could not have been done within the limited time I had at my disposal. I must specially mention the Centre's Director at that time, Prof. V.B. Singh, who made this possible. Sujit Deb, the Centre's Librarian at that time also extended every possible support for my research work—then and ever after. The institutional support made available to me by *Lokniti*, the Programme on Comparative Democracy, with which I worked as honorary Associate Fellow initially and later by the Sarai Programme of the Centre with which I worked as Fellow for over a year, was indispensable for my being able to continue my work. I also wish to thank the entire staff of the CSDS, for the ready help and the visible and not-so-visible support that one could always count on. I wish to especially thank Himanshu Bhattacharya, K.A.Q.A. Hilal, Ghanshyam, Ruddar Singh, Bhuvan Chandra, Jabbar Singh, Jayashree, Hemlata, Purnima, Kanchan, and Ramesh. I also wish to express my gratitude to my present colleagues in the CSDS faculty for continued intellectual exchanges.

I also want to thank the Nehru Memorial Museum and Library, Teen Murti and all the staff who extended all manner of cooperation for my work during the long months spent there.

I am grateful to South-South Exchange Programme for Research on the History of Development (SEPHIS), the Netherlands, whose financial support was critical for the research and writing of the thesis, which has now taken the shape of this book. During that period I also received a visiting fellowship to the South Asia Visiting Scholars Programme, Queen Elizabeth House, Oxford in March to June 1998. In 1999, I had the opportunity of a visiting fellowship at Birkbeck College, University of London. Both of these provided an opportunity to work in libraries in England as also to interact with various scholars in these institutions.

I am extremely grateful to Shahid Amin whose intellectual and practical support in the publication of this book has been invaluable.

My editors at Oxford University Press, Delhi, have been accommodating and efficient, for which my thanks.

I wish to thank *Economic and Political Weekly*, where what is now Chapter 5 was initially published: 'Secularism, Modernity, Nation: An Epistemology of the Dalit Critique', *Economic and Political Weekly*, vol. 35, no. 48, 25 November 2000.

I cannot adequately thank Manjari and Milon Chandra Gupta, for their selfless support in difficult times. My special thanks to Manjari Gupta for her hospitality during my field trip to Calcutta.

I am grateful to Vishwas Satgar and Langa Zita, for the long nights of endless discussions on the problems of the South African Revolution and the new horizons for socialism in the twenty-first century. My thanks to them also for their hospitality and for introducing me to other leaders of the South African Communist Party and the African National Congress.

My deepest gratitude to my family members: my mother Santwana, her partner Rajinder Nath, my sister Aditi and brother-in-law Shankar Raghuraman and their daughters, Anya and Trina who have been a constant source of strength and sustenance in more ways than one. Also Devaki and B.M. Menon, Pramada, Lara, and little Naima.

To Susheela, our everyday back-up.

To Monobina Gupta, I owe a personal debt such that it is difficult to adequately acknowledge. To Anirban, who begins his adventure in the life of ideas in an uncertain and catastrophic world.

Finally, to Nivedita Menon, with whom this intellectual and political journey acquired special meaning.

Introduction

The object of this book is the entity called 'secular-nationalism'. As the ruling ideology of the postcolonial Indian state and elite, it represents a specific, historically constituted, ideological configuration. At the same time, it has a kinship with other similar ideological formations elsewhere in the postcolonial world. Equally important is the wider kinship it enjoys with the two great ideologies of modernity—secularism and nationalism—that it draws from but with which the exact nature of its relationship is unclear. The common-sense understanding seems to be that it is the direct descendant of the marriage between the two—standing in opposition to both Hindu and Muslim communal nationalisms. Much of the recent debate in India has centred on the ideology of *secularism*.[1] *Nationalism* as a category, on the other hand, has been relatively less debated, except among Marxists in the 1970s but here too, the category of the 'nation' itself has not been put to any serious scrutiny and the central preoccupation has been with the question of the 'right to self-determination' and whether India is *a* nation.[2] More recently, from the mid-1980s onwards, political theorists in India have focused on the discourse of Indian nationalism and its formation in the late nineteenth century.[3] Some valuable historiographical work on the construction of nationalism has appeared subsequently. However, the conjunctive term *secular-nationalism*, has been used more descriptively and there has not really been much discussion about it. Since my concern here is not merely the object called 'secular-nationalism' but more specifically, its *crisis* in the last two decades, it is necessary to situate the discussion of the problem within the overall context of the moment that constitutes this crisis.

I believe this context to be a larger, global condition that marks our times, a condition I describe, drawing on a Foucauldian expression, as the 'insurrection of little selves'.[4] This condition could be said to mark a deep crisis of the political project of modernity that became manifest in the penultimate decades of the twentieth century. It is a phenomenon that has been referred to by many other names depending upon the intellectual orientations of the authors concerned—namely 'identity politics', 'politics of particularisms', or more generally the 'crisis of modern universalisms'. Jean-Francois Lyotard, in his well-known—and often misconstrued— description of the postmodern condition, described it as the 'incredulity towards metanarratives'.[5] Though Lyotard used the term in the context of the situation of knowledge and its legitimizing structures, it also clearly refers to the larger context of politics. This 'incredulity towards metanarratives', particularly the modern metanarratives of emancipation, applies in equal measure, to the two great visions of the modern West— the liberal project of abstract citizenship and the Marxist project of a 'new man' (sic) and a classless society. From the ruins of the former Soviet Union and the East European bloc to the entire postcolonial world, we have been witness to the rise of these myriad assertions of Selfhood, in what seems to be a perpetual war against one another—often giving the impression of a kind of Hobbesian 'war of all against all'. Even the supposedly 'mature' Western liberal democracies have not been immune to the assertion of identities that had so far been thought to be already relegated to the domain of the 'past'. The liberal democracies in the West are suddenly faced with the emergence of what one may call, paraphrasing Stuart Hall, the *other* Europeans, or the *other* Americans who 'come from Jamaica, Pakistan, Bangladesh and India',[6] endangering the very idea of abstract citizenship. Further, the problem is not just due to the more recent large-scale immigration from former colonies, but equally to the fresh assertion of identities such as the Scottish and Welsh in Britain, in the recent past. Racism and anti-Semitism have of course been old problems of liberal democracies but until recently, there was still the hope that one day, humanity would leave all these markers of identity behind, and the great dream of abstract citizenship would be realized. At the beginning of the twenty-first century that dream seems further away than ever before. A deep chasm seems to perennially divide the enlightened, 'progressive' elite whose dream this is, and the 'backward', sectarian 'masses' who continually frustrate its fulfilment. The actual dynamic of the way in which this chasm manifests itself, is of course infinitely more complicated than the formulation above allows. For the activity of the 'masses' is never free of elite interventions, nor are they internally homogeneous. Further, there is a divide between the 'masses' of the majority and dominant cultures and those of the minority cultures.

This experience is as global as modernity itself; it is something that marks modern politics everywhere. In the postcolonial world this chasm appears in the context of the attempt in different societies to build a 'modern nation'. This book explores the crisis of the secular-nationalist project in India in the context of the experience described above.

One of the claims of this study is that this vision of the Enlightenment project is ridden with a fundamental aporia because of at least two interrelated, underlying problems. First, the emancipatory project is fundamentally tied to the agency of the enlightened elite, which is seen as the carrier of Reason and Progress. This idea is based on the assumption of the inertia and backwardness of the masses who have to be delivered from darkness and brought to light. The second, related problem is that this vision is virtually innocent of any understanding of power. As a result, it is unable to comprehend the possibility that *these 'inert masses' could actively resist attempts at 'enlightenment'* for reasons that may have to do with the asymmetries of power and the privileges enjoyed by this elite. The Marxist variant of this project did try to address both these questions but its metaphysical resolution of the problem which arbitrarily made the 'working class' the sole privileged agent of History in effect avoided addressing the problem in any meaningful sense.[7] It seems to me that this question has become one of the most fundamental political and intellectual questions of our times. Undoubtedly, the trajectories of the West and the postcolonial world differ in very fundamental ways and one of the objectives of this book is to understand the specificities of the postcolonial predicament. Nevertheless, the fact remains that the global spread of modern ideas and institutions has made some of these questions live and burning ones, notwithstanding their origins in the West.

This study, therefore, argues that none of these assumptions of the Enlightenment are unproblematic and at the root of the impasse of its vision lies the notion of subjectivity inaugurated by it. The modern subject that was expected to simply ascend from the constitutive attachments of community life into the realm of citizenship, actually followed a very different trajectory and revealed in the process, the complex nature of 'free will' and disengaged agency. It is worthwhile therefore to lay out the terrain of the problem of modern subjectivity that frames all the subsequent discussions that will follow. I must state quite clearly that I will not make the larger claim that all that the Enlightenment represents is therefore, passé.[8]

In the rest of the introduction, I will set the stage for the discussions that follow in the subsequent chapters. In the first section, I will discuss what appear to me to be the most critical problems of modern subjectivity and the deeply problematic nature of the assumption that 'individuation' inevitably leads to the dissolution of community attachments and the emergence of the rational, autonomous subject. Through a reading of a number of different texts, I will discuss how such moments of transformation defy the simple schema of change from *gemeinschaft* to *gessellschaft* formations and lead to new imaginations and constructions of community. In the second section, I will discuss nationalism as one of the paradigmatic forms of this new community, linked to modern subjectivity. In the third section, I will focus on the ways in which this experience actually takes shape in the postcolonial context and where it diverges significantly from the European experience. In the fourth section, I will discuss nationalisms' attempts to create homogeneous national cultures, within the larger question of the new time-consciousness of modernity. I will especially be concerned in this section with the question of 'minority cultures' and their extremely problematic relationship with the project of nationhood. In the fifth section, I will examine the problematic concept of a 'totality' upon which, I argue, arise both the idea of a nation and that of 'World-History'. In the final section, I will return to the problem of the so-called opportunism of minority cultures through a discussion of two specific cases—one in relation to nationalism from India, and the other in relation to 'World-History', taken from the Balkan experience.

The Travails of Modern Subjectivity

Following a whole tradition of the critique of modern subjectivity, I argue that it is in the institution of 'man' as the measure of all things, as the knowing Subject, that some of the most fundamental problems of contemporary politics can be located. Here I draw from the tradition extending from Nietzsche and Heidegger to some more recent poststructuralist critiques of subjectivity. Second, I suggest that as a corollary of this, the entire edifice of modern politics is in crisis today as a consequence of its rationalist assumptions based on the idea of subject-centred Reason. It is on this basis that modern politics erects the entire theoretical logic of liberal democracy and its concomitant vision of abstract citizenship—to which the idea of nationhood itself is historically tied.[9] It is the latter that we shall be more directly concerned with here but it is necessary to outline some of the fundamental points of the critique of the very concept of subjectivity before proceeding further.

Heidegger describes the 'modern' as that period 'which is defined by the fact that man becomes the measure and centre of beings'. 'Man', he says, 'is what lies at the bottom of all beings; that is in modern terms, at the bottom of all objectification and representability'.[10] According to David

Kolb, Heidegger contends that the modern self affirms itself in and through giving measure to other beings. 'To be a subject in the modern sense is precisely to be capable of bringing things to presence before oneself, to be able to represent the world to oneself.' Modern subjectivity, he argues in his exegesis of Heidegger, exists as a subject when it imposes order. 'To impose a self-originated order on other things is an act of will.'[11] This understanding of the subject as a creature of will is what we will encounter in the course of the discussion that follows.

Charles Taylor describes modern 'rationalism' as a certain conception of reason wherein 'the thinking agent' had been 'shaped by a kind of *ontologizing of rational procedure*.' He elaborates this further, arguing that 'what were seen as the proper procedures of rational thought were read into the very constitution of the mind.'[12] The result of this operation, according to Taylor, 'was a picture of the human thinking agent as disengaged—as rationally thinking and without constitutive cultural attachments.'[13] It follows that individual thinking agents must share common ways of thinking—these being innate qualities of the mind. Individual agents who have attained to reason cannot, in other words, be seen as located or embedded in different moral-cultural worlds. Their emergence from their narrow moral universes, as individuals, was precisely the precondition for this idea of disengaged agency. The emergence of this individual, that is the individuated self, becomes the critical precondition of modern democracies, for it is this individual subject who is to be the citizen, the bearer of rights in modern society. In the dominant understandings till very recently, this subject was considered to be the ideal unmarked, abstract citizen. This idea of the modern subject is intimately linked to the understanding of the space of modern institutions as constituting the rational public sphere where reasonable discourse will lead to a resolution of differences of opinion. The parliamentary institutions of deliberations and open discussion assume this disengaged rational subject. However, the problem is that the individual produced by modern society is often not this kind of individual. Modern society also produces, through its workings, a very different kind of disembedded individual that inhabits these societies, as we shall see below.

There are two problems here that we need to reckon with. First, the assumption behind the *telos* of the individuated, abstract citizen was that all human beings 'naturally' desire freedom. Needless to say, this assumption was based in turn on another, that of the innate rationality of the individuated mind and the fairly straightforward relationship that was posited between Reason and Freedom. In relation to this, Erich Fromm for instance, argued, in the wake of the Nazi experience, of the need to 'recognize that millions in Germany were as eager to surrender their freedom as their fathers were to fight for it.'[14] Fromm put forward the idea of the 'ambiguity of freedom', where he argued that freedom from the old structures also led to the loss of community, roots, meaning, and security that the old world provided. This loss of meaning and security was experienced differently by different social strata—the wealthy and powerful adjusted to the new world much more easily. It was 'the "masses" who did not share the wealth and power of the ruling group' who lost their security and 'became a shapeless mass'—always to be manipulated by those in power.[15] Fromm, however, does not stop here. He proceeds further to argue that it was in the need of these insecure, rootless, and powerless masses that impulses arose 'to give up one's individuality', assuming the form of *submission to some authority outside of him/herself*.[16] If Fromm sounds too archaic, let us recall that Deleuze and Guattari too have, in more recent times been preoccupied with this 'fundamental problem of political philosophy', namely, why people desire their own repression.[17] We shall return to this aspect later.

The second problem to be noted here is the nature of the agency that the disenchanted world of modernity inaugurates. It is to this that we turn now. Hannah Arendt, like Erich Fromm, in her celebrated study of the rise of totalitarianism alludes to the 'rise of the mass man' as the key factor in the emergence of totalitarianism.[18] In the historical trajectory of democracies of the West, this 'mass man' as Fromm points out, defies the notion of the *disengaged rational subject*. Carl Schmitt, an inveterate enemy of liberalism, from a very different perspective, also pointed out in the early decades of this century that 'the parliamentary system' was in crisis because of 'the rise of mass democracy'.[19] Schmitt's argument rested on two major absences/silences in the constitutions of democratic states and in liberal political theory. The first was the political party, unrecognised except in empirical or sociological studies on democracies. Arising out of an inability to understand this organism, is the second silence, on the nature of political participation. With the emergence of political parties, Schmitt argued, '(T)he masses are won over through a propaganda apparatus whose maximum effect relies on an appeal to immediate interests and passions'.[20] We may add here that these appeals often enough, are directed not so much at any given, objective, immediate interests but on the contrary, they *constitute* these 'interests' through propaganda: The 'mass man' acts through the process of mobilization, of mediations that *produce him*, not as a disengaged, rational subject but as an extension of an always-already constituted collectivity—the nation, community or simply the 'mass'—moved by passion and perceived self-interest. The 'self' here, it needs to be underlined, is more than merely individual, conceived as it is as an extension of a collective self of the nation or the community. This collectivity, we will see later, is no more the old community but *a modern political collectivity made up of atomized, disembedded individuals*. This collectivity must be therefore seen as something new. This new community is based on what Balibar calls 'fictive ethnicity' in the context of the nation-form, and represents a complex articulation of the modern disembedded individual into a recreated community.[21] As social formations are nationalized, the populations included within them, argues Balibar, 'are ethnicized—that is, represented in the past or future *as if* they formed a natural community.' Without this, the nation would appear only as an idea or an arbitrary abstraction; 'patriotism's appeal would be addressed to no one.'[22] With the people thus constituted as a fictively ethnic unity, 'one can then be interpellated, as an individual, *in the name of* the collectivity whose name one bears.' In the history of nationalism, Balibar suggests, the production of 'peoplehood' becomes a crucial factor. Because no modern nation, however 'egalitarian' it may be, ever leads to the extinction of class differences, 'the fundamental problem is, therefore, *to produce the people*'.

Arendt describes the 'chief characteristic' of the mass man as 'his isolation and lack of normal social relationships'—in other words, already uprooted and disembedded, that is, individuated.[23] There is a larger history to the whole body of work done around the rise of 'mass society' and the 'mass man' who comes to embody its 'essence'. Most of this work is of course, reflective of the 'fear of the masses' that many theorists of the nineteenth and early twentieth centuries in Europe nurtured. Nevertheless, there is something interesting and insightful in the way these intellectual responses to the rise of mass society understand the conflict between reason and the 'masses'. Ortega y Gasset among many before and after him, for instance, discusses the phenomenon, also from a considered conservative political position. He talks of the rise of what he calls 'hyperdemocracy' in which the masses *act directly, outside the law*.[24] 'In our time' he says, 'it is the mass-man who dominates', in contrast to universal suffrage. For, 'under universal suffrage, the masses do not decide; their role consists in supporting the decision of one minority or other' he says in a revealing observation. In that dispensation [of universal suffrage], according to him, 'the masses were invited to accept the line of the decision'.[25] But here 'he' acts directly. He claims that there are two 'fundamental psychological traits' that distinguish the mass-man: first, '*the free expansion of his vital desires, and therefore of his personality*' and second, '*his radical ingratitude* towards all that has made possible the ease of his existence'.[26] These two traits, it is clear from his preceding discussion and from the way he formulates these traits, are incontrovertibly *extensions of modern notions of selfhood, predicated on the emergence of the individual subject*—the unencumbered self, as it were. He further links this mass man to the phenomena of syndicalism and fascism, alongside which, 'there appears for the first time in Europe, a type of man who does not want to give reasons or to be right...This is the new thing: *the right not to be reasonable, the reason of unreason.*'[27] This 'new thing' that Ortega points out in his discussion is crucial, I believe to the understanding of the travails of modern subjectivity, for the refusal to be reasonable is clearly not a simple manifestation of the 'irrationality of the backward masses'. What does happen with the great changes that take place in the centuries since the Renaissance and the Reformation is that there emerges a secularized conception of the world, with 'man' at its very centre. As Hans Kohn remarks, it was the breakdown of 'medieval universalisms' that 'opened the gates wide for a new individualism', which along with 'secularism' 'paved the way for the rising national consciousness.'[28] The 'man' that emerged from this newly disenchanted world then, was not only the rational citizen; it was also the man who became part of the mass, the crowd: lost, lonely, powerless, and yet no longer answerable to any other-worldly authority outside 'himself'. 'He' was answerable only to the community that he now affiliatively made his own—or to the new figures of authority he desperately sought and submitted to.[29]

Tocqueville, in his attempt to explain the rise of 'mass-like' society, astutely and insightfully links this development to the majority's having become '*delirious with' its passion for equality.*'[30] In this remarkable phrase, we can probably sense the entirely unanticipated turn that this unprecedentedly emancipatory idea of 'equality' takes—and is capable of taking. If we are to appreciate the full meaning of Tocqueville's 'delirium', however, it is necessary to see it in the context of the elitism of the practitioners of democracy, that is, the new political class of representatives. As Zeev Sternhell remarks, the petit bourgeoisie and the industrial workers 'did not recognize either the pattern or the language of parliamentary politics as their own'. This politics 'reflected the psychology of the nineteenth century elitist politics, which had been rationalistic and utilitarian...'[31] In such a situation, it is hardly surprising that the 'delirious passion for equality' could easily turn against the forces of 'progress' and 'reason'. I am not suggesting here that this mass man has only an antagonistic relationship to parliamentary democracy. What I want to underline however, is that 'he' enters the arena of parliamentary politics, with a very different language and set of notions, often totally at variance with those on which its institutions are based. And more often than not, 'his' relationship to these institutions is framed by a revulsion against the power and privilege that they seem to embody. It is worth bearing in mind that even a phenomenon like fascism capitalizes on this sense of exclusion from power experienced by the ordinary person.

This is, I suggest, a phenomenon far more complicated than something that can be explained as either a residue of the past or simply as a pathology of modernity. But one thing seems clear: the main character of this drama, the 'mass man' is a product of modern society, uprooted from his old contexts, habitat, and community—of which he retains but a trace in his memory. He is an agent, nevertheless, who is fully constituted by modernity's 'radical secularity', its self-gratifying egocentric individual. Hence the traits that Ortega mentions: endless proliferation of desire and 'radical ingratitude' for its fulfilment. For this man, no God is any more responsible for 'giving us this day our daily bread'. It is also evident that this 'mass man', coming as he does from the lower depths of society, is always at odds with the elitism of Reason.

We are brought face to face then, with the circumstance that the subject of modern liberal democracy—the rational autonomous citizen—is not the inevitable product of an individuated, radically secular idea of self.[32] We need only recall here Erich Fromm's studies on Nazism and his conclusion that the easy assumption that all human beings 'naturally desire freedom' may be entirely misplaced. The 'fear of freedom' reflected in the fascist mobilization of the masses points towards the entire domain of the inner world of human beings that we might need to consider.

Now if we take Schmitt's suggestion regarding the transformation of the logic of politics with the emergence of political parties seriously, we need to look more closely at the technologies of political mobilization directed at drawing this man into action, and also to the ways in which they constitute him as such, in the first place. Since these technologies are developed and deployed primarily by the political party, we also need to understand this crucial institution/organism of modern polities. That, however, is a question that lies beyond the scope of our discussion. But it would be worthwhile to refer here to another figure, related to the political party and closely allied to the 'mass man', whom Hyppolite Taine calls the *jacobin*. This figure, according to Taine, is 'a certain human type', 'a political animal possessed of the "*espirit Jacobin*".' 'Absurd utopia and mad ambition' are, in his view, the main ingredients of the jacobin mentality.[33] Typically, Taine thought, such figures could be found neither in the upper orders who were the beneficiaries of the social system, nor among the 'vast popular and rural mass' for 'they are unable to understand the ideological abstractions of the revolutionary ideologues...and [their] constant worry about sheer survival sets them apart from the realm of jacobin fanaticism.' Rather, they 'originate *among uprooted men on the fringe of the two main classes*'—the *déclassé*.[34] Notice the reference to the 'uprootedness' of the déclassé. Also notice the reference to absurd utopia and mad ambition—both qualities that could only become generalized once the modern subject was in place with 'his' spirit of world-mastery. There is possibly a hyperbolic element in these descriptions, and it is important to remember that most theorists of 'mass society' were precisely the representatives of the liberal or conservative elite against whom the ire of mass society was directed. They nevertheless point towards an aspect of modern subjectivity that crucially concerns us. It is also relevant that in this context, Habermas notes the despair of Mill and Tocqueville, at the 'public opinion determined by the passion of the masses' and its need of 'purification', in their opinion, by enlightened and 'materially independent citizens'.[35] What is important for our purposes, in all these accounts, is a recognition of two aspects: a) that the split between the elite and the masses corresponds in a significant sense with the split between 'reason' and 'passion'/unreason, instituted by the discourse of Reason, and b) that the individuated subject produced by modern politics is not always the rational disengaged individual.

Nationalism and the New Community

It is this disembedded individual that Hegel links to nationalism. Charles Taylor has called this Hegel's dilemma for modern democracy:

The modern ideology of equality and of total participation leads to a homogenisation of society. This shakes men loose from their traditional communities, but cannot replace them as a focus of identity. Or, rather it can only replace them as such a focus under the impetus of militant nationalism or some totalitarian ideology which would depreciate or even crush diversity and individuality.[36]

It is with this mass of atomized individuals that nationalism, in instituting the new community, attempts to create a kind of peculiar *gemeinschaft-in-gesellschaft*. As we will see in the next chapter, the historical link of the nationalist idea with the notion of citizenship was severed early in its career. Germany was probably one of the early instances of the insertion of nationalism within a discourse of organic community. Much of our discussion in this book will relate to the subsequent trajectories of nationalism, especially in the postcolonial world. We will therefore, need to qualify Taine's understanding of the jacobin personality in the context of anticolonial nationalisms. The corresponding figure here is most often not the *déclassé* element, but the elite who is in contest with the colonial power. The second qualification that we need to make here with reference to the preceding discussion is that nationalisms in the postcolonial world have at their disposal, not the fully individuated 'mass man' but communities in transition—caught somewhere between the old and the new, between '*gemeinschaft*' and '*gesellschaft*'.

To the extent that modernity is a general condition that envelopes all third world societies, even if with inflections specific to those societies, the phenomenon of individuation and the emergence of the 'masses' are very much part of their social and political landscape.[37] To that extent, the question of the relationships between individual, community, and nation, discussed above have a relevance for these societies too. It is necessary here therefore, to note that there are many other interesting *dislocation effects* in the way in which older communities meet the challenge of modernity, as we shall see later in our discussion, that makes a kind of alternative mobilization possible, alongside the nationalist ones. In this context, it will be worth noticing that this new individual—the man of the mass—is not available only to hegemonic nationalism; contending nationalisms and 'community'-based mobilizations too have him ready at hand. It is to this aspect of modern politics that we now turn.

In his rendering of Heidegger, Charles Taylor makes a distinction between the disengaged subject versus the *embedded self*. This distinction is important for our discussion because it is this idea of the disengaged subject, derived from a naïve and unproblematic understanding of the individuation process, that lies at the root of the great *telos* of modernity, that of the abstract, unmarked citizen.[38] But modernity did not always produce this disengaged, rational individual subject, disembedded from commitments of community and religion. Far less did colonial modernity succeed in producing this subject. In Taylor's rendering, unlike the 'knowing subject' who treats the world simply as an object of knowledge and use, the 'embedded self' 'knows its way around... moving around, dealing with things, handling things with understanding'.[39] This idea of the subject seeks to recover, according to Taylor, 'an understanding of the agent as...

embedded in a culture, a form of life, a "world" of involvements...'[40] This notion of self or agency is related to Heidegger's notion of the 'world' and Fred Dallmayr explicates this idea of the 'world' as one that 'signifies a non-objective and *non-objectifiable background* of experience which is 'always-already' assumed by subjects relating to objects...'[41] In Heidegger's own account the term has both, an ontical, pre-ontological sense as well as an ontological one that relates to the 'interpretation of Being'. It includes 'that "*wherein*" a factical *Dasein* as such can be said to "live".'[42] In Heidegger's discussion this distinction is meant to lay the basis for a stepping back from the diremption between the 'knowing subject' and the 'objective world' instituted by modern epistemology. I am interested in using this idea for a somewhat different purpose.

Heidegger's notion of embedded agency or *Dasein* is largely a theoretical abstraction, not meant to be simply read into the empirical world. And yet it is nothing other than empirical wo/man for the very idea of *Dasein* or 'Being-there' would cease to make any sense without any relation to the real/empirical. Now the idea of embeddedness assumes a 'world' that is given. This should not however be understood to mean that the world is therefore unchanging and static. *Dasein* always ever encounters a 'world' in the throes of change. Embeddedness then becomes a more complex matter. I read the critical significance that Heidegger accords to the categories of 'anxiety', and 'uncanniness'—that is, 'not-being-at-home'— as the modality through which the world is disclosed to *Dasein*, to be a reference to this ever-changing-ness of the world.[43] Such was after all, the 'real world' of Heidegger's youth— 'a period of sudden, wrenching change, a time when Germany was transformed from a relatively backward and predominantly agricultural nation into one of the greatest industrial powers of the world?'[44] This, after all, is the world of the formation of nations, of sudden transformation from traditional agricultural societies their emergence into the new world.[45] This is also the world of the emergence of the mass man. This world, as I have suggested, does not simply register a move from *gemeinschaft* to *gesellschaft*, but in fact, sees the emergence of the novel political community of the nation - a curious gemeinschaft-in-gesellschaft.

In this rapidly changing world where 'old ties are being torn asunder' and individuals/ communities are uprooted *en masse*, the idea of 'being-in-the-world' acquires a different meaning. To look at the world in turmoil or change is to also look at the subject's inner world, for the subject is what s/he is *in that world*. I suggest that we can understand this process by referring to the twin notions of *filiation* and *affiliation*, that I borrow from

Edward Said. Said talks of the transformations in the forms of modern consciousness and underlines the 'difficulties and ultimately the impossibility of natural filiation' in that context.[46] *Filiation*, according to him refers to the largely 'natural' or 'biological' attachments that an agent carries with her—but occasionally he uses the term simply for inherited cultural attachments.[47] We could in some sense even see this as alluding to Heidegger's 'world'. The difficulties or even the 'ultimate impossibility' of retaining these in the modern world lead the agent however, to what Said believes is an imperative of modern existence—the search for 'new and different ways of conceiving human relationships', which he calls '*affiliation*'.[48] Said reads in T.S. Eliot's work the move to an affiliation with the 'enfolding presence of the English church', as he does in Lukács' *History and Class Consciousness* and the notion of class consciousness, 'an insurrectionary form of an attempt at affiliation' that could 'possibly break through the antinomies and atomisations of reified existence in the modern capitalist world-order'.[49] In these expressions of the cultural products of modern Europe, Said finds 'the deliberately explicit goal of *using that new order to reinstate vestiges of a kind of authority associated in the past with filiative order.*'[50] In 'Freud's psychoanalytical guild' and Lukács' vanguard party, he sees attempts at finding a restored authority.

It is worth noticing therefore that in this discussion of the filiation/affiliation dialectic, the subject of Said's discussion is already the modern, individuated, rational, disengaged subject—in the persons of Eliot, Freud, and Lukács. Therefore, the kind of affiliations that Said conceives of are affiliations to modern institutions, ideologies, parties, and belief-systems. Nevertheless, *here too* he finds in them the desire to *restore some kind of authority*. Affiliation is in his understanding, then, not simply an attempt to find a new community of equals but also to find a new figure of authority on whom *at least a part of the agent's agency may be delegated or transferred.* Recall here Fromm's idea of submission and surrender of individuality and Deleuze and Guattari's 'desire for repression'.

What if we step outside these binaries of the filiative (community) and affiliative (modern institutions) and cast a glance at the 'other subject'—not an individuated Lukács, Freud, or an Eliot but the 'ordinary' person? This ordinary person could be the already-individuated 'mass man', or more likely, one who is still retains strong links with the filiative order, but is lodged irrevocably *in the process of individuation*, beginning to learn the new languages of modernity? What kind of affiliation would such an agent seek? Understood in the context of embedded agency, we can see how the agent who 'adjusts to the new order', realizes that something frightening is happening to his/her 'world'—something new, often unrecognizable and unintelligible, speaking a new language, is tearing it apart—might step in to 'preserve' her old world by 'using' its language, its own discourse, its institutions. Of course, historical experience shows that this 'filiative order' can never really be 'preserved', for modernity has already transformed the very conditions of its existence; but we do have, as a consequence, different modes of articulation of the traditional and the modern. This agent is an agent who is neither fully 'traditional', nor 'fully modern'. S/he 'mobilizes' the community and reinvents it such that it can live a powerful after-life in the new world. The only language that this agent finds 'ready-at-hand' is the language of community, always at odds with the abstract universalist language of modern politics. In fact, s/he can only understand the new language in terms of her old received languages. Characteristically, mobilizations in postcolonial modern polities take place around such widespread experiences of dislocation, rather than around the more 'rational' differences of opinion that are presupposed by parliamentary politics. The coming together of the 'propaganda apparatus' of the political party, 'manned' by the jacobin, and the 'masses', often produced by this apparatus, forms one of the potent challenges to the very institutions of democracy, given the sharp division between the 'elitism of Reason' and the unreason/passion of the masses. The problem is complicated manifold if the new world is ushered in through the agency of an alien colonial power. For, in this world, the elite interventions in mass politics are shaped by the experience of subjugation by the very forces which claim to represent Reason. This experience also produces another 'type' that inhabits the terrain of anticolonial nationalisms, whom I will discuss in Chapter 4. That is, the agent who, already 'individuated', 'decides to return' to the filiative order.

The foregoing discussion shows how the contemporary crisis of the political project of modernity, also throws into question in the process, the very idea of an undifferentiated 'people' or 'masses'. It provides a glimpse of how, in a very profound sense, this crisis reveals the continuing resilience of the idea of 'community', even if it is no longer the community of the old type.

The Nation and Postcoloniality

There are different ways in which the idea of a community surfaces in the historical trajectories of the Western liberal democracies and in the postcolonial democracies that had to embark on the project of nation-building in the context of colonial subjugation. Its emergence in the West seeks to transform the contours of existing liberal notions of citizenship and redefine institutional practices in tune with these redefinitions, while for the latter, the forging of a *national political community* becomes crucial. For postcolonial democracies, this is the way they can emerge on the scene of 'World-History' as equal partners with their former colonial masters—never mind the fact that the very idea of a nation had its roots in the specific history of the West. As David Gordon notes, '(A)s for [Albert] Memmi, for [Frantz] Fanon the exploitation by the colonized of his past, his cultivation of his uniqueness mythically, is only a moment, historically, in his access to universality...a dialogue among free peoples.'[51] This is true not only of emerging nations seeking liberation from colonial rule but also of smaller or marginalized communities that have found it difficult to adjust on equal terms within the dominant majoritarian articulations of nationhood. It is no accident then, that throughout the twentieth century, community identity has been articulated in the non-Western world in terms of a *search for a different nation*, within the subjugated 'nation'. The 'right of nations to self-determination' reflects primarily a desire to form *another nation*, different from the dominant one, rather than think in terms of an alternative set of political arrangements for many of these countries for which the historical option of the European kind of nationhood was not available. European nations forged a national culture by obliterating other local, non-literate cultures through an enunciation of a high culture of nationalism and assimilating the former into the latter. In countries like India, on the other hand, the nationalist elites were faced with a twofold difficulty. On the one hand were the innumerable, more or less developed linguistic cultures (both Hindu and Muslim), and on the other hand, the fact of colonial subjugation which demanded the broadest unity across all these cultural communities. Indian secular-nationalism therefore, had to opt for a different model even though the desire that animated its elites was still lodged within the European imagination of nationhood. 'Unity in diversity' was its way of negotiating this difference and secularism became, in this context, not merely a name of religious neutrality but also for enunciating the idea of an India that stood above all differences of religion, language, caste, and community. It did not demand the dissolution of all identities into an Indian one but pleaded for a primacy of the Indian over other identities. However, it made a distinction between linguistic communities on the on the hand and those of religion and caste on the other. While linguistic diversity was recognized as being more benign, and strictly speaking not incompatible with the demands of modern life, it forbade the articulation of caste and religious difference as something that was antithetical to the very project of nationhood. Its secular self-image prevented the articulation of the voice of communities like the Muslims, who were feeling increasingly marginalized by the nationalist struggle. How else but in the language of community could this sense of marginalization be articulated? In the event, the north Indian Muslim elite had to turn to a different definition of nationhood. Its demand for a separate Muslim homeland—Pakistan—showed yet again the over-powering hold of the idea of the nation even among those who challenged the dominant construct of nationhood. I examine the dynamic of these two kinds of 'communities'—religious and caste-based—and their relationship with the hegemonic project of nationhood, in the chapters that follow.

The nation-form thus becomes the vehicle, simultaneously, of the universal and the particular. It is the precondition of ascent to the universal but becomes inevitably lodged in the logic of the particular—that of self-determination. There lies in the play of the universal and the particular, a whole range of serious intellectual and political questions that need to be examined in today's world. The most crucial question here is, of course, the claim of modern universalisms to be available to all in a straightforward and transparent way. It is the argument of this book that this claim has been shown through our experience of its practice to be false, for it hides beneath its surface all the privileges of the dominant culture, counter-claims to which can only be articulated in the language of cultural difference and subalternity. Through an examination of two such marginalized/oppressed communities, namely the Muslims and the Dalits, during and after the anticolonial struggle, this book argues that in a sense, the project of Indian nationhood was/is an impossible project. For nations, if they are to be nations, must become so by creating a homogeneous national cultural identity.[52] Thus, one of the problems we encounter with this focus on nationalism and nation-building in a context like India's is that the concept seems riddled with difficulties from its birth. We are faced with the problem of confronting an impossible 'totality' and a notion of time that ruptures the 'homogeneous empty time' of modernity. It may be apposite, therefore, to discuss the larger theoretical questions involved here before proceeding with the specific discussion of the project of Indian nationhood. It is also worth mentioning that this notion of time has a wider relevance to that other idea that we encountered earlier, that of World-History, as another impossible totality. I explore this link further in the next section.

Nation, Time, and Minority Cultures

Benedict Anderson, in his path-breaking work *Imagined Communities*, suggests that one of the crucial conditions of possibility of the idea of nationhood, is the emergence of a modern conception of time. This conception of time was marked by a certain linearity and a clear-cut separation of the past from the present on the one hand, and the possibility of thinking simultaneity in a radically different way, on the other.[53] If the medieval conception of time thought of the past and the present as simultaneous, the modern conception is premised on the idea of a homogeneous empty time, where simultaneity is 'transverse, cross-time', 'marked by temporal coincidence and measured by clock and calendar'.[54] Anderson suggests that the '*idea of a sociological organism moving calendrically through homogeneous, empty time is a precise analogue of the idea of the nation which also is conceived as a solid community moving steadily down (or up) history.*'[55] Anderson also refers to the 'discovery', in the sixteenth century, of 'grandiose civilizations' like those China, Japan, Southeast Asia, and the Indian subcontinent—or those of Aztec Mexico and Incan Peru—and argues that these 'suggested an irremediable human pluralism'. How could the European deal with these different entities 'whose genealogies lay outside of, and were unassimilable to, Eden'? Anderson's suggestion, in passing, is that only homogeneous, empty time 'offered them' accommodation: That is, by making possible the idea that others too could exist alongside 'us' [the Europeans], *in the same time*. In other words, it was not merely possible to 'think' the idea of the nation; the new conception of time now made it possible to think the notion of 'World-History'.

Reinhart Koselleck has shown in his fascinating studies of the idea of historical time, that 'history' itself is a word of mid-eighteenth century vintage and talks of 'History' as being 'experienced as a new temporality' alongside which 'specific dispositions and ways of assimilating experience emerge'.[56] One of the modalities through which this new temporal experience is grasped is the idea of what he calls the 'contemporaneity of the noncontemporaneous', that is *simultaneity* in Anderson's sense.[57] Koselleck argues that this 'contemporaneity of the noncontemporaneous was initially a result of overseas expansion' [read colonialism] and soon became 'a basic framework for the progressive construction of the *growing unity of world history*'.[58] Towards the end of the eighteenth century, the notion of Progress as a collective singular was coined in the German language—inaugurating a whole new series of notions like 'earlier than', 'later than', etc. Elsewhere, commenting on the new experience of historical time, and with reference to a text written in 1775, Koselleck refers to the history of Hindustan, 'which had first been introduced into a world-historical context by the English twenty years earlier'.[59]

Put differently, what both Anderson and Koselleck are saying, often explicitly, is that this new conception of time makes possible the idea of something called World-History. When Koselleck, for instance talks of the 'growing unity of world-history' what he is hinting at is the idea that the World is now 'One' singular entity—a totality in the philosophical sense. What this means in theoretical terms is that there is a certain coherence, a certain logic—a *logos*—that governs this totality, much as it does the different parts or constituents of this totality. Different parts of a totality, in philosophical terms, are internally linked in a manner that provides coherence to the whole. In its stronger version, different parts of a totality are mere carriers of the whole with no internal logic of their own 'development' or movement. That is why Hegel could talk of a World Spirit that governed the movement of World-History. We need to recall here Anderson's suggestion that the 'idea of a sociological organism moving calendrically through homogeneous, empty time is a precise analogue of the idea of the nation'. The idea of 'society' then, conceived as an organism that is moving forward through such homogeneous, empty time, according to some internal evolutionary logic, becomes that fundamental idea upon which arise both the idea of World-History and that of the nation—depending upon whether one is talking of 'national' societies or 'human' society (in the singular) as a whole.

What I will refer to as the 'paradigm of nationhood' arises on this epistemological ground. Its central problem is of aggregating what have been, till then, so many different social, cultural, and geographical entities into a single entity of the nation. It must weld together all these different entities—let us call them 'localities'—with different pasts and different presents, into one big modern Nation. The claims of the Nation's sovereignty can become real and tangible only to the extent that the pasts of the localities are either erased or reproduced within a narrative of the Nation's history. The road to the realization of abstract universal citizenship necessarily passes, in this paradigm, through the production of a homogeneous national culture and a unified national consciousness. As Renan puts it, the defining feature of nations is the 'fusion of their component populations'. 'No French citizen knows whether he is a Burgundian, an Alan, a Taifale or a Visigoth, yet every French citizen has to have forgotten the massacre of Saint Barthelomew or the massacres that took place in the Midi in the thirteenth century.'[60] History as the new 'science' becomes the weapon of the nation in its fight to produce a common past and thereby posit a common destiny, against the claims of the locality. The Nation becomes sovereign over its territory first, before it can be acknowledged as such in its external relations to other nation-states. The nation, as Renan argues, *presupposes a past*, even though he believes that there is a continuous need to forget the violence that lies at the origin of this unity or fusion of populations that eventually becomes a nation. Clearly then, what he emphatically claims is that *certain pasts* need to be forgotten for a nation to live.

If we are to go by this classical paradigm of nationhood, elaborated and put into practice in Europe, many postcolonial societies would be, as Ranabir Samaddar has suggested, forever suspended in the space between the 'former colony' and the 'not-yet nation'.[61] It is this 'lack'—this failure to be a nation—that can often be seen to drive the most xenophobic and virulent nationalisms of the postcolonial world. This is a feature of anticolonial nationalisms that I will be centrally concerned with in Chapters 1 and 4 and I will not probe it further here. For the present, I will underline the fact that this idea of a nation and the paradigm of nationhood arise on the theoretical ground of a totality—a single whole, governed by a single logic. In order to interrogate the paradigm of nationhood, therefore, we need to take a closer look at the idea of totality. I will suggest that theoretically dismantling the idea of totality will enable us to see our postcolonial condition in radically different ways such that it is not haunted by what it is not. In the remainder of this chapter, therefore, I will look at this problematic notion of totality.

The Nation as 'Articulated Totality'

In what relation do the different histories/pasts stand to the homogeneous empty time of the nation? In other words, how do they relate to the idea that different 'societies' within the nation may have their own 'preferred futures'?[62] Can we really assume that the 'national societies' which came to acquire their specific form and structure through entirely contingent factors, are really governed by some singular logic? On the other hand, if we reject the idea of a social totality in the sense discussed above, that is as one that is governed by a singular logic, are we left with just so many 'little selves', continuously at odds with each other?

If we reject the self-perception of nationalist elites that there is something 'natural', 'given' and eternal—at least about *their* nation—then we must reckon with the possibility that there can be different contending imaginations of the idea of nationhood or imaginations of identity that *contest or disturb given ideas of nationhood*. If we take Anderson's suggestion seriously that communities are to be distinguished 'not by their falsity/ genuineness' but by the 'style in which they are imagined' then there is no reason why this criterion may not be extendable in principle, to all communities.[63] In other words, we also need to understand the ways in which other histories ran—now alongside, now against—the current of 'the nation's' history. We need, in other words, to understand the different times inhabited by these different histories; we need to delve into 'the type of articulation, displacement and torsion which harmonizes these different times with one another' to produce the totality called the 'nation'.[64] We need, in other words, to see the nation as an 'articulated totality'.

I derive this notion of an 'articulated totality' from Althusser, who develops a notion of time that is linked to the nature of social totality, where each 'level' of the 'totality' has its own time, its own history. The *term* 'articulated totality', of course, is not his, because in his highly structuralist version of Marxism, the 'levels' are always eventually subordinated to the totality, the 'ever pre-given structure-in-dominance'. In the structuralist Marxism of Althusser, these 'levels' refer to the economic, political, philosophical, and scientific. Each level has its own specific past and present. The 'time' of politics or the 'time' of philosophy have their own logic, not reducible, in principle to the 'time' of the economy. In his rendering of the notion of time, the idea of a social totality that has only one *historical 'present'*, expressing the essence of all the levels within it, becomes unacceptable. There are different times, different presents, different histories, and the articulation of these into a totality involves a process of displacement and torsion. Althusser argues that these different times are 'punctuated with different rhythms' that mark them out as different times. We can no longer then, see the history of a social totality as one moving through the continuum of a homogenous empty time; this notion forces us to direct our attention to the different histories of the different elements that constitute the totality. As can be seen, this notion of time lies in uneasy truce with the notion of totality that he assumes— 'ever pre-given' and 'in-dominance'. Uneasy, because, despite heroic efforts to assert the idea of 'determination in the last instance', we may recall, Althusser has to acknowledge in the end that the 'lonely hour of the last instance never arrives'. This is not the place to go into a discussion of his notion of totality. Let us merely note, that to accept the existence of these different times, irreducible to any other more privileged one, is to argue for a fundamentally different kind of contingent totality, that has no singular logos that governs all its levels. Althusser argues, for instance, that there cannot be a vertical slice of any point of time, which he calls an *essential section*, cut out through an intellectual operation, in which 'all elements of the whole revealed by this section are in an immediate relationship with one another...that expresses their internal essence.' Such an 'essential section', we may note is the basis of all notions of *periodization*, that historiography bases itself on. So for instance, the 'age of Louis XIV' or the 'age of Louis XV' are not expressions that can reveal, in one single logos, the essential relation of all the parts. We can at best, see them as describing a *conjuncture*, which represents a complex historical unity of such different temporalities. Extending his logic, one might argue that the 'age of nationalism' inaugurated by the French revolution, in the time of world-history, does not and cannot reveal the 'truth' of what was going on in the colonies in *that precise present*. For Europe's 'age of nationalism' was the 'age of subjugation' for large parts of Asia and Africa. A totality that allows for such a notion of time, I suggest, can only be one that is always incomplete—always threatened by the 'play' of these different temporalities.

Later in the text, Althusser suggests the importance of this notion of time, not merely in relation to the different levels of the totality, like politics, economics etc., but also, quite explicitly, its indispensability,

'(I)f we are to establish the status of a whole series of notions which have a major strategic role in the language of this century's economic and political thought, e.g., the notions of *unevenness of development*, of *survivals*, of *backwardness* (in consciousness) in Marxism itself, or the notion of 'under-development' in contemporary economic and political practice.'[65]

In a companion essay, Etienne Balibar has explored this notion of time in the context of the history of the capitalist mode of production in Marx's *Capital* and *Grundrisse*. Here Balibar shows how the history of capitalism as a mode of production, that is, as a social totality, is constituted through the coming together of two different histories: that of 'free' labour and capital. This history of the capitalist mode of production cannot be thought of as a simple 'transformation' of the feudal mode into a capitalist mode. This transformation cannot be seen as the necessary evolution of the structure of the feudal mode into the capitalist. 'Instead of being thought at the level of the structures [i.e. totality], it [this history] must be thought at the level of the elements', for '(t)he two elements necessary for the constitution of the structure of capitalist production each have their relatively independent history.'[66] Balibar thus concludes through his reading of *Grundrisse*, that the 'elements combined by the capitalist structure have *different and independent origins.*'[67]

It will be evident from the discussion above that this notion of time enables us to do away with an evolutionary view of society that sees the totality of the structure itself as evolving through homogeneous empty time. At the same time, it allows us to retain a notion of a totality such as the 'national polity' or 'social-formation' or the 'world-economy' where different logics and dynamics play themselves out. We can then still talk, in some sense, of 'non-capitalist' or 'non-modern' structures within the overall universalizing logic of capital and modernity, without placing them on a continuous flow of linear time—without seeing them as 'backward' or 'forward'. Their historical articulation into a larger totality of the nation or the world-economy does not authorize us to see them as 'remnants' or 'survivals'.

I have found it useful to see the 'nation' as such an articulated totality, where the totality is not an *a priori* given, but is formed out of different communities and social groups that have their own histories. Their coming together into a 'nation', involves precisely a displacement and torsion of different times, of the type suggested by Althusser. This notion helps to dismantle the problematic but nevertheless common sense idea whereby each history of the so-called fragment can be reduced to a part of the nation's history. Or, at another extended level, the idea that following the insertion of 'individual nations' into world-history, all national histories can be reduced to a mere episode of the former: in Hegel's famous rendering, there is only one world-historical people, who at any point in time represent the World Spirit.

Let us return briefly to Koselleck through a discussion of his ideas by Habermas' and Paul Ricoeur. Habermas, in his discussion of 'modernity's consciousness of time', refers to Koselleck's work where he argues that 'the "new age" lent the whole of the past a world-historical quality': Even Hegel's use of history in the 'collective singular' was a coinage of the eighteenth century. Koselleck's contention, says Habermas, is that following the break instituted by the Enlightenment and the French Revolution, there emerges a new sense of time that involves, apart from this idea of a universal singular history, a sense of a decisive break, a 'newness'. This gives rise to a whole series of terms like revolution, progress, emancipation, and development.[68]

Koselleck argues, says Habermas further, that modernity's consciousness as a new age has distanced the 'horizon of future expectation' itself 'from all previous experience'—the experiential space of the peasant and the craftsman. These now stand devalued.[69] With this break, in Paul Ricoeur's rendering of Koselleck, appear three new 'topoi of modernity': the idea of a new age, the idea of acceleration and the idea that history can now be 'made'. It now becomes possible to believe that 'if progress can be accelerated, it is because we can now speed up its course and struggle against what delays it, reaction and harmful survivals.'[70] We need to remember that in Koselleck's discussion, the 'space of past experience' refers to the experience of the still existing peasants and craftsmen of Europe, who then still live in a different time-consciousness. We can also read it from *our own present*, and find many resonances of the themes touched upon and elaborated by him. However, both Habermas and Ricoeur are interested in salvaging modernity from this indictment. So Ricoeur seeks to 'resist the seduction of *the purely utopian expectation*' and salvage modernity by insisting on the 'permanent ethical and political implications of these metahistorical categories of expectation and experience.' He, therefore, wants to retain the idea that '*humanity as a whole*' must be the subject of history '*as a collective singular*.'[71] He sees the 'threats of oppression linked to the very idea of a universal history' as resulting from some 'confusion' of universal history with the 'hegemony of one society or a small number of dominant societies.'[72] However, Ricoeur passes off as 'confusion' *between two different phenomena*, entities that are inextricably linked though the idea of a totality. The empirical question of the 'hegemony of one society or a small number of dominant societies' cannot be separated from the notion of a World-History (or universal history) as that totality can only be governed, in any particular age, by the internal logic of that whole. In a Hegelian rendering, it is the World Spirit represented by the world-historical people; in the Marxist version it could be the logic of the advanced productive forces. In the liberal theorists of the Empire, there was the civilizing mission—the white man's burden. It is precisely against this kind of an understanding of totality that I invoke Althusser's notion of time.

Habermas too, does not answer Koselleck's charge against the new time-consciousness of modernity but brings in a counter-charge in his bid to extricate and salvage modernity: 'Koselleck overlooks the fact that the notion of progress served not only to render eschatological hopes profane and open up the horizon of expectation, but also to *close* off the future as a source of disruption with the aid of teleological constructions of history.'[73] Habermas seems to be thinking of religious teleologies here, against whose possible disruption, he seems to think, the notion of progress provides a guarantee—by 'closing off' the future to them. This proposition itself is debatable in our time/space, but more important is the fact that this critique of traditional/religious eschatologies cannot by itself validate the modern notion of progress as a collective singular, and free it of responsibility from the violence that *it* carries within it.

It is against this kind of view that Althusser's notion of time, in my view, offers a way of fracturing the idea of an essential, expressive totality—be it the nation or world-history—and recovering the idea of differential temporalities.[74] Let me also add that, in my reading, these different times being different 'apprehensions' or reckonings of time, are not objectively given. Notions of time are related to notions of Selfhood and the ways in which different histories are narratively constructed and *lived*. If time is not merely an empty container, within which human beings live, then it needs to be seen as a particular configuration of past, present and future, as it belongs to a particular Self. This configuration, marked by its own rhythms, bearing its own modes of reckoning, must be seen as relating to particular Selves whose pasts and presents it narrates. To that extent, even while relating to the 'real' experience of lived time, these are not reducible to any 'objective time'.

The 'Opportunism' of Minority Cultures?

Let me illustrate this idea of time further with two instances. Javeed Alam discusses the state of Muslim politics in India in the late nineteenth and early twentieth centuries—especially its distance from the politics of anticolonial struggle.[75] The struggle of the Muslims was for equality, not *vis-à-vis* the British but in relation to the Hindus. The logic of the situation, he argues, was such that their staying with the British 'could tilt the flow of concessions in their favour'. Consequently, the pattern of politics that emerged among them 'was not, by and large, anti-colonial'. He then goes on to argue that what happened in the case of the Muslim elite was nothing new and that the modern Hindu elite, *in its own time*, had gone in for a similar collaboration with the British. It was also so in the case of the Dalit/Depressed caste leaders, as well as important leaders of the Bihar tribals of the Jharkhand region.[76] But then, he goes on to argue that '*If we are not interested in an all-India view* but are looking at *a specific community*' then '*the date of the formation of such an elite will vary*.' The significant factor that Alam then points out is that there was no anticolonial movement in existence when the Hindu elites were collaborating with the British. However, when the Muslim elite came to its own—and we could say the same by extension, of the Dalits/Depressed castes—'nationalist and proto-nationalist tendencies were clearly consolidating into an anti-colonial critique' and a corresponding politics was already emerging. It is therefore, '*the timing of the development* rather than its content', that, says Alam, was of 'decisive' importance. 'It is the atemporality of this ["dominant, nationalist, including the Left"] mode of understanding' which Alam then finds problematic. In order to de-communalize our understanding, the temporal factor must be factored into our understanding, he concludes.

We already have here in Alam's account, the elements of a fractured notion of time. However, there is a further theoretical operation that needs to be performed here. For, by merely asserting that the development of the Muslim elite—or the Dalit elite—lagged behind that of the Hindu elite, we are still within the notion of a linear, homogeneous, empty time. All we can say is that they were 'latecomers'. Within this notion of time, we can merely think the simultaneity of the Hindu elite's nationalism and the Muslim/Dalit elite accommodation with colonialism. In order to make sense of them in their interrelationship, we can then only 'explain' the 'backwardness' of the minority elites in terms of their 'cultural deficiency', 'insulation', or 'resistance to change', as many nationalists—not to mention progressives and Leftists—did for decades. Alternatively, we might try to explain this 'lagged development' with reference to specific historical antecedents, like exclusion from education in the case of the Dalits, which still leaves us within the same notion of a singular linear time—the time of the nation, which is also the time of world-history. It is this conception of time that Nehru, for example, articulates when he says that:

We in India do not have to go abroad in search of the past and the distant. We have them here in abundance. *If we go to foreign countries, it is in search of the present.* That search is necessary, for isolation from it means backwardness and decay. The world of Emerson's time has changed and old barriers are breaking down; life becomes more international.[77]

Our real, *lived present* becomes in this homogeneous empty time, a past that 'we have in abundance'—because of it we are immersed in 'backwardness and decay'. The Present is 'in foreign countries', precisely, in Europe, for that is the context of Nehru's discussion. We are then faced with the possibility that homogeneous empty time, or the time of world-history is hegemonized time. For, it does not merely 'offer accommodation' to other cultures, as Anderson suggests, it does so by inserting them into a larger totality where they represent mere survivals of the past. The only way in which we can recover the real meaning of the supposedly 'late arrival' of the minority elites is by recognizing their history as a separate history, not as a part or a section of the history of the nation that is yet to be instituted. In other words, the only way in which these times can make sense, then, is by dispensing with the notion of totality upon which this notion of homogeneous empty time is erected. It is in the subsequent institution of 'the nation' as an entity that we see the subsequent articulation of different times, with considerable displacement and torsion.

My second instance is based on J.L. Talmon's fascinating discussion of Engels' reflections on the 'national question' in the Austro-Hungarian empire. Talmon here discusses Engels'(and Marx's) oft-quoted distinction between 'historic nations' and 'peoples without history'. This understanding, we know, is based on the Hegelian idea that 'In the state alone has man rational existence'. 'Those men who live outside a state, in patriarchal tribal societies, for instance, are totally on the margins of history.'[78] Talmon notes that Engels' reflections are based on the idea of 'being in what they considered revolutionary times [i.e.1848 and 'long after'].' He says:

In that confrontation [between revolution and counter-revolution], no quarter could be asked for or given... . You were either a revolutionary or a counter-revolutionary. Whatever the causes, reasons, motives, intentions of the Czechs or Croats were, once they decided to support the Austrian monarchy, they chose to ally themselves, indeed to serve Russia in her crusade against the revolution. Once they decided to give preference to their nationality over revolution, they had signed their death warrant.[79]

And then he quotes Engels himself:

In the first victorious uprising of the French proletariat...the Austrian Germans and the Magyars will liberate themselves and wreak bloody revenge upon the Slav barbarians. The general war, which will follow, will crush that Slav league, and *not even the name will be left of these small, stubborn peoples.... And this too will be progress.*

And again, from Engels:

Among all the nations and tribes of Austria only three were the carriers of progress, actively entered history and are still today capable of continued existence: the Germans, the Poles and the Magyars. This is why they are revolutionary nations. The *immediate destiny of all others, the big or small tribes is to perish in the revolutionary world storm.* This is why they are today counter-revolutionary.[80]

For Engels then, the aspirations of these minority or 'history-less' cultures can only be opportunist. Even as late as in 1882 in a letter he wrote to

Karl Kautsky, he justified his condemnation of the Slav nations as 'tools of Russian Tsardom', and condemned their nationalism as 'fraud' and 'imaginary'. It mattered little, says Talmon, that the 'Slavs were trying to use an international situation to find allies where they could', even if, embarrassing ones, to help them gain independence, in the hope of getting out of their clutches eventually. 'I do not care to look for reasons why the Slav peoples have come to regard the Tsar as their only liberator. It is of no importance…' said Engels in that letter.[81]

What I want to draw out of this discussion of Engels' attitude is precisely the way in which here, the notion of an expressive totality called World-History operates, whose essence is expressed in a single Spirit—the world-revolution. In the face of that 'objective' logos of World-History, it is the destiny of all those who resist, even if out of the desire for their own freedom, to perish. It does not matter why these 'small, stubborn peoples' see their fate tied to that of Tsardom. Notice the similarity here with the smaller, equally stubborn minorities in Alam's discussion, who refused to throw their lot with the dominant 'spirit of the times'—that of nationalism—and collaborated with the reactionary forces of colonialism. If these people had, by some historical accident, arrived on the scene *earlier*, and become 'more developed', like the bigger nations, they could have been redeemed. *Now*, they had no choice. What we have here is once again, different histories and different times, articulated into a single time of a single totality—World-History.

One of the consequences of thus understanding the idea of time has direct bearing on our understanding of a 'troubling' feature of many anticolonial nationalisms, that we can see in the above discussion. This is the question of the 'opportunism' of smaller cultures: their refusal to throw in their lot with the 'larger cause', often to the extent of allying with reactionary forces. In discussions of anticolonial nationalisms, these are generally attributed to the 'divide and rule' strategy pursued by the colonial powers to keep 'the people' or the 'nation' divided. There is no doubt that such strategies are routinely adopted by colonial powers. But simply to reduce the phenomenon to this strategy is to undermine the agency of these marginal cultures and their desire for freedom. We have seen a glimpse of the problem in our two instances above, namely that of Alam and Talmon. I will just add two more instances to underline its importance.

The first is mentioned by Anderson in his discussion of the Venezuelan case. Anderson quotes Simon Bolivar to say that a Negro revolt is a thousand times worse than a Spanish invasion, a position that Bolivar later changed. In the same discussion, Anderson notes that,

It is instructive that one reason why Madrid made a successful come-back in Venezuela from 1814-1816 and held remote Quito until 1820 was that she won the support of the slaves in the former, and of the Indians in the latter in the struggle against the insurgent creoles.[82]

The second instance appears in Michael Taussig's work among the Cuna Indians in what was the former Colombian nation-state. Taussig says that although technically part of the Colombian nation-state for most of the nineteenth century, 'the Cuna inhabited a political backwater at the farthest extreme imaginable', in the mountainous interior of the deep south. They were generally left to themselves, till things suddenly changed in 1903, with the United States' 'orchestration of secession from the Republic of Colombia by the province of Panama' followed by the US construction, 50 miles from the Cuna, of the Panama canal.

Now the governing circles of the fledgling nation-state of Panama, in certain respects an 'imagined community' of the U.S. and certainly its de facto colony, began to play out their love-hate relationship with the colossus of the north on a Cuna theatre, enacting on the Indians what had been enacted on the Panamanians—aping hideous little reconstructions of civilization-versus-savagery dramas on the frontier and vigorously attempting to demolish... the most visible signs of difference, notably the clothes and adornments of the women...

Lying close to the border, the Cuna were initially able to set the Panamanian government off against the Colombian government. But with the consolidation of schools and police in Cuna territory by the Panamanian government, the Cuna found that the global pattern of international power politics and racist energies provided the perfect occasion for their trump card. Using their very Indianness vis-a-vis 'civilization', they played the United States off against the Panamanian State, finding ready allies with Americans from the Canal Zone and from the members of the scientific establishment of Washington D.C.- many of whom were eugenicists committed to racist theories of society and history, especially anti-negro theories.[83]

As can be seen, this is a particularly complicated case, as it involves one subaltern identity arrayed against the other.

This is, however, an aspect that will concern us throughout the discussion on India, particularly in relation to the Dalits and Muslims. How do we understand the aspirations of minority cultures that often perish in the process of nation-building and the consequent attempt to construct homogeneous national cultures? How do we even begin to appreciate their own agency, if we are to avoid pronouncing, like Engels, that it is their destiny to 'perish in the revolutionary storm'? On the other hand, what do we do when a subordinated culture seeks its liberation in the context of the neo-colonialist or imperialist manoeuvres to 'divide and rule' and confronts in the process, other subordinate cultures pitted against itself, thwarting its aspirations to nationhood? In other words, there is, involved here, a dialectic of universality and difference that defies a simple answer that will always privilege one or the other: *either* universalism *or* the right to minority culture. What is required, I will argue, is that we need to specifically locate the discussion of minority cultures in the context of their own subjectivity and agency. We need to understand whether there is really a popular aspiration behind such assertions, or whether it is the agency of a colonizing power, that props them up with the help of some small section of self-seeking elites—that is, when 'differences' between cultures are fetishized by an imperialist or colonialist power, in order to challenge the growing nationalist assertions of a subjugated culture. In the last analysis, cultures need to be understood not as eternal or timeless givens, but as social constructs and it is of crucial significance what the communities think of themselves at a particular historical juncture. Do they see themselves as part of a nation-to-be, or do they see their future as distinct and different from that of the majority? It is also necessary here to emphasize that I am not suggesting that the 'they' should include the 'majority' of the particular minority concerned, with the minority being defined in terms of some objective criteria. In the case of the Muslims of India, for instance, there is no doubt that a majority of them did not support the demand for Pakistan. It was initially a demand of the elite of northern India and in the best of times, enjoyed the support of only a section of the north Indian Muslims. Yet, it was a support that was big enough not to be ignored. The fact is that politically, the opposition in the form of the 'nationalist Muslims' to the Muslim League platform, was rapidly marginalized, leaving the Muslim League as the only legitimate voice of the 'community'. That within a few years of the formation of Pakistan, assertion of Bengali sentiment should have begun to fracture the putative 'Muslim' community, leading to the formation of Bangladesh in a little over two decades, shows how 'community' was/is understood differently over different historical contexts. It is worth considering the following possibility as a counterfactual: If the aspiration of the minorities could have found adequate reflection within the mainstream, would the Muslim League, for instance, have ever become the force that it did? And would that inclusiveness have called for a different notion of identity than the one provided by the paradigm of nationhood?

The rest of the book will explore some of the themes raised in this introduction at greater length. In Chapter 1, I will focus specifically on the question of nationalism as it has been discussed by the theorists of nationalism. My discussion of these theorists' work will however, focus on the questions that seem directly relevant for our concerns in the postcolonial context. Anticolonial nationalisms and the deep xenophobia that marks them will be one of my central concerns in this chapter. In this chapter, I will also discuss the broad contours of the ideological formation called secular-nationalism in India. I also bring in a discussion there of the South African case as that helps to complicate the question of universality and difference that emerges as a critical question in the earlier discussion in the chapter. The South African case represents one of the most interesting instances of a 'nation-building' process that seeks to go beyond the paradigm of nationhood—at least in some crucial respects.

In Chapter 2, I examine the conjunctures of the 1980s and 1990s, in order to understand the unravelling of the nation and the crisis of the secular-nationalist imaginary. This chapter basically maps the major developments in these decades, through a reading of parliamentary debates and newspapers of this period. Chapter 3 examines the Indian debate on secularism in detail and suggests that despite sharp ideological polarizations between the different positions, there are certain areas of agreement between them. On the whole the differences relate to different conceptions of what is meant by secularism in the Indian context.

Chapter 4 deals with different historical imaginations that are unleashed in the wake of the discovery of the Self in the late colonial period. I deal specifically with certain imaginations of community and history among the Dalits and the Muslims, which reveal very different notions of Self. I argue in this chapter that the project of Indian nationhood was really an impossible project. Chapter 5 discusses what I have called the Dalit critique of modernity, with particular reference to secularism and the nation. In this chapter, I offer a reading of some of Ambedkar's writings and of some contemporary Dalitbahujan writings to argue my case.

The last chapter discusses another form of secular practice—that of the Marxist left, based on detailed interviews with communist activists. In this chapter I argue that actual secular practice on the ground diverges in significant ways from the official pronouncements of the party. In this context, I also raise the specific question of the agency of what I have called the bilingual activist, who simultaneously inhabits the ground of the community and that of modern political institutions. This gestures towards a significant arena of political activity that is left untouched within general discussions on political theory. For understanding such practices, I use Partha Chatterjee's notion of political society, which I then discuss at greater length in the conclusion.

Notes

1. Chapter 3 of this book deals with the debate in detail.

2. This debate received fresh impetus with the beginning of the Assam movement in 1979 and the demand for the restructuring of centre-state relations initiated by the Left Front government of West Bengal in 1978. Much of the debate was carried out in the *Economic and Political Weekly*. Earlier contributions by Javeed Alam, Ajit Roy, Partha Chatterjee can also be seen in a special issue of the *Social Scientist* (August 1975, no. 37). The later ones include contributions by Amalendu Guha, Hiren Gohain, Sanjib Baruah. See for instance, issues of the *Economic and Political Weekly*, vol. XV, nos 8, 11, 16, 20, 21, 31, 32, 41, 42, 43, 49, (1979), among other contributions.

3. Important contributions in this connection are those by Sudipta Kaviraj on the structure of nationalist discourse and by Partha Chatterjee on the relation of nationalist thought and colonial domination, including a re-reading of many nineteenth-century nationalist texts. See Kaviraj (1992, 1998) and Chatterjee (1986).

4. In a lecture delivered in 1977, Foucault once used the expression 'insurrection of subjugated knowledges' to refer to the emergence in the recent past, of knowledges once made illegitimate by the canons of scientificity. See Foucault (1977).

5. See Lyotard (1984/92), p. xxiv. This expression has somehow been routinely construed as the *death* of metanarratives.

6. Hall (1996), p. 347. Hall calls this phenomenon the 'return of the repressed'.

7. It is useful to recall the way in which both problems were sought to be resolved in a single stroke: by postulating that the working class, by virtue of its being tied to the most advanced mode of production and being the most exploited class, was therefore the most historically advanced (and the carrier of the most advanced ideas) and objectively more interested in changing the world and transcending capitalism.

8. It should be emphasized that a critique of modernity does not entail, as is so often thought to be the case, a return to some pristine past. In fact, most poststructuralist and 'postmodernist' critiques, as I understand them, are attempts at interrogating our own subject-positions from within modernity. There is no outside to modernity, and its critique therefore is immanent. Its resources cannot be drawn from any external position.

9. I will discuss this relationship of nationalism with democratic citizenship at length, in Chapter 1.

10. Heidegger, *Nietzsche*, cited in Kolb (1986), pp. 137–50. Also see, Heidegger (1982).

11. Kolb (1986), p. 141.

12. Taylor (1993), pp. 317–18.

13. Ibid., p. 318.

14. Fromm (1942/2001), *The Fear of Freedom*, Routledge, London and New York, p.3.

15. Ibid., pp. 34–42.

16. Ibid., p. 24.

17. Deleuze and Guattari (1983), p. 29.

18. Arendt (1968).

19. Schmitt, (1992) p. 6.

20. Ibid.

21. Balibar (1991), p. 96. Balibar describes fictive ethnicity as the 'community instituted by the nation-state'. I think it is necessary to modify this description. It is nationalism, even before it assumes a state form, that creates this fictive ethnicity, by undoubtedly drawing on pre-existing communities of culture, usually hegemonic ones.

22. Ibid.

23. Arendt (1968), p. 15.

24. Gasset (1932), p. 18.

25. Ibid., p. 52.

26. Ibid., p. 63, all emphasis added.

27. Ibid., p. 80, emphasis added.

28. Kohn (1944/67), p. 120.

29. On filiation and affiliation, see the discussion later in this chapter.

30. Cited in and discussed by Giner (1976), pp. 47–8.

31. Sternhell (1976), p. 348.

32. Although this may not have been explicitly asserted as the only possible outcome of the radically secular idea of the self, the entire pedagogical project of democracy has been geared to the production of the rational, rights-bearing citizen.

33. Giner (1976), p. 51.

34. Ibid., pp. 51–2. Emphasis added.

35. See Habermas (1992), pp. 133–7.

36. Taylor (1975), p. 414.

37. Here I am clearly resisting an argument such as Dipesh Chakravarty's which is suspicious of any idea of 'transition'. 'Transition' he claims, is a notion that invokes a telos, such that the subject of all history always remains Europe. All other histories remain in that case, he argues, versions of that real history. My argument here is that once modernity and its institutions, practices, knowledge etc., become globalized, a certain transition becomes inevitable. Except that we do not really know what the transition will be towards, because the larger processes are continuously interrupted by other histories.

38. I use the term *telos* here in the more general sense of aim, purpose, or goal, though it is used elsewhere in this book also in its stronger sense of immanence, of some kind of inevitability.

39. Taylor (1993), p. 327.

40. Ibid., p. 318.

41. Dallmayr (1996), p. 77, emphasis added.

42. Heidegger (1962), pp. 91–3.

43. For Heidegger's elaboration of these categories see ibid., pp. 226–34.

44. Guigon (1993), p. 27.

45. See Gellner (1983). For a more detailed discussion see Chapter 1.

46. Said (1991), pp. 16–17.

47. The problem with Said's formulation, however, is that it places too naïve an emphasis on the binaries of filiation and affiliation, or of *gemeinschaft* and *gesellschaft*—often even casting this distinction in terms of a nature (filiation) and culture (affiliation) division.

48. Ibid., p. 17.

49. Ibid., pp. 17, 19.

50. Ibid., p.19, emphasis added.

51. Gordon (1971), p. 18.

52. I discuss the centrality of the production of a homogeneous national culture to the project of nationhood in the next chapter.

53. Anderson (1991), pp. 22–31.

54. Ibid., p. 24.

55. Ibid., p. 26, emphasis added. Anderson takes this idea of 'homogeneous empty time', as we know, from Walter Benjamin.

56. Koselleck (1985), p. xxiv.

57. Ibid., p. 94.

58. Ibid., p. 256, emphasis added.

59. Ibid., p. 141.

60. Renan (1996), p. 44–5. Saint Barthelomew's day on 24 August 1572, it will be remembered, was the day when thousands of Huguenots were said to have been massacred by the Catholics in France, over 2000 in Paris alone and about 3000 in the provinces. For details see Mack (1997), pp. 90–5.

61. Samaddar (1999), p. 108.

62. I borrow this expression from Alam (1999b).

63. I say this despite Anderson's claim that 'nation' and 'ethnic' community arise on two different grounds—those of unbounded and bounded seriality. See Anderson (1998), p. 40. It seems to me that it is almost impossible to fix the boundaries between the two, given the seamlessness with which each seems to move into the other in different historical moments.

64. See Althusser and Etienne (1977), pp. 94–100.

65. Ibid., p. 105

66. Althusser and Balibar, Ibid., pp. 279–80

67. Ibid., p. 281

68. Habermas (1995), pp. 6–7.

69. Ibid., p. 12.

70. Ricouer (1990), p. 211.

71. Ibid., p. 215.

72. Ibid., p. 216.

73. Habermas (1995), p. 12.

74. I should mention here that Althusser proposes this idea as against what he calls the Hegelian idea of an expressive totality. For my part, I think the idea is valuable irrespective of its polemical value—of which I am not quite sure.

75. Alam (1999b), see pp. 90–6. All emphasis in the quotations added.

76. Alam relates this to what he builds as a general thesis about the formation of the modern elite in colonial conditions. In this thesis Alam posits a kind of sociological law that all colonially dependent elites begin with collaboration with the alien rulers. I do not agree with this thesis in its present form because it is based on a somewhat superficial, empirical correlation between colonial rule and the formation of elites. However, cast differently, it can be related to the Fanon-Memmi thesis of the moment of mimesis (which I discuss later), but that is not relevant here.

77. Nehru (1946/82), p. 565.

78. See Taylor (1975), p. 390.

79. J.L. Talmon (1981) *The Myth of the Nation and the Vision of Revolution*, Seeker and Warburg (London and Univ. of California Press, Berkley, p. 43

80. Ibid., pp. 43–4, emphasis added.

81. Ibid., p.56.

82. Anderson (1983/91), p. 49.

83. Taussig (1993), pp. 138–9.

1

Nationalism, Democracy, and the Postcolonial World

Introduction

In this chapter, I will examine the discursive configuration called secular-nationalism, in order to pose the problem of its crisis in the 1980s. I will do so by exploring the relationship between secular-nationalism and nationalisms in general, and postcolonial/anticolonial nationalisms in particular. Nationalist discourses being discourses of modernity *par excellence*, I will try to explore their complicated relationship to a specifically colonially imposed modernity and the problems that result from this circumstance. I will first look at the phenomenon of nationalism through the writings of some of the leading scholars and theorists in the field. I look especially at the experiences of large-scale dislocation that accompany modern development, creating in their train, huge sectors of population that live a highly volatile existence. The dislocations, coupled with the emergence of modern democratic politics for the first time in history, constitute these populations into 'the masses'—composed mostly of uprooted, atomized individuals. The specific experiences of dislocation in colonized societies, creates, apart from such 'masses', also a very different kind of elite that becomes the vehicle of anticolonial nationalisms.

I also look at the South African experience of nation-building and use it to complicate the dialectic of the universal and the particular that we discussed in the introduction, and which, in a way, animates the entire book. In the penultimate section, I discuss the entity called secular nationalism at some length. Finally, I give a provisional description of the key terms that I use in the book—some of which are elaborated at different places in different chapters.

It is customary to study social/political movements, organizations, and discourses in the period of their ascendance. The 'sudden' appearance on the political stage of certain trends—the Hindu right or the Dalit tendencies for instance—becomes the occasion for a process of social scientific inquiry of 'explaining' the rise of those tendencies. Characteristically, these explanatory exercises have to draw on the general mood of triumph or high levels of self-confidence of the movement, that retrospectively produce its growth as some kind of inevitability. Internally, these moments of growth or victory mean a silencing of dissenting voices and an unprecedented legitimization of the hegemonic voice. Thus it is only in what Marx described as the moment of self-criticism—in other words, the moment of the first initial defeats or retreats—that the hitherto silenced voices begin to get heard.[1] Typically, this leads either to the hegemonic discourse recasting itself, restructuring its terms, or to opening out of the conflict within. However, it is only in moments of extreme crisis and serious decline, that the myriad silenced voices find expression and the possibility of a no-holds-barred introspection opens up. I believe that it is at such times that a more fruitful understanding of movements is made possible. The discourse of secular-nationalism is not best understood at its Nehruvian 'moment of arrival'.[2] Then and in the subsequent decades of its hegemony, it is precisely that discourse that *produces* common sense. It is that which provides the elements and language of critique—the critique of tradition, of oppressions of the old order, as well as of colonialism and imperialism. At such times it is capable of producing only hagiographies and self-congratulatory autobiographies. Its weapon of criticism is addressed elsewhere—it is directed outwards and incapable of being wielded for self-correction. It is the moment of crisis that forces re-examination and opens out possibilities for the re-emergence of the marginalized voices, if in entirely new forms. A moment of crisis then is also a moment of immense possibilities.

Secular-nationalism in India was nationalism in its 'moment of arrival', that is at the point when through a kind of 'ideological reconstruction', nationalism was transformed from the hegemonic discourse of a movement, to a state ideology. However, the main presuppositions of this discourse were already present within the movement, represented especially in the person of Jawaharlal Nehru. Nationalism in India was born in the dual moment of its struggle against colonial domination and the encounter with modernity. Its emancipatory ideals too, were effected largely, though not exclusively, through this encounter with modernity. In a sense, India was inserted into 'world-history' through the encounter with modernity. This insertion made available ideas from other dissenting and critical traditions to the Indian elite, ideas that it imbibed, from its own subjugated location. This location made for a necessarily critical and selective reception of the ideas of modernity. Confronted with 'world-conquering Western thought', it was forced to articulate its position *against* many of the presuppositions of this thought. It was in this conflict-ridden and often contradictory situation, that the discourse of Indian nationalism was formed.[3] I will argue, however, that *secular-nationalism* came to be the ruling ideology of the postcolonial Indian state by keeping itself relatively insulated from the severe contestations *within the incipient nation*, precisely in its bid to fashion a modern democratic polity. Nationalism, under the hegemonic leadership of Gandhi, fought the battle for liberation from colonial rule, while at the same time, negotiating different impúlses of emancipation among the different sections of the population like the Muslims and Dalits. Nehruvian secular-nationalism, on the other hand, managed to keep itself insulated from the latter. Gandhian nationalism, it needs to be noted, represented an extremely complex phenomenon, which we cannot go into in detail here. Suffice it to note however, that Gandhi was the lone leader whose nationalism sought to include, rather than exclude, other streams like the Muslims and Dalits, if often in extremely misplaced ways. Further, Gandhian nationalism sought to accomplish this task by soft-pedalling the question of 'independence' by defining 'swaraj' in somewhat metaphysical ways. Gandhi seems to have understood that rushing the agenda of freedom and self-determination of the nation, without first resolving the great potential and manifest conflicts within—among the Hindus and Muslims and Hindus and Dalits—would jeopardize the very cause of freedom. He seems to have realized that the more stridently he raised the question of independence, the more difficult it would be to win over these sections. Yet, the very vocabulary of Gandhi's political mobilization, the very articulation of his moral world in the language of Hindu religious categories, endangered the project he strove to accomplish. Nonetheless, Gandhi and Indian nationalism under his leadership, even though it failed to bring the Muslims and the Dalits into the movement, did succeed in welding together the diverse linguistic groups into the common struggle and the Indian nation.

In the process then, the nation that was born was, in many ways, very different from the nations as they emerged in the West, particularly Europe. The Indian nation managed to preserve the linguistic diversity of its culture but failed in other respects. Amidst serious contestations and efforts to construct the nation along the lines of the Hindi-Hindu-Hindustan slogan, the combination of the Gandhian and Nehruvian streams posited 'unity-in-diversity' as the essence of Indian nationhood. At its root, however, nationalism remained embedded in the discourse of high modernity, of rationalism and order. Gandhi himself remained an irritant to most Congress leaders who thought his fads needed to be checked, once swaraj was achieved.[4] In the post-independence period, it was Nehru and the modernists' vision that took over. It is not surprising therefore, that in its moment of crisis, it seems to share the fate of many of these ideals of modernity. The unravelling of the Indian nation in the 1980s and 1990s, and the continuing attempts at redefining its cultural contours by marginalized groups, points to the hypothesis that I seek to explore in the discussion in this chapter and more generally in the book: that nationalisms—and modern universalisms in general—being predicated on an erasure of cultural difference, can at best only be privileges of the dominant and the already powerful.[5] They may or may not succeed in erasing difference but they do relegate it to the realm of the unspeakable and in so doing, they render marginalized subaltern cultures, voiceless. Consequently, I will argue, the power that they preserve and consolidate, is always the power of already entrenched social groups; a power, in other words, that is always founded on the history of racial, religious, ethnic, caste, gender, and class privilege. At the heart of the most secular of nationalisms and universalisms then, lie embodied the non-secular privileges of the 'past'. At a more specific level, I will also try to understand the problem of anticolonial nationalisms in the third world in the context of their complex relationship with modernity—their articulation of these universalisms with the hegemonic narratives of selfhood. Secular-nationalism too, I will suggest in the final section of this chapter, carries this burden of modern universalisms, sharing thereby, a common ground with Hindu nationalism—insofar as they both preserve the same power even if in different ways. I leave a further elaboration of this idea to later chapters of the book. Chapters 4, 5, and 6, in particular, illustrate this 'Hindu' character of secular-nationalism.

I draw specific empirical instances to argue my point from the experiences of India and South Africa. Bringing in the South African experience helps, I believe, in understanding more clearly and in a more nuanced way, the question of cultural 'difference'. In the apartheid conditions, an especially fetishized/reified form of difference was made to serve the purposes of one of the most brutal of regimes the twentieth century has known. A discussion of South Africa helps, I believe, to put the question of universality and difference in perspective. We will return to a more detailed discussion of anticolonial nationalisms and secular-nationalism later. Before that it is necessary to first turn to the phenomenon of nationalism in general.

Nationalism and Its Discontents

There exists a large body of work on the phenomenon of nations and nationalism, not all which is directly relevant to our concern here.[6] My concern in this chapter, I have mentioned, is specifically with anticolonial or third-world nationalisms—terms which I will use interchangeably. Most of the authoritative work on nationalism is located within a specifically European context and related to developments almost two centuries old. The concerns that animate those debates and writings are specifically European/Western. In any case, questions that most such studies address such as whether nationalism was a by-product of industrial society or capitalism, or whether language is the 'true' principle of nationhood, as opposed to any other cultural attribute like religion, are not what this book is interested in. It is also not the task of our discussion here, to *define* nationalism, assuming that such a definition is at all possible.[7] Any attempt to define, it seems to me, is fraught with the danger of reducing it to some 'universal' features, which like all universalisms, will instate some nationalisms as the norm and others as deviations from it. Nevertheless, it is worth looking at some of the literature mentioned above in order to draw out issues and trends relevant to our concerns. Methodologically speaking, however, we need to exercise some caution in the way we read that body of work. It seems to make more sense, in my opinion, to read the Western scholarship and debates in relation to the specific question that we seek to address, rather than to discover the 'truth' about nationalism. It should be clear that I am not arguing that the European experience is irrelevant for us, but only that we need to read it from our own location and on our own terms—without first accepting it as the norm. Often, this will mean that we must look at the work done in other contexts in order to find out where our concerns and histories diverge from those of the West. However, because the language of politics in the modern world is inextricably linked to the language of nationalism and nation-states, there *is* a sense in which the general idea of nationalism is important as a reference point. Since all third world nationalist elites routinely drew upon the European experience, if selectively, we cannot in any case, avoid a reference to that experience and simply fall back on some kind of third world exceptionalism—not to speak of Indian indigenism.

In what follows, I will bring in a reading of some of the writings referred to above, from this point of view. I will discuss the question of nationalism in the context of what I believe is the fundamental impasse in many anti-colonial nationalisms. To anticipate the argument that follows, this impasse is embodied in what appears as the almost insurmountable opposition between nationalism and marginalized or minority cultures. For, if it is true that nationalism universalizes dominant cultures, as the following discussion argues, then the resistances offered by smaller cultures to assimilation must be understood as democratic impulses. To the extent, therefore, that nationalisms are predicated upon an intolerance of difference, its universalizing drive can also be understood as being directed against democracy itself. However, the opposition between nationalism and democracy must not be understood as a simple opposition to the institutional forms of democracy. Rather, it should probably be understood as the expression of a deep-rooted paradox within the structure of nationalism. This paradox is embodied in the contradictory impulse of nationalism to 'invite the masses into history'—to borrow Tom Nairn's evocative phrase[8]—on the one hand, and the equally elemental impulse to homogenize and obliterate difference. This is a paradox that is in some senses integral to all nationalisms but as we will see, it acquires a special salience in the context of anticolonial nationalisms.

It is generally agreed upon by most theorists of nationalism—as diverse as Hans Kohn, Ernest Gellner, Eric Hobsbawm, and Benedict Anderson—that nationalism is not merely a European, but also a specifically modern product. Whether it is seen to be related to the arrival of 'universal history' (Kohn), industrialism (Gellner), print capitalism (Anderson), or simply capitalism, all theorists agree on its modernity. What all of them also point out, with differing degrees of emphasis, is the imperative of *cultural homogenization* that accompanies nationalism. Of course, not all of them share Gellner's celebration of it. Gellner argues forcefully that cultural homogenization is the very 'objective, inescapable imperative' of industrial society: it is not that nationalism 'imposes' homogeneity, but on the contrary, this imperative of homogeneity takes the form of nationalism. He therefore advises that, for this reason, 'we had better make our peace with it.'[9] Culture, in the industrial age, is a 'necessary shared medium, the life-blood', the 'minimal shared atmosphere within which alone members of society can breathe and survive and produce.'[10] It is the medium through which education and training so indispensable to industrial society, is now imparted. For a given society, therefore, 'it must be the *same* culture' and more importantly, 'it must now be a great or high culture' which 'can no longer be a diversified, locality-tied, illiterate little culture or tradition.'[11] In Elie Kedourie's view too, nationalism is a specifically European doctrine, 'invented...at the beginning of the nineteenth century.'[12] But Kedourie emphasizes that the deep roots of the desire for cultural homogenization lie in *European culture* itself, rather than in modernity or industrialism—and that these roots can be traced back to the sixth-century Roman Empire under Emperor Justinian. Since then, the tendency to deprive 'pagans, heretics and Jews of all rights in the body politic' has been an abiding feature of Roman law and government.[13] It was the codification of this law by the Byzantine emperors that became the foundation of European medieval law. He argues against Arnold Toynbee who he says, believed 'quite wrongly', that 'this intolerance of heterogeneous beliefs, is a Judaic legacy to Christian politics of Byzantium and Europe.' As evidence he cites the instance of Islam—'another religion, perhaps more closely affiliated to Judaism than Trinitarian Christianity', which despite its warlike beginnings, 'never demanded religious uniformity and from the start made a place within its polity for those of a different belief...a place recognized and sanctioned by law.'[14] Kedourie specifically mentions the 'highly developed *millet* system' of the Ottoman Empire and adds: 'And what is true of Muslim lands is equally true of the lands of Hinduism and Buddhism. In none of these areas, before the coming of European influence, was a homogeneous population considered a religious or political ideal...'[15] However, if we read Kedourie's own account closely, even in Europe, the generalization of the desire for homogeneity into the dominant norm takes place in the modern era when nationalism is invented in the nineteenth century.[16]

For Hans Kohn, the age of nationalism 'represents the first period of universal history.' Before that, according to him, there was the 'long era of separate civilizations and continents among which little, if any, intercourse existed.'[17] We have discussed the notion of 'universal history' and some of its implications earlier; for the present let us note that 'universal' here connotes more than what Kohn implies. We need to understand 'universal' here in a dual sense. It was not simply 'an ever-widening process of acculturation, economic exchange and intensification of communication' that enveloped the entire globe.[18] This age was also 'universal' in the sense that the word is used in 'universal suffrage' and 'universal education'. It was universal in the sense that for the first time, the 'masses were invited into history', thus enveloping all classes and sections of 'national societies'. Tom Nairn, in fact, explicitly relates the arrival of nationalism to 'the political baptism of the lower classes.'[19] This political baptism of the lower classes, however, meant, among other things, the forging of a common language and culture—a common medium of 'communication'. This is what appears in Gellner's more ruthless rendering: 'most cultures are led to the dust-heap of history by industrial civilization, *without offering any resistance.*[20] On Gellner's account, these cultures went into the dust-heap of history because, once uprooted by industrialization, they willingly identified themselves with, and 'yearned for' 'incorporation into some *one* of the cultural pools which already (had) or look(ed) as if it might acquire a state of its own, with the subsequent promise of full cultural citizenship, access to primary education, employment and all.'[21] Kohn's 'acculturation' and Gellner's ominously teleological 'dust-heap of history', refer then, to the same process of cultural homogenization, though the context of Gellner's discussion is internal to the prospective 'nation', while Kohn's is more explicitly external and global. This homogenization, also evident in the emergence of the print-culture and the rapid standardization of certain vernacular languages, that Anderson talks of, is in fact the prerequisite as well as the consequence of the emergence of nationalism. To the extent that in its initial phases it is not a state-enforced process, it is at least non-coercive in an explicit sense. There was no identifiable oppressor; it was accomplished through the impersonal 'forces of the historical process'. In case it *was* explicitly coercive, as Ernest Renan in his classic essay concedes it was, it was still a case of the 'cunning of Reason', as Hegel would have put it. For, 'historical enquiry brings to light deeds of violence which took place at the origin of all political formations, even of those whose consequences have been altogether beneficial.' 'Unity', continues Renan, 'is always effected by means of brutality; the union of northern France with the Midi was the result of massacres and terror lasting for the best part of a century.'[22]

We can safely assume then, that this process of developing a homogeneous national culture was central to the project of nationalism. This is not to say, of course, that in each case, it was equally successful in the same way. Historical antecedents did certainly modulate the ways in which this national culture was imagined and finally took shape. Etienne Balibar provides a more nuanced understanding of this homogenization when he suggests that differences are not always suppressed; often they are relativized and subordinated to the national culture.[23]

What is important here is the fact that this project of the construction of a homogeneous national culture was considered liberatory, in that it enabled the imagination of a larger political community within which the ideal of citizenship and democracy, of rights and equality was to be, and generally was, realized.[24] 'The growth of nationalism is the process of integration of the masses into a common political form', says Kohn.[25] Tracing its beginnings to the French revolution, he argues that 'nationalism is inconceivable without the ideas of popular sovereignty preceding—

without a complete revision of the position of the ruler and the ruled, of classes and castes.'[26] For him, this is the 'original' impulse within nationalism—the one that was born in Western Europe and was 'connected with the concepts of individual liberty and rational cosmopolitanism current in the eighteenth century.'[27] To Eric Hobsbawm too, 'the element of citizenship and mass participation' was central to the phenomenon.[28] Benedict Anderson seems to make an exception in the case of the 'creole pioneers' of the Western hemisphere, where 'far from seeking to "induct the lower classes into political life", one key factor spurring the drive for independence from Madrid, in such important cases as Venezuela, Mexico and Peru, was *the fear* of 'lower-class' political mobilizations.'[29] The icon of Venezuelan liberation Simon Bolivar, says Anderson, himself stated that a '"Negro revolt" was a thousand times worse than Spanish invasion'. But even in this exceptional case, Anderson observes that Bolivar subsequently changed his mind about the slaves, and that 'his fellow-liberator San Martin decreed in 1821 that "in the future the aborigines shall not be called Indians or natives; they are children *and citizens* of Peru and they shall be known as Peruvians."'[30] Anderson's exception, in that case, does not seem to be much of one. The point that Anderson finds himself in agreement with more generally, and which is the key issue I wish to point to, is that historically, the arrival of nationalism in the West was tied to the overall question of citizenship and the creation, clearly by force, of a homogeneous national community: it would in a Rousseauesque way 'force the people to be free'. About this relationship to citizenship, and the massive transformations initiated by the advent of mass print culture and the 'accumulating memory of print', following the French revolution, Anderson is clear: 'Out of this American welter came these imagined realities: nation-states, republican institutions, common citizenships, popular sovereignty, national flags and anthems.'[31] Invoking Tom Nairn's phrase, he continues:

Even backward and reactionary Hungarian and Polish gentries were hard put not to make a show of 'inviting in' (if only to the pantry) their oppressed compatriots...If 'Hungarians' deserved a national state, then that *meant* Hungarians, all of them; it meant a state in which the ultimate locus of sovereignty had to be a collectivity of Hungarian speakers and readers...[32]

This when half the subjects of the kingdom of Hungary were non-Magyar, the high Magyar aristocracy spoke French or German and the middle and lower nobility conversed in a dog-Latin strewn with Magyar, Slovak, Serb, and Romanian expressions as well as vernacular German.[33]

While the above discussion illuminates the relation between nationalism and the quest for modern democratic citizenship, it should also alert us to the other implicit meaning of this relationship. The idea of citizenship is tied to the notion of the individual self—it can only be an attribute of the individual. Communities and social groups or classes cannot be 'citizens'. Yet that is precisely what the idea of nationalism has to deal with in many of its subsequent incarnations. Nationalism did not retain its original associations intact in all its later incarnations. As Kohn points out, already by the time it reached central and eastern Europe, it had become detached from this origin:

Nationalism in Germany did not find its justification in a rational conception, it found it in the 'natural' fact of a community, held together not by the will of its members nor by any obligations of contract, but by traditional ties of kinship and status. German nationalism substituted for the legal and rational concept of 'citizenship' the infinitely vaguer concept of the 'folk'.[34]

This is the form, according to him, that the search for indigenous 'originality' took, in German, Russian, and Indian nationalisms—albeit drawing inspiration from certain marginal West European traditions. However, it did retain one crucial aspect of the initial impulse: 'the invitation of the masses into history' remained. Only, it was now articulated in a different language that tore it 'out of its semantic field of origin' and deployed it in a different one,[35] but it retained *some* notion of the 'enfranchisement' of the people. With that idea, its relationship continued in most subsequent incarnations. Of course, once the link with the idea of citizenship was severed, 'people' themselves could be imagined in different ways. We have seen one version of this German nationalism, expressed in its most violent form subsequently in the history of Nazism. What this transformation, the severance of its links with the idea of citizenship, and its insertion into a discourse of community, did to nationalism has as much to do with nationalism as with the system of representative parliamentary democracy and its allied idea of citizenship that prevailed in nineteenth-century Europe. Zeev Sternhell, for instance, in his study of fascist ideology, quotes from a significant observation by Eugen Weber:

Eugen Weber has pointed out that the liberal politics of the nineteenth century were representative and parliamentary. *But the representative system of which parliament is the symbol, functioned adequately only in a deferential society*, where distinction of achievement and wealth had replaced distinction of birth, but where the concept of distinction as such survived...*The parliamentary representative system had been worked out by and for an elitist society* not much more inclusive than the aristocratic society it replaced. In the mass society that took over at the end of the nineteenth century, with its democratic structure and its egalitarian ideology, parliament either did not, or was no longer felt to, work properly.[36]

In other words, the revolt against the elitism of representative parliamentary democracy was to some extent at least, responsible for the break with the idea of citizenship and the emergence of a different kind of nationalism in the subsequent period. This period towards the end of the nineteenth century was also marked, we may recall, by the intellectual and philosophical revolt against Reason which surely made its contribution to the process and runs parallel as an intellectual revolt against the *elitism* of Reason. It is important to note the effect of a 'dislocation' (*decalage*) that the history of nationalism carries—in this transference of the ground from that of citizenship to that of 'natural' community (the *volk*).[37] For this dislocation continues, in different ways, through different histories of anticolonial nationalisms. It is to this specific nature of these nationalisms that we now turn.

Anticolonial Nationalisms

Anticolonial nationalisms, born in the struggle against imperial domination and often led by left-wing nationalist elements, as in much of Asia, Africa, and Latin America, have had a deeply democratic content. Very often, combined with moderate to radical socio-economic programmes, as in the case of China, Vietnam, Cuba, Angola, Mozambique, Nicaragua, and such other countries, they have not only led to a wide transformation of the globe by ushering in the era of decolonization; in some cases they have also succeeded in transforming the life of ordinary people within these countries. In many others, they have not had that same degree of success in socio-economic terms. However, these aspects of anticolonial nationalisms—national liberation struggles in Marxist parlance—do not concern us here directly. For our purpose here is to explore the relatively under-explored aspects of anticolonial nationalisms that relate to the cultural-political level. The discussion here is not meant to be a 'total' assessment of the nationalist phenomenon but intends rather, to understand its present crisis in the face of the overall anxieties regarding identity. The specific concern of the following discussion will be the relationship of these nationalisms to minority cultures.

Much of what has been discussed in relation to nationalism in Europe, which is nationalism as an 'invitation to the people into history', and following upon it, its close relationship to democracy and citizenship, remains relevant to some extent in this context too. However, this much has been widely acknowledged and I will not go into those aspects here. The real questions in relation to the nationalist phenomena, however, have emerged in the close relationship of postcolonial nationalisms with a deep xenophobia. That is what I seek to explore below.[38]

Our discussion of the mass man and the allied figure of the jacobin in the Introduction becomes relevant in our discussion here because the kind of large-scale dislocations that modernity brings in its train, creates a highly unstable and volatile mass, open to different kinds of mobilizations. However, it must be stated at the outset that it is more the second figure— that of the jacobin personality—that we will be concerned with here. The mass man as such, does not really figure in our discussions, except incidentally. The figure of the jacobin is important to bear in mind however, in the context of the nationalist elites and their interventions in political mobilizations in general in India too. For it is the experience of widespread dislocation of different kinds, along with the emergence of an elite in a world of rapid transition, that provides the backdrop to the activity of these elites, re-inventing community life, now imagined as a nation. Such elites could only have been modern, individuated people, yet connected in some ways to their respective filiative orders. It is not simply fortuitous that the two great leaders of the Hindu and Muslim nationalisms, Vinayak Damodar Savarkar and Mohammed Ali Jinnah, were atheists and rationalists, and the third, the 'father of the nation', Gandhi, almost became one.[39] It is also important to bear in mind that while the bulk of the nationalist mobilizations in colonized countries came from the peasantry, it is the urban centres, increasingly inhabited by people dislocated in the recent past, which have been the theatre of all 'spectacular' forms of politics, then disseminated by the media to become country-wide phenomena. These include communal or sectarian tensions and violence through a large part of the late colonial period. We will discuss the Indian situation later, but let us note the following observation made in the African context, by Frantz Fanon:

The working class of the towns, the masses of unemployed, the small artisans and craftsmen for their part line up behind this nationalist attitude [of the native bourgeoisie]; but in all justice let it be said, they follow in the footsteps of their bourgeoisie. If the national bourgeoisie goes into competition with the Europeans, the artisans and craftsmen start a fight against non-national Africans. In the Ivory Coast, the anti-Dahoman and anti-Voltaic troubles are in fact racial riots... From nationalism we have passed to ultra-nationalism, to chauvinism, and finally to racism.[40]

The experience of dislocation involving the urban-dweller, who forms a critical part of nationalist, and subsequently, chauvinist mobilization is evident from Fanon's description. It is also worthwhile to recall the emphasis in both Fanon and Mao Tsetung on what came to be known as the *lumpen-proletariat*, especially on its susceptibility to counter-revolutionary and as well as revolutionary mobilizations.[41] My point is that certain kinds of discourses are received with enthusiasm in mass audiences because they speak, if in highly mediated and often pathological ways, to such widespread experiences of multiple dislocation.

However, we need to be careful in stretching the argument too far. Beyond this level of generality, we will need to explore the specific experiences of dislocation and the ways in which specific discourses are produced that gain currency and establish themselves as hegemonic, by speaking to these experiences. As Ernesto Laclau puts it, from this structural dislocation, 'new possibilities of historical action emerge', for, 'the world is less "given" and must be increasingly constructed.' And this involves not merely a construction of the world, but 'of the social agents as well' 'who transform themselves and forge new identities as a result.'[42] And it is entirely possible that the 'historical action' may take any form—moving, as Fanon suggests, between nationalism and chauvinism.

I have discussed in greater detail, in Chapter 4, what can be called the Memmi–Fanon thesis about the constitution of the subjectivity of the colonized. Both Albert Memmi and Fanon in their own ways identify two moments of this constitution. The native intellectual, who is marked by a 'cultural schizophrenia', consequent upon colonial rule, starts off by mimicking or emulating the colonizer, in the first moment. 'He' achieves self-realization, in the second moment, when he 'decides to remember' who he is. This begins the phase of recovering a 'memory' that he has long lost. In this phase, he therefore imagines a past, dug out of old legends, interpreted in the light of 'a conception of the world discovered under other skies'. This is a past that is erected in radical alterity to the colonizing power—predicated on the 'essential difference' of the native from the colonizer. The imagination of the new nation, in the consciousness of the colonized, always carries, therefore, the mark of this experience of subjugation. I will not anticipate the entire discussion of this question here, but suffice it to note that beneath this consciousness lies another very specific experience of dislocation, within which it is entirely possible for a democratic anti-imperialism to co-habit with a latent xenophobia. For the purposes of this chapter, it is enough to note here that the resurrection of Khmer glory in the Marxist-Leninist discourse of the Khmer Rouge in Cambodia and the 'reinscription' of the 'construction of socialism within the frame of the return to the ancient Inca empire' by the Sendero Luminoso in Peru, do not represent exceptional cases.[43] It is also not without significance that Pol Pot, before becoming a revolutionary was a professor at a French lycee at Phnom Penh, 'known for his subtle reading of Rimbaud and Mallarme' and Abimael Guzman, leader of Sendero Luminoso was a philosophy professor who did his thesis on Kant.[44] This co-habitation of indigenism/xenophobia alongside a rational, democratic anti-imperialism is not a characteristic of these communist leaders alone; it is something that is more generally observable in the histories of postcolonial nationalisms.

Much of the recent work on nationalism has followed the rich and textured insights of Benedict Anderson, on the idea that nations are imagined communities. In Anderson's rendering, print-capitalism and the emergence of a secularized world where 'the legitimacy of the divinely-ordained, hierarchical, dynastic realm' was destroyed,[45] appear as the conditions in which a certain kind of imagination became possible, which eventually took the shape of nationalism. A somewhat similar idea is put forward by Ernest Gellner, according to whom 'nationalism is not the awakening of an old, latent, dormant force' but rather something that 'takes pre-existing cultures and turns them into nations, sometimes invents them, and often obliterates pre-existing cultures.'[46] However, as both Anderson and Gellner point out, to say that nations are imagined or invented does not mean that they are in some way unreal or artificial.[47] If we accept nations as 'imagined communities', we must also keep open the possibility of their being imagined along any of the available markers of cultural identity. There are, after all, innumerable ways in which empirically existing nations can be seen to be constructed along such widely differing axes.

Partha Chatterjee has argued, against Gellner and Anderson, that their understanding of nationalism converges, despite important differences, on a kind of sociological determinism whereby third-world nationalisms are reduced to mere copies of the 'original', European ones—of 'modular' character, in Anderson's phrase.[48] If nations are to be distinguished by the styles in which they are imagined, then, strictly speaking, this insistence on the 'modular' character of third-world nationalisms, leaves little by which they can be distinguished, according to Chatterjee. Anderson is, of course, the most sophisticated of all the theorists of nationalism, but he too, says Chatterjee, seems to share the opinion of others like John Plamenatz, Hans Kohn, Elie Kedourie, and Ernest Gellner in this regard. The burden of Chatterjee's argument is that by confining the discussion to the 'modular character of twentieth-century nationalisms' he fails to notice 'the twists and turns, the suppressed possibilities, the contradictions still unresolved.'[49] What interests Chatterjee is the question of the autonomy of third-world nationalist elites. Talking of third-world or anti-colonial nationalisms, he therefore argues that this nationalist ideology is 'inherently polemical' and 'shot through with tension':

It [this polemical tension] is part of the ideological content of nationalism which takes as its adversary a contrary discourse—the discourse of colonialism. Pitting itself against the reality of colonial rule—which appears before it as an existent, almost palpable historical truth—nationalism seeks to assert the feasibility of entirely new political possibilities...Only a vulgar reductionist can insist that these new possibilities simply 'emerge' out of a social structure or out of the supposedly objective workings of a world-historical process, that they do not need to be thought out, formulated, propagated and defended in the battlefield of politics.[50]

It is Chatterjee's contention that merely outlining the historical process and the coordinates of the emergence of nationalism, without attention to the specific contexts and ideological configurations of the formation of nationalist discourse in the colonial world, carries within it the danger of always reducing it to a distorted copy of the 'original' model. Even sophisticated theorists like Anderson can then simply point to the emergence of print capitalism and other coordinates of European nationalism and be content to read the trajectories of anticolonial nationalisms in that light.[51]

By focusing on the self-representation of the nationalist elite and trying to understand Indian nationalism on its own terms, while delinking it from the 'autobiography' that the nation retrospectively gives to itself, Chatterjee actually effects a major break in the study of anticolonial nationalisms. This dual move gives to his intervention the space to interrogate both the Eurocentric discourse on nationalism, as well as many of the common-sense assumptions of this 'autobiography of the nation', now 'uttered in a single and unambiguous voice', glossing over the 'contradictions and divergences of the past'[52].

It is from this position that Chatterjee launches on his project of understanding the formation of the *hegemonic discourse of nationalism*. In order to understand this process he deploys Gramsci's idea of the 'passive revolution of capital' where capital, in adverse conditions, finding itself unable to take head-on the former dominant classes and 'unable to establish complete hegemony over the new nation', resorts to a strategy of slow, molecular transformation. Passive revolution, he argues, is the general form of transition from colonial to postcolonial states in the twentieth century. In this context, he reads nationalist thought in India as *one complex unity*, that goes through three specific 'moments'. The 'moment of departure' represents the coming to self-awareness of nationalism in the late nineteenth century, whereby it demarcates its difference from the colonialists and more generally, the West. The 'moment of maneouvre' represented by Gandhi, is the moment of appropriating the popular, of 'consolidating the national by decrying the modern'; and finally the 'moment of arrival' represented by Nehru, being the moment when nationalism prepares to become the ideology of the postcolonial state. At this last moment, it is the discourse of order, of the rational organization of the state.[53]

In a later elaboration of his argument, Chatterjee makes it explicit that nationalism in its moment of departure, underlines its difference from the West by demarcating an inner spiritual-cultural domain, where it declares itself sovereign. In the outer material domain it is in a position of subordination and subject to the colonial state. By thus rendering the structure of nationalist thought, Chatterjee points to the most crucial move made by it in terms of establishing its hegemony over the incipient nation. It is here that Chatterjee opens out the immense possibilities for a more nuanced study of nationalism. For, once this is done, it becomes possible to really understand how nationalism then 'deals with' all aspirations for internal reform that were characteristic of much of the nineteenth century. Chatterjee has discussed, in particular, what he calls the 'nationalist resolution' of the women's question, which was centrally a part of the early and mid-nineteenth century debates over social reform. The 'sudden disappearance of this question in public debate towards the close of the century' is explained by him as a consequence of 'nationalism's success in situating the "women's question" in (the) inner domain of sovereignty'— the domain of national culture, moreover, that 'was constituted in the light of the discovery of "tradition".'[54] By situating the 'women's question' now in the inner domain, nationalism thereby refused to make it 'an issue of political negotiation with the colonial state'.[55]

However, it is also here, that the possibilities opened out by Chatterjee's framework seem to be pushed to the margins by the further direction of

his inquiry. For one thing, in his inquiry there are only two players—the colonial state and the nationalist elite. He, therefore, fails to push the implications of the 'refusal to negotiate' further. There are, I believe, two sides to this refusal that follows from the construction of the inner domain of sovereignty. Like all sovereignties, this one too, must be seen as having an external and an internal dimension: one in relation to the colonial state and the other, in relation to what it believes to be the future nation. Its sovereignty in relation to the nation has two further aspects. The first aspect, that Chatterjee deals with, is the bid to produce the 'new woman', different not only from the Western woman, but also from her traditional position—cultured, educated, and properly 'socialized'.[56] The second aspect, its relation to the emergence of women's subjectivity outside the pale of nationalist politics, and often in defiance of it, is relegated by him to a position of no analytical significance. If the subjectivity of women does appear historically, as marginal in this period, this fact is by no means devoid of analytical significance.[57] But our point would become clearer with reference to lower caste assertions. For, in nationalist thinking, caste reform too was a matter of the inner domain. It was this that led to acute frictions and clashes between the nationalists and the leaders of the lower castes, with Tilak and his followers threatening to burn down the *pandal* of the Social Conference that used to take place till 1897, alongside the sessions of the Indian National Congress. The Social Conference, it is well known, dealt with questions of internal social reform. Not that the nationalists were always casteist, but they saw the issue of caste reform too as an internal problem of the nation, to be taken up after independence was gained. The 'refusal to negotiate' in this case was not simply a matter of producing a 'new' version of caste, it was enforced by ruthless suppression and, in Gandhi's case, by 'emotional' blackmail. The caste question defied the resolution that nationalism worked out for the women's question.

Similarly, Ayesha Jalal has recently raised some questions in this respect, in relation to the Muslims. I do not agree with her contention that the inner/outer distinction made by Chatterjee is meant to 'skirt around the problem of dismantling the binary opposition between "secular nationalism" and religious communalism', for here, I think she misreads him. It is, in the first place, not 'Chatterjee's distinction', but his rendering of a distinction he argues is implicitly made by nationalism. It is precisely by rendering explicit this implicit distinction in nationalist thought, that he is able to *overcome* the straightforward progressive/reactionary, or secular/communal-revivalist binaries which characterized the histories produced by nationalism in its moment of arrival. However, there is some substance in Jalal's charge that Islam is virtually absent in Chatterjee's rendering of nationalist discourse.[58] Her objection is that he leaves 'unexamined the myriad subaltern contestations of an emerging mainstream nationalism'.[59] It may be argued in Chatterjee's defence that the object of his inquiry in the above two texts is hegemonic nationalism, not its contestations. However, there is still a problem that remains insofar as nationalist discourse itself, especially in its moment of maneouvre, can hardly be fully appreciated without reference to the 'myriad subaltern contestations' referred to by Jalal. Of particular importance, in this context, are the emerging dynamics of Muslim and Depressed Caste (henceforth, I will use the term 'Dalit') politics, not to mention the other stream of privileged upper caste Hindu politics in the shape of the Hindu Mahasabha. Secular-nationalism would not have been what it was, were it not faced with these counter-currents.

A part of the problem, as Aamir R. Mufti points out, is that in 'one important sense', Chatterjee's work 'continues to replicate the autobiographical assumptions of the postcolonial nation-state: it assumes an essential continuity of "Indian" polity from pre- to post-Partition times.'[60] If as Mufti says, the crisis over Muslim identity appears in Chatterjee's book as a marginal event in the life of nationalism, it is, I suggest, a consequence of the fact that he continues to think in terms of 'the nation' and '*its* fragments'. As a consequence, he does not direct his vision to the different imaginings of Selfhood that take place at the same time, many of them not quite compatible with the imagined nation. After all, in the context of the resolution of the women's question, he does notice responses among the Muslims of Bengal, very similar to the nationalist one, in terms of attitude to social reform. One can argue, as Ambedkar did, that among Muslims this response was probably due to their minority status and the fear of being swamped by the Hindus, rather than due to colonialism. That question, however, does not become part of Chatterjee's quest. The fundamental question that underlies his investigations is that of the relationship of the *nationalist elite* to modernity.

It is this silence that Edward Said, in my opinion, points to, when he says that while Chatterjee successfully demonstrates that anti-imperialist nationalism can 'become a panacea for not dealing with economic disparities and social injustice', he fails to emphasize enough 'that the culture's contribution to statism is often the result of a separatist, even chauvinist and authoritarian conception of nationalism.'[61] Though somewhat vague, this comment of Said's can be understood with reference to his immediately preceding discussion where he refers to George

Lamming's and Cuban critic Roberto Fernandez Retamar's discussion of *The Tempest* and the invocation of Caliban as the figure of resistance. The basic question, says Said, that the Latin American discussion seeks to address is, how does a culture seeking to become independent imagine its own past? According to Said, the choice opted for by radical nationalisms that produced concepts like *Negritude*, Islamic fundamentalism or Arabism, represents a particular rendering of the figure of Caliban—one 'who sheds his current servitude and physical disfigurements in the process of discovering his *essential precolonial self*.'[62] Said then goes on to observe that while the awareness of 'one's self as belonging to a subject people is the founding insight of anti-imperialist nationalism' and thus immensely productive in terms of giving rise to new movements, literatures, and political parties, one must remember Fanon's observation about the pitfalls of nationalist consciousness: it can very easily lead to frozen rigidity. 'The dangers of chauvinism and xenophobia... are very real.' 'It is best', he therefore adds, 'when Caliban sees his own history as an aspect of the history of *all* subjugated men and women...'[63] The hegemonic discourse of nationalism being his object, it is this aspect that Chatterjee seems to miss out.

The discussion above underlines the possibility of chauvinism and xenophobia present within the structure of anticolonial nationalisms. It also indicates that this possibility might be linked to the very experience of colonial subjugation. There is at least one case of a postcolonial nationalism where there has been an explicit attempt, in my opinion, to avoid the pitfalls of national consciousness by taking a different route. This is the experience of post-apartheid South Africa, which has sought to locate its project of nation-building not in the hoary, pristine past but in the present. This experiment is still in its infancy and we do not really know where it will go. Nevertheless, it seems an important landmark in the history of modern political communities in the postcolonial world. It is to this experiment that I shall now turn. There is another reason why a closer look at the South African experiment is important for us. It provides an altogether different perspective to the whole question of universality and particularity that we have been discussing. For, despite its conscious attempt to avoid the nationalist ambition of producing a homogeneous national culture, the new regime is deeply suspicious of any excessive emphasis on identity, given the way in which apartheid had fetishized cultural difference. And yet, a look at the public debates in contemporary South Africa, as the following section will show, reveals the same logic of universalism. It is the privilege of the powerful white sections of the population to speak in the language of universalism. The voice of the blacks can only be articulated in the language of cultural difference.

Post-Apartheid South Africa

The South African case is particularly complex because of the specific history of colonialism's intervention in native society. Post-apartheid South Africa is a postcolonial third world country, with the first world right in its midst. Nowhere else did the European imagination graft itself so thoroughly, creating a Europe in the middle of the displaced and dispossessed native space. On the one hand, there is this first world in South Africa that lives in 'world-historical time' and whose history goes back to Portugal, Holland and Britain. On the other is the vast sprawling native space of the black townships and the former 'homelands', compressed into barely 13 per cent of the land, whose history has till recently been denied and who, even today, live like the majority in the rest of the third world.[64] As de Klerk put it in 1990, on the eve of the transition process: 'We have this large Third World component, with the typical Third World problems which are slowly strangling the rest of Africa. We have them in our midst.'[65] This native space is inhabited by a number of tribes, large and small. Then there are the South Africans of coloured and Indian origin whose history goes back to the nineteenth century when they were brought in as indentured labourers. Their memory of a history prior to their arrival in South Africa, is practically non-existent and they do not seem to have integrated fully into the mainstream, although there are the more affluent Indians also, primarily Muslims, whose integration into South African society has been smoother.

The specific problem of South Africa has, of course, been the legacy of apartheid. Although the formal institution of the system of apartheid came about only in 1948, with the Nationalist Party coming to power and the passage of the Group Areas Act in the 1950s, the roots of the system go much farther back—to the period of British rule. As Mahmood Mamdani has argued, it was the British colonialists who discovered the authoritarian possibilities in "native custom" and harnessed it for the purpose of indirect rule, that is, rule of the natives through a *reconstituted* Native Authority. And it was under Louis Botha's 'government of conciliation' (between Afrikaners and Britons), that it was given shape from the time of the formation of the Union of South Africa.[66] Jan Smuts, as Mamdani shows, was the pioneer of the effort to 'rule natives through their own institutions'.[67] Smuts' argument, it is interesting to note, was based on the need to 'recognize' the particularity, difference rather than identity, of the natives with the Europeans. His complaint was that the European rulers in South Africa 'had ruthlessly destroyed' the 'political system of the natives, in order to incorporate them as equals into the white system.' This was unwarranted, and for 'Africa to be redeemed', Smuts argued, a strategy needs to be adopted that will not simply force European institutions on her but one that 'will preserve her unity with her own past'. The result of this policy of indirect rule, Mamdani suggests, has been to freeze the population into so many tribes, each under its 'own' native authority, as if they were put into different containers.[68] Here then, is the embryo of the policy of segregation, on which apartheid was to subsequently build. The continuity of the temporal dimension in Smuts' insistence on preserving Africa's 'unity with her own past' and de Klerk's 'Third World in our midst that is strangling Africa' should not be missed. The first-world-within-the-third-world was quite conscious of the different histories that constituted it and it was a recognition of this difference, embodied in the tribal cultures of the natives, that it made its basis of segregation. This strategy, it would seem on the face of it, takes care of the various later-day critiques of colonialism in countries like India, to the effect that colonialism imposed its own institutions and value-systems on the colonized, in its drive to homogenize.[69] It is necessary therefore to consider this aspect of the so-called preservation of 'native cultures' more closely.

Mamdani suggests that the British reconstituted Native Authority before handing over rule of 'its own people' to it, and in so doing, of the many traditions that existed, it privileged the 'one with the least historical depth' as 'custom'. In this way, custom was already marked by the presence and activity of the colonial state. The ways in which native authority was constituted is certainly important in understanding how colonialism instituted its so-called 'indirect rule', described as 'decentralized despotism' by Mamdani. The advent of colonialism however, not only redefined custom for its own purposes, its very presence introduced a wholly new dynamic in South African society. For now it was not merely a question of horizontal relationships between different tribal communities that mattered, it was also the fact that all relationships between these communities were now mediated vertically, by the existence of the colonial state. More importantly, Smuts was shrewd enough not to extend his idea of cultural difference on to the white population. So, at the very time of the creation of the Union Constitution of 1910, he envisaged the formation of a single *white* nation. 'The whole meaning of Union of South Africa' he said, is that 'we are going to create a nation—a nation which will be of composite character, including Dutch, English, German and Jew, and whatever nationality seeks refuge in this land will be welcome.'[70] Barely two years after this, in 1912, the African National Congress was formed, expressing the desire for the formation of a single black nation that would include all native peoples. The actual formation of a black nation however, was a formidable task, given the activity of the ever-present colonial state to thwart it. There was then, the continuous production and reproduction of the white nation sponsored by the state and the simultaneous drive to block the formation of the black nation. The white nation of settler-colonialists was now pitted against a native population to whom the very possibility of nationhood was denied. In strictly enforcing segregation at different levels, in various phases of their programme like the Group Areas Act, or the prohibition of inter-racial marriages, at one level, and the supposed conferring of 'national autonomy' and 'right of self-determination' through the 'bantustan programmes' from the 1960s onwards, on the other, two purposes were to be simultaneously accomplished. First, through racial segregation, the 'purity' of the white nation was to be ensured, and second, through what Mamdani calls 'containerising' the native population into tribal communities, the possible emergence of a black national consciousness was sought to be prevented. The colonial authorities effectively arrested and confined the native populations not merely in spatial terms. By preventing horizontal interaction among black communities, so necessary for the imagination of a black national consciousness, they also froze these communities in time. It was as if they had to remain not only where they were but also *what they were*—or what colonial rule made them to be. The so-called 'separate development' plan pushed through the so-called 'complete sovereignty' of the ten bantustans or native 'homelands', sought to effectively 'divide' the native population into so many different 'nations'. The step was therefore justifiably seen by native leaders as a move to 'boost up as much as possible, the intertribal competition that is bound to come up' and to exacerbate mutual hostility.[71] Much of the problems of post-apartheid South Africa follow directly from such interventions of the colonial state. The rise of leaders like Mangosuthu Buthelezi in KwaZulu, as leaders of the homelands, and hostile to the ANC and the liberation struggle, owes a lot to such manoeuvres.

We also know that in subsequent years when the apartheid era was drawing to a close, it was the idea of minority cultures that was invoked by the government, in order to challenge the native claim for majority rule.

As an official broadcast of the government put it in 1987: 'Majority rule is nonsense in South Africa *as there is no majority. The key issue is the protection of minority rights.* There are ten African nations, plus Whites, Coloureds and Indians, and all insist on their right to self-determination.'[72]

Here we get, then, a very different perspective on the dialectic of universality and difference. In the South African context we see the attempt by colonial authorities to essentialize native cultures and segregate them into separate spaces. It is also worth noticing that because there were practically no hierarchical relations *between* the native tribes before colonialism, we also find little evidence of prior aspirations for self-determination. The animosities that we see subsequently in the form of the Inkatha Freedom Party (IFP), therefore, flow directly from the 'homelands strategy' of apartheid. It is equally relevant to note that the 'concern' of colonial authorities for the cultural distinctiveness of the native tribal communities, goes hand in hand with the de-essentialization of the European cultures that are sought to be welded into a single nation—to the extent that the impossible Other, the Jew, too is seen by Smuts as a potential part of the white nation.

It is this context that provides the backdrop to the suspicion of the post-apartheid South African leadership about the question of minority rights—sometimes taken to the extreme of denying their importance in principle. The entire struggle of the South African liberation movement to construct a black identity that would eventually include the coloured populations as well, is a struggle to transcend smaller 'ethnic identities'. The most audacious part of the South African project, however, is one that seeks to move now, even *beyond the idea of a black nation*, to fashion a nation that includes the whites and blacks within it. The attempt is audacious because it is unprecedented. It is audacious because it seeks to locate the basis of such a nation, not in some antiquity, but in the living present. In that sense, we could see it as an attempt to transcend the nation-form itself.

Speaking on the occasion of the adoption of the Republic of South Africa Constitution Bill, 1996, on 8 May 1996, Thabo Mbeki, now President of South Africa made his famous speech 'I am an African'. In this speech he described his 'Africanness' in fairly unusual terms:

I owe my being to the Khoi and the San whose desolate souls haunt the great expanses of the beautiful Cape—they who fell victim to the most merciless genocide our native land has ever seen, they who were the first to lose their lives in the struggle to defend our freedom and independence and they who, as a people, perished as a result.

I am formed of the migrants who left Europe to find a new home on our native land. Whatever their own actions, they remain still a part of me.

In my veins courses the blood of the Malay slaves who came from the East...

I am the grandchild of the warrior men and women that Hintsa and Sekhukhune led, the patriots the Cetshwayo and Mphephu took to battle...

I come of those who were transported from India and China, whose being resided in the fact, solely, that they were able to provide physical labour...[73]

In this remarkable passage, Mbeki gives a poetic rendering of the proclamation of the Freedom Charter adopted in June 1955 at the Congress of the People, convened by the African National Congress, along with the South African Indian Congress, the Coloured People's Organization, and the Congress of Democrats, that 'South Africa belongs to all those who live in it, Black and White'.[74] The recognition in the Charter and more specifically, in Mbeki's speech of the different histories, different pasts that flow and merge into the present entity called South Africa, and the bold attempt at defining the nation in terms of *this* present, gives this experiment in nation-building a certain uniqueness. There is no call here to resurrect *an* imagined great past; no call to exclude thereby, sections of the population that do not share *that past*. It is also worth noting that it is an 'African nationalism' that is invoked by Mbeki, even if he is explicitly talking of South Africa. In another famous speech, Mbeki gave his call for an African Renaissance. Even that does not hark back to the great antiquity of Egyptian civilization in the way that Europe's renaissance recalled the great Greek heritage. The accent of his speech, on the contrary, is entirely on the 'present of the nation': 'Africa cannot renew herself where its upper echelons are a mere parasite on the rest of society' and whereby Africa endlessly 'reproduces itself as the periphery of the world-economy'. So, '(T)he African Renaissance demands that we purge ourselves of the parasites...'[75] The regeneration of Africa rests not on digging out its pristine past but on purging its present of the exploiters and parasites.

However, despite what we have quoted from Mbeki above, it is undoubtedly the case that modern South Africa seeks to build a nation that transcends narrow tribal and ethnic loyalties. Mbeki's emphasis on the diversity of streams that go into the making of contemporary Africanness, should not be understood as implying that these different identities are to be frozen where they are. In fact, given the history of forced cultural segregation under apartheid, the new leadership of postcolonial South Africa is extremely wary and suspicious of particularistic loyalties. It represents an effort, rather, to arrive at a kind of 'unity-in-diversity' that will blend into a future African nation. In this effort, the present leadership has also managed to win over the IFP and Buthelezi. Whether this will develop into a long-term collaboration remains to be seen but as many activists of the African National Congress (ANC) and the South African Communist Party (SACP) see it, for the time being it has 'neutralized the contra option.'[76] The ANC general secretary, Kgalema Motlante, in fact emphasized the need to win over such leaders who had moved away but who, he asserted, had an important role in nation-building. The most crucial problem that the nation-building project faces, however, concerns the negotiation of the problem of racial difference. The emergence of the post-apartheid era has, to a certain extent, made it possible to deal with the question of black identity but the problem of the relationship with the whites remains.

Apart from the forced segregation into tribes, one of the key questions that the liberation struggle in South Africa had to face in terms of its self-definition was one that related to the peculiarity of its situation arising out of the specific nature of settler colonialism. The ANC and the SACP described it as 'colonialism of a special type' or 'internal colonialism'—where colonialists and the colonized occupied the same territory. The successive waves of colonization had each left their deposits in South African society for the liberation struggle to come to terms with. Then there were the various other sections of the native and immigrant population. To build a nation out of this formidable diversity was a stupendous task by any standard. As Joe Slovo, the secretary-general of the SACP put it as late as in the 1980s: 'Are we already "one people" or are we, as yet, only a nation in the making? In the light of the undoubted existence of ethnic differences, is the cementing of our diverse communities into a single South African nation both desirable and realisable?'[77] Slovo's answer is unequivocally in the affirmative. For the nation to be, it is necessary to shun all talk of 'right of nations to self-determination' for other smaller ethnic or tribal groupings. On this Slovo almost echoes the call of Samora Machel of Mozambique: 'For the nation to live, the tribe must die.'[78] In what follows, however, I will briefly discuss the problem of nation-building in the context of the problem of race. Here, we will encounter a different dynamic of the problem of universality and difference.

Slovo outlines his position in opposition to Stalin's definition of nations as communities of language, culture, territory, common psychological traits, and economy, with which he has serious problems. His primary objection is that it tends too much towards recognizing nations on the basis of common culture, and applying it mechanically, 'we might even be tempted to lend theoretical respectability to neo-colonial-inspired secessionary tendencies.' In making this statement, Slovo is reacting against a Comintern resolution of 1932, calling upon the Communist Party of South Africa (as it was then called) to 'advance slogans for the immediate and complete independence for the people of South Africa' especially to recognize 'the right of the Zulu, Basuto etc. nations to form their own independent republics.'[79] Countering the 'mechanical application' of the idea of the right of nations to self-determination, he asserts: 'There is no absolute ethic about nation formation.' The consolidation or fragmentation of disparate ethnic groups into one or into several entities, he goes on to argue, cannot be judged by any universal formulas as to what constitutes a nation.[80] While Slovo justly criticizes the above resolution of the Comintern in this discussion, he does not refer at all to the 1928 discussions and recommendation made by it regarding what has come to be known as the 'black republic' thesis. Comrade Mzala, an SACP leader from Zululand recalls this set of recommendations where the Comintern put forward the slogan of 'the creation of an independent native republic', *which was opposed by the SACP delegation* of white leaders, for they thought that 'it would be criticized by the *white working class*' back home. According to Mzala, this proposal was understood by the SACP leaders as subordination of the principles of class struggle to the support for black nationalism. 'In their eyes the Party was being asked to emphasize African nationalism instead of the equality of all workers, black and white.'[81] This abstract equality of all workers, we may note, had turned out to be a serious problem from the very inception of the communist and trade union movement in South Africa. Ever since the well-known Rand Rebellion of 1922, where the white workers in Witswatersrand struck work against the attempts to treat them at par with the black workers, through the removal of the colour bar, it had dogged the activity of the communists. There is no doubt that the intent behind the government's attempt to dismantle the colour bar was simply to attract cheap black labour to push down wages, rather than any egalitarian concern. For the communists who were just beginning to organize themselves, this strike of the white workers was after all, a working class action from which they could hardly stay away, whatever their discomfort about its explicit racism. It was an occasion that revealed the inability of the white communist leadership to handle the problem of race and it was this that prompted the Comintern's intervention. Mzala's reference must be seen in this highly charged context.

This difference of emphasis between the position of Joe Slovo, a white leader of the SACP and Comrade Mzala, a Zulu leader from the same party, illustrates what I found to be part of a wider phenomenon in my interviews with leaders of the ANC and the SACP. While it is true that the SACP did adopt the 'black republic thesis' in all seriousness subsequently, there are different emphases and inflections that one can see in the pronouncements of the whites and the blacks—irrespective to a certain extent, of whether they are political leaders or ordinary folk. Almost invariably, white opinion relies on the idea of abstract equality and notions of class that Mzala refers to and black opinion emphasizes colour difference and the legacy of race discrimination. As would be expected, this difference becomes most clearly visible on the question of affirmative action and the controversial 'Black Empowerment Programme' undertaken by the post-apartheid state. This programme is seen by many in the ANC as a way of spawning a 'black bourgeoisie' which will contest white domination in the economy. A problematic part of the deracialization programme in South Africa today, arises from the fact that economic assets, including newspapers and publishing houses, are largely owned by the whites. Repeatedly, I came across activist opinion that felt that much of the intellectual production and public debate is also determined by the fact that apart from the state-owned radio and television networks, white domination continues[82]. In some senses, civil society itself, has been so far split into a white and a black civil society.

In my discussion with Jeremy Cronin, the assistant general secretary of the SACP, it was evident how this question appears, even today, to the white leadership in the party. Cronin believes for instance that the conditions of relatively advanced capitalist development in South Africa had 'produced the infrastructure' of a nation, by having created 'a single national market'—if 'with peculiar distortions'. The prospect for a single nation seems to him therefore, much less problematic than to many others. He also believes, quite categorically, that there 'is no possibility of forming a black bourgeoisie' as a class distinct from the white bourgeoisie and sees any such bourgeoisie as being an integral part of a single capitalist class. He considers the problem as one of the deracialization of a single South African capitalist class, which is 'undoubtedly stratified' and whose development has been 'somewhat distorted', but which nevertheless remains a single class. He emphasizes that the bourgeoisie, black or white, is driven fundamentally by class interests. Kgalema Motlante, the ANC general secretary, also a functionary of the SACP, however, sees the Black Empowerment Programme as 'critical to the task of nation-building' as it helps 'unravel the skewed ownership structure' within the economy. Motlante sees the development of black entrepreneurs and business people as central in many ways to the future of the national project but he presents the importance of the programme as extending beyond that of generating a 'black bourgeoisie'. He underlines the importance of the initiative taken by trade unions and workers' groups in the form of forming collective investment companies as a key component of this process. The initiative taken by the National Union of Mine Workers to form an investment company, was mentioned by him as a major instance in this respect.

In public discourse too, this white relationship to universalism finds some particularly interesting manifestations. In sharp contrast to the early twentieth century attempts at constructing a white nation to the exclusion of blacks, in public discourse today, it is precisely white opinion that talks of a single South African—or African—nation. There was a lot of discussion in the press, for instance, over Thabo Mbeki's renewal of the old two-nation theory, which in a sense, formed the basis of the formulations about 'colonialism of a special type'. In this speech, made in the National Assembly in May 1998, Mbeki talked of 'this reality of two nations', where 'white minority domination constitutes the material base which reinforces the notion that we are not one nation, but two nations'. 'And neither are we becoming one nation', he adds.[83] Parenthetically, it is interesting to compare this statement with Cronin's. For Cronin, the single capitalist economy provides the 'infrastructure' for a single nation; to Mbeki, on the other hand, it is white minority domination that provides the material basis for the split of South African society into two nations. It is this speech that has been at the centre of a lot of controversy in the last couple of years.

In a recent and symptomatic exchange, for instance, David Atwell, a professor of English at the University of Natal, attacked this description of contemporary South Africa as comprising two nations. Atwell argues that in drawing from Disraeli, Mbeki is hopelessly mistaken, because Disraeli in *Sybil or the Two Nations*, is talking of *class distinctions*, of the gap between the rich and the poor: 'Disraeli was addressing class division in the context of racial and cultural unity, Mbeki is talking about race.'[84] Atwell justifies his argument entirely at the level of a class universalism. It is justified, in his view, to talk of class, but talking of race is divisive, for it contains the 'strategically polarizing language of the Black Consciousness era'. After all, not all poor are black and not all black are poor, he argues and points towards 'ostentatious black consumerism' to buttress his claim. Not unexpectedly, this brought forth a volley of reactions from black

intellectuals. I take up two of them. M. O. Phayane of the University of
Cape Town for instance, responded by pointing to the continuing economic
misery of and lack of opportunities for the blacks, and the tendency among
whites 'to cite every minor example of black success' as evidence of a
change in their conditions. He goes on to argue that Mbeki's thesis does
not 'entrench disunity' but 'exposes it'. Dan Ojwang of the University of
Witswatersrand, accuses Atwell of 'historical revisionism' in his attempt
to 'single out the Black Consciousness movement for popularising the
divisive, polarising language that proclaims South Africa's racial-national
duality.' Ojwang accuses Atwell of 'hair-splitting' while agreeing that the
'two nation' thesis needs to be criticized—though for different reasons. It
needs to be criticized 'because it might detract attention from the country's
multiple realities that defy neat and easy conclusions.'[85] Ojwang, like
Phayane suggests that in bringing in the 'ambiguous categories of people'
Atwell is obfuscating matters; rather than squarely recognizing the
continuing existence of racial discrimination.

To take another instance, let us look at the way commentator Darrel
Bristow-Bovey discusses slavery. In his long article in the same paper, he
argues that 'It is...a comforting myth to imagine the meeting of Europe
and west Africa as a clash between sophisticated plunderers and primitive
plundered. *It is a racist myth.*'[86] Bristow-Bovey is no defender of slavery. He
in fact, considers 'slave trade as one of civilization's most shameful chapters'
and believes that 'the Atlantic slave trade is a blot on every maritime
European nation and every country of the Americas.' But he argues, slavery
was a *universal phenomenon*. 'Slavery was an established institution in Africa,
as it was everywhere else' and cites the instance of the existence of slavery
in West Africa in 1000 BC. While one does not deny the existence of different
forms of slavery in antiquity, what the commentator does here that is
relevant to our argument, is to assimilate the specific form of modern
slavery that accompanied the colonization of the world by Europe, into a
universal history of all humanity. The point here is not whether Bristow-
Bovey is stating the truth or not. I am only interested in highlighting the
way in which all debate in South Africa gets set up along predictable
channels, with the whites almost invariably espousing an abstract,
universalist-egalitarian idiom while it is the lot of the blacks to underline
specificity and difference. It is not an accident that while the ANC has to
push measures for affirmative action, the opposition to it from the
Democratic Party for example, is expressed in the language of 'freedom
of the individual' and 'merit' 'fairness' etc.:

The Democratic Party stands for an opportunity society where *individuals have the freedom* and the physical means to improve their lives and the lives of their children.
We will continue to *oppose the new racism*. We want a country built on opportunity, fuelled by peaceful commerce, driven by the spirit of enterprise, *founded on justice, fairness and merit*, protected by the law.[87]

The South African attempt to fashion a nation-state then, involves an intricate interplay of universality and difference: the attempt to overcome difference and construct a single black identity on the one hand, and a simultaneous attempt to weld the blacks and whites into a single nation, but one which nevertheless, must be based on a recognition of difference that also involves reverse discrimination. While it may be too early to say whether this attempt will bear the expected fruit in the long run, it is nevertheless an unprecedented attempt at forging nationhood. It is particularly unprecedented in the context of Africa where the miserable failure of postcolonial nation-states to deliver has been particularly noteworthy. Given the overall experience of the failures of postcolonial nation-states everywhere, the need is to rethink the very form of the nation-state and its relevance for these societies. Indeed I venture to suggest that if the South African experiment does fail, the reason, to some extent, would be that this project remains within the confines of the nation-state.

In the concluding section of this chapter, I discuss the problem of another equally creative and bold project—that of Indian nationalism. The rest of this book is of course, about the fate of Indian nationalism, but here I will trace the transformation of that nationalism from an ideology of a movement to a state ideology— in short, to secular-nationalism.

Secular-Nationalism in India

Drawing on C.A. Bayly's study of Allahabad in the late nineteenth and early twentieth centuries, Gyanendra Pandey has elaborated on the historical link between the emergence of secular-nationalism and the rise of the concept of 'communalism'. Bayly refers to the development of a secular tradition in the person of Ajudhia Nath Kunzru, inherited later by Motilal Nehru, alongside 'the close connections of the radical Congress leadership of the 1910s with 'Hindu sectional interests and groups'. He also refers to the "strong revivalist strains" in early nationalism.'[88] Bayly refers to the Madhya Hindu Samaj, for instance, whose annual sessions 'were held concurrently with the Indian National Congress until 1891 or 1892.' Pandey furnishes further evidence to buttress the claim that community concerns were central to the imagination of the future nation. This coexistence of the 'secular strains' within nationalism alongside 'strong community concerns' are seen by Bayly as a kind of split that existed between the high discourse of 'Congress publicity and official pronouncements' and the 'idiom adopted by their orators'. Pandey suggests that this combination of 'two idioms' was more characteristic of early nationalism in its formative stages. In this stage, 'the emerging Indian nation was conceived of as a collection of communities: Hindus + Muslim + Christian + Parsi + Sikh and so on'; that it was 'sometime around the 1920s [that] this vision was substantially altered and India came to be seen very much more as a collection of individuals, of Indian citizens.'[89] Pandey argues that it was in the 1920s, the period of the 'entry of the masses' into nationalist politics, that a veritable reconstruction of nationalist discourse took place whereby it was no longer considered legitimate to mobilize 'Hindus' and 'Muslims' for the nationalist cause. Nationalists thenceforth, saw such tendencies as 'distorting and distorted'. '"Hindu" and "Muslim" politics...became from the 1920s the chief flogging horse of Indian nationalism—divisive, primitive and, in a far more general nationalist judgement, the product of a colonial policy of Divide and Rule.' This, he argues, 'was the birthplace of the nationalist version of the concept of "communalism".'[90] In other words, Pandey suggests that it was this emergence of a secular-nationalism that created the other in the concept of 'communalism': 'the age of communalism was concurrent with the age of nationalism; they were part of the same discourse'.[91] From now on, he claims, nationalism, in the persons of Lala Lajpat Rai, Gandhi, Ganesh Shankar Vidyarthi, or Nehru, would emphasize the larger unity of the nation and call for the 'privatization of religion', for distinguishing the essential parts of religion from the inessential. Pandey thus highlights the important common assumptions underlying the nationalist discourse from the 1920s onwards, assumptions that are shared alike by leaders of the Hindu Mahasabha like Madan Mohan Malaviya and Lajpat Rai, and secularists like Ganesh Shankar Vidyarthi and Nehru.

While there is a great deal of truth in Pandey's reading of nationalism since the 1920s, it is not very helpful, in my opinion, to see this phase as the *secular-nationalist* phase, unless we are to so expand the notion of secular-nationalism as to divest it of its specificity. This phase of mass nationalism is very much the phase of Gandhian hegemony, the peculiarity of which lies in the fact that it is the enigmatic figure of Gandhi that becomes a mass phenomenon; other currents within nationalism remain in this respect, marginal figures. And Gandhian discourse is very much a discourse of community and religion. Gandhi's discourse, in sharp contrast to that of other leaders of the Congress, is a discourse of a mass movement par excellence, one that rejects the project of the nation-state in all its essentials. It neither shares the call for the privatization of religion nor rejects the notion of community. His emphasis on the removal of untouchability, an 'inessential part of Hindu religion' according to Pandey, is also a call to the 'Hindu community', not an appeal to the 'individual citizen' who resides in the realm of civil society. Gandhi's point, on the contrary, is that all religions, in their essence, preach the same universal values and hold the same universal truth. Once that is realized, communities can live together as communities, without having to dissolve their separate identities. Pandey's suggestion that Gandhi changed his position in this respect, "when the full impact of the Mappilla outbreak was beginning to be seen" insofar as he started asserting the primacy of the nation over community identities, is an indication, to my mind, of the fact that it was community rather than the individual citizen that formed the basis of his thinking.[92] To that extent, it was not really as drastic a shift as he seems to suggest. Undoubtedly, there is a shift in the thinking of many individual leaders but on the whole, I will argue against Pandey, that the very evidence that he marshals suggests a very different reading of the situation.

On the one hand, we find the assertion of Madan Mohan Malaviya, one of the most important Congress leaders associated with Hindu Mahasabha, made as early as in 1905, that it is 'not the Hindus alone who now live in Hindustan' and that 'Hindustan is no longer exclusively their country...it is of the Muslims too.'[93] This is not very different from statements by people like the secular Vidyarthi in the mid-1920s. In one such quotation, which Pandey takes from an article in 1924, Vidyarthi argues that because '(t)he Muslim League and the Khilafat Committees, the Hindu Sabha, the Arya Samaj and the Sanatan Dharma Sabhas...exist and will continue to exist for a while', 'it is the clear duty of every single follower of the Congress... desirous of Indian independence to attach no importance to these organizations.'[94] However, if this contrast between the emphasis on community by one person and on the individual by the other seems to substantiate Pandey's point, what are we to make of this other statement from Vidyarthi quoted by Pandey? Two years later, the same Vidyarthi 'responded to a Bengal government order of June 1926, banning the playing of music outside mosques in Calcutta at the time of *namaz*, by declaring that the right to play music had now become a matter of *dharma*, i.e. of duty of religion in the larger sense.' He therefore, 'stressed the need for Hindu organization and reform and urged the Hindu

Mahasabha to convene a special session of its general body in Calcutta' in order to oppose the order.[95]

How do we read this evidence? How do we understand the relatively 'secular' position taken by the Hindu Mahasabhaite Malaviya as against the wholesale defence of Hindu dharma by the relatively secular Vidyarthi? Admittedly, Vidyarthi's 'secularism' is a limited one and quite unlike that of say, Nehru's. Even so, there is no dearth of evidence to show that such apparently contradictory positions keep emerging from time to time. How does this evidence square with Pandey's suggestion about the wholesale reconstruction of nationalism and the emergence of a citizen-based, secular-nationalism as the dominant tendency from the 1920s? I will argue that this highly problematic part of Pandey's reading arises from an inadequate appreciation of: (a) the close kinship between Hindu nationalism and secular-nationalism, and (b) the specificity of secular-nationalism. For one thing, Pandey's discussion fails to recognize sufficiently that Hindu nationalism was itself a secular ideology, hardly concerned Hinduism as a religion. As Ashis Nandy and Partha Chatterjee have argued, it was concerned primarily, with a certain construction of the modern nation.[96] For another, what Pandey designates as the emergence of secular-nationalism, seems to be more of a conjunctural shift, as nationalism acquired a mass character. At this stage of its development, nationalism must be seen as an acutely contested and contradictory terrain when all the different impulses were playing themselves out. It had not yet acquired the singular voice of the monochromatic discourse that emerged subsequently. In this moment of acute contestation, when it was full of contradictory possibilities, we often encounter the same individuals exhibiting different impulses on different occasions.

What we may call secular-nationalism proper, I will suggest, emerged only towards the final phases of the anticolonial struggle and managed to establish its hegemony with the transfer of power. This secular-nationalism too, was a nationalism that was Hindu in some of its essentials, even when articulated in the language of secular citizenship, born as it was within a purely Hindu universe. This is so, I will argue in the rest of the book, because its insistence on an abstract universalism produced the dominant culture as the norm by default. Yet, it was different from Hindu nationalism in certain key respects, the most important being its insistence on the idea of the nation as a 'unity-in-diversity', alongside the insistence on the idea of the secular unmarked, abstract citizen. While Hindu nationalism also saw citizenship as abstract and unmarked, it nevertheless insisted on a prior and explicit acceptance of Hinduness as the essence of nationhood.

Another crucial area where the two differed was with respect to the understanding of Indian history where secular-nationalism insisted on a syncretic reading of tradition and culture, in opposition to the blatantly communal reading of that past by Hindu nationalism. This secular-nationalism remained, in ideological terms, a marginal discourse till the penultimate phase of the anticolonial struggle, despite the important role that its ideologues, like Nehru, individually played in this struggle. The first of the above propositions, namely that Hindu-nationalism was basically a secular ideology, has been argued at length by Nandy and Chatterjee and I have discussed these positions in Chapter 3. It is primarily the second of these propositions that I want to discuss in the remainder of this chapter—that secular-nationalism, thanks to its universalist assumptions, was basically a 'Hindu' nationalism, insofar as it produced *that* as the norm.

The ideology of secular-nationalism as the ideology of the postcolonial nation-state in India, is closely related to the figure of Jawaharlal Nehru, the first prime minister of the Indian republic. He was the ideologue and theoretician of independent India and thanks to a constellation of circumstances, remained its unchallenged leader till his death in the mid-sixties. It is necessary therefore, to explore Nehru's discourse in order to understand the fundamental features of this ideology.

Nehru wrote his autobiography in the mid-thirties. By that time, the contours of the various strands of the anticolonial struggle had appeared with sufficient clarity. The Muslim League was already pitted in opposition to the Indian National Congress. The virtual lack of participation of the Muslim masses in the civil disobedience movement, and their further alienation from the 'mainstream' were becoming clear. The Round Table Conferences had already taken place, Ramsay MacDonald's 'Communal Award' and Gandhi's subsequent fast-unto-death had brought the issue of the Dalits to the forefront as issues of fundamental significance—with Ambedkar's insistence on separate electorates for them. It is therefore interesting to notice that Nehru is practically oblivious of the question of Dalit emancipation. In the entire autobiography, there is not a single reference to this struggle of the Dalits/Depressed Classes, except in the section where Nehru narrates how he went into fits of depression at Gandhi's fast-unto-death. I have discussed this question at length in Chapter 5, but suffice it to note here that Nehru found this 'mere question of electorate' immensely irritating and was angry that Gandhi 'chose this side issue for his final sacrifice'. To Nehru, it was an 'insignificant' question. The blindness to the question of Dalit emancipation is further evident in

the fact that not once in the entire autobiography do the names of
Ambedkar or Periyar appear even in passing. Even when he refers to the
Poona Pact, it appears thus: 'A "pact" was signed by various people gathered
in Poona...'[97] He also felt 'irritated by the Harijan movement because it
had come in the way of civil disobedience.'[98]

If Nehru is blind towards the aspirations of the Dalits, what he has to
say of Muslim politics is illuminating in a different way. On the 'communal
question' Nehru's reflections often tend to put the blame on 'Muslim
political reactionaries' for being unnecessarily obstreperous. Their constant
insistence on the 'safeguards' in political representation, appear to him as
unnecessary obstacles in the normal course of the national movement for
independence. There is not a moment's hesitation in his mind; he makes
no attempt to understand the anxieties that may have led them to take
certain stances. It is interesting to contrast Nehru's unproblematic vision
of Indian independence, with Gandhi's tormented soul struggling to bring
the Muslims and Dalits into the mainstream of the movement, if in often
misplaced ways.[99] So Nehru talks of 'the Muslims' taking objection to
'music or any noise which interfered with their prayers'. 'In every city
there are many mosques, and five times every day they have prayers, and
there is no lack of noises and processions (including marriage and funeral
processions). So the chances of friction were always present.'[100] The
'Muslim political reactionaries', 'helped in the process by the British
government', having emerged into prominence following the non-
cooperation fiasco, were clearly behind these fantastic demands. 'From
day to day, new and more far-reaching communal demands appeared on
their behalf, *striking at the very root of national unity and Indian freedom.*' In order
to maintain the 'secular balance', he then adds that "on the Hindu side
also" political reactionaries were active in vitiating the atmosphere.[101]

What is interesting here is that to Nehru it was 'national unity' and the
cause of 'Indian freedom' that was paramount; it mattered little to him,
privileged Kashmiri Brahmin that he was, that the entire ethos of that
'unity' and 'urge for freedom' was under-girded by a Hindu nationalism.
He is quite aware of this fact but nevertheless, unruffled by it. 'Indian
nationalism was dominated by the Hindus and had a Hinduized look', he
says, in *The Discovery of India*, which can be considered the foundational
text of secular-nationalism, and continues:

So a conflict arose in the Muslim mind; many accepted that nationalism, trying
to influence it in the direction of that choice...and yet many others began to drift
in a separatist direction for which Iqbal's poetic and philosophic approach had
prepared them.

This, I imagine, was the background out of which, in recent years, arose the cry for a division of India.[102]

'*Political* reactionaries' in his terminology were those he thought were obstructing the cause of freedom. By constantly deploying this category, he could condone the Hindu Mahasabhaites who, 'despite their communalism' worked for the 'freedom movement'—and were therefore *not* political reactionaries. Thus Nehru, talking of Madan Mohan Malaviya can say: 'So long as he had been one of its leading spirits, the Mahasabha, in spite of its communalism, had not been politically reactionary.'[103] And further: 'Muslim communal organizations are notoriously reactionary from every point of view—political, economic and social. The Hindu Mahasabha rivals them, *but is left far behind in this backward-moving race* by the Sanatanists...'[104] The implication here is that because many of the Mahasabha leaders are active in the 'freedom struggle', their communal outlook is not as bad as that of the Sanatanists.

How does all this fit in with Nehru's 'progressivism', socialism, and secularism? Nationalism, defined as the project of the future independent nation-state, is the ground on which Nehru's universalism blends with his essentially Hindu ethos. It was Marxism that brought the light of History into Nehru's life:

History came to have a new meaning for me. The Marxist interpretation threw a flood of light on it, and it became an unfolding drama with some order and purpose, howsoever unconscious, behind it... I was filled with a new excitement and my depression at the non-success of the civil disobedience grew much less. Was not the world marching rapidly towards the desired consummation? There were grave dangers of wars, catastrophe's [and one may add, communal conflagrations], but at any rate we were moving...Our national struggle became a stage in the longer journey...[105]

The anticolonial struggle was but a stage in the great telos of History and whoever, for whatever reason chose to stay away from it, was reactionary and therefore, doomed. Nehru is quite clear that:

The new nationalism then grew up from above—the upper class English-speaking intelligentsia—and this was *naturally confined to the Hindus*, for the Muslims were educationally very backward. This nationalism spoke in the gentlest and most abject of tones, and yet it was not to the liking of the Government, and *they decided to encourage the Muslims more and keep them away from the new nationalist platform*.[106]

And then, continuing with the Marxist interpretation of Indian history:

The Muslims were not historically or ideologically ready then for the *bourgeois* nationalist movement as they had developed no *bourgeoisie* as the Hindus had done...The Muslims were still wrapped up in a *feudal* anti-democratic ideology, while the rising middle class among the Hindus had begun to think in terms of the European liberals.[107]

On the stage of World-History then, the Hindus represented the progressive, bourgeois forces of nationalism while the Muslims were still caught in the mire of feudal conservatism. For Nehru then, the Hindu Mahasabhaite Malaviya, was more tolerable than the 'political reactionaries' of the Muslim League. Nehru, unlike many later-day secularists, was clearly aware of the bourgeois-modern inspiration that animated Hindu Mahasabhaites like Malaviya:

The *sole change* he desires, and desires passionately, is the complete elimination of foreign control in India. The political training and reading of his youth still influence his mind greatly, and he looks upon this dynamic, revolutionary post-war world of the twentieth century with the spectacles of the semi-static nineteenth, of T.H. Green and John Stuart Mill and Gladstone and Morley, and a three-or-four-thousand-year *background of old Hindu culture and sociology*. It is a curious combination, bristling with contradictions.[108]

There is little doubt, of course, that Nehru was an uncompromising secularist, quite intolerant of what he thought was the 'backward-looking' politics of religious communities. As will be evident from the above discussion, his sight was singularly focused on the independence of India and the new nation-state to emerge, and all his positions derived from the passionate secular-nationalism that he espoused. All his arguments were drawn from the theoretical arsenal of Marxism and anti-imperialism. Yet, Nehru shared, through his belief in the *telos* of Universal History, many of the positions of the Hindu nationalists. The last quotation from his autobiography, where he assesses Malaviya's intellectual world, also provides us a glimpse into the secular inspirations of Hindu nationalism. His Hindu baggage, in Nehru's reckoning, was of Hindu culture and sociology, *not religion*. It is worth noting here that Malaviya was not the only one among the Hindu nationalists who was inspired by the secular-modern ideas of leading European thinkers. In fact, as Gyan Prakash has recently shown in his fascinating and well-documented study, a massive intellectual effort went into the fashioning of a nationalism that would blend Hindu traditions with science. Whether it was the work of religious reformist-publicists like Dayanand Saraswati, or the scholarly tracts like Prafulla Chandra Ray's *History of Hindu Chemistry*, and G. Srinivasa Murti's scientific defence of *ayurveda*, the intellectual ferment of the late nineteenth and early twentieth centuries was animated by the desire to synthesize Hindu traditions with science that was to be deployed in the service of a modern India.[109] In fact, it was more than synthesis. As Prakash argues, it was the attempt to prove that 'India was the original home of science', an 'attempt to re-signify traditions to position them as knowledge relevant to their contemporary world'.[110] To that extent, it was a colossal intellectual effort to make India, by definition Hindu, equal to the challenges of the modern world. Prakash notes that this 'scripting of India in Hindu texts proved so compelling that even secular nationalists such as Jawaharlal Nehru could not entirely escape.'[111] In that sense, there was a continuity between the Hindu nationalists and secular-nationalists.

My argument seeks to go beyond what this formulation allows. I have been arguing that not only was Nehru a Hindu by default, and drew on the work done by Hindu scholars before him, but that there is something in the abstract universalism of secular modern politics and its understanding of Progress and History, that, in its effort to erase markers of difference, privileges the dominant/majority culture as the norm. By de-legitimizing such difference and disallowing articulations of 'different' voices, modern secular universalisms reproduce the common sense of the dominant/majority cultures as hegemonic. This is the tendency we see at different points in time and space—in the development of nationalism in Europe, in Engels' attack on 'stubborn' minority cultures, in the way the whites in post-apartheid South Africa seek to shift public debate into abstract universalist categories, and in the activities of the early white communists in South Africa. As I will argue in Chapters 5 and 6, it is this modernist universalism that underlies the Marxist/secular-nationalist silence with regard to caste and accounts for the easy integration of these discourses into the hegemonic nationalism, that as Nehru remarks, was Hindu.

In the penultimate years of the anticolonial struggle, Gandhi—that inveterate opponent of the nation-state form—was rapidly marginalized. The desire to build a modern India brought together Nehru, Ambedkar, and the Hindu nationalists—their influence, particularly in the Constituent Assembly was profound. In the last years of the anticolonial struggle, it was Nehru who emerged as the impatient and often intolerant state-builder. It was he who, in his unseemly haste to 'get freedom' seemed ready to allow the last possibilities of an understanding with Jinnah and the Muslim League to go under.[112] I discuss some of this dynamic in Chapter 4. What we need to underline here is that Nehru was of course no communalist but on the contrary, a convinced, unwavering secularist. All the same, his single-minded fixation with the cause of independence and his intolerance of any 'diversion' from it, put him more often that not, in the company of the Hindu nationalists. This was the fundamental problem that secular-nationalism never faced, but which recent developments in Indian politics force us to turn our gaze to.

Secular-nationalism undergoes a further transformation in the postcolonial phase. Nehru's impatience for independence that underlay his entire political practice and thinking, was now replaced with the concrete agenda of building the new nation-state. As Pakistan became a reality, large masses of Muslims left behind—including those who consciously chose to remain here—began to adjust themselves to the new realities. Nehru initially continued to deal with the Pakistani state in his characteristic intransigent way, especially on the question of Kashmir and in relation to the release of Pakistan's share of Rs 550 million of the Reserve Bank's cash reserves. Gandhi's final threat of a fast-unto-death eventually made him and Patel relent.[113] Gandhi's subsequent assassination at the hand of a fanatic Hindu nationalist as well as the wave of indignation and repentance that followed it, gave the new state under Nehru's stewardship, the opportunity and the moral weapon to clamp down on his enemies, on sections of the Hindu right. Having achieved control over the new nation-state, his single-point agenda realized, Nehru could now see the question of inter-community relations in a different light. He could now afford to be magnanimous to the Muslims for whom the only option now was to throw their lot with the Congress. For the Dalits of Ambedkar's Scheduled Caste Federation (SCF), who had been in alliance with the Muslim League, the scenario had changed too. Ambedkar had emerged as one of the architects of the Constitution and took office as a minister in Nehru's cabinet. In the 1946 elections, the SCF had suffered a major defeat. This defeat was partly due to the system of joint electorates hammered out in the Poona Pact. But that was only one part of the story. The other part was that with the new dispensation having become a tangible reality, many leaders of the SCF now realized that making common cause with the Congress was their best bet.[114]

With the Hindu right now silenced, and all other forces thus effectively brought within the fold of the Congress, nationalism under Nehru now turned to write its autobiography. The new nationalist historiography would now take the cue from Nehru's *The Discovery of India*, and produce historical tracts that spoke in a single and uncomplicated voice. It needs to be stated here that Nehru in his magnum opus had laid the outlines of a secular history which, even while harking back to the 'five thousand years' of essentially Hindu history, had successfully produced a narrative that demonstrated its composite character. This composite character was not merely a blend of 'Hindu' and 'Muslim' culture—categories that he refused to entertain—it was evident in the ancient traffic of ideas and cultures between India and the Greeks, the Chinese, and the Iraqis/Persians. Nehru's historical narrative was undoubtedly a major effort to show that India, timeless and eternal, had always been an ocean of tolerance and an exemplar of openness, ever willing to absorb different cultures. Whatever the truth of this idea, it undoubtedly gave secular-nationalism a narrative within which it could negotiate its Hindu origins with the requirements of a culturally diverse, independent India. All the rest of the problems were now left to the future, to be resolved themselves. Residing in the interstices of this secular-nationalist narrative of Indian history, however, were many of the modern Hindu beliefs—those that saw evils like the 'hardening of the caste system', 'growth of the purdah' and 'fall in the status of women', as the consequences of Afghan and Turkish (Nehru was careful not to refer to them as 'Muslim') rule.[115]

Whatever may have been the salutary effects of this kind of syncretic reading of Indian history, it also effected certain closures. For one thing, embarrassed references to caste apart, it became impossible to talk of the continuing salience of caste oppression in public. Caste was seen as a matter of the past, the last remnants of which would be swept away by the advance of modern education, scientific temper, and growth of an industrial economy. Likewise, the question of communalism too, understood in the narrative of Progress, became merely a matter of the economic progress, and particularly, of the Muslim community. That economic growth and industrial development would automatically bring all communities to an equal level, now that the imperialists were no longer there to divide and rule, leading to the elimination of sectarian strife, became the assumption of secular-nationalism.

Nehru made a point of emphasizing that '(I)t is wrong and misleading to talk of a Moslem invasion or India or of the Moslem period in India, just as it would be wrong to refer to the coming of the British to India as a Christian invasion.'[116] While this again may have had a political purpose behind it, such an understanding prevented any serious investigation of the ways in which sectarian conflicts fed on feelings of injury and hurt that were, rightly or wrongly, seen to be associated with such aggressions. We know today how missionary discourse in the nineteenth century was instrumental in the colonial campaign against certain practices of the

Hindus and Muslims. The task today, as Shahid Amin has recently pointed out, is not to produce syncretic histories as much as to write non-sectarian histories of sectarian strife.[117] What secular-nationalism did, by effecting these closures, was to make such articulations of caste and community conflict unspeakable in the public domain of civil society. It could not eliminate them; it only pushed them 'underground' so to speak—to smoulder in the depths of political society and erupt at its moment of crisis.[118] It is these that have occupied the centre-stage of Indian politics in the last two decades.

Conclusion

To recapitulate, I have argued in this chapter that nationalisms, and particularly anticolonial nationalisms, despite their close connection with the project of democracy and citizenship, have a paradoxical character. Their impulse of 'inviting the masses into history', repeatedly comes up against their impulse of creating a homogenous national culture. I have also argued that following the early severance of nationalism's links with the quest for democratic citizenship and its subsequent insertion into the discourse of an organic national community, there has been an ever-present possibility of subversion of the democratic project within nationalism.

Since nationalism is coeval with certain modern developments in industry, it is also a discourse that must speak to the multiple effects of dislocation that these developments bring in their train. This goes side by side with the rise of a particular kind of atomized individual who has lost past moorings and awaits the new in anticipation, always ready to be mobilized by often contradictory discourses of new kinds of community identity. This circumstance is further complicated in the context of anticolonial nationalisms where the experience of colonial subjugation permanently marks their discursive universe, leading to extreme forms of xenophobia and chauvinism.

I have also discussed the Indian and South African (post-apartheid) nationalisms in order to argue that while abstract universalisms tend to privilege the dominant culture as the norm, the dialectic of universality and particularity can assume very different and unexpected forms in different historical contexts. With regard to secular-nationalism in India, I have argued that the insistence on such an abstract universalism has led to a production of Hindu culture as the norm. As a result, despite the uncompromising secularism of its architects, especially Jawaharlal Nehru, it has remained a creed under-girded by a Hindu ethos.

In conclusion, I want to offer a provisional description of certain key terms that appear often in this book:

Abstract citizenship: This term refers to that general construct of political theory and constitutional practice, where the individual qua individual, is considered as the rights-bearing citizen. Such a citizen is supposed to be unmarked by any other identity, so far as constitutional practice is concerned. This concept, now seriously under question, has been closely linked to the idea of formal equality. The question of racial and gender identity being rendered unspeakable in the name of formal equality and abstract citizenship, has been a matter of intense controversy in the context of affirmative action by the state, in different parts of the world.

Nation/nationalism: By these terms, I mean historically existing nations and nationalisms, especially where my critique of these is concerned. I refer to the historical entities called nations (and nationalist discourses) as homogenizing and repressive of marginalized cultures, in the specific context of my inquiry. That does not exhaust all that there is to nationalism. Nor do I intend to present nationalism as an unmitigated evil. It is also important to mention that my critique of nationalism is not one of abstract principle, though I do think that there are what appear to be insurmountable barriers to its future redemption. However, my attempt to think of the nation as an articulated totality, is in fact an attempt to imagine the nation form differently.

Secular-nationalism: As will be evident from the foregoing discussion, this term describes the ideological-discursive configuration represented notably by Nehru but one that achieves its fullness at the time of independence/partition. This discourse represents the final victory of this nationalist current over both Gandhian mystical nationalism and the Hindu Mahasabhaite Hindu nationalism. On the eve of independence, it also acquired coherence with the coming together of hitherto discordant and more problematic voices like those of Ambedkar and the Hindu Mahasabhaite sections within the Congress. This discourse was different because of its representation of the nation as a unity of diverse cultures and its emphasis on a secular syncretic reading of India's history and tradition. However, I have argued throughout that by default, it remained Hindu, born as it was within a Hindu universe. In this its modern universalist vision played an important part.

Political society: I have taken this term from Partha Chatterjee and slightly modified/expanded its use. As distinct from civil society, that is, the domain of citizenship governed by the language of rights and rules of contract, this domain represents what can be called the 'underground' of civil society.

This is the domain marked by a constant translation between the language of citizenship and rights and the more traditional language of community. It is the domain of the invisible, which nurtures all marginalized political and cultural dissent that cannot find accommodation in dominant political consensuses. The ground for their sudden irruption on to the institutional arena of modern politics is prepared in this relatively invisible domain. I have discussed this idea in greater detail in the concluding chapter.

Notes

1. This is a relatively untheorized notion of Marx's. I have discussed this in a separate article; see Nigam (1999).

2. The term 'moment of arrival', as well as the description that follows, is taken from Chatterjee (1986).

3. I draw some of the crucial insights of this argument from Chatterjee (1986).

4. Nehru mentions in his autobiography, that 'for the time being, at least', 'we gave him a blank cheque'. 'Often we discussed his fads and peculiarities among ourselves and said, half-humorously, that when Swaraj came, these fads must not be encouraged.' See Nehru (1936/98), p. 73.

5. Here I am referring to the *project* of nationalism as universalist. However, it must be underlined that this project has to deal with pre-existing communities of culture, all of which cannot be either assimilated or excluded or excised from the body of the new nation. Definitions of Selfhood, therefore, characteristically involve, a production and reproduction of cultural difference, of notions of the Other, as simultaneous preconditions of national identity. I have discussed this idea of nationalism as universalism at length later in this chapter.

6. Some of the key works in this domain are those of Kohn (1944/67), Kedourie (1960, 1970), Seton-Watson (1977), Gellner (1983, 1994), Anderson (1983/91), Hobsbawm (1990). The list is by no means exhaustive and there are many books and important essays which include Breuilly (1992), Smith (1986), and Nairn (1977/81).

7. As Seton-Watson has observed, there is really no 'scientific' way of establishing what all nations have in common. Quoted in Brennan (1995), p. 47. Ernest Gellner, on the other hand seems to disagree and tries to provide a rigorous definition. One whole chapter of his *Nations and Nationalism* is therefore devoted to definitions of state, nation, and nationalism.

8. Quoted by Anderson (1983/91), p. 80.

9. Gellner (1983), p. 39.

10. Ibid., pp. 37–8.

11. Ibid., p. 38.

12. Kedourie (1970), p. 28.

13. Ibid., pp. 31–2

14. Ibid., p. 33.

15. Ibid., pp. 33–4.

16. Ibid., p. 32. Here, Kedourie talks of this tendency being given new life in the Crusades and the massacre of Jews, the wars of religion in the sixteenth century—the turning point is the revocation by Louis XIV of the Edict of Nantes, a century before the French revolution.

17. Kohn (1944/67), p.vii.

18. Ibid., p. vii.

19. Nairn (1977/81), p. 41.

20. Gellner (1983), p. 47.

21. Ibid., p. 46.

22. Ernest Renan, 'What is a Nation?' in Geoff Eley and Ronald Gregor Suny, op. cit., p. 45.

23. Balibar (1991), p. 94.

24. Here we must make an exception of what Anderson, after Seton-Watson, calls official nationalisms—for these were *responses* by 'primarily dynastic and aristocratic' ruling groups, to popular nationalisms. Anderson sees them as conservative—if not downright reactionary—*policies* 'adapted from the model of largely spontaneous popular nationalism that preceded them'. He quotes Jaszi (1929) to the effect that one may ask 'whether these late imperialist developments of nationalism really emanate from the genuine sources of the national idea' and not from the monopolistic interests of certain groups, 'alien to the original conception' of national aims. Anderson (1983/91), p. 110. Consequently, they must be treated as a different category of nationalisms, with very different projects.

25. Kohn (1944/67), p. 4.

26. Ibid., p. 3.

27. Ibid., p. 330.

28. Hobsbawm (1990), p. 19.

29. Anderson (1983/91), p. 48.

30. Ibid., p. 50.

31. Ibid., p. 81.

32. Ibid., p. 82.

33. Ibid.

34. Kohn (1944/67), p. 331.

35. See note 37.

36. Sternhell (1976), p. 348. Emphasis added.

37. I have borrowed the term *decalage*, from Althusser, who uses it to denote various kinds of dislocations: in relations between concepts and their real objects, between different practices, between different 'levels of the totality' etc. (See Althusser and Balibar [1977], p. 312). Althusser also uses this term in relation to Marx's use of Hegelian terms where they introduce an effect of *dislocation 'between the semantic field of origin'* and *'the conceptual field to which they were applied'* (p. 121). It is in a wider and slightly altered sense of this last version that I use this term here.

38. I should make it clear here that when I talk of nationalism/s, I am talking of historical nationalisms and not of ideal-typical forms. I am consequently not interested in the question of whether all nationalisms must always, inevitably, be hostile to minority cultures, even though I personally think that if we were to ever invent a nationalism that is accommodative of minority cultures, it would make little sense to call such a thing by this name. This for the simple reason that without a homogenous national culture, a mythology of a common history, and a common destiny, nationalism would not really remain nationalism.

39. Gandhi (1927), p. 29. Here Gandhi mentions that he had no living faith in any god and that he was more inclined to atheism in his early youth.

40. Fanon (1971), p. 125.

41. Ibid., p. 109 and Mao Tsetung (1977) *Selected Works*, vol. 1, p. 19.

42. Laclau (1990), p. 40.

43. The expression in quotes is from Zizek (1993), p. 224. However, Zizek makes this observation in the context of a different argument. It may not be out of place to mention that immediately after liberation in April 1975, at a Special Centre Assembly for cabinet ministers and zonal and regional secretaries of the Khmer Rouge, Pol Pot while initiating his breathtaking 'communist regime' decreed along with abolition of all markets and currency, in the same breath that the entire Vietnamese population be expelled. See Kiernan (1985), 416.

44. Zizek, (1993), p. 224.

45. Anderson (1991), p. 7.

46. Gellner (1983), pp. 48–9.

47. Anderson (1991), p. 6 and Gellner (1983), p. 56. Anderson critiques Gellner in this passage for conflating invention with 'falsity' and 'fabrication', basing himself on his earlier work, *Thought and Change*. In the work cited above though, Gellner is categorical that it would be erroneous to conclude from his formulation that nationalism is 'artificial' and an 'ideological invention'—though occasionally he does seem to suggest artificiality, too (p. 56).

48. Chatterjee (1986), p. 21.

49. Ibid., p. 22.

50. Ibid., p. 40.

51. In a later work, Chatterjee also elaborates how both the emergence of print culture and cultural products like the novel, have a very different history in

a country like India. See Chatterjee (1995), p. 7–9. It is worth mentioning here, in passing, that Chatterjee's has been a highly misread argument. Even serious scholars like Sumit Sarkar seem to read in it precisely the obverse of what he is arguing. For instance, Sarkar says in an obvious reference to Chatterjee's argument, 'Colonial-Western cultural hegemony...tends to get homogenized, abstracted from internal tensions, and presented as all-pervasive, virtually irresistible within it own domain—those touched by it become *capable of only "derivative discourses"*.' In the footnote that follows the paragraph, he says this explicitly: "The 'derivative discourse' argument was elaborated by Partha Chatterjee in *Nationalist Thought...*' (Sarkar, 1997, pp. 4–5). Similarly, Javeed Alam believes that it is Chatterjee's argument that because nationalism 'latches onto the idea of progress' and borrows from the Enlightenment, it remained 'derivative'. 'However hard one may try, one somehow gets dragged into the domain of the derivative. Gandhi, who waged a titanic struggle to achieve autonomy of mind and thinking, did not also entirely succeed in being out of its domain.' (Alam 1999b, Chapter 4, note 27, p. 101). I may mention that regarding Gandhi, Chatterjee clearly holds that his thought lay 'entirely outside the framework of post-Enlightenment thought'. It might be interesting from the point of view of a sociology of knowledge, to find out why this particular text was misread so thoroughly.

52. Chatterjee (1986), p. 51.

53. Ibid., See pp. 49–51.

54. Chatterjee (1995) *Nation and Its Fragments*, Oxford University Press, Calcutta, Delhi etc, pp. 116-7

55. Ibid., p. 32.

56. Ibid., pp. 126–7.

57. One might refer here to the work on women like Pandita Ramabai and Savitribai Phule and such others who took on the nationalist leaders in their attempts to educate women. See for instance, Chakravarti (2000).

58. Jalal (1998), p. 2183.

59. Ibid.

60. Mufti, (1998), p. 118.

61. Said (1994), p. 262.

62. Ibid., pp. 257–8.

63. Ibid., p. 258.

64. The provision to confine the black native population within a small area was made in the Native Land Act, 1913. The percentage varied since then till, in 1936, the native population was allotted this area of 13 per cent. See Biko (1996), p. 81.

65. Quoted in Altbeker and Steinberg (1998), p. 66.

66. See Davenport (1992), pp. 231–6.

67. Mamdani (1996), pp. 5–7.

68. Ibid., p. 51.

69. In India too, the British emphasis was on ruling the natives through 'their own laws', though of course, it was no native authority that would administer it; most often it was British authorities ruling on the basis of a codified 'customary' law, that was in any case, reconstituted through the elimination of its diversity and subordination to the dominant Shastric law in the case of the Hindus and the Shariat law in that of the Muslims.

70. Quoted in Mzala (1989).

71. Biko (1996), pp. 83–4.

72. Quoted in Slovo (1989), p. 147.

73. Mbeki (1998), pp. 31–2.

74. 'The Freedom Charter' reprinted in *New International*, no. 5, Fall 1985, p. 63.

75. 'The African Renaissance' in Mbeki (1998), p. 298. To be sure, there was a voice of considerable significance in the sections of the Black Consciousness movement and particularly, the Pan-Africanist Congress that opposed this accent, of the Freedom Charter, on the democratic state. The PAC sought, on the other hand, to focus exclusively on the mobilization of black people for the building of the future nation. See Meli (1989), p. 73. The fact that the PAC never really managed to make the kind of headway, shows that the ANC's construction of the idea of nationhood has much greater acceptability.

76. This comment was made by Vishwas Satgar, Gauteng provincial committee member of the SACP in a personal interview. Much of the insights and information in this section are derived from discussions and interviews with activists and leaders of the ANC and the SACP. In particular, my interviews with Kgalema Motlante, secretary general of the ANC, Jeremy Cronin, assistant general secretary of the SACP, Langa Zita, central committee member SACP and ANC member of parliament, Vishwas Satgar, Gauteng provincial committee member of the SACP helped me understand the issues involved. Extensive discussions with the last two, and the opportunity provided through them to attend workshops and meetings helped in getting a textured feel of the current issues.

77. Slovo (1989), p. 142.

78. Quoted in Mamdani (1996), p. 135.

79. Slovo (1989), p.143.

80. Ibid., p. 144.

81. Mzala (1989), pp. 48–50.

82. This is an opinion that is strongly held among the non-white activists I spoke to.

83. Mbeki (1998), p. 72.

84. David Atwell, 'Simplistic "two nations" thesis lacks moral clarity and should be abandoned', the *Sunday Independent*, 4 June 2000, Johannesburg, p. 9.

85. Both these letters to the editor appeared in the *Sunday Independent*, 11 June 2000, p. 9.

86. Darrel Bristow-Bovey, 'Enslaved by a man-made myth', the *Sunday Independent*, 11 June 2000, p. 13.

87. Quoted in *Umrabulo—Let's Talk Politically*, no. 8, Special edition of the ANC document for the National General Council to be held in Port Elizabeth from 11–15 July, 2000. Document prepared by the Political Education and Training Unit of the ANC, p. 22. All emphasis added.

88. Quoted in Pandey (1992), pp. 206–7.

89. Ibid., p. 210.

90. Ibid., p. 235.

91. Ibid., p. 236.

92. Ibid., p. 238.

93. Quoted in ibid., p. 212.

94. Quoted in ibid., p. 238.

95. Quoted in ibid., pp. 256–7.

96. For details, see Chapter 3.

97. Nehru (1936/98), p. 372.

98. Ibid., p. 384.

99. I discuss this in detail in Chapter 4. Suffice it to note here that with regard to the Muslims, when finally the question of a prime minister came up under the Cabinet Mission's plan, Gandhi proposed that Jinnah should form the first government. (See Wolpert [1996], p. 362.) Likewise with regard to the Dalits he would constantly soft-pedal the nationalist movement to take up the cause of untouchability abolition, even though the ways in which he sought to do so irritated Ambedkar and Periyar greatly. For further details see Chapters 4 and 5.

100. Ibid., p. 135.

101. Ibid., pp. 135–6, emphasis added.

102. Nehru (1944/89), p. 351.

103. Ibid., p. 458.

104. Ibid., p. 382, emphasis added.

105. Ibid., pp. 362–3.

106. Nehru (1936/98), p. 460, emphasis added.

107. Ibid. p. 462.

108. Ibid. pp. 157-8. Emphasis added.

109. See Prakash (1999).

110. Ibid., p. 118

111. Ibid., p. 119.

112. See the discussion in Wolpert (1996). Wolpert's fascinating biography of Nehru documents his position on this matter with great clarity. He refers to Maulana Azad's observation in later years, that it was the 'greatest blunder of my political life' to nominate Nehru as the Congress president in the crucial year when the Cabinet Mission plan was to be finalized. Azad's regret was that in deciding not to stand for the post himself, if he had even nominated Sardar Patel instead, he would have ensured the successful implementation of the Cabinet Mission plan and never committed Nehru's mistake. Nehru's great mistake that, according to Azad, gave 'Jinnah the opportunity of sabotaging the plan', of course included the irresponsible statement to the press, that 'we agreed to go into the Constituent Assembly...and have agreed to nothing else'. Ominously for Jinnah and the Muslim League, Nehru declared that 'we are entirely free' to do what we want, in the Constituent Assembly. That it was this that finally led to Jinnah's call for observing the 'Direct Action Day' on 16 August 1946, is well known—along with all the disastrous consequences that followed. See especially pp. 362–70.

113. For a graphic description of the events, see ibid., pp. 408–32.

114. For a detailed discussion of the SCF and Dalit politics in the partition period, see Rawat (2001). I have discussed this entire dynamic at greater length; see Nigam (2004b).

115. See Nehru (1944/89), pp. 242–3.

116. Ibid., p. 241.

117. See Amin (2002), pp. 24–43.

118. I draw this distinction between civil society and political society from some recent writings of Partha Chatterjee and discuss it at greater length in the concluding chapter.

2

Nation and Infra-Nationalisms
Secular-Nationalism Comes Apart

Introduction

In this chapter I will discuss the conjunctures of the 1980s and early to mid-1990s. It is in these conjunctures that we can see the logic of the unravelling of the nation playing itself out in the face of severe contestations within. With respect to the 1980s, I will especially look at the return of the repressed discourses of caste and community, the eruption of 'subnational' assertions, the emergence of the women's movement as a major political force and finally, the challenge to the ideology of developmentalism posed by ecological movements.

I will then look at the unravelling of the Congress that begins alongside these processes and around the turn of the decade, the rise of the Hindu right, represented by the BJP and the RSS. In a subsequent section I will also discuss the immense transformation in the imaginative possibilities that unfold before the expanding middle classes and their effect on a re-imagination of the nation as a 'global nation', following the revolution in communications technology and its relationship to the assertions of Hindu nationhood.

Finally, I will discuss the discursive break or rupture that marks the onset of the 1990s, when the entire terms of public discourse are refashioned, even turned upside down. I suggest that the 1980s represent one moment of rupture and the 1990s another. The first moment ruptured the secular-nationalist discourse 'from below', the second, 'from above', representing the nation striking back.

I should clarify here that by 'unravelling of the nation' I do not mean that the nation is finally and irrevocably came apart. What is important here is the way in which the nationalist imagination constantly runs up against what I will, for want of a better term, call 'infra-nationalisms'. These infra-nationalisms are probably better understood as those subterranean currents that inhabit the life of the postcolonial nation-to-be and often burst forth on the political stage, continuously threatening its project of nationhood. They should be understood as different from 'subnationalism' in that *they need not ever* express themselves in the desire for *another nation*. Some by their very geographical spread cannot articulate their aspirations in terms of a separate nation but they nevertheless insist on redrawing the internal cultural boundaries of the nation-in-the-making. The different lower caste movements, including the Dalit movement, the ecological movements and various other currents discussed below can be seen as instances of such infra-nationalisms. Infra-nationalisms, I will also suggest, borrowing from Ranabir Samaddar, represent 'a particular kind of postcolonial anxiety: of a society suspended forever in the space between the "former colony" and the "not yet nation"'.[1] Samaddar uses the notion of 'cartographic anxiety' in the context of external boundaries of the nation that are made and unmade in the encounters between the state and the people—the former striving to fix the territoriality of the nation, while the latter see it as 'one more minefield to be navigated safely', maybe even profited from.[2] My argument is that this anxiety over borders is equally internal. I should also clarify that by 'internal borders' I mean two things: first, the physical borders between different regions, the drawing and redrawing of which has been a perennial source of tension in the project of Indian nationhood. This has also meant a perennial tension over the distribution of natural resources like the sharing of river waters. Second, by this term I also wish to refer to the anxieties about cultural borders between communities or between different caste groups, since these boundaries also codify power relations between them. In the cases of so-called separatist movements these anxieties are about actual territorial borders, as the discussion of Assam and Punjab will demonstrate; in the case of other movements, they are about the cultural boundaries, which codify power as the instances of the lower caste assertions and ecological movements will show. Recent attempts to redefine relations between the Hindus and Muslims, Hindus and Christians, or Hindus and Dalits represent in different ways attempts at redrawing such borders. The case of the women's movement is, of course, more complicated, for it is not about borders as such. Nor has the women's movement really made nationalism the explicit object of its interrogations. However, as the argument in that section will show, it does eventually open up different vantage points for the critique of patriarchal power relations embodied in the institutions of the nation-state. Later critiques by feminists of the masculinist project of nations, reflected in militarism and war, certainly provide more radical vantage points for theoretical critiques of the nation-form itself. Infra-nationalisms then can be understood to represent the failure of the impossible project of nationhood in the postcolonial context.

In July 1984, Atal Behari Vajpayee, leader of the Bharatiya Janata Party (BJP) remarked: 'We have still not been able to *become a nation*, this is not a good thing (*hum abhi tak ek rashtra nahin ban paaye, yeh koyee achhee baat nahin hai*). Pakistan was formed on the basis of religion, but it got divided. We decided not to make religion our basis. We said our country will be religion-neutral (*dharma-nirpeksha*), secular. It will be for the believers of all religions. And yet, India has come to the brink of another division.'[3] This was said during a discussion on the White Paper on Punjab presented in parliament, in the aftermath of the notorious 'Operation Bluestar', by the government of Indira Gandhi. By that time the idea of a nationhood in the making was already badly shattered. The immediate context of Vajpayee's anxiety was of course provided by the developments in Punjab. The sudden escalation of the situation, going completely out of control, was evident from the White Paper itself, according to which, 'right from 1981 to June 2 1984, there were 561 incidents'. Of these, 'from the 20th March 1981 to 21st December 1981, there were only 28 incidents. From 21st January 1982 to 24th December 1982, there were 32 incidents'. Then from 10 January 1983 to 26 December 1983, there were 130 incidents. And thereafter, within five months time from January 5 1984 to June 2 1984, the number of incidents was 363.[4]

An interesting aspect of this debate was the way in which the question of Punjab immediately raised the question of Indian 'nationhood'. The parties in parliament were no longer prepared to discuss the issue in terms of the specifics of the Punjab situation, or to see it as a law and order problem. Intervening in this debate, C.T. Dhandapani from Tamil Nadu (Pollachi) remarked that the White Paper mentioned, '[that] The people of India do not accept the proposition that India is a multinational society'. This he claimed was completely irrelevant and unnecessary and went on to register his sharp disagreement from such a position. Dhandapani had no doubt that India *was* a multinational country.[5] Many other members including the Speaker, pounced on him, one of them even reminding him that he, as a member of parliament 'was under oath' to consider the nation sacrosanct. While the speaker reminded him that this was a matter of the Constitution, another luminary chided him on his 'lack of knowledge' of English.[6] Dhandapani, on his part, pointed out that there are fifty nationalities in China even though it is one nation. Similar was the case with the USSR. He added, '(T)herefore, this is a debatable point. I would like to say this more particularly when we talk about Centre-State relations.'[7]

In fact, the anxieties about the nation were so pervasive in that debate that Vajpayee even grilled the prime minister, Indira Gandhi, reminding her of her alleged statement made in the USSR that there were many nationalities in India, to which his party had objected. Mrs Gandhi had to clarify that she had used the word 'qaum' to mean communities and not nationalities.[8]

It is also interesting that in her intervention in the debate, the then prime minister, Indira Gandhi, spelt out a scenario that seemed to carry intimations of the unravelling of the structure of secular-nationalism. The creeping sense of doom felt by the Congress Party, which was supposed to have been an embodiment of secular-nationalism, was evident in her intervention. She reiterated that the Congress had always fought communalism and all types of extremism. Emphasizing that it would continue to fight it in its new garb, that of fundamentalism, she went on to say:

...[I]n our country we have to fight it all the harder, because our society is far more vulnerable. This fundamentalism [...] is not in any one community. I am not referring only to Sikh fundamentalism but also to Hindu fundamentalism and Muslim fundamentalism and even to Christian fundamentalism. Every religion feels it has to take an extreme view. Sikhs are not considered real Sikhs because they do not belong to the Akali Dal. What do the Muslims say? That those Muslims who are in the Congress or Communist [party] are not real Muslims, because they do not belong to the Muslim League... This is what our party is suffering from because we have kept to our ideal of secularism, because we have kept to certain wider goals.[9]

In her speech, Indira Gandhi returned, of course, to her favourite theme of the 'foreign hand': 'The links between communalism and neo-imperialism are deep-rooted.'[10] She went on to expand on her favourite theme of how the imperialists could not stand the idea of an independent India and therefore, fomented trouble. That however, is not immediately relevant for us. What is important is her acknowledgement that the Congress was by then already feeling besieged by the rapid erosion of secularism and the rise of religious sectarianisms. Hindus, Sikhs or Muslims were now seeking their own platforms and to that extent, the Congress was suffering. Also important in her speech is the reference to the fact that the Sikh and Muslim 'fundamentalists' do not consider 'secular' or Congress/communist Sikhs and Muslims as real Sikhs and Muslims. Her exclusion of the Hindus here seems significant. If the later trajectory of the Congress is any guide, the realization had probably already dawned that it could not be all things to all people, if things continued the way they did. This was all the more significant, because as we shall see in subsequent chapters, whenever nationalism was under strain, it revealed its Hindu colours.

That the onset of the 1980s represented a change of qualitative dimensions is by now widely acknowledged. Take for example the following observations from the writings of secular-liberal and left-wing scholars, surveying the developments of the decade towards it end.[11] The first observation:

While the official ideology of the state is generally hesitant to recognize cultural and political diversities, it is quite willing to accommodate primordial institutions like caste and religion. These institutions...have gained *fresh legitimacy* owing to the entente between the state and revivalism. *This is particularly noticeable in the 1980s which has witnessed unprecedented upsurge in religiosity, an exacerbation of sectarian tensions* and increased polarization of Indian society along caste and communal lines.[12]

The second, and equally telling observation of a Marxist:

The decade of the 1980s in Indian politics has so far *been one of violent sectarian upheavals which have,* relatively speaking, *pushed back the growth of democratic forces into the background...*
...(T)he 1980s stand in sharp contrast to the 1970s. The 1970s, too were years of struggle, turbulence and crises, notwithstanding the great hopes of renewal with which they started. But the struggle and crises were of a different nature. Whether in Gujarat or Bihar, or later in the all-India JP movement, they were essentially secular and wholly social in nature.[13]

It is evident then, that the onset of the 1980s was widely perceived as a watershed in Indian politics. Opinions may differ on the exact meaning of these developments and their analysis. Some scholars like Achin Vanaik have seen it as a 'crisis of legitimacy of the state'.[14] Others like Atul Kohli have understood it as a 'crisis of governability'.[15] Still others like Bhabani Sengupta have seen it as the state superseding the nation: 'The State grew, the nations declined. Then, the 'nations' within the Nation began to assert themselves with their demands for political and cultural recognition.'[16] Another group of scholars, surveying the developments in the early 1980s, saw the transformation as a consequence of the growing 'devaluation' of 'the conventional forums through which the "masses" attempt to participate in decision-making...forums which include the State and its developmental agencies, and the political parties and their mass fronts.'[17]

It should also be mentioned here that some of these scholars like Kohli and those associated with the Lokayan initiative, traced the origins of this crisis back to the late 60s and early 1970s. Kohli takes 1967, the period of the beginning of the decline in Congress hegemony, as his reference point in understanding the crisis of governability. Rajni Kothari, a theorist of the Lokayan initiative, refers more specifically to the emergence of 'non-state actors on the one hand and non-territorial crystallizations on the other,' at a global level, including voluntary and non-governmental organizations. Kothari sees the 'grassroots movements launched by the non-traditional Left—Chipko, the miners struggle in Chhattisgarh, the Ryot Coolie Sangham in Andhra Pradesh, the Satyagraha led by the peasants movement in Kanakpura in Karnataka against the mining of granite, the Jharkhand Mukti Morcha...' as bringing within the domain of politics, issues that were hitherto not considered political. These included issues of health, rights over forests, and the rights of women within the family.[18] Harsh Sethi includes in his list of such non-party struggles, the Bihar and Gujarat agitations in 1973–74 and the then ongoing textile strike in Bombay under the leadership of Datta Samant.

All these positions highlight the process of the crisis of legitimacy of the state in general and the 'Congress-system' in particular, and note correctly in my view, that the process had begun much earlier. In fact, the imposition of the Emergency in 1975 can also be seen as a nervous response to that crisis. However, these positions do not adequately recognize the change in the language and terms of protest that Hasan and Alam draw our attention to. It is the argument of this chapter that the developments indicated not just the coming apart of the 'Congress system'; they portended the unravelling of the nation as it was imagined in the course of the anticolonial struggle and built in the post-independence period. While earlier protests and mass movements raised economic demands and allied issues like those of corruption, they did not question the cultural boundaries of the nation. Some of the tendencies mentioned by Kothari did, of course, begin to raise issues that would eventually lead to such interrogations—especially by the ecological movements through their emphasis on the control over local natural resources. The tendencies I wish to discuss, either directly challenged the idea of India inherited from the anticolonial struggle, or at the very least, insisted on redrawing the cultural boundaries of the nation in explicit and implicit ways. The roots of the developments of the 1980s lie in an immediate sense in what happened in the period of the Janata Party government, but in a more profound sense, in the very construction of Indian nationhood, as a distinct cultural-political entity, built during the anticolonial struggle and the immediate post-independence phase.

In the remainder of this chapter, I will trace the developments of this period and map the 1980s, with a view to exploring the manner in which this unravelling took place. To anticipate the argument briefly, I will suggest that there were at least two distinct moments of the rupture of secular-nationalism. The beginnings of the first moment can be placed around the period of 1978–80, when caste and community erupted on the political scene as autonomous actors. This period also saw the emergence of the issue of centre–state relations and increasing 'sub-national' assertions, particularly the Assam and Punjab movements, as well as an intensification of the conflict in Kashmir and the North-East. Issues of gender and ecology also start coming to the fore subsequently. The second moment of rupture can be located around the years 1990–92, when around three events—the anti-Mandal agitations, the structural adjustment programmes, and the demolition of the Babri Masjid—the entire discourse of Indian politics undergoes a major transformation. All the basic assumptions of political discourse that were till then thought to be sacrosanct are, as we shall see, turned around into their very opposite. I will also suggest that the emergence of the Hindu right in the late-1980s was not a response to the situation arising out of a rapid 'global integration' of the Indian economy as suggested by some scholars; it was rather the response of the hitherto privileged upper-caste Hindu elite to the challenges posed by the nation's repressed selves. To that extent, these developments point to a certain kinship between the hegemonic secular-nationalist discourse and the resurgent right, at least in terms of maintaining the privileges cornered by this elite. The real meaning of this kinship will be explored in Chapter 5.

Return of the Repressed: Caste and Community

The end of the Emergency regime of Indira Gandhi and the coming to power of the Janata Party could be said to have heralded an unprecedented interrogation of the nation. The entity called India, as it had come to be in the three decades since independence, was for the first time examined in its internal structure by a relentless assertion by the various smaller entities which constituted it. In a way, of course, the official discourse of the Janata Party was as nationalistic as that of the Congress and there were powerful sections within it that had learnt their politics in the Congress of yore. Yet, there was a sense in which the Janata Party became the vehicle for the expression for a wide array of forces that had been marginalized during the three decades of Congress rule. To that extent, therefore, the endemic conflicts within the Janata reflected contestations between some of these very diverse currents.

One of the occasions within the parliament on which this conflict came to the fore was the debate on a private member's Bill, moved by Roop Nath Singh Yadav, entitled the 'Indian Social Disparities Abolition Bill 1977'. The debate on this Bill continued intermittently for more than a year and eventually led to the formation of the Scheduled Castes and Tribes Commission. The debate on the issue provides fascinating insights into the kind of conflicts that were emerging as well as to the modes of their articulation with the discourse of secularism, or more precisely, secular-nationalism. Shambhu Nath Chaturvedi, a Brahmin member from Agra,[19] argued against this Bill advocating reverse discrimination for backward castes, on the grounds that it would not 'be conducive to promotion of the *feeling of nationhood or integration* in our community.' Another crucial consideration he said, 'is whether the benefits of reservation reach the weakest or the most backward sections of the community or are monopolized by a small section thereof...' Next in his armoury was the argument, equally well-known today: '...whether these reservations do not destroy the *espirit de corps* of the administrative services and bring down their efficiency and morale.' On all these counts, the member felt that the Bill would 'prove harmful'.[20] It is important to note that all these arguments marshalled by Chaturvedi are of nationalist and secular provenance. As against the non-secular categories of caste, they invoke issues of nationhood, of the *espirit de corps* of the services, so important for the nation's advance and of the interests of the *economically weakest* sections. Chaturvedi went further. 'Concessions once enjoyed', he argued, 'are never given up'. 'We have the experience of our own country. *We gave certain concessions* and, ultimately, they went on and on and led to the division of the country. The same has been the experience of other countries also. In Czechoslovakia, the Sudeten minority agitated and ultimately it led to an armed invasion and the outbreak of the Second World War.'[21]

On the other side, Ram Naresh Kushwaha, a backward caste leader speaking for the Bill, argued that the whole system was dominated by vested interests who resisted the entry of the dispossessed into education, jobs, and ownership of land were responsible for the bloodshed that was taking place. He accused those in charge of providing employment of being 'anti-Harijan, anti-Backward, and anti-Muslim'—which was why quotas were never filled up.[22] It is worth noticing that Kushwaha was forced to articulate his demand in opposition to the universalist-modernist language of Chaturvedi, precisely in the vocabulary that had been rendered unspeakable by the etiquette of secular-nationalism. In the same vein he also referred to the notorious incident where the upper castes, led by Congress leader Kamalapati Tripathy's son, washed the statue of Sampurnanand with Ganga water because it had supposedly been polluted by the Dalit leader Jagjivan Ram's presence.[23] Kushwaha went on to argue that 'the Hindus' had no right to oppose reservations as they had been availing of them since ancient times, thanks to the *Manusmriti*. Another intervention of considerable sophistication came from Kanwar Lal Gupta, an RSS member of the BJP opposing the Bill. He argued that, *in principle*, he supported the Bill because there are crores of people who, even over thirty-two years after independence do not get a square meal. 'Particularly, our Harijan brethren have suffered untold indignities at the hands of our ancestors, not only after independence but for thousands of years, and for that we are guilty and it is urgently necessary to rectify the situation. I respect the feelings of those who have brought this Bill...I have only one objection. Even if there is a millionaire (*crorepati*) from the backward classes, will his child get free education and a Brahmin's child, even if hungry, unclothed, thirsty, will be deprived of bread?'[24] At this point, another member, Ram Awadhesh Singh, interjected to say: 'This you will never understand'. Kanwar Lal Gupta continued to make his speech: '*I only want to say that we should not talk about caste...* We should say that those who are poor, hungry, and unclothed... The way a casteist struggle has been unleashed today in the name of the Backwards, this will set the country on fire. Any struggle today, in the name of caste, language, or religion is going to push the country backwards, not take it forward.'[25] Notice again, how the argument is cast in terms of a sanitized and universalist language where it is possible to talk of socio-economic deprivation, but forbidden to mention caste, language, or religion. Put differently, for those whose caste, religious, or linguistic interests are preserved within the existing structure of the nation, secularism seems to be an eminently affordable creed. This might incidentally give a clue to the accusation of 'pseudo-secularism' levelled by the Hindu right on its secular opponents: they are incomplete seculars because they continue to talk of minority rights in some fashion, whereas this logic of secularism demands that they excise any talk of minorities, such as caste.

Two more things are noteworthy about this debate. Recurrent in the debate is the sense of restiveness among the representatives from the Dalit and Other Backward Classes (OBC) backgrounds. Repeated mention is made of the fact, most notably emphasized by Roop Nath Singh Yadav, the mover of the Bill, that though the Kaka Kalelkar Commission was appointed in 1953 and gave its report in 1955, it remained unimplemented twenty-three years down the line [26] Also important is the fact the arguments in the debate anticipate more than twelve years in advance, all the arguments that were to be deployed in public discourse after the implementation of the Mandal Commission. That they nevertheless took the secularists by surprise is understandable, considering that they remained absent from this significant debate in 1978. This is a point we will come back to later.

It may be useful to go back briefly to the Kaka Kalelkar Commission itself to see that the arguments that were being rehearsed in this debate have a much more exalted and hoary lineage. Christophe Jaffrelot has fascinatingly recounted the entire story in his recent volume.[27] Kaka Kalelkar, who headed the first Backward Classes Commission, was a noted Gandhian Brahmin. His team in the commission consisted of eleven members. It was supposed to identify the backward classes and suggest means of redressing their backwardness. Among its recommendations was a scheme of differentiated reservations varying from 25 per cent of the jobs in class I employment to 40 per cent in classes III and IV.[28] The report was of course, not unanimous and even at the time of its submission, five of the eleven members dissociated themselves from it. The most interesting thing was that Kalelkar himself did a last minute *volte face*. In these final moments he was overcome with anxiety: was he doing the right thing? Did backwardness have to identified on the basis of caste? What would it mean for the nation? Kalelkar's own words are eloquent: 'the nation has decided to establish a classless and casteless society, which also demands that backwardness should be studied from the point of view of the individual and at the most, that of family'.[29] Equally revealing is the resort to the 'economic' criterion in his note, which he advocated so as to 'remove the bitterness which the extremely poor and helpless amongst the upper classes [*sic*] Hindus feel…'[30] G.B. Pant, who was then Home Minister and to whom the report was submitted, dismissed it with the following words: 'With the establishment of our society on the socialist pattern…social and other distinctions will disappear as we advance towards that goal.' It was Nehru who finally sealed the fate of the report with arguments that will by now seem only too familiar: 'If we go in for reservations on communal and caste basis, we swamp the bright and able people and remain second-rate or third-rate'.[31]

Let us now return to our earlier discussion. It is while the debate on the private member's Bill was taking place, a month before the formal debate but long after the tabling of the Bill, that the 'scheduled caste and scheduled tribes MLAs decided to put up their own candidate in the contest for the leadership of Janata Legislature Party in Madhya Pradesh'.[32] It is significant that while the formal modes of representation were still encoded in secular and universalist language and parties sought to speak in terms of 'nation', 'class', or simply 'people', this development presaged the emergence of one that would become far more widespread and in fact, acquire a centrality in a little over a decade. No more would such categories retain their efficacy in mobilization; caste, community, and language would become the main modes of political representation. But some more developments of this period need to be mentioned. In fact, on the same day as the newspapers carried this report, they also reported a statement by the All-India Council of Indian Christians which expressed disappointment over the 'decreasing representation to Christians in the Ministry at the Centre and in the States'. The Council resolved to request political parties to nominate a Christian candidate for vice-presidentship when the then vice-president B.D. Jatti retired.'[33]

In the last week of December, the same year (1978), a Muslim Conference was held in Lucknow. The Conference raised demands for reservations in elected bodies and in public appointments. It also demanded the disbanding of the Provincial Armed Constabulary of Uttar Pradesh, which had earned notoriety during communal riots, as an anti-Muslim outfit.[34] Lok Sabha debates during this period, as well as news reports, testify to the increasing incidence of communal violence in large parts, particularly of north India. The growing sense of restiveness and alienation among the Muslims is also evident in the speeches made in parliament. One of the leaders, G.M. Banatwalla, for instance, raised the matter that several reports of the Commissioner for Linguistic Minorities had never been discussed in the House. He mentioned that from the Fourteenth Report for 1971–72 onwards none had been discussed.[35] Clearly, this was a reference not to the alienation caused by the immediately existing situation but to an accumulated grievance. Later on Banatwalla raised the question of representation during the debate on the presidential address.

The Muslim population today constitutes 11.2 percent of the population. We are assured everyday that fair and adequate representation will be given to them in the services, but in the midst of these assurances, the situation is deteriorating. Take the figures for IAS officers. In 1965 the percentage of Muslim IAS officers was 5.8 percent; today it is only 3.09 percent. Take the case of IPS. Muslims in 1965 accounted for 5.6 percent, today it has fallen to 3.19 percent [...]Take the total number of clerical cadre in the Central Secretariat. The total number of clerks [...] is 9,900. Muslims number only 21[...] (that) is hardly 0.02 percent.[36]

This was also the time when the central government set up a Minorities Commission 'to safeguard the interests of religious and linguistic minorities, towards preserving the secular traditions, promoting national integration and to remove the feeling of inequality and discrimination against them.'[37] Three days later, the president of the Akhil Bharat Hindu Mahasabha (ABHM) S.R. Date, issued a statement criticizing the government's decision. He opposed the setting up of the commission on the grounds that, 'it would discourage "Muslims and other minorities from joining the national mainstream."' The statement also lamented that the Janata government had fallen prey to threats of some Muslim leaders and taken a retrograde step: 'which even the pro-Muslim Nehru and Indira governments dared not do'.[38] The thrust of Date's criticism, it will be noted, was once again that this step would discourage the minorities from joining the 'national mainstream'. The idea of the 'minorities joining the mainstream', as we shall see, is fundamental to the Hindutva project of building a modern nation-state with a uniform and homogeneous national culture. Equally importantly, Date's statement draws attention to the fact that the Janata government, with sizeable Jana Sangh presence, had to do what the 'pro-Muslim' Nehru–Indira regimes had not dared to. In other words, it draws attention to the acute struggles and conflicts that were going on within the government and the party—something that may have been impossible to conceive of during the Congress regime.

The extent to which the formation called the Janata Party concealed its contradictory social forces is also evident from the struggle, or 'caste-war' as it was called, that burst forth in Bihar within a couple of months. In mid-March, with Karpoori Thakur, the chief minister of the state, implementing 26 per cent reservations for the Backward Castes, the state went up in flames. As the minister of state for home affairs, Sushila Sahai resigned amidst violent clashes between pro- and anti-reservationists, the conflict escalated. Jayprakash Narayan, the unchallenged leader of the 1974–75 Bihar movement had to face the ire of the assertive backward castes, for his advocacy of the so-called 'economic criteria'. Karpoori Thakur was the icon of the backwards, while JP became the banner of the upper castes. Slogans like *'Karpoori Thakur nahin ghabrana, Tere peechhey naya zamana'* and *JP shahi nahin chalegi*[39] showed the rapidity with which the icon of yesterday, Jayprakash Narayan came to be seen as a representative of the old system. So vicious was the anti-JP sentiment that a group of youths went to a bookshop on Fraser Road and burnt books on JP. Bookshop owners were threatened if they kept books on JP.[40] The reason why JP became the object of attack was that he had expressed himself in favour of reservation on the basis of *economic backwardness.*[41] Here were two forces vying for supremacy—rather, one was trying desperately to retain control over the assets, resources, and institutions of the state while the other, having found its voice for the first time, was staking its counter-claim. The language in which the claims and counter-claims were being articulated were clearly resonant of those being rehearsed inside parliament, and those that had acquired a legitimacy from the time of the Kaka Kalelkar commission controversy itself—that is, the claim to existing privilege in secular humanist terms, the counter-claims in the illegitimate language of caste. As if to leave no further doubt as to the point we are making, twelve Janata Party MLAs openly backed a demonstration in favour of job reservations *on the basis of economic backwardness* rather than caste and typically, the organization sponsoring the demonstration was called *Manav Adhikar Raksha Samiti* (Committee for the Defence of *Human* Rights).[42]

Violent conflicts continued during this period in different parts of the country.[43] Significantly, even Jagjivan Ram, a conventional 'Dalit' leader in the Congress mould, addressing the Bharatiya Dalit Varg Sammelan (Indian Dalit Classes Conference) in West Bengal, described the continuing violence as a sign of peoples' awakening. In June, the Uttar Pradesh (UP) government also announced a quota of 35 per cent for backward classes in services and posts in urban local bodies. This reservation, it was claimed, would be available to members of the 58 listed backward classes in the state—37 Hindu and 21 Muslim.[44]

It is interesting that while these assertions met with strong opposition from the entrenched upper caste sections now in control of power and institutions, left and secular forces watched the developments with increasing despair. The different ways in which the entrenched interests reacted were interesting replays of the oft-repeated dramas of the national movement. So for instance, in the beginning of 1979, a *Vishva Hindu Sammelan* (World Hindu Conference) was held in Allahabad, where apparently, delegates from seventeen countries collected to declare 'their resolve to fight untouchability and other weaknesses so that the Sammelan's aim to make the world "Arya" was achieved.'[45] In another characteristic move of incorporation and appropriation, the organizers succeeded in getting the Dalai Lama to inaugurate the conference, thus 'washing away' the 'thousands of years of acrimony between Sanatani Hindus and the Baudhs, after Buddha was denied entry into the holy city of Kashi.' It was declared in the Conference that untouchability must be declared untouchable. The untouchables shall be exalted to the highest form of Hindu salvation.[46]

Meanwhile, inside parliament, the manoeuvre made was equally significant. The prime minister Morarji Desai, in order to deflect and defer the matter of 33 per cent reservations for backward classes as promised in the Janata Party manifesto, appointed the Mandal Commission. The argument was that this commitment was based on the Kaka Kalelkar Commission report that was already twenty-two years old.[47] In the event, of course, the Mandal Commission Report was to become the new banner of struggle eleven years later.

Clearly, the question of representation was by now assuming proportions that were not till now imaginable. Communities were no longer satisfied 'being represented' by parties or organizations that claimed to speak in the name of abstract categories—for these categories had rendered certain kinds of experiences of marginalization or oppression unspeakable. It was necessary to blurt it out now in the 'crudest' of ways. The question of public employment and the question of political representation must be seen here as performing the same function; they must be seen as continuous with each other. Representation in employment was emphatically not simply about jobs, or as economists are fond of saying, the size of the cake; *it was about the political voice of the community*.

At this point, it is necessary to point out that almost around the same time another set of movements began to burst forth on the political stage, namely the assertions of subnational identity. These challenged the nationalist imaginary in a different way. Sometimes they were explicitly articulated in non-secular, religious terms like the demand for Khalistan in Punjab. But quite often they simply challenged the nationalist idea by foregrounding their subnational identity. By the mere act of foregrounding subnational identity, they brought forth the deep anxieties among nationalists of all hues, thus revealing the extent to which they were at least seen to be questioning nationhood.

It was also around 1980–81 that the resurgent women's movement came to an unprecedented high. In terms of its own self-consciousness, the women's movement was both secular and expressed a reliance on the nation-state. But as we will see later, as the identity of 'women' became the criterion on the basis of which all institutions were critiqued, it potentially carried the elements of a critique of the nation-state within itself, which started becoming manifest in the latter half of the 1980s. It is to the first of these that I will now turn.

Centre-State Relations and Subnational Assertions

If the coming to power of the Janata Party opened up opportunities for the assertions by hitherto repressed Dalit and Backward Caste voices, it also provided an opportunity for its allies to raise other questions crucial to the future of Indian democracy. One of these was the question of the restructuring of centre-state relations, initiated by the Left Front (LF) government in West Bengal. On 1 December 1977, the LF government adopted a memorandum demanding more powers for the states. The demand naturally involved major constitutional changes. This memorandum was then sent to the chief ministers of other states like Sheikh Abdullah of Jammu and Kashmir and Prakash Singh Badal of Punjab. This of course tied in with the demand for autonomy that was expressed for instance, in the Anandpur Sahib resolution adopted by the Akali Dal in 1973. Now that there were many non-Congress governments and in comparison to those of the 1960s, more homogeneous, the question could be taken up more seriously. It is an index of the hegemonic influence that the ideology of nationalism wielded over the educated middle class, trained and socialized to become good citizens of free India, that this relatively moderate and entirely constitutional demand was not only misunderstood by the leaders of the bigger parties, but was also misread by intellectuals and the media. So, for instance, a news report entitled 'Akali Extremists Put Pressure on Badal' states: 'A threat to Mr. P.S. Badal, Chief Minister of Punjab, is growing because of his refusal to "toe the extremists' line which supports Mr Jyoti Basu", Chief Minister of West Bengal and Sheikh Abdullah, Chief Minister of Jammu and Kashmir, in their demand for greater autonomy to States.'[48] Of course, history had yet to 'unfold' for the concerned correspondent to fully see what 'extremism' really meant and how extremism really fed on the intransigence of the powers-that-be. There was, to be fair, a hint of this in the report concerned. It pointed out that '[T]he stiff posture adopted by the Prime Minister over the transfer of water head –works[...]has made things worse for Badal.'[49] The extremists till then were the likes of Gurcharan Singh Tohra and Jagdev Singh Talwandi—a far cry from the extremism of a Bhindranwale. Expressing similar prejudices, a leading journalist declared in a lead article in the *Times of India*, that the 'CPM Plan Will Emasculate [*sic*] Centre'.[50] The supposedly Gandhian prime minister, Morarji Desai even ruled out any possibility of debate. 'There was "no need" for any debate on Centre–State relations' he said, asking 'What is the number of Chief Ministers [demanding it]?'[51] The right-wing external affairs minister, Atal Behari Vajpayee, on the other hand, was more diplomatic, stating that the Janata Party stood for decentralization of political and economic powers upto the village level. He said a review could be done provided it was not done in a spirit of confrontation with the Centre. However, he went on to add, quite gratuitously, 'He [Jyoti Basu] must realize that his concept of India being a multinational state is not acceptable to the Janata Party…We are a multilingual and multi-religious state and we regard India as being one nation and the Indian people as one people.'[52] The overall tenor of reactions to the very suggestion of review of centre–state relations was so charged that at one point the education minister of Punjab, Sukhjinder Singh had to publicly say that '[T] hose who opposed the demand for autonomy betrayed lack of confidence in the minorities of the country.' He further charged that the critics of autonomy 'had challenged the loyalty of the Sikhs to the nation. The Sikhs were second to none in their patriotism', he affirmed, 'but at the same time they wanted to maintain their religious and cultural identity.'[53] The issue of centre–state relations kept simmering and could not make much immediate headway due to the fall of the Janata Government. Much later though, the issue would come up more seriously.

Within a couple of years of Indira Gandhi's return to power, came the period of a new phase of opposition politics. E.M.S. Namboodiripad has described this as 'a sea-change in national politics', when in 1983, the Congress lost Andhra Pradesh and Karnataka, which along with West Bengal, Tripura, Tamil Nadu, Jammu and Kashmir, took the total of non-Congress governments to six. Namboodiripad acknowledged that 'an immediate consequence' of this was that the debate on centre-state relations was intensified. A conference of non-Congress chief ministers was held and the demand was raised 'that the whole structure of centre-state relations be recast'.[54] This time round, however, the lead was taken by the new Andhra Pradesh chief minister, N.T. Rama Rao to call a meeting of opposition political parties. In May 1983, the first of the series of 'conclaves' took place in Vijaywada. The CPI(M) found itself making common cause with the 'regional' parties whom it was simultaneously coming to view with increasing suspicion. For instance, the state unit of the CPI(M) in Andhra Pradesh had opposed NTR's platform of 'Telegu national pride' an opposition for which the party had to pay heavily in electoral terms. The Central Committee then seriously criticized the state leadership, asserting that the understanding of the Andhra Committee 'was wrong when it was made, and it was again proved wrong during the course of the elections'.[55] And yet the fact is that the Andhra Committee only reflected the overall suspicion of the rest of the party. The difference was really one of degrees, as was to be revealed very soon.

In the Vijaywada conclave, where the BJP too was present, a general resolution was adopted on the need for opposition unity and expressing concern over the 'growth of communal and divisive forces'. Between then and the Srinagar conclave, which was the third and the penultimate one, the issue of centre-state relations became highly contentious, with the advocates of change themselves differing sharply. Namboodiripad writes, '(d)ifferences arose at this conclave between *the national and the regional parties, the former standing for a set-up in which a strong centre would be based on strong states, while the latter called for a weak centre*'.[56] This really misrepresents the position of the so-called regional parties, who were certainly demanding a much more radical recasting of centre-state relations. The fear of 'disintegration of the nation' was really what was behind this misrepresentation and by this time, it was increasingly taking hold of the left as well. Writing in this background in *The Marxist*, the theoretical journal of the party, B.T. Ranadive elaborated once again his party's understanding on what is called the 'Nationality Question in India' in Marxist parlance. Here he candidly stated 'it will be *thoroughly reactionary* to present the nationality problem in isolation from the struggle for people's democratic revolution...*That will lead to regionalism, separatism and secessionism*'. He further added, echoing what has been a favourite nationalist theme: 'Today it is the strategy and tactics of imperialism to encourage secession and separatism wherever national inequalities exist'.[57] Writing two years later, another ideologue of the party, M. Basavapunnaiah made the position clearer still: '*Centre–state conflict is not only being exploited by certain separatist and secessionist forces in the country, but is also being exploited by the imperialist forces*'.[58] The party that had pioneered the demand for the recasting of centre–state relations, was now afraid of pressing the issue any further, when for the first time since independence, there was widespread support in favour of this demand.

Once the issue of federalism was opened for negotiation, and given the atmosphere that was developing, the articulation of many other subnational or 'regional' assertions of autonomy also became possible. However, often due to the nationalist reaction, many of these like the movements in Punjab and Assam were beginning to take on a definitively 'secessionist' colour. It is not necessary to go into all the details here but it will be useful to look briefly at the issues raised by these two movements, in order to see how they constitute an important aspect of the postcolonial anxiety about nationhood referred to earlier.

Curiously, the agitation in Assam owed its immediate stimulus to an official move. It was in October 1978 that the 'Chief Election Commissioner told a conference of Chief Electoral Officers at Ootacamund that "an alarming situation had arisen in the North-Eastern states because of the large-scale inclusion of foreign nationals in the electoral rolls" and suggested issuing identity cards to voters in line with what was being done in Sikkim. It was this statement by the CEC that gave a new sense of urgency to the problem and the stage was set for the present agitation.'[59] According to Sanjib Baruah, one of the prominent intellectuals associated with the movement, 'the controversy over the by-election [to the Mangaldoi parliamentary constituency] became the proximate episode that led to the six-year long Assam movement.'[60] He claims that there were 'reports' that the number of voters in Mangaldoi 'had gone up phenomenally' since the previous election which 'sent alarm bells' ringing among many 'ethnic Assamese'. This was a constituency that had a fairly large concentration of Bengali Muslims—ostensibly from across the Bangladesh border. On June 8 1979, the all Assam Students' Union called for a twelve-hour general strike, signalling the beginning of the movement which demanded the 'detection, disenfranchisement and deportation' of foreigners.[61]

The 'influx of foreign nationals' was certainly not a new development. The presence of a large Bengali population in Assam has been a continuous source of anxiety for the Assamese elite. It is one of those issues that has marked the very beginnings of Assamese nationalism. From the very birth of the 'Axom Xonroknwini Xobha' (Assam Preservation Society) in 1926, under the leadership of one of the spiritual fathers of Assamese nationalism, Ambikagiri Raychaudhuri, two major issues formed the core of its programme: the separation of the Bengali-speaking Sylhet district from Assam and the control of immigration from East Bengal.[62] In a sense this fear was understandable, given the fact that colonial rule had made Bengali the administrative language of Assam.[63] Early Assamese nationalists like Raychaudhuri and Gyananath Borah had in fact called for a 'federation of linguistic nationalities' with dual citizenship.[64] Primarily, these Assamese nationalists were concerned with the preservation of a linguistic nationality, with its own culture and identity, even if their attention was primarily directed at the dominance of Bengalis. The implication of the Bengali language in colonial rule, as far as the Assamese were concerned, was what was at work behind these demands being articulated by them.

This point is more clearly articulated by another account. This account, also sympathetic to the movement, traces the history of Assamese nationalism to the discriminatory policies of the British who not only excluded the 'Assamese oligarchy' from the exercise of power, but also 'set up an administration, the lower rungs of which consisted almost wholly of Bengali Hindus imported mainly from Sylhet. Assamese nationalism which began as a rage against foreign imperialist domination acquired through this exclusion, an added anti-Bengali, anti-non-Assamese (Indian) character ...British policy makers, with the support of Bengali chauvinists in administration made Bengali the official language of Assam in the 1830s.'[65] The same commentator also notes that this colonial legacy had another dimension: 'the encouragement of missionary activities among autochthonous tribes' leading to the reversal of 'the historical process through which these tribes were getting assimilated into the Assamese nation.' He sees this reversal, combined with the loss of power, and 'the disastrous effects of civil wars', as a setback to the development of the Assamese nation.[66] Sharma also draws attention to the phenomenal increase in the Assamese-speaking population in the state, precisely in the period when it is claimed that there was a massive influx of Bengalis, that is, between the 1931, 1951, and 1961 censuses. His answer is that 'this miracle' was achieved by registering what he calls the 'Black Tribals' (i.e. tribal workers from Bengal, Bihar, Orissa, Central India, and the Madras Presidency brought by the British 'in lakhs' to work in the tea plantations) and autochthonous tribals within the Assamese-speaking category. This, he argues, 'was legitimate enough at that time in that these ethnic entities were moving towards assimilation with the Assamese.' Then the process was disrupted, he argues, due to the 'narrowest chauvinism', which is left unexplained. In an interesting observation, Sharma adds that: 'Indeed, before or during each decennial census, there have been widespread riots in Assam.'[67]

Another leading intellectual associated with the movement, cited earlier, suggests that it is likely that the Muslim League Ministry might have encouraged the land-hungry peasants from East Bengal to settle in the fertile plains of Assam 'out of purely communal consideration' but in his view, there 'were important economic considerations too that contributed to the migration, including the need of the British-owned jute mills for cultivators who could grow jute, and of the local Assamese gentry for cheap labour.'[68] He suggests that in later years, this had been 'underplayed by successive Congress governments because the immigrants, often illegally present and always afraid of exposure, blindly voted for the ruling party...'[69] Many Congress leaders connived in the settling of the foreigners, according to this commentator. 'It was only after the Janata government under Golap Borbora took over, that the issue of influx came to be highlighted. In several statements towards the later part of last year, the CM made clear his government's intention to deport *the infiltrators*.'[70] A vital move is thus accomplished with the almost imperceptible transformation of the 'illegal presence of the foreign nationals' into *infiltration*.[71] 'Infiltration' suggests a diabolical motive that mere illegal presence in a foreign land need not.[72]

Whether one agrees with the political viewpoint of the above commentators or not, it is difficult not to see the agitation in Assam as the residue of a failed anticolonial nationalism. All the motifs are there: the presence of the colonial power, the differential access of different groups to the institutions of political and administrative power, large-scale migrations of labour for working the colonial enterprises like the tea plantations and jute cultivation for their mills, the experience of large-scale dislocations, the politics of enumeration ('riots before and during censuses') and the desire to 'become majority', the real or imaginary threat to cultural distinctiveness. Even if one agrees that the fear of the Assamese middle classes was entirely misplaced, how do we discount the fact that it moved large masses of the province's population? In order to *recognise* this, one does not have to *endorse* the extreme xenophobia that marked the movement. At one level, my argument about nationalisms in general and anticolonial nationalisms in particular is that xenophobia is built into its very structure. So long as nationalism continues to be the language in which subordinate cultural or social groups imagine their selfhood, it will be an always-present threat within them. My point here is not to present a case *for* the Assam movement or for Assamese nationalism generally, but to show that the very project of an Indian nationalism was an impossible one, fraught with difficulties that it could only perpetually defer but never quite 'resolve'. One of the difficulties in dealing with the immense diversity of cultures, languages, religions and so on was of course internal to the nationalist imagination itself. It was the desire to make India *a nation*, with a homogeneous national culture, that led to continuous attempts by the leadership of the nationalist struggle to brush aside questions of cultural and linguistic identity. It is interesting in this context that Sanjib Baruah refers to the first Linguistic Provinces Commission that was constituted in 1948, which after prolonged hearings of petitions from different groups, gave its recommendations against the idea of linguistic states. Its rejection of the idea was based on the otherwise sound plea that this would create new minority problems, given that in no state would there be more than 70 to 80 per cent people speaking one language. In the bargain, it meant that it would leave colonial arrangements like those in Assam, intact. The work of the commission, said Nehru, 'was an eye-opener for us' for 'we were simply horrified to see how thin was the ice upon which we were skating', referring to what he called the 'ignorant prejudices engaged in mortal conflict.'[73]

I do not wish to go into the debate often passionately conducted among Marxists of different persuasions, about whether language can be a basis of nation or nationality.[74] My own position is that if one sees nations as imagined communities, in the manner of Benedict Anderson, then there is no sense in saying that there can only be one way or a set of ways in which they can be imagined. The relevant point here is that in the Indian context, as it happens, language did become an important axis along which the nationalist imagination took shape—and this did not always sit well with the pan-Indian nationalist project. It is also worth noticing in the above account that it was with the ascent to power of the Janata Party under Golap Borbora's leadership that the controversy was stirred up afresh. As I have been arguing above, it was the forces marginalized under the Congress dispensation that got together under the banner of the Janata Party and it was these forces that in different ways initiated the process of a wholesale interrogation of the nation as it had been thought of till then. Cultural boundaries within the nation were to be redrawn afresh, thereafter.

If one follows the developments within the movement and the extremely rich debate among Assamese intellectuals on it, there is no denying the fact that it constitutes one of the many unresolved problems of the nation-building project in India. It was the erosion of the legitimacy of the Congress government at the centre and the crack in the official discourse of secular-nationalism that made possible the articulation of one more of the problems that had been rendered unspeakable by it.

If the Assam crisis was marked by cultural anxieties around issues of citizenship, definitions of Self and the fear of the Bengali Other, the one in Punjab was marked by questions of territory, resources, and the problem of Sikh 'nationhood'. Like Assam, here too, the politics of enumeration played out around censuses, figures quite prominently. Unlike Assam however, where cultural nationalist anxieties of the Assamese middle classes extended right from the late nineteenth century, Punjab did not have a long history of Hindu–Sikh strife. Punjab generally, and the Sikhs in particular, have always been more closely integrated into Indian nationalism from the beginning, and the two communities have enjoyed a close relationship for a long time. Except for a short period when the demand for a separate Sikh homeland or the *Sikh Suba* was voiced in the early 1940s by the Akali Dal under Master Tara Singh, there has never been any hostility or even tension between Sikh identity and Indian nationalism. This demand for a Sikh homeland was short-lived and was later modified to one for a 'Punjabi speaking province in which the Sikhs should be at least 60 per cent of the population.'[75] In the process, the Akalis tried to claim the Punjabi language, spoken by both Sikhs and Hindus, as a part of Sikh religion, which the Hindu extremists countered with the assertion that Hindi and not Punjabi was their mother tongue. This was the context in which the Arya Samaj and the Hindu Mahasabha had campaigned for Hindus to return Hindi as their mother tongue in the 1951 and 1961 censuses.[76] To cap it all, in order to oppose the demand for a *Punjabi Suba* they made the demand for a *Maha Punjab*, so that the Sikhs could be turned into a small minority.[77]

According to some accounts though, the origins of the conflict did go back to the days of colonial rule and Khushwant Singh for instance has argued that 'the real seeds of Hindu–Sikh separatism were sown by the British by conferring minority privileges on only *keshadhari* Sikhs in the matter of recruitment to the services and later introducing separate electorates and reservation of seats in legislatures.'[78] However, according to Singh, it was the 'Hindu renaissance ushered in by the Arya Samaj', which tried to 'reabsorb Sikhs within the Hindu fold' that aggravated the situation. For Arya Samaj leaders, especially Swami Dayanand Saraswati, 'used intemperate language to denigrate Sikh Gurus and the *Granth Sahib*'.[79] It was the common threat of Muslim communalism, says Singh, that kept the conflict between the Hindus and the Sikhs in check. Once that threat was out of the way with partition, the divide began to widen. On Singh's account, the Hindus managed to rebuild their lives after independence, being largely urban people who were able to salvage some of their property and cash. Sikhs, on the other hand, being basically farmers lost their homes, cattle, and lands. From being the richest landowners in undivided Punjab, they were reduced to poverty, trading places with the landless Muslim peasantry of East Punjab. 'With rustic logic they maintained that while Hindus got Hindustan, and the Muslims got Pakistan, all they got was poverty.'[80] What is more, with independence, they also lost the privileges they had enjoyed under British rule, in terms of employment in the defence services and reservations in legislatures. Nonetheless, past episodes of friction notwithstanding, there was actually never a serious conflict between the Hindus and the Sikhs. For the most part, it remained a conflict that was played out within a small minority within the two communities. It is worth noting, for instance, that even during the height of terrorism and militancy, throughout the 1980s, there was no mass communal conflagration between the two communities in Punjab.

Given the fact that a divide between the two communities was already being cultivated, the deferral of the question of reorganization of the state was becoming fraught with serious consequences. There is enough evidence now to show the cynical game being played by the Congress under Indira Gandhi's leadership right from the days of the Punjabi Suba agitation in the 1960s. And yet, this cynical game cannot be put down merely to the whims of Indira Gandhi, for it reveals once again how the Congress brand of secular-nationalism has time and again revealed itself to be a Hindu creed—whenever it has come under pressure. It is well known, for example, that the Punjabi Suba was conceded after a full decade of the states reorganization and that too after much violence. By the time the state was reorganized, enough fires had been stoked on both sides to lead to large-scale violence. Finally when the Punjabi Suba did materialize, 'furious Hindu mobs in the state ran berserk. Hindu-Sikh clashes took place in many towns. Government offices and vehicles were attacked and burnt.'[81]

A.G. Noorani uses the account given by Sardar Hukum Singh, former speaker of the Lok Sabha, and then chairman of a parliamentary committee on the Punjabi Suba, to detail how Mrs Gandhi tried to sabotage the proposal. He also quotes from Mrs Gandhi's own book *My Truth* where she reveals, 'I went to Y.B. Chavan and said I had heard that Sardar Hukum Singh was going to give a report in favour of the Punjabi Suba and *that he should be stopped.*' He quotes further: 'But then I was very bothered and went around seeing everybody'. Why? Mrs Gandhi is candid: 'To concede the Akali dilemma [*sic*] would mean abandoning a position to which it (the Congress) was firmly committed and *letting down its Hindu supporters in the projected Punjabi Suba.*'[82] It is for this reason, probably, that when the Boundary Commission was appointed on April 23 1966, 'to examine the existing boundaries of the Hindi and Punjabi regions of the present state of Punjab' and 'to recommend changes, if any', it was directed by the government to 'apply the linguistic principle *with due regard to the census figures of 1961.*' (emphasis original). This, when it is well known that in the communally charged atmosphere of the period, and following the campaign of the Arya Samaj and the Hindu Mahasabha, large numbers of Punjabi speaking Hindus had returned Hindi as their mother tongue in the 1961 census and that it was therefore massively skewed.[83]

Even when the reorganization of Punjab did take place, many vital issues were left hanging, namely the question of transference of Chandigarh to it, resolution of the question of river water distribution between Punjab and neighbouring states, and settlement of other territorial disputes. Satyapal Dang calls this an 'unjust reorganization' where many Punjabi speaking areas were given to Haryana, primarily because the *tehsil* rather than the village was taken as the unit. These were the issues then that the Anandpur Sahib Resolution took up subsequently.

It was in 1973 that the Shiromani Akali Dal passed its well-known Anandpur Sahib Resolution, which demanded among other things a federal structure for Indian polity and a fairly radical devolution of powers. In this sense, the first demand for restructuring of Centre–State relations was raised by the Akalis but as it happens the resolution remained more or less an inert document for the next five years. It was only in 1978, once again with some amendments, that it was revived and taken up with some urgency. It was a document that was drawn up with the involvement of some prominent Sikh intellectuals, along with a sub-committee of the SAD formed to formulate a 'policy programme' under the chairmanship of Surjit Singh Barnala, the general secretary of the party.[84] In 1973, the working committee of the SAD adopted this document but it was only in August 1977, after the lifting of the Emergency, that it was issued for wider discussion, and eventually adopted by the 'General House of the Party'.[85] The finalized document was adopted in 1978. Even a cursory reading of the document is enough to show that it was hardly the kind of 'secessionist' and 'antinational' document that the Congress government at the Centre sought to portray it as. All it called for was a radical restructuring of Centre–State relations such that the centre retains only 'Foreign Affairs, Defence, Currency and Communications (including means of transport)', letting the states deal with all other matters.[86] In fact, a large part of the document consists of economic demands pertaining to the industrialization of the state, remunerative prices for agricultural produce, settlement of pending territorial and river water disputes, and so on. Dipankar Gupta rightly notes with regard to the Resolution that all its demands were 'straight-forward regional and secular.'[87] As Kuldip Nayar says, Chandigarh was never an issue, and on other territorial issues like that of Abohar and Fazilka, even though the Akalis claimed them to be Punjabi speaking, they also agreed to a territorial commission to settle the dispute. The sharing of river waters was of course a 'ticklish issue'. The Akalis argued that river water was all that Punjab had; it had no resources, no coal, oil or iron ore. Nor did the state have any industry. Everything therefore depended upon its water resources. Nevertheless, on this matter too, they agreed to abide by the decision of a Supreme Court judge.[88]

What probably raised the hackles of the centre was the Akali claim, made in the Resolution as well, that the Sikhs are 'a Nation', and that therefore they 'should enjoy special rights as a nation.' The document, however, makes it clear that there was no secessionist intent involved in this claim and the existence of the Sikh nation was not seen as something incompatible with the larger entity called India. In the logical structure of the Resolution, the very demand for autonomy was seen to take care of the national sentiments of the Sikhs. The centre of course completely misread it. We have already seen in the earlier discussion the violence with which the demand was received by the prime minister Morarji Desai and the powers-that-be. We can now see the continuity of that reaction with the reaction of the Indira Gandhi regime. This reaction on the part of the Congress is not surprising. Any demand by any minority for any degree of autonomy was always anathema to it. Only the 'majority' community had the privilege of being unproblematically nationalist in that sense as far as the central government was concerned. It was this Hindu public that the Congress always had in mind, as we have seen.

The later developments, especially the way in which the Congress under Indira and Sanjay Gandhi's leadership dealt with the situation was once again, classic. On the one hand, the Congress, then out of power, condemned as 'anti-national' the All India Akali Conference resolution demanding constitutional reforms for ensuring state autonomy;[89] on the other it egged on the extremists and encouraged the creation of the Dal Khalsa in order to outflank the Akali Dal from the fundamentalist side. It is well known, for instance, that Jarnail Singh Bhindrawale was consciously egged on by the Congress under Sanjay Gandhi's leadership. Sanjay Gandhi's aide, Kamal Nath is even reported to have said later that they used to give him money, off and on.[90] The Dal Khalsa, which later became an important vehicle for voicing the demand for 'an independent sovereign Sikh state' was blessed on its foundation, by Zail Singh, former Congress chief minister of the state.[91] Once the game of competitive populism was thus set up and the centre was clearly not going to allow the moderate leaders of the Akali Dal to have their way, the stage was set for the militants to surge ahead.

It is also worth mentioning that the following years saw a deterioration of the situation with regard to these, as yet unthreatening, movements. It also saw the emergence of other conflicts that had so far been dormant. Some of them were explicitly directed at the state and administration, demanding autonomy while some others expressed themselves in the escalation of sectarian strife. So for example, in the beginning of 1979, we see the escalation of sectarian violence on the Naga–Assam border, with rebel Nagas killing 50 people just two days before the chief ministers of the two states were to meet to discuss border issues.[92] On the same day, the Marxist chief minister of Tripura, Nripen Chakravarty, alleged that 'foreigners', especially the 'evangelist Church leaders' were instigating tribals against the left government of the state.[93] A few months later the prime minister, Morarji Desai arrived in Darjeeling only to be greeted by a total bandh, called by the All-India Nepali Bhasha Samiti, to press for the inclusion of the Nepali language in the VIIIth Schedule. The bandh resulted in zero attendance in government offices, tea gardens remained closed, and telephone and telegraph links with the rest of the country were snapped.[94] The list of such incidents could be endless.

It needs to be kept in mind that none of the events or incidents mentioned above can be said to be *exclusive* to this period. What was characteristic was the fact that these were now becoming the main form of expression of mass discontent. What is also important is that they were all, in some form or the other, aimed at redrawing the cultural-political boundaries of the 'Indian nation'. It is not really relevant for our purposes that many of these may have petered out subsequently or that they were crushed by sheer force. For as we have seen in the case of both Assam and Punjab, unless these problems are squarely addressed, they have the capacity to linger on for decades and burst forth afresh once the situation is conducive for them to do so. 'Squarely addressing' such problems, however, may not be an easy task within the overall nationalist project.

There were broadly speaking, two other types of movements and struggles of this 'fragmentary' kind, that came to the fore during this period, namely, the struggles relating to gender and environmental issues.

Gender Issues to the Fore

Like many other struggles and movements of this period, the beginnings of the contemporary women's movement can also be traced to the radicalized atmosphere of the first half of the 1970s. It was the overall radicalization of this period, with the Naxalite movement, the Gujarat Navnirman Movement, and the Bihar students' movement that acquired an all-India character later, and many other movements between the late 1960s to the mid-1970s that first drew women in large numbers into them and subsequently opened up spaces for their own autonomous activity on specifically women's issues.[95] To that extent, the beginnings of this 'third wave' of the women's movement, as Shah and Gandhi call it, can be actually traced to the period 1972–3. But at that time, there were just some small embryonic groups emerging in different parts of the country. In 1974, the Commission on the Status of Women in India (CSWI) gave its reports on extremely low status of women, alongside important recommendations like 30 per cent reservations for women in legislatures. There was a brief debate too on this recommendation.[96] The following year was observed, according to the United Nations' call, as International Women's Year and this became an opportunity for serious intellectual debate on gender issues—even if much of it was still overshadowed by the Marxist rhetoric of 'larger socio-economic structures' and 'production relations'.[97] During the Emergency, however, there was no possibility of any open public debate on political questions.

It was therefore, precisely in the period immediately after the Emergency, when the Janata government came to power, that the women's movement really came into its own. Women's groups were formed at least in the major cities and mostly with an explicit feminist orientation.[98] While many organizations and groups of an autonomous nature came to the fore, this period also saw, symptomatically, the formation of party-affiliated organizations like the Mahila Dakshata Samiti formed by the socialist women in the Janata Party, or the CPI (M) controlled All India Democratic Women's Federation, which until then had only a couple of state level organizations.[99] More importantly, this is the period when the women's movement acquired a mass character on specifically gender issues. Prior to this, there had been women's participation in general social and political movements but gender issues were hardly ever separately articulated. The struggles of the women's movement of this period centred around questions of the growing spate of dowry deaths in the country at large and in the capital in particular; on questions of rape and custodial rape; sexual harassment and eventually, marital rape as well.

The anti-dowry struggle began after an initial investigation by the Mahila Dakshata Samiti, of supposed 'suicides' and 'accidental deaths' of women ('catching fire' in kitchen accidents) revealed that these were in fact pre-meditated murders.[100] In early 1978, the Mahila Dakshata Samiti published its findings, which were widely publicized and opened up a whole world of women's oppression within the family to public scrutiny. Protest actions followed in major cities. What was really shocking was that many urban women who were reported murdered for dowry were found to be from middle-class and lower middle-class families—quite a few of them even being independent salary earners.[101] Their economic independence too, could provide no protection to them. Clearly, there were other structures, those of patriarchy that operated in hundreds of different ways that needed to be uncovered. Thereafter, intervention on specific cases by the various autonomous groups began, joined by party-affiliated women's organizations. This process continued to gather momentum and peaked in the early 1980s. Through the 1980s, the women's movement registered its presence by intervening on major issues of gender discrimination.

The other important issue that came up in the agitations during this period was the question of sexual violence, which ranged from harassment on streets and public places to rape. However, it was police rape or custodial rape that became the focal point of political action.[102] One of the earliest cases was that of Rameeza Bee, who was taken into police custody when she was returning from the cinema at night. She was charged with prostitution and beaten and raped by four policemen.[103] Her husband was beaten to death when he protested. This was in 1978. In 1980, the Maya Tyagi case in western UP became another emblematic instance of police brutality. This young woman was first molested by policemen and when her husband and his friends fought back, the police left but returned soon to take revenge. They pulled them out of a marriage party that the couple were attending and Maya was stripped, paraded through the marketplace, and finally raped in the police station.[104] Even more bizarre was the case of the rape of a fifteen-year old tribal girl, Mathura by the police who were let off by the Supreme Court after being convicted by the Bombay High Court.[105] Legal procedures and the judiciary itself now came under scrutiny.

Madhu Kishwar is probably right when she suggests that it was because of the general anger and deep mistrust of the police in this period immediately following the Emergency, that most of these issues struck such a vital chord among people.[106] The overall political climate thus allowed expression of the women's movement. But the movement certainly did not stop at critiquing the state and the police. Once it began to examine the issues of dowry and custodial rape, questions about the deeper structures of patriarchy were bound to come up. Issues like rape could not be confined to custodial rape alone and along with questions of dowry deaths, sexual harassment, often within the family and eventually marital rape, they could not but raise larger questions about the very nature of all institutions—from the family to the state. Shortly thereafter, in 1982, the question of amniocentesis and the abortion of female foetuses further brought a whole array of institutions and practices under scrutiny.[107]

It is significant, however, that the women's movement, unlike the other movements referred to in this chapter, was self-consciously secular and not in the business of interrogating the nation/nationalism. On the contrary, its manifest discourse placed enormous reliance on the nation-state and its legal and judicial apparatuses. In fact, the edge of this phase of the women's movement was primarily addressed to the state, demanding enactment of certain laws and its intervention in society for their execution.[108] It is a measure of the change in the perception of the women's movement that the recommendation of the CSWI on 30 per cent reservation for women in parliamentary bodies, which was rejected in 1974, was to become a major issue in the 1990s. Nivedita Menon has suggested that the earlier confidence of the movement was predicated largely on the faith in the ideal of universal abstract citizenship, where 'women' did not need to be treated as a special category. In a way, it also reflected a faith in the nation-state itself. The subsequent change, on the other hand, is based on the realization that given the pervasive operation of patriarchal structures, women as a separate category need to make their own special claims.[109]

Even though not articulated as such, the elements of the subsequent, more thoroughgoing critique of family, law, the medical establishment, the judiciary, and the executive, were all potentially present in the early developments. As two activists of the women's movement, Nandita Gandhi and Nandita Shah surveying the movement some years later put it, the concerns of this 'third wave' women's movement had shifted decisively from the concerns of the earlier efforts such as the social reform movements. In their words, this time round too, issues were of violence against women, but the focus was not on *sati* and ill treatment of widows but on rape and wife battering; on marriage but not on widow or child marriages but rather, divorce, maintenance and child custody; on law but not on enactment of more laws but in critiquing existing ones, demanding amendments within them and seeking their implementation; on education but not on extending educational facilities to women but critiquing sexist and stereotyped textbooks.[110] For, as one pamphlet of the Forum Against Rape put it, the very bastions of justice had turned out to be defenders of the criminal insofar as in its practices, the prosecutor was invariably turned into the defendant and the accuser into the accused.[111] In other words, the institutions of family, marriage, education, and law were themselves subjected to the most thorough scrutiny for their gender bias. The experience of these initial critiques and their subsequent results were to lead to far more radical conclusions in the coming period.

To the extent that the movement privileged the identity of 'women' as the lens of such critiques, and opened the way for the subsequent, more throughgoing interrogations of the nation-state, it too could be said to belong to this moment of rupture of the secular-nationalist discourse. If the 'women's question' and the idea of sovereignty in the 'inner cultural domain' was the central site on which nationalist imagination had conceived of the future Indian nation,[112] then the eruption of this question in the 1980s, must be seen as belonging to the moment of rupture in a more fundamental sense. One of the most dramatic instances of this can be seen, for instance, in the shift within the women's movement, on the question of a uniform civil code. Until the first half of the 1980s, the self-confident women's movement insisted on a gender-just and secular uniform civil code, but things began to change quite clearly from 1985 onwards. The Shah Bano case, the subsequent capitulation of the government to the Muslim fundamentalists, the rise of the Hindu right—all played their role in initiating a drastic rethinking. It has been noted for instance, that while the early demand for a uniform civil code was articulated in terms of its being necessary for the achievement of full nationhood, this phase 'marks the beginning of rethinking in the women's movement on the legitimacy of the national integrity argument'.[113] Flavia Agnes has noted for instance, that the apparent conflation of national identity with gender justice before this rethinking began was probably a consequence of the unproblematized relationship of the women's movement with the idea of the nation-state.[114] The emergence of the woman as a subject in her own right, coupled with the diverse impulses that opened out the public space for her, was a feature of this period.

Ecological Struggles

Symptomatic of the investments of the modern nation-state in the ideology of Progress and Development was India's first prime minister, Jawaharlal Nehru's claim that large, multipurpose dams and modern industry were the temples of modern India. By the early 1970s the magic of development had started wearing out. Protests were beginning to break out against specific development projects. By the late 1970s, the Silent Valley dam project came in for major opposition in one of the first ecological struggles, led ironically by the Kerala Shastra Sahitya Parishad—a popular science movement linked to the CPI (M), which as the party heading the state government, had in fact agreed to the project. This project would have inundated one of the last surviving tropical rainforests, in the name of generating electricity and facilitating industrialization of the state.[115] Harsh Sethi argues that this struggle was most significant because it was fought entirely on ecological grounds as the project was to cover uninhabited land and involved no mass displacement. By the end of the 1980s, almost all other dam projects were facing prolonged agitation from those likely to be displaced by them: the Tehri and Pong dams in the north; the Kosi, Gandhak, Bodhghat, and Koel Karo in the east; the Narmada in central India; Bedthi, Bhopalpatnam, and Ichampalli in the west and the Tungabhadra, Malaprabha, and Ghataprabha schemes were all facing resistance.[116]

Another early ecological struggle to break out in this period was the well-known Chipko movement, which 'began as a movement to save the local forest resources from commercial exploitation by outside contractors'. The initial demands says Sethi, 'were mainly for local control of local resources.'[117] Given the fact that most adult males from the region have to migrate to the plains for employment, it was hoped that by demanding a stop to the timber contracts being given to outside businessmen by the nationalization of forests, provision of contracts to local cooperatives and such measures, male outmigration could be checked.[118] The struggle actually burst forth after the forest department refused the local people permission to cut ash trees to make agricultural implements, and later allotted the same patch of land to a sports manufacturer.[119] The later demands of the movement were for a complete ban on felling of trees, for a substantial step-up in afforestation efforts based on tree species that were environmentally suitable and locally useful. Most importantly, the demand was raised in this phase for the *'control of local forests to pass into the hands of local village communities'*.[120]

Gail Omvedt has designated the Jharkhand movement as the first environmental struggle. Nominally, the beginnings of the Jharkhand movement were in 1972, when the Jharkhand Mukti Morcha was formed 'almost as a direct result of events following the nationalization of coal mines in 1971 when—due to the prospect of a rise in wages and benefits for government workers—nearly 50,000 local miners lost their jobs and were replaced by North Biharis.'[121] For this area represents what A.K. Roy, the miners' leader of the Dhanbad region called 'internal colonialism'. As Omvedt puts it, the industrialization of this Jharkhand area, the centre of India's coal and iron mines, was 'visibly a parasitical enclave', based on grabbing the land of the local population, and destroying much of the rest through deforestation and pollution, thus 'sucking the life of the native communities to turn their men into unskilled workers and their women into prostitutes sent all over India.'[122] Roy himself believed that the organized working class too shared in the exploitation of the Jharkhandi peasantry.[123] In a different way, here too the question of local control over local resources was becoming a central issue. Among the initial steps of the movement was therefore 'a forcible harvesting of crops in a land-grab movement focused against the outsider money-lender-landlords'.[124]

From there the movement moved on to focus on a different notion of development where local water resources would be tapped for irrigation, local resources would be tapped for providing organic manure, each village would have a grain-bank, village disputes would be settled within the village itself, each village would run a night-school, and the status of women would be elevated through bans on child marriages, polygamy, indiscriminate divorce, etc.[125]

However, as Omvedt herself says, this early phase quickly 'faded away, with its leader Shibu Soren temporarily won over by Indira Gandhi during the Emergency and drawn into direct government-sponsored developmental programmes.'[126] This was replaced later by the resistance to displacement through two large dams in what was called the Subarnarekha Multipurpose Project. These were the Koel Karo and the Icha dams in Ranchi and Singhbhum districts respectively. This movement was one that has been described as 'near guerrilla warfare leading to police combing operations' resulting in the death of twenty people in 1978–9[127], and in this phase it belonged to the period that we are discussing. While the Chipko and the Jharkhand movements could be said to have been the early intimations of the ecological movements, they were clearly not articulated as such, that is within a larger critique of Development and Progress. It was only in the post-Emergency phase that they started becoming more widespread and impacting upon public discourse by questioning the very model of development.

It is again in this period, in 1978, that the National Fishworkers Forum came into existence, leading major and intense struggles of fisherfolk, especially against deployment of ecologically destructive technology. The struggle of the fisherfolk 'caught in the throes of destructive development' became possible with the confluence of liberation theology and the common people's struggles in the coastal regions of Kerala. In the 1980s, it became a powerful movement opposing the opening up of traditional fishing spaces to mechanized trawlers. Something that was supposed to be confined to the deep sea was now allowed access to shallow waters where the traditional fisherfolk did their fishing. This 'over-fishing' was leading to a decimation of young fish and destroying any possibility of breeding and spawning.[128] Once again the question was of protecting the space of local access to local resources and not allowing big commercial interests to colonize all domains of life. This question remains one of the most recurrent motifs in the ecological struggles of this period, focusing on the symbiotic relationship between the local people and nature.

Subsequently, by the latter half of the 1980s, powerful movements like the Narmada Bachao Andolan (Save Narmada Movement) appeared on the scene, challenging not merely the damming of Narmada river but the entire model of development. As these movements, along with many of those mentioned by Kothari, such as those for forest rights and against destructive mining, acquired a more coherent character, their initial hesitant critiques articulated in terms of rehabilitation and cost-benefit, moved towards a more fundamental interrogation of the development paradigm itself. As we have seen, the notion of local access and later, local control, over natural resources was the key idea around which the new critiques were now being articulated. 'Hamara gaon, hamara raj' (our village, our rule) was a popular slogan in some parts of the country. Whether it was the thrice displaced people of Singrauli—displaced through construction of dams and thermal power plants—or whether the more recent instances of the struggles of people of Jadugoda suffering physical deformities due to uranium mining for nuclear plants, they all expressed the refusal of a people to 'suffer for the sake of the country, as Nehru had once advised them.'[129] There were other struggles in this period which focused on other aspects of development. Noteworthy among them were the struggles against devastation of the Gandhamardhan hills by the aluminium-mining project undertaken by a public sector company and the struggle against the development of the Baliapal missile testing range in a rich and fertile coastal area, in 1985.[130] It may not be out of place to mention here, therefore, that according to one recent estimate, when we talk of people displaced by developmental projects, we might be talking of somewhere in the range of 213 lakh people in the pre-1990 period itself.[131]

It is worth noticing from our point of view that the idea of local sovereignty has important consequences for the idea of the nation itself, whose sovereignty over its realm is supposed to be undivided and uncontested. To the extent, therefore, that these movements and struggles challenge the internal borders of the nation, they add another important dimension to the interrogations of the nation in the discourse of the 1980s.

As Omvedt notes,

> By the early 1980s this diffuse but pervasive environmental destruction began to have a wide impact throughout India, and the hitherto silent struggles of the rural poor against drought and being evicted for irrigation and development projects began to get a new hearing from the press, media, and other sections of intellectuals. The localized struggles began to take on a 'national' scope as part of a movement: environmentalism.[132]

Omvedt also discusses at some length, another kind of movement that came to the fore during this period, namely the farmers' movements that broke out in different parts of the country in the early 1980s. Among them were the movement led by Sharad Joshi in Maharashtra, by Mahendra Singh Tikait in western UP, Narayanaswami Naidu of Tamil Nadu, and such other militant struggles in Punjab and Karnataka. The issues were mainly of remunerative prices and prices of inputs like fertilizers and electricity, questions of debt, and bureaucratic corruption.[133] While it is possible to understand these agitations as some kind of class issues or at any rate, issues that do not in any way challenge the secular-nationalist framework, there is one striking factor about them that situates them squarely within this conjuncture: they too erupted on the political scene *outside the framework of existing political parties and organizations.* To that extent, they share a dissatisfaction with the kind of representational modes that were specific to the parties of that time—parties which claimed to be all things to all people but ended up only defending dominant interests.

Unravelling of the Congress and the Rise of the Hindu Right

It is with the return of Indira Gandhi in 1980, after the failure of the Janata experiment, however, that we can begin to see the changes in Congress politics clearly. At least as a government party, the Congress became more reckless about its commitment to the ideals of secular nationalism. In fact, as a weekly very close to the Congress and more thoroughly wedded to Nehruvian ideals put it in the early 1980s, 'a new elite of Congress (I) leaders' had emerged by then [1982], which was characterized by 'three distinctive features'. These distinctive features were described by the journal as firstly, lacking in political experience, especially of mass politics; secondly, having close links with the landowning classes; and thirdly, '*the new Congress(I) elite has no knowledge of either the national movement or the Nehruite ideology.*'[134] The anonymous analyst underlined that this new elite does not believe in any 'ism', but hastened to add that 'this does not mean that they are not secular and nationalist'. In the astute observation of the analyst of this avowedly left-Nehruvian journal,

...Another significant change in Indian politics which has taken place in the post-Nehru period is that the social base of the Congress (I)... has started changing. In the Nehru era, the Congress relied for its success on the popular support in the Hindi-speaking belt, particularly among the Harijans and the Muslims. Muslims, scheduled castes and the scheduled tribes came to believe in the Nehru era, that the Congress was their friend and protector...The Congress started losing ground in this area in 1967 itself and this trend reached a new high in 1977...In the five Hindi-speaking states including the largest state UP, where almost half of the SC reserved seats are located, the Janata Party, in 1977, *eased out the Congress by winning all the 38 SC reserved seats.*[135]

It is important that it was precisely these social groups, once the bastion of the Congress, that were increasingly feeling dissatisfied by its performance and which then found expression in the opportunity provided by the formation of the Janata Party. It was the unravelling of its mass support and the increasing pressure from the margins that were tempting the Congress elite to pander to all kinds of sectarian politics for very short-term gains. The fact that this elite had no commitment to any 'ism' of course, made this eminently possible. No pangs of conscience were involved in doing this. It has been noted and meticulously documented by various scholars in recent years that this turn in Congress politics was defined by an overarching move to cater to Hindu majoritarian sentiments—which was but an aspect of this tendency. The process received a major fillip with the assassination of Indira Gandhi, after which the Congress then led by her son Rajiv Gandhi, openly utilized Hindu 'fears'. His notorious statement in response to the massacre of Sikhs that 'when a big tree falls, the earth shakes', was a clear and blatant admission of the fact that thenceforth, the party would have no qualms in using majoritarian sentiments to the maximum. Naturally, the results in the elections brought forth the following assessment by the RSS, whose mouthpiece, *Organiser* commented that '[I]t was a conscious Hindu vote, consciously and deliberately solicited by the Congress party as a Hindu Party. And this is what steered the party to a grand victory, decimated the "revisionist" BJP and reincarnated the Cong (I) as the BJP.'[136] As the decade rolled on, the Congress showed itself to be increasingly fickle and compromising on this matter.

So, according to Arun Nehru, formerly one of Rajiv Gandhi's close confidantes and advisors, the Congress High Command had taken a decision in early 1986, to 'play the Hindu card': 'The Muslim Women's Bill was passed to play the Muslim card; and then came the decision on Ayodhya to play the Hindu card.'[137] Rajiv's biographer, Nicholas Nugent, also notes that in August 1989, Nehru hinted in an interview that Rajiv not only played a key role in negotiating the Hindu side of the deal, but also arranged the televising of Hindus worshipping at the newly unlocked shrine.[138] In 1989, Rajiv initiated his party's campaign for the Lok Sabha elections, by ritually breaking a coconut at Ayodhya and claiming that only the Congress could usher in the utopia of *Ram Rajya*.[139] The role of the Rajiv-led Congress in making possible the foundation-stone laying ceremony (the *shilanayas*), at Ayodhya, is known to have been one of the most dangerous episodes in this game of placating the Hindu communal platform. Christophe Jaffrelot also documents that the RSS position barely a year ago was expressed in its chief Balasaheb Deoras' 'readiness to support Congress (I) "in a good cause"'. He holds that it was the RSS' official position in 1988, that 'only the Congress (I) could govern India.'[140]

These developments in Congress politics need to be read in conjunction with (a) the fact that its base was fast eroding due to the protests from the 'fragments', outlined in the earlier sections and (b) the fact that the leadership of the Congress, especially after Indira Gandhi, represented a much more accentuated form of the elite referred to by the *Link* commentator—completely without any connection with or any memory of, the 'national movement'. Its links with the ideological configuration described by secular-nationalism, as well as with the tradition of anti-imperialism were by now, tenuous. The possibility of a complete rupture afforded by the assassination of Indira Gandhi, certainly made things easier for this new elite.

The emergence of the Hindu right as a major political force belongs to this later phase. It was in the late 1980s that the BJP started emerging as a serious contender for power at the centre. For a period after the collapse of the Janata government in 1979, the BJP went through a process of reinventing itself. Reluctant to go back to the Jana Sangh past, the party made desperate efforts to gain an acceptable and inclusive character. It sought to establish continuity with the Janata Party legacy, not simply by adopting the new name of the Bharatiya Janata Party, but equally importantly, by emphasizing the link with the Gandhian legacy of the former by declaring its commitment to 'Gandhian socialism'.[141] In July 1980, Ram Jethmalani with the support of Sikander Bakht, 'introduced a

Bill in the Lok Sabha that would once again legalize religious conversion. His justification for this initiative was the need to dispel anxieties engendered by O.P. Tyagi's Freedom of Religion Bill and to give credibility to the secularist image that the BJP wanted to promote.'[142] In this period, the BJP concentrated on raising mass issues like price rise. In fact, it is interesting that the Meenakshipuram conversion case, that was retrospectively produced as a major event, was hardly noticed publicly by the BJP at that time. The conversions took place on 19 February 1981. The *Times of India* reported the incident on 21 March, while others like the *Statesman* reported the event for the first time on 25 May. From 23 February to 8 May the parliament had been in session but the issue was never raised. In fact a perusal of the newspapers of this period shows that the BJP was at this time seriously involved in conducting mass agitations against price-rise—what was called the *loot roko, jail bharo andolan*. The party's national executive meeting was held in Shimla at the end of June but there was silence on the conversion issue. Among the demands raised in the resolutions at the meeting were issues like fixation of procurement prices for wheat and rice, free movement of grain throughout India, and expansion of the number of items distributed through fair-price shops, to include vanaspati ghee, soap, tea, and match-boxes etc. The only explicitly political part of the resolutions was the condemnation of the Khalistan demand.[143] However, the conversion issue certainly animated the RSS and the VHP, and the growing rift between the BJP and these organizations in those years has been noted by scholars. In fact, in mid-1984, Bal Thackeray told correspondents that the BJP was 'also following the same policy of Indira Gandhi' and that it had also 'started wooing the Muslims'. 'There is a rift between the RSS and the BJP on this issue', he said.[144]

The point I wish to make here is that already by the mid-1980s, the old grammar of Indian politics had irrevocably changed and national parties were finding it increasingly difficult to operate in old ways. To some like the Congress, whose hegemony was fast eroding, the old language of secular-nationalism appeared to be of no use. And to the BJP, after years of being in the wilderness with the fall of the Janata government, could not revive its old Hindu platform easily. National parties were grappling for their way ahead in an uncertain situation. Very soon, by the turn of the decade, the language of political mobilization and representation was to change drastically. This situation, in my opinion, was the consequence of the logic of the unravelling of the nation, of the emergence of infra-nationalisms and the increasing unintelligibility of the language of secular-nationalism that had provided, till then, the basic framework of Indian politics.

Imagining the Global Nation[145]

The decision to tap NRI (non-resident Indian) money and technical resources was taken a few years ago when the government realized that NRIs have a financing potential. A rough estimate puts the number of NRIs spread across the world at 10 million [...]Although it is difficult to quantify total NRI resources, a rough estimate has put their annual savings at around $ 100 billions—a sizeable amount by any standard.' *Business India*, 20 Aug.–2 Sept. 1990, p. 49.

The emergence of the figure of the non-resident Indian (NRI) in political and economic policy discourse can be traced to around the mid-1980s. Its emergence was certainly given a fresh impetus due to the rapidly dwindling foreign exchange reserves in the later part of 1990, in the face of a phenomenal hike in oil prices in the international market, thanks to the brewing tension that was soon to lead to the Gulf War.[146] It will not be correct, however, to assign the rise of this ubiquitous figure of the NRI to something as instrumental as its financial capacities. What was inaugurated in the mid-1980s, with the advent of Rajiv Gandhi, was a new way of imagining the nation. Rajiv Gandhi of course, should be seen as a milestone—and an usher of this new mode—rather than the cause. For the advent to power of Rajiv Gandhi and his 'computer boys' came in the backdrop of certain breathtaking changes in the world economy, especially in the 1980s.[147] The revolution in communications technology had already begun with a bang. As his biographer put it, 'Rajiv [is] guided by the thought that India missed out on the industrial revolution which gave Europe its pre-eminent position and he believes it is vital not to miss out on [...]the electronic or computer revolution.'[148] Rajiv himself belonged to the emerging globalized elite and crucial to his entourage was another important player, Sam Pitroda, himself an NRI, with his post-graduate education in Illinois, who 'had made a fortune in the United States'.[149] This new elite that was gathering around Rajiv was powerful enough—or potentially so, in some cases—not to want to simply migrate to the West. It was important to wield power within the nation and this elite was therefore fired with grand visions of equipping India to enter 'the twenty-first century' as a modern technologically advanced nation. They saw their power in representing such an India, rather than living a relatively powerless existence in the West. And so they assessed their strengths and weaknesses.

India had the knowledge and technical skills necessary but its brain-power, so the nationalists of yore had noted, was being drained off to the West. While nationalists in the past had thought more in terms of reversing the pernicious 'brain-drain', the new elite represented by Rajiv, saw these overseas Indians as a 'brain bank'.[150] Some like Sam Pitroda would probably have been attracted back to India if they had the chance of putting their plans into action and wielding the power they did. But it was not central to this new imagination to get these non-residents back. In fact, it could be argued that it was precisely their location abroad that made them so important, because there they would be in touch with the frontiers of technological advance. The nation was now everywhere; no more was it a territorially bounded entity. Even citizenship of the nation would soon be delinked from territoriality. The figure of the NRI is emblematic of this new imagination of nationhood.

The austerity of the old nationalist vision that seemed to demand individual sacrifice 'for the nation', including refusal of greener pastures abroad, was now replaced with a reverse vision: the diaspora as the extension of the motherland, forced to separate from her but tied to her with a thousand invisible ties. This was the version of the NRI that became so crucial in the rise of the Vishwa Hindu Parishad (note the name: *World Council of Hindus*) in its second phase in the 1980s, providing it unlimited funds and a favourable audience abroad. If this was initially an elite vision of the new, de-territorialized 'global nation', there were enough ingredients in the socio- economic, political, and cultural life of the 1980s that ensured its rapid acceptance as a mass, if exclusively middle class, phenomenon.

In material/economic terms, two developments mark the decade of the 1980s. It was a period of high growth, based on the pent-up consumerist urges of the middle-class sections of the population, who had by then come into their own. Overall industrial growth and especially the consumer durables sector within it, recorded unprecedented—even if skewed—growth. What is perhaps, of crucial importance is that this entire development became possible due to the availability of free flowing credit, even to the lower rungs of the middle class.[151] It is an index of the vastly changed lifestyles of the middle classes—and therefore, of the stakes it began to have in the global economy—that by the end of the 1980s, the number of investors in the capital markets was over a whopping 40 million. At the beginning of the decade, the number was barely a million. Interestingly, of the Rs 36,000 crores worth of approvals by the Controller of Capital Issues, for the entire decade, almost half belonged to the last two years of the decade.[152]

The rapid expansion of the state-controlled television network, reaching out to the remotest corners of the country, had of course, been accomplished by Indira Gandhi herself during her tenure. Begun initially as a part of the overall developmental drive, in order to extend the reach of the state's message to the innermost corners of the country, it saw huge investments by the government, during the 1980s. From 1983 onwards, since Doordarshan started accepting sponsored programmes, it acquired more than a mere developmental profile. No longer would it beam only boring pedagogical programmes for children, peasants, and women—laden with messages on national integration, hygiene, or family planning! It was rapidly becoming an important entertainment medium. Already, during the late 1980s, cable television had arrived surreptitiously, first in luxury hotels and then in the elite colonies of Bombay.[153] More importantly, it facilitated the advent and widespread use of the video. Much before the arrival of cable television, the explosion of the video culture had overtaken the middle classes of the country. By the mid-1980s, the culture had also spread to poorer sections at least in the urban areas. Cinema audiences had fallen considerably and even remote small towns in northern India were running video parlours showing the latest films from Hollywood, which could not have come to the cinema halls till two years later. Video viewing on hired videos was common in the resettlement colonies of Delhi. The important thing about this circuit of cultural consumption was that it operated in almost 'capillary fashion' through the body of society, without any regulation or censorship. Viewing here was completely unrestrained and comprised objects ranging from the latest Hindi films to unadulterated hard pornography, made almost entirely in the West.[154] Whatever the overall result of these developments might have been, there was certainly one change that had taken place long before cable TV finally made its way into Indian city life in 1992: a new and different experience of the world in rapid transition was becoming available and at extremely low and affordable costs, even to the poorer sections in the cities. Central to that experience was a kind of explosion of consumerist desire, but presumably, desire more generally, for, what was 'being sold' in advertisements and through soap operas, was a new lifestyle: the dream of individual fulfilment was at hand. The nation mattered no more—not in the old way at any rate. This easily synchronized with the direction in which the economy itself was headed, especially in the latter part of the decade.

The second half of the 1980s therefore, saw scramble for such consumer durables. Clearly, these were also signs of changed investment priorities. Gone were the days when the investment priority of the import substituting model was capital goods and infrastructure; when self-reliance was the key word and individual consumption was encouraged only to the extent that 'the nation could afford it'; when hard work for nation-building was idealized and individual consumption was constantly deferred in the larger interests of the nation. The new regime of 'consumer sovereignty' was already a sign of the times that in the 1980s, 'the nation' was on the way out in the imagination of the articulate, vocal middle classes. Or at least, one might say, there was a significant change in the way the nation was now imagined. If the Nehruvian dispensation 'enshrined' 'the economy as the synechdochic representation of the nation', the period since the mid-1980s represents a stage 'when the economy is being evacuated of the collective conception of the Indian nation.'[155]

It is important to remember that the imagination of this 'global nation' provided the resources for eventually appropriating the new technologies of media/communication for the Hindutva campaign in the late 1980s and early 1990s. Simultaneously, the use of these new technologies aided the new imagination. The unhesitating and skilful use of audio and video cassettes in the construction of this imagination can hardly be underestimated. The well known and fiery speech by Sadhvi Ritambhara, according to one estimate by a HMV official, had already sold 15 lakh copies by the beginning of 1991.[156] Other accounts have noted the role played by the video cassettes produced by Jain Studios, depicting the state repression on *kar sevaks* in 1990.[157]

The Discursive Break

The year 1989 could be said to have inaugurated the beginning of a decisive shift in the intellectual climate of the country. So fundamental would the shift prove to be in the coming three years that it can hardly be called a *shift*. Indeed it marked a *break* and that too of a bewildering intensity. The important thing about this conjuncture is that it sees the coming together of three distinct discursive strands into a single constellation. First, the argument against reservations rehearsed daily through the scores of anti-reservation riots in different parts of the country, articulated in the secular language of 'economic deprivation' started merging in the late 1980s, with the argument of individual merit and accomplishment, pushed forward by the logic of free-market reforms. Secondly, the argument against reservations became an aspect of the argument for free and unbound labour markets and against protection. Finally, the argument against protection and affirmative action could now, in the conjuncture of the end-1980s and early-1990s, flow seamlessly into the argument of another projected 'protection'—that of the minorities. The 'minorityism' that the RSS and the BJP had been talking of for years, was but the argument that under the Nehruvian dispensation secularism was 'not genuine'—for it was not based on non-discrimination. It was claimed that this was pseudo-secularism because it provided for a kind of positive discrimination for the religious minorities. At the heart of the three arguments was the 'socialist, secular Nehruvian welfare state', which had through misguided ideas of intervention created new privileged sections—the organized working class, the 'reservation-elite', and the 'pampered minorities'.

Symptomatic of the coming together of these different discursive strategies into a single constellation, was the fact that this period saw the rapid movement of intellectuals to the side of the Hindu right. Intellectuals who till the other day, saw themselves as secularist or leftist, suddenly seemed to move over to the other side. All at once, things that were unspeakable in public discourse were now being openly discussed in the media. It might, therefore, be helpful to map some of these shifts as expressed in and through the media to get a sense of the developments. In this process, I hope to demonstrate the coming together of these diverse arguments into a single discourse on the Nehruvian state.

In January 1989, Swapan Dasgupta, a former leftist journalist working at that time with *The Statesman*, and later to become a spokesperson for the BJP, wrote a lead article in his paper. It is worth quoting some parts here:

...there is a sense of *deja vu* in encountering the shibboleths of India's 'progressive' lobby. The most recent example of this is the policy statement of the seven-party National Campaign for a Left Democratic Alliance. Prefacing its 15-point programme with a characteristic overstated appeal to strengthen the 'sinews of national unity' and overcome the national mood of 'cynicism, concern and anxiety', the campaign restates its faith in traditional *Indian socialist wisdom*. There is the demand to 'vigorously propagate the policy of national self-reliance to be achieved through the planning process, the anxiety over 'the concentration of economic power and growth of big monopoly houses' [...]and the distress caused by the 'so-called liberalization policy package' and the elitist 'new education policy'. *Minor variations aside the document could well have passed off as an archival relic from 1969 when Mrs Gandhi re-discovered socialism...*

The trip down nostalgia lane is not confined to the so-called left of centre. The professed votaries of the 'centrist' alternative in the Janata Dal did try to consciously break the rhetorical mould in its policies and programmes [...]but the task proved too onerous in the face of competing pressures. The 'public sector' was once again identified as 'the sheet anchor' in the development of the economy...

To be fair, the JD did express misgivings over the planning process, which it claimed is 'an instrument of patronage by the ruling party' [...]Unfortunately, this attempt to break the mould *was offset by its hasty decision to implement the Mandal Commission report...*[158]

It is interesting to note here that Dasgupta, not yet a 'proud Hindu', is clearly a free-market enthusiast by this time. Later in the same article, he praises Rajiv Gandhi for having posed the real challenge 'to the consensus established by Mrs Gandhi'. He also notes how, being 'untutored in Congress culture' he was impatient with established conventions and therefore 'questioned inefficiency and corruption'. However, by this time the link between the liberalization argument and the anti-reservation argument is clear in Dasgupta's article. Less than three months later, responding to the ban on *Satanic Verses* by the government, Dasgupta wrote once again, this time on 'the rage of Hindu India'. 'Thanks to the sanctimoniousness of "progressive" thinking in India' he argued, 'the intellectual climate has turned hostile' to any re-examination of concepts like "secularism". The intolerance is such that any attempt to raise such question brought forth accusations of "communal bias" and the "mere use" of terms such as "minorityism" 'entails a grave risk of being lumped together with the rabid members of the Vishwa Hindu Parishad'. In this article too, Dasgupta is careful not to yet appear closely aligned to the 'Hindu' right-wing. He therefore, says: '...grassroots opinion in what can loosely be described as "Hindu India" is turning menacingly against the existing secular consensus. *Because the political mainstream refuses to acknowledge this phenomenon, it is dangerously exploited by people like Bal Thackeray and the Shankaracharya of Puri.*'[159] Even though there is an attempt here to distinguish his position from that of the more virulent fascist ones like Bal Thackeray's, it is evident that the third argument about the 'pseudo-secularist protection' of the minorities (note the use of the term 'minorityism') has already made its appearance in Dasgupta's discourse.

Late into 1990, after the outbreak of the anti-Mandal agitations, a columnist in a leading business monthly drew the connections between the discourse of liberalization and that of an anti-reservation platform:

Even when competition is fair, members of the scheduled castes believe they stand little chance against those who will be perceived to possess better educational and social qualifications. The power of prejudice is felt very much more devastatingly in the labour markets than in the market for goods. To redress the balance they seek protection against competition just as our industries do, and this is what reservation in the job market is all about...

Indian producers in both the public and private sector should understand these arguments, because for the last 40 years and more, they have been pleading a similar case and have succeeded in persuading the government that they deserve protection in the goods market. The reasons they give are similar to those put forward by the reservationists. How can a poor country compete against a rich country? How can a technically backward nation be asked to pit its people's skills against the experience and power of the developed world? Then there is the familiar 'infant industry argument...

To put it in purely economic terms, how is the case for reservations different from the case for industrial protection?

The time has come to put an end to the nonsense of protection in all its forms. We must push, and push hard to make the economy competitive...[160]

Another important journalist to move over to the right was the veteran, Girilal Jain. A former Royist (a Radical Humanist), Jain made his shift to the side of the Sangh 'parivar', precisely in this period. Writing a few years later, looking back over this development, he notes:

This is a relatively new development in my life [...]I do not believe it would have crystallized to the extent it has, if the Vishwa Hindu Parishad's campaign on he Ramjanmabhoomi temple in Ayodhya had not acquired the sweep it had by the time of the *shilanyas* in 1989; if this sweep had not translated into support for the Bharatiya Janata Party in the election that followed the *shilanyas* [...]if the popular response to L.K. Advani's *rath yatra* had not been overwhelming as in fact it turned out to be.[161]

So widespread was the appeal of the Hindutva platform in its new incarnation, that the turn of the decade saw not merely sections of the intelligentsia shifting sides, but the overall shift in the intellectual climate made the hitherto unspeakable, respectable and chic. As one discerning report in *India Today* put it: 'The Hindutva battle cry is no longer coming from those with dhotis and chotis, or from the temples. It's also being echoed, however softly, by those sitting in high-rise air conditioned offices, discussing foreign exchange and media planning.' One multinational executive in New Delhi, for instance, claimed that though he 'moves in a circle where people would be loath to admit that they could root for a party which is communal' 'now' he could openly say so.[162] The most classic illustration of this shift and the underlying concern at the 'disintegration of the nation' is of course the phenomenon of ex-armed forces officers joining the BJP, witnessed in 1991. Jaffrelot has listed them as follows: 2 air marshals, 6 lieutenant-generals, 4 major-generals, 4 brigadiers, 1 air commodore, 4 colonels, 1 lieutenant-colonel, 2 wing commanders, 2 majors, 3 captains, 1 squadron leader and 1 flying officer—apart from a retired inspector-general and 2 retired director-generals of police.[163]

That the overall climate was registering a shift is evident from the fact that not merely those who finally changed sides, but also those who did not, were in an 'introspective' mood. Dileep Padgaonkar of the *Times of India* wrote for instance, that no party save the BJP had come to grips with the dominant role played by religion in Indian society, even though it took a narrow and parochial view of religion. He went on to express a common fear: 'Unlike in the past, pinning the label of communalism on the BJP may no longer guarantee rich dividends in the elections. After the traumatic events in Punjab and the grim developments in Kashmir, the country simply does not want to take any chances with those who exploit religion to promote sectional interests'. He concluded the article by saying that '[T]he answer... cannot be a nebulous concept of secularism and much less a policy of appeasement of fundamentalists of varying hues.'[164] Despite his attempts to distinguish his positions, the themes he raised frighteningly echoed the ones being raised by the campaign of the Sangh forces.

Perhaps the most significant statement of the shift can be seen in the following statement by a contributor to the open page edited by Chandan Mitra, in the *Times of India*. Referring to the serialization of the *Mahabharata* on television, she wrote:

As an Indian Hindu, I am relieved finally at sharing a common identity with millions within the privacy of my own home, and without having to extend an apology to the likes of Syed Shahabuddin. For many of us Hindus, these telecasts provide an opportunity to shed our self-consciousness and come out of the closet and relish our heritage.[165]

It has been suggested that the rise of the Hindu right had something to do with the anxiety of entering the new global dispensation in the 1980s.[166] In the late 1980s at least, that does not seem to be the case. At the time it was *the internal threats to its 'integrity'* that were causing anxiety to the 'Hindu nation'; what it was afraid of was the collapse of the hegemony of the upper caste, north Indian Hindu over the nation.

Nothing captures these anxieties better than the advertisement put out by the BJP in the run-up to the 1991 election, in a leading fortnightly. It runs like this:

For years we allowed the congress to divide our nation.
　　Sacrifice our stability for its self-interest and dynastic rule
　　State after state was alienated from the rest of the country,

As it stuck to its seats of power.
Congress and corruption became two sides of the same coin
And then the Congress defectors took over.
They too split and splintered.
Defected and discriminated....
If the Congress used minorityism to divide us,
Their worthy successors chose casteism to tear us apart.
Turning Indians against Indians.
Brothers against brothers.
And now things have gone too far.
Terrorism and militancy have become tools for separatism.
A Janata Dal chief minister wants his state to secede from the Nation.
His party wants recruitment to the police and para-military forces on religious
basis.
The Congressmen, past and present, want to protect infiltrators in Assam and
West Bengal
But are blind to the sufferings of Hindus in Kashmir...
Over 200,000 Kashmiris have had to flee their homes for want of protection—
The single biggest failure of pseudo-secularism.
Today our pride is in peril. Our identity is at stake.[167]

What stands out is the whole set of fears that the Hindu mind was gripped
with at the end of the 1980s—the fear of the 'disintegration of Hindu
society' thanks to 'divisive slogans' like reservations; the fear of the Muslim
Other, always ready to take advantage of internal divisions, now getting
more organized after the worldwide resurgence of Islamic fundamentalism;
the fear of the nation being torn to shreds especially by terrorism in Punjab
and Kashmir. And so the 'nation' betrayed by its secular champions, now
prepared itself to strike back.

This could be termed as the second moment of rupture. If the first
moment ruptured the secular-nationalist discourse 'from below', the second
moment could be said to have done so 'from above', representing the
nation striking back. The 'socialist welfare state' now becomes the target
for having—through policies of affirmative action, an interventionist
economic role and a 'pseudo-secularist' appeasement of the minorities—
created new privileged classes/groups: the 'reservation elite', the 'organized
working class', and the Muslim.[168] The sections enjoying the privileges
under the secular-nationalist dispensation, curiously start finding it
problematic precisely when those oppressed by it were either beginning to
stretch it to its limits as in the case of the Mandal Commission, or to find
other avenues of self-representation, outside those sanctioned by the
discourse of secular-nationalism.

Notes

1. Samaddar (1999), p. 108.

2. This citation as well as the notion of 'cartographic anxiety' is borrowed by Samaddar himself from Krishna (1994), pp. 507–21.

3. *Lok Sabha Debates*, Seventh Series, vol. XLIX, no. 3, Lok Sabha Secretariat, 25 July 1984, p. 243.

4. Ibid. Quoted by C.T. Dhandapani of Tamil Nadu in his speech on the White Paper, pp. 258–9.

5. Ibid.

6. Ibid., 258–9. This comment was made by Vikram Mahajan.

7. Ibid., pp. 258–9.

8. Ibid., pp.303–4.

9. Ibid., pp. 282–4.

10. Ibid., p. 289.

11. In describing these scholars as secular-liberal or Marxist, rather than attribute any position, I am going by what I believe is their self-description.

12. Hasan et al. (1989), Introduction, p. 23, emphasis added.

13. Javeed Alam, 'Political Articulation of Mass Consciousness in Present-Day India' in ibid., pp. 238–9.

14. Vanaik (1990), p. 102.

15. Kohli (1991), pp. 4–6.

16. Sengupta (1996), p. 36.

17. Sethi and Kothari (1983), p. 93.

18. Ibid., p. 31.

19. It is interesting to note that records of Indian parliamentary debates identify members only by the constituency they represent. So thoroughly imbued with the liberal idea of individual citizenship are they that they do not even mention the party affiliation of the members. Party affiliations and caste/community backgrounds of the members have to be ascertained from other sources. This is something that illustrates the point that Carl Schmitt makes about constitutional-parliamentary politics, which we discussed in the introductory chapter.

20. *Lok Sabha Debates*, Sixth Series, vol. XXII, no. I, Lok Sabha Secretariat, 23 February 1978, pp. 340–3.

21. Ibid., p. 341.

22. Ibid., p. 344.

23. Ibid., p. 345.

24. Ibid., pp. 358–60.

25. Ibid., p. 360.

26. Ibid., p. 373. The Kaka Kalelkar Commission had been appointed to look into the problems of the Backward Castes.

27. Jaffrelot (2003).

28. Ibid., p. 222.

29. Cited in ibid., p. 225.

30. Cited in ibid., p. 226.

31. Nehru's letter to chief ministers, cited in ibid., p. 228.

32. The *Statesman*, 16 January 1978, p. 1.

33. Ibid., p. 7.

34. The information was sought by M.N. Govindan Nair of the CPI, in a starred question to which the home minister furnished this information in his reply. See *Lok Sabha Debates*, Sixth Series, vol. XXII, no. I, Lok Sabha Secretariat. 21 February 1979, pp. 34–5.

35. Ibid., no. 6, 26 February, p. 292.

36. Ibid., pp. 327–8.

37. Ibid., p. 7.

38. The *Statesman*, 18 January 1978, p. 3.

39. For details see The *Times of India* (Bombay), 15 March 1978, p. 1. The rough translation of these slogans would be: Fear not Karpoori Thakur/For the New Age is behind you; and JP-rule will not be tolerated.

40. Ibid.

41. The *Times of India*, 16 March 1978, p. 1.

42. Ibid.

43. Conflicts along class lines too occurred throughout this time, notable among which is the firing on Bailadila workers or the major clashes of the peasants with the police, in Tamil Nadu. This latter struggle had a statewide spread. There was also the massive police agitation of all-India proportions in 1979.

44. The *Statesman*, 8 June 1978, p. 4.

45. The *Statesman*, 28 January 1979, p. 2. The VHP was 'relaunched' in this second conference, till then it had barely managed to exist. For details, see Jaffrelot (1999), Chapter 10. Also see, Katju (2003). It is a matter of some interest that the re-launching of the VHP was in reaction, characteristically, to the increasing restiveness of the backward castes and that it actually pre-dates the Meenakshipuram conversions, retrospectively produced as an instance of the great threat to the Hindu community.

46. The *Statesman*, 28 January 1979, p. 2.

47. Statement by Ram Awadhesh Singh, MP, at a rally of the All India Backward Classes, Scheduled Castes, Scheduled Tribes and Religious Minorities Federation. See The *Statesman*, 25 March 1979.

48. The *Statesman*, 3 February 1978, p. 1.

49. Ibid., p. 1. Two days before that report, Morarji Desai had supposedly asked Badal to hasten the transfer the irrigation headworks at Ropar, Harike, and Ferozepur to the Bhakra Management Board as that was entailed in the Punjab Reorganization Act. See The *Times of India*, 1 February 1978, p. 1.

50. A.S. Abraham, 'A Question of Autonomy–CPM Plan Will Emasculate Centre', The *Times of India*, 1 February 1978, edit page.

51. The *Times of India*, 8 February 1978, p. 1.

52. The *Times of India*, 21 February 1978, p. 9.

53. The *Times of India*, 9 April 1978, p. 1.

54. Namboodiripad (1994), p. 284.

55. 'Resolution on Andhra Elections', adopted in the Central Committee meeting held in Calcutta, January 25-28, 1983. Politburo circular no. 3/1983 (upto district committees). This document was meant for internal circulation only.

56. Namboodiripad (1994), p. 285.

57. Ranadive (1983), p. 25.

58. Basavapunnaiah (1985), p. 37.

59. U.M. (1979), p. 1993. This point is corroborated by Baruah (1999), p. 121.

60. Baruah (1999), p. 121.

61. Ibid., p. 121.

62. Ibid., pp. 78–9.

63. Ibid., p. 71.

64. Ibid., pp. 79–80.

65. Sharma (1980), pp. 1321–2.

66. Ibid., p. 1321.

67. Ibid., p. 1322.

68. U.M. (1979), p. 1993.

69. Ibid.

70. Ibid.

71. This is characteristic of the slipperiness of language, although it also it hides an underlying politics. It is not simply one article or one author who slides between these terms at will. See another report, the *Statesman*, 17 January 1979, p. 9, for the same kind of slippage. Often the vernaculars have the same term for

both (for instance, *bahiragata* or *anuprobeshkari*) but the English translation unfailingly makes it 'infiltration'.

72. For an interesting discussion of such transborder migration, see Samaddar (1999).

73. See Baruah (1999), p. 95.

74. See for one point of view, Vanaik (1990), p. 5. This was, however, a much more debated issue in the 1970s and most Marxists in India would hold a position contrary to Vanaik's.

75. See Dang (1998), p. 10.

76. Nayar and Singh (1984), p. 43. See also Noorani (1990), pp. 354–6.

77. Noorani (1990), p. 10.

78. Nayar and Singh (1984), p. 21.

79. Ibid.

80. Ibid.

81. Kumar and Sieberer (1991), p. 185.

82. This part of the discussion is based on Noorani (1990), pp. 354–6 and Kumar and Sieberer (1991).

83. Noorani (1990), p. 356. Also Kumar and Sieberer (1991), p. 177.

84. All the details in this section on the Anandpur Sahib Resolution here are taken from the document issued under the signature of Sant Harchand Singh Longowal, by an organization styled Society for Integration, Kindness and Humanity (SIKH), New Delhi, in the wake of the anti-Sikh massacres in 1984. The document is dated December 1984, entitled *Anandpur Sahib Resolution*, and was made available to the non-Punjabi speaking public for the first time in English through this version.

85. Ibid., p. 3.

86. Ibid., p. 10.

87. Gupta (1997), p. 74. I do not of course agree with Gupta's reading of the entire 'context of ethnicity', as he calls it. My disagreements are largely theoretical but they also pertain, for that reason, to the manner in which he presents his facts. However, this is a larger question which we cannot go into here.

88. Nayar and Singh (1984), pp. 61, 49.

89. The *Statesman*, 2 November 1978, p. 2.

90. Kuldip Nayar in Nayar and Singh (1984), p. 31.

91. Ibid., p. 34. See also Kumar and Sieberer (1991), and Grewal (1998), p. 72 and pp. 84–5.

92. The *Statesman*, 6 January 1979, p. 1.

93. Ibid., p. 2.

94. The *Statesman*, 30 May 1979, p. 1.

95. Gandhi and Shah (1992), Kumar (1993), and Omvedt (1993).

96. Omvedt (1993), p. 81.

97. For an interesting discussion of this early period see ibid., pp. 76–87.

98. Kumar (1993), p. 106.

99. Ibid., p. 111 and Omvedt (1993), pp. 84, 88.

100. Kishwar and Vanita (1984), p. 31.

101. Ibid., p. 32.

102. Ibid., p. 34.

103. Gandhi and Shah (1992), p. 39.

104. Ibid., p. 39.

105. Omvedt (1993), p. 87.

106. Kishwar and Vanita (1984), p. 32.

107. Datar (1983), p. 299, discusses the involvement with the amniocentesis issue.

108. Mazumdar (1999).

109. See Menon (2004), *Recovering Subversion: Feminist Politics Beyond the Law*, Permanent Black, Delhi.

110. Gandhi and Shah (1992), p. 21.

111. Cited in ibid., p. 37.

112. This is Chatterjee's (1995) argument which we have referred to in Chapter 1. According to him, it was on the site of gender that the nationalists declared their sovereignty in the inner cultural domain, refusing to make it an issue of negotiation of the colonial state.

113. Menon (1998), pp. 251–3.

114. Quoted in Menon (1998), p. 251.

115. Sethi (1993), p. 132.

116. Ibid.

117. Ibid., p. 127.

118. Ibid.

119. Omvedt (1993), p. 132.

120. Sethi (1993), p. 127, emphasis added.

121. Omvedt (1993), p.128.

122. Ibid., p. 127.

123. Ibid., p. 129.

124. Ibid.

125. 'Agrarian Revolution in Dhanbad' by R.N. Maharaj and K.G. Iyer, quoted in ibid.

126. Ibid., p. 130.

127. Ibid.

128. Sethi (1993), p. 136.

129. This was Nehru's advice to those facing displacement in the Hirakud dam project in Orissa. Quoted from the *Bombay Chronicle*, April 12 1948, in Kothari, (1995), p. 10.

130. All these instances are also from Omvedt (1993), pp. 134–40.

131. Fernandes and Chatterjee (1995), pp. 30–1.

132. Ibid., p. 139.

133. Ibid., Chapter 5.

134. 'Congress Culture and Nehruism' cover feature, *Link*, 14 March 1982, pp. 8–15.

135. Ibid., pp. 13–14.

136. Quoted in Jaffrelot (1999), p. 314.

137. Quoted in Jaffrelot (1999), p. 371. Also see Nugent (1991), p. 187.

138. Nugent (1991), p. 187.

139. Ibid., p. 195.

140. Ibid., p.374.

141. See Jaffrelot (1999), Chapter 9, for details. Jaffrelot notes that this found expression in the fact that the word 'Hindu' did not make a single appearance in the party's constitution.

142. Ibid., p. 317.

143. The *Statesman*, 30 June 1981, p. 9. Neither the resolutions of the national council session in Cochin held from 25–27 April, nor the resolutions of the national executive (mentioned above) published by the party separately refer to the conversion issue.

144. *Link*, 3 June 1984. Interview to Madhu Shetye and John Dayal.

145. I owe this term to Ravi Vasudevan, who suggested it in a conversation.

146. There were other important reasons too as to why the foreign exchange reserves got depleted, especially the high import content of the growth of the 1980s.

147. I have elaborated the argument presented in this section elsewhere. See Nigam (2004a).

148. Nugent (1991), p. 68.

149. Ibid., pp. 63–4, Presumably under their inspiration, a new computer policy was already underway while Indira Gandhi was alive. After her death the process was speeded up.

150. Ibid., p. 68.

151. This is evident from a perusal of the business journals of the 1980s. As companies geared to meet the new competitive environment, following the liberalization of the mid-1980s, many companies started hire-purchase schemes and even provided finance, loans to consumers. Bajaj Auto Finance Ltd for example, was started in 1987 for such a purpose (*Business India*, 18 September–1 October 1989, p. 63). Similarly, when Maruti 1000 bookings opened in late 1989, three multinational banks, namely Citibank, American Express, and Bank of America, grabbed the opportunity, offering loans for booking the vehicles at rates of interest as high as 16.5per cent to 18per cent (*Business India*, 27 November–10 December 1989). The developments also parallel the rise of big finance companies providing corporate finance, in the same period. Credit cards also made their appearance at this time.

152. The *Statesman*, 1 January 1990, p. 11, economic review of the decade by 'Pennywise'. See also Editorial, *Business India*, 6–19 August 1990.

153. Poduval (1999), pp. 107–18 and Prasad (1999), pp. 119–29.

154. Most of this information was collected first-hand by me, in the early to mid-1980s, in Delhi and Himachal Pradesh.

155. For a fascinating elaboration of this argument, see Deshpande (1993).

156. Quoted in Simran Bhargava, 'Audio Cassettes—On a Fast Track', *India Today*, 15 January 1991 pp. 90–3.

157. This was the time of the first *Rath Yatra* organized by the BJP, which was supposed to culminate in the dismantling of the Babri Masjid that was prevented by the state government under the chief ministership of Mulayam Singh Yadav. This naturally involved some use of force by the police.

158. Swapan Dasgupta, 'Post Politics—Who Will Break the Mould?', the *Statesman*, 28 January 1989, edit page. All emphasis added.

159. Swapan Dasgupta, 'Quiet Rage of Hindu India' edit page, second article. Emphasis added.

160. Sudhir Mulji, 'The Economics of Reservation', *Business India*, 15–28 October, p. 49.

161. Jain (1994), pp. 1–2.

162. Jain and Banerjee 'BJP Supporters: Invasion of the Scuppies', *India Today*, 15 May 1991, pp. 38–9. The article is based on interviews with people of this new 'globalized' middle class.

163. Jaffrelot (1999), pp. 433–4.

164. Dileep Padgaonkar, 'Election Strategies: Barking up the Wrong Tree', the *Times of India*, 15 August 1989, edit page.

165. Neera Kuckreja Sohoni, 'The "Mahabharata" Gives Hindus Common Identity', the *Times of India*, 14 September 1989, p. 11 (Agenda).

166. This argument has been made by Hansen (1999).

167. *India Today*, 15 May 1991, pp. 48–9, two-page advertisement entitled 'Enough is Enough'.

168. Newspaper commentaries of that period are replete with attacks on the 'socialistic' policies of the Nehruvian era which led to 'labour market rigidities' and vitiated the 'investment climate'. The poor investor had become a hostage of unionized labour as he could not 'hire and fire' at will.

3

Antinomies of Secularism
The Indian Career of the Concept

Introduction

In this chapter I will look at the Indian debate on secularism that has been raging since the mid-1980s. Through this exercise I hope to identify some common misreadings of the various positions that have become prevalent in recent years. It will also become clear that the ideological polarizations mask substantial areas of agreement among the opposing viewpoints. The field that I have laid out in the previous chapter through a mapping of the various developments since the late 1970s, will form the backdrop in our reading of the debate.

As I have already suggested, there was a period that lasted until the late 1970s and early 1980s, when the nationalist imaginary and the secular-nationalist discourse fashioned in the course of the national movement remained hegemonic. During this period there were undoubtedly assertions, of smaller, particularly linguistic identities, but they did not really challenge the overall institutional framework set in place by the founding structure of the Indian republic, the constituent assembly.[1] The various movements for the reorganization of states, therefore, never transgressed the limits of the nation and its institutional structures. Their demands were almost always articulated within the given institutional forms of redressal and within the larger entity called India. The violence that accompanied some of the movements for reorganization had more to do with the intransigence of the central government rather than with a rejection of the institutional framework of centre–state relations. Those assertions that were not amenable to this framework remained an embarrassment and were generally marked out as aberrations, namely Kashmir and the North-East. They were at best ignored in mainstream discourse or constituted as problematic objects constantly interrupting and disturbing the harmony of the 'nation', such that the use of force against the local populace could be justified. Gradually however, the fragile nation began to unravel under the impact, both of its unredeemed promise of freedom and the emancipation of the 'little selves' that comprised it, as well as from reactions against the consolidation of old brahminical hierarchies within the new 'secular' nation. Three decades down the line, the inherited idea of nationhood was under serious challenge from all sides. This is the conjuncture within which I will locate the debate on secularism.

This is so also because this debate is, in my view, an important entry point into the problem of nation-building itself. For even though the manifest concern of such a debate is necessarily the question of religion and religious communities, there are wider implications in that it is the same issue of handling plurality and difference that lies at the core of the assertion of local or particularistic identities too. This can be elaborated through an example: something peculiar happened in the highly charged days of the anti-Mandal agitation. Many people who considered themselves secular modernists suddenly found it necessary to defend caste-based reservations and find intellectual justifications for it. Of course, protective or positive discrimination had 'always' been there for the Dalits and tribals but it was generally understood by the secular-modern mind as merely one specific *temporary measure*. In time, individuals from these communities would be brought at par with the others and the great liberal dream of abstract citizenship—the erasure of all markers of difference in public life—would be realized. That more than four decades after independence, we would have to think of bringing in *more and more* social groups into the fold of reservations and positive discrimination was something most people had not anticipated. Equally peculiar was the fact that while secularists were forced to talk of caste-reservations, the most sophisticated *brahminical* arguments came clothed in impeccably secular and modernist language— that of merit and efficiency. Thus secularists were accused of casteism and of disrespect to the principle of equality. Then, during the Babri Masjid campaign came the slow and almost chilling realization that even though they thought they were secularists, the Hindu right's attack on them was that they were *pseudo-secularist*—that they pandered to minority communalism, to casteism and what have you. The entire language had been turned over. Meanings were inverted and suddenly the world looked very different. What was thought to be the resurgence of Hindu 'revivalism' did not find itself ill at ease with a secular-modernist self-representation.

On the contrary, it was speaking that language in a way that made many secularists pause and think. Further, it was during those troubled days that many secularists started realizing what the women's movement was already having to grapple with—the great secularist demand for a uniform civil code, raised so forcefully during the debates in the constituent assembly, was now the war cry of the resurgent 'Hindu' right: 'How dare the minorities *be different?*' In other words, secularists were being forced to grapple with the possibility that uniformity and 'unmarkedness' were not necessarily always good things. It wasn't as if 'difference' was always undesirable either.

In this sudden twist of language lie deeper questions that one then has to begin asking. I do not find sufficient the explanation offered by scholars like Achin Vanaik that this is simply a case of 'vice paying tribute to virtue'.[2] This argument could have been valid in a period of the general advance or hegemony of secular democratic politics, but it is certainly not an adequate explanation in the times of its worldwide retreat. There was something more serious happening here in this play of difference and universality—the insistence on erasing all markers of difference no longer had the self-evident emancipatory ring to it that it once had. Clearly, meaning was not simply internal to the word or even to the entire manifest levels of discourse. And this experience was showing once again that words, discourses, and languages are never faithful to their origins, that there is always an accretion and/or deficit of meaning, a surplus that keeps attaching to them or something that keeps wearing off, till very often they can become difficult to recognize.

Fifty years after independence, nation-building, modern education, and technological advance, 'Indian' identity—presumably the last step before the emergence of a truly universal citizen—itself stands threatened, deluged by hundreds of other identities, Hindu communalism being only one of them. Somewhere along the line it seems, large universalist, abstract categories passed on to us by the old secular-nationalist discourse, became very easily available for being articulated into the overall structure of the new Hindu nationalism, now rapidly acquiring a hegemonic character. This is the conundrum of secularism that I wish to explore, through an examination of its historical complicity with the nationalist project. That is why the debate on secularism seems to provide the best entry point theoretically, having been also by far the richest political debate in Indian scholarship.

The Debate on Secularism

The recent Indian debate on secularism[3] is important not only for the richness of the ideas thrown up by it, but equally for what it does not say. It is important because it has involved scholars from across the spectrum, from diverse political and intellectual traditions. It has been unlike many of the earlier debates which were either esoteric in the extreme, like the mode of production debate and the debate on the 'nationality question' among the Marxists of the 1970s, or were specific and internal to some disciplines. Most protagonists of this debate have been politically engaged public intellectuals and theorists, the primary impulse animating whom was the alarming rise of the 'Hindu' right-wing in the late 1980s and the 1990s.

It was sometime in the mid-1980s that the first salvoes were fired, sparking off the debate that continues to rage today with unabated ferocity. First, there was the colourful attack launched by Ashis Nandy[4] which was soon followed by the more sober terms of T.N. Madan's critique[5]. This was the time when, it needs to be remembered, the rise of the various 'secessionist'/'divisive'/'fissiparous' movements was an accomplished fact of life and some of them had already challenged the inherited idea of nationhood. Special mention can be made in this regard of the Assam and Punjab movements whose distinct edge by the mid-1980s was already anti-'India', in the sense that whether or not they were explicitly secessionist, they sought to renegotiate and redraw India's cultural-political boundaries. Also visible on the horizon was the rise of the Hindu right, especially after the intensification of the Ayodhya movement, following the opening of the locks of the mosque on the orders of a Faizabad district court. The period 1986–87 also saw sharp controversies on the Shah Bano case and the *sati* incident in Deorala (Rajasthan) come to the fore and occupy the attention of secularists. These were the early signs that the terms of political discourse were on the way to being irreversibly transformed. Not only were the terms of discourse being transformed, secularism itself was under tremendous pressure to defend itself in an atmosphere that was becoming increasingly inhospitable for it.

As it happens, it was this breakdown of its hegemony that necessitated as well as opened up the space for a fresh look at the entire set of political-theoretical assumptions that underlay secularism. 'Necessitated', because there was an increasing realization that the way it was constituted, secularist discourse was fighting a losing battle, that there was a need to re-examine many of its assumptions afresh; and 'opened up', because till then the unchallenged hegemony exercised by this discourse had made it impossible to raise any questions about these assumptions without being considered 'backward' and 'reactionary' in some ways.[6] The attack opened by Nandy and Madan was followed later by an equally powerful critique launched from within the ranks of former secularists, especially those of a Marxist persuasion. Important among these are Partha Chatterjee and some of the historians of the Subaltern Studies group, as well as Sudipta Kaviraj, to some extent.

A word of clarification, before I step into the debate: I will be reading the various contributions to the debate occasionally against the grain and maybe also against the explicit sense of the protagonists' arguments. For my intention is not just to read the manifest meaning of what is being said but equally importantly, to interpret the quiet shifts, the silences, and the slippages which often enter the text.

To begin with Ashis Nandy's argument. He opens his attack by distinguishing between two types of secularisms, or two meanings of secularism current in contemporary India. The first, he says, was known to every modern Westerner—and in his language, this would mean every 'modern' person. This was the idea of secularism as a separation of religion and politics. The second was an Indianism, best embodied in the figure of Gandhi, who said he was secular but thought poorly of those who wanted to separate religion and politics, for he claimed, they understood neither the one nor the other.[7] In this second meaning, secularism was *not the opposite of sacred but 'of ethnocentrism, xenophobia and fanaticism'*. True secularism, according to this second meaning, opts for equal respect for all religions rather than equal disrespect for all of them. This was the meaning given to it by the anticolonial mass mobilization in India.[8] Nandy further argues that religious tolerance by the state need not mean tolerance in society at large and in fact, given the 'condition of the Indian state', its loss of credibility and its alienation from the people at large:

Few will believe that Hinduism, Sikhism or Islam has any moral lesson to learn from the Indian state. For the same reason, the hope that the state can be an impartial arbiter among different religious communities in its present state appears a rather pallid one.[9]

He points out that the second sense of secularism implicitly accepts 'that the growth of vested interests in a secular public sphere is *an insufficient basis* for the long-term survival of a political community.' Otherwise, he continues, 'the Scots, the Welsh or, for that matter, the Sikhs and the Assamese would not be creating so many problems for their countries.'[10]

Elsewhere Nandy has vehemently argued the reverse: not that this growth of vested interests in the secular public sphere is *insufficient* but that it is precisely its excess that is responsible for the rise of all kinds of fundamentalisms. This argument comes immediately after the assertion that state toleration can only ensure short-term survival of 'a political community' (which presumably means something like a nation, Indian for instance, as distinct from religious and cultural communities). I take this to mean that Nandy is arguing that a secular public sphere *alone cannot suffice* for the survival of the 'national community'; that this larger community must find its own way of living in harmony, recognizing difference within. There is however, another equally compelling part of his critique that is directed at the very nature of secularism understood in its first sense as separation of religion and politics. For this political community to recognize difference within and be tolerant to it, it is the modernizing state elite that has to come to terms with difference. It is this elite, rather than the religious believers, which is intolerant. An important part of his critique of what he calls official secularism—that is, secularism in the first meaning—is that it sees the believer as someone with an inferior consciousness and as a consequence:

Such secularism fails to sense that critical social consciousness, if it is not to become a reformist sect within modernity, must respect and build upon the faiths and the visions that have refused to adapt to the modern worldview.[11]

Nandy surely, is not unaware that the 'critical social consciousness' that he talks of is a modern (though not necessarily modernist) consciousness and he is therefore, clearly identifying here what is an explicitly modern agenda: re-forming faiths and visions and helping them to 'adapt to the modern worldview'. Precisely in order that critical social consciousness may be able to undertake the immense task of cultural transformation—and not merely remain a sect—is it necessary, Nandy then suggests, that it enter into a creative engagement with lived faiths. And yet, his entire attack centres on a vigorous critique of modernity, which he sees as the root of all evil. It is too simplistic, and I believe a common misreading of Nandy to think of him as an inveterate 'traditionalist'. Nandy is a modern critic of modernity, even if an avowed anti-modernist, drawing from tradition.

Nandy's ire against modernity is directed against the nation-state form and its attendant ways. It is for this reason that he then brings in his second distinction, this time between 'religion-as-faith' and 'religion-as-ideology'. The latter, that is, religion-as-ideology, is in his view a direct consequence of the forms of modern politics. Modernity, with its drive to create a homogeneous, sanitized, and rational public sphere governed by the rules of contract, he argues, forces a split in the personality of the citizen, *only part of whom is represented in politics*. And here, only *religious ideology* (as distinct from faith), secularized and excised of all spirituality can be effective. Officially religions (and cultures and visions) are subjected to growing marginalization, forcing them, however, to enter through the back door. Ruled by instrumental rationality and the secular interests of power, the only religion accepted in the public sphere is this secularized religion-as-ideology, shorn of the value concerns that govern everyday religion, where the great resources of toleration are lodged, according to him. Nandy (1990) presses this argument further. Everyday religion is 'definitionally non-monolithic and operationally plural' but that is not conducive to ideological mobilization around power interests or the need of religion-as-ideology to centralize and homogenize around some canonical texts. More importantly, he argues, 'the modern state always prefers to deal with religious ideologies rather than with faiths. It is wary of both forms of religion but it finds the ways of life more inchoate and hence, unmanageable' even though it is the latter that has always shown greater catholicity.[12] The secular desire of the modern nation-state to create a sanitized public sphere is seen by Nandy as *primarily responsible for the rise of communalism*. In that sense, this assertion stands in contradiction to the 'insufficiency argument' mentioned earlier. Its homogenizing desires make it 'definitionally ethnophobic' and often ethnocidal. This ethnophobic tendency is naturally complicated by virtue of secularism's historical complicity with Western culture/s, which makes it all the more intolerant of non-Western cultures that it sees as 'backward' and 'irrational'. And yet, since modernity is the very condition of life, the only resistance to it stems from within it, he argues:

Much of the fanaticism and violence associated with religion comes today from the sense of defeat of the believers, from their feelings of impotency, and from their free-floating anger and self-hatred while facing a world which is increasingly secular and desacralized.[13]

It is as though he is arguing that if political resistance can only come within the terms set by modern politics, at least intellectual critique need not be bound by that imperative.

The other aspect of Nandy's critique is epistemological and flows directly from the understanding of the cultural hegemony exercised by the modern West. In his characteristic style, he labels it as 'the imperialism of categories'. And since the problem is epistemological, it cannot but be linked to other ways of seeing things and also as part of that larger package of 'development, megascience and national security'. But it may also be useful to remind ourselves that he does not deny that this 'Western concept of secularism *has* played a crucial role in South Asian societies; *has* worked as a check against some forms of ethnic intolerance and violence, and *has* contributed to humane governance at certain times and places.'[14] What he is arguing then is that, despite deep epistemological problems, the concept or the idea was not worthless—that it was 'crucial' at a certain historical moment, in dealing with certain kinds of intolerance, even in South Asian societies. However, it cannot cope with the *new kinds of fears and intolerances*, and certainly not when genocide is justified in terms of the logic and ideology of the modern state. To quote once again:

As the modern nation-state system and the modern thought machine enter the interstices of even the most traditional societies, those in power or those who hope to be in power in these societies begin to view statecraft in fully secular, scientific, amoral and dispassionate terms.[15]

This then, is why *merely relying on* expanding the secular public sphere with the state's intervention is insufficient. That is why he would much rather focus on this infirmity of official secularism and deal with questions of toleration in everyday lived religion.

It is also useful to mention here Nandy's crucial distinction between the organizers and instigators of communal and sectarian violence and the 'mob': the former are the analogues of the state elite operating purely on the basis of secular rationality. This distinction, it is worth noting, clearly resonates with the idea of the 'jacobin personality' that we discussed in the introductory chapter, and 'his' connection with modern subjectivity in a disenchanted world. There are different psychological motivations for each of these groups to join in the phenomenon of communal violence. It is the instigators and the planners who are Nandy's target, and they, he insists, operate already *as if they are the state*. There is nothing pious or religious or even unscientific about how they operate. The 'mob' on the other hand he holds, acts out of some degree of faith, even if misdirected and perverted. In my view then, Nandy is not arguing simply that secularism per se is bad and undesirable, an argument that he does seem to make in relation to the nation-state and the modernizing elites. What makes secularism problematic is its transformation into a state ideology and its close alliance to the workings of the modern nation-state. He continuously builds his argument in terms of the new governmental and mobilizational technologies linked to the logic of the nation-state, and of the modern elites who then find in secularism a handy instrument to give themselves the status of sole arbiters among different religious and cultural communities. This explains his insistence on the second meaning or model of secularism—simultaneously more tolerant and unhinged from the reasons of the state.

T.N. Madan's argument is relatively more straightforward and simple. He finds 'secularism in South Asia as a generally shared credo of life impossible, as a basis for state action, impracticable' because it is culturally specific to Christianity. Hindus, Buddhists, Muslims, or Sikhs simply do not know what it means to privatize religion—for them, it is the very basis of their being in this world.[16] It is not merely that these religions do not have any notion of separation; the distinction that these four religions do make between the religious and the 'secular' is structured in a hierarchical way where the spiritual/religious authority is supreme and temporal/secular power is always subordinated to it.[17] His point seems to be that it was the specific context of the Reformation that provided late Christianity with a model of separation and,

secularism as an ideology emerged from the dialectic of modern science and Protestantism, not from a simple repudiation of religion and the rise of rationalism. Even the Enlightenment—its English and German versions in particular—was not against religion as such but against revealed religion or a transcendental justification for religion.[18]

This is a point, as we shall see, many secularists will readily agree with. Sumit Sarkar and Javeed Alam at least have argued this at length.[19] Madan concurs with Nandy that it is the marginalization of religious faiths with the growth of the secularization process that is responsible for 'the perversion of religion' though he does not seem ready to go with him all the way in his attack on modernity. After having first posited the 'impossibility of secularism' in the South Asian context, he then seems to argue that 'secularism must be put in its place: which is not a question of rejecting it but of finding the proper means for its expression.'[20] This is an unresolved contradiction in his argument. For he goes on to defend not merely a different meaning of secularism but makes an argument Nandy would never agree with: that a modern state can be differently constituted such that it runs on other principles than rationalist ones.

In multireligious societies, such as those of South Asia, it should be realized that secularism may not be restricted to rationalism, that it is compatible with faith, and that rationalism (as understood in the West) is not the sole motive force of a modern state.[21]

We will see that in Rajeev Bhargava's reconstituted notion of an alternative ethical secularism, he seems to recommend precisely such a notion of the state. Madan, while stating in unqualified terms that secularism is impossible in South Asian contexts, is at the same time, keen to extricate himself from any possible charge of cultural essentialism. He pleads for the need for cross-cultural translation, difficult though such a task admittedly may be. Cultures do exist in dialogue and

creative individuals and dominant minorities play [a part] in changing and shaping the course of history...even in the simplest of settings, cultures, ways of life are not merely reproduced but are also resisted and changed.[22]

Despite this caveat, it seems to me that Madan's argument about the impossibility of secularism as a shared credo of life in South Asia cannot hold unless he presses the cultural untranslatability argument to its logical essentialist end. On the other hand, if one is to agree with him that cultures change as indeed Christianity did—for Madan recognizes that pre-Reformation Christianity hierarchized spiritual over temporal authority—then it seems difficult to sustain the position he takes. In his subsequent more detailed examination of the phenomena of secularism and fundamentalism, Madan seems to rely heavily on essentialized notions of culture and of Islam and Hinduism in particular.[23] We may note that statements like the following abound:

The edge to these struggles between Sunni orthodoxy and different kinds of heterodoxy...was provided by the character of the Muslim masses, who were mostly converts and who never completely forsook their original faiths and ways of life. This is quite understandable because conversions had a multiplicity of causes and *were not generally the result of strong religious conviction alone*. Coercion, opportunism, economic and ecological pressures...were also influential in different degrees in various places and times.[24]

The argument that if conversions were really a result of conviction, they would lead to a complete adoption of the new faith, leaving no trace of the old, suggests a strongly essentialist notion of culture. It is as though he is arguing that Hinduism or Islam can only be pure or not be true religion at all. The residues of the old in the new faiths, always appear to Madan as *lacks*, or as *impurities* carried over from the past faiths. And such impurities can only result from conversions that are fraudulently effected through 'coercion, opportunism', etc. That such traces of past beliefs have continued to co-exist in most belief systems is a point that need not be laboured and all of these cannot be explained away by representing them as outcomes of fraud. It is on the basis of such essentialized notions of pure religion that Madan erects his argument—the 'cultural impossibility thesis' as Rajeev Bhargava has aptly termed it.

A third and very powerful critique comes from Partha Chatterjee. Unlike Nandy's externalist attack, Chatterjee's can be considered an internal critique of secularism. Nandy's attack, as we have seen, can be read as a strong defence of different cultural communities in the face of the homogenizing impulses of the modern nation-state and therefore of the need to find resources of tolerance that are not ethnophobic *vis-à-vis* non-Western cultures. Chatterjee's response, on the other hand, shares in the project of modernity to the extent that by his own admission, he is 'looking for political possibilities *within* the domain of the modern state institutions as they now exist in India.'[25] It seems to me, however, that Nandy too is aware that there are no possibilities available outside modernity at least, if not outside the institutions of the modern state. The crucial difference is that Nandy the psychologist and analyst, *is not looking for a political solution* in the first place. He is concerned with analysis and in that task he finds the imaginary space of the non-modern a useful reference point to highlight the violence of the modern nation-state and its drive towards homogenization.

Chatterjee is more immediately concerned with the rise of the Hindu right in the recent past and with the need to resist it. It is from this standpoint that he asks: 'Is secularism an adequate, or even appropriate ground to meet the political challenge of Hindu majoritarianism?'[26]

His argument begins by building on the analogy drawn between the Hindu right and Nazism in Germany by many contemporary commentators. He suggests that just as 'the Nazi campaigns against the Jews and other minority groups did not call for an abandonment of the secular principles of the state in Germany' but were on the contrary, 'accompanied by the attempt to de-Christianize public life', so the 'majoritarianism of the Hindu right...is perfectly at peace with the institutions and procedures of the 'western' or 'modern' state.'[27] Chatterjee argues further:

Indeed, *in its most sophisticated forms*, the campaign of the Hindu right often seeks to mobilize on its behalf, the will of an interventionist modernizing state in order to erase the presence of religious or ethnic particularisms from the domains of law or public life and to supply, in the name of 'national culture', a homogenized content to the notion of citizenship. In this role, the Hindu right in fact seeks to project itself as a principled modernist critic of Islamic or Sikh fundamentalism and to accuse the 'pseudo-secularists' of preaching tolerance of religious obscurantism and bigotry.'[28]

Chatterjee makes it clear that, in his view, this is a specific strategic possibility available to the *Hindu right in India*, quite unlike the situation of Islamic sectarianism in Pakistan and Bangladesh or Sinhala chauvinism in Sri Lanka. Even in the context of the Hindu right, he takes the *most sophisticated forms* of its campaigns, implying thereby that there may be/are many other cruder strands. His argument it seems to me, is not that secularism will in all circumstances lend itself to such a mobilization on behalf of a majoritarian chauvinism. Rather, there is a historical specificity to the fact that the Hindu right is able to present itself as the 'principled modernist critic' of other sectarianisms, which has to do with the specific history of India, its nationalist struggle, and the contestations that it had to face within. However, even though he makes a more limited argument here, there are reasons to believe, as we will see later, that his critique is situated on a bigger canvas that relates to the crisis of the liberal-democratic state itself, resulting from its inability to handle difference.[29] In other words, it is a critique that seeks to think of other forms of the modern state, based on different principles.

Clearly, the sophisticated forms of the Hindu right's discourse that Chatterjee talks of, are the dominant ones that determine the main direction of attack of their campaigns. So even if this does not exhaust the entire spectrum of its positions, it does prompt us to consider, he argues, that if what is happening is not really an attack on the secular principles of statecraft but their mobilization to target specific minorities then the threat might be located *elsewhere*: the ground where the attack is being launched is 'on the duty of the democratic state to ensure religious toleration'.[30] That then, is also the place where the challenge should be met. It is evident that there is, at this point, a shared ground between his position and that of Nandy's, as both see the secular principles of statecraft as 'being mobilized against minority communities' and therefore as complicit in the project. Yet, there is a crucial difference between the two. While for Nandy there is a *necessary connection* between these principles and the rise of sectarianisms, for Chatterjee this is *a possibility* that may or may not be realizable everywhere—as indeed it is not, possibly, with the Taliban kind of movements. If the crisis is located on the terrain of one form of the modern state, that is the liberal-democratic one, then what he seems to be suggesting is that there is a need today to think of alternative ways of constituting the modern state. In other words, there is a need to think of different principles on which the practices of the state could be grounded. It is from this perspective that he asks his basic question: if the basis of secularism is lost when serving as the neutral space for arbitration between communities, then what can be a workable idea of toleration, which will form the basis for mutual intelligibility between different communities?

Two things are implied in Chatterjee's argument so far. First, that the idea of secularism no longer represents in a self-evident manner, at least in the Indian context, the emancipatory meanings that are attached to it historically. Second, that the principle of mutual toleration between communities too, even if it is assumed to exist in the principles of everyday religion are not of much help, where it concerns the business of modern politics. In order to function, modern societies and their public institutions need other principles too—those that do not belong to a particular community. They cannot, therefore, simply wish away the state. Principles of toleration for the state lacking in any single common principle of intelligibility that are consonant with the otherwise different normative worlds of different communities must be evolved. The problem is complicated by the fact that these communities live in a world where power is unequally shared. In such a situation, Chatterjee would appear to say, we might need to return to the secular public sphere, in order to reorganize it along different principles. Chatterjee, unlike Nandy and Madan, holds that the problem is not simply one of the cultural specificity of either South Asian (Madan) or non-Western cultures (Nandy), but that the bind is in some sense much wider and resonates with the crisis of the liberal-democratic state and its inability to handle cultural difference. He draws attention to the raging debate within liberal theory and philosophy, on the politics of multiculturalism, on the question of collective and group rights of cultural communities, and to the consequent impasse in the discourse of rights. Chatterjee sees the possibility that there may be times when communities may refuse to enter the domain of 'reasonable discourse' as very real. These are institutions of the rationalist public sphere, undergirded by the large 'universalist assumptions of post-Enlightenment Reason'. The problem with the liberal solution, he claims, is that it can, at best, resort to platitudes about respecting diversity, valuing the different ways of life and trying to understand the Other. But in the final analysis, it cannot but fall back on the very universalist values that are at the root of the crisis, to act as final arbiters between communities and their different normative worlds. Notions like 'deliberative universalism' too do not seem to fit the bill because, though they do talk of evolving common ground, they do not take the 'strategic context of power' into account.[31] Such notions assume that different groups always enter into reasoned deliberation on an equal footing, where mutual give and take is possible and contentions can be resolved by merely providing for a space where such deliberation can take place.

If this is not really the case, Chatterjee argues, '(I)t is naive to think of secularization as simply the onward march of rationality, devoid of coercion and power struggles'. Here he seems to concur with Nandy and Madan that:

(E)ven if secularization as a process of the decreasing significance of religion in public life is connected with such 'objective' social processes as mechanization and segmentation of social relationships...it does not necessarily evoke a uniform set of responses from all groups...contrary phenomena such as religious revivalism, fundamentalism and the rise of new cults have sometimes also been explained as the consequence of the same process...[32]

What does this bringing in of the context of power mean and what does it do to our understanding of the question of secularism in India? There are two aspects of this context of power that are central to his argument. In the first place there are power relations as between colonialism and nationalism, which structured the very form and content of nationalist ideology and which continue to be present in the way postcolonial elites have dealt with cultural difference within the nation. Secondly, there are unequal power relations between communities comprising the 'nation'. Chatterjee works out his argument through the experience of the implication of the state and the modernizing elites in the process of religious reform. It is not necessary to rehearse the details of his argument here, but the critical point he makes through a detailed reading of the empirical/historical material is the following: there has been a strong desire among the modernizing elites in the country to push for religious reform, which has sometimes been expressed in the name of reforming religion, but most often in the name of certain crucial universal principles like rights of equality and personhood, such as temple-entry laws, those banning the Devadasi system, and the practices of untouchability and bondage, throughout much of the nineteenth century. The arrival of nationalism in the penultimate decade of that century changed much of that. It denied the colonial state the prerogative to intervene in and reform Hindu society. Nonetheless, the desire for reform and modernization remained and accumulated throughout the nationalist struggle. This accumulated desire burst forth in the late 1940s in a spate of legislations—first in the provinces, then in the constituent assembly and the subsequent actions of the independent Indian state. The desire for reform and uniformity was as much evident within the Muslim community and through the 1920s and 1930s there were a series of legislations to this effect. The very diversity of practices and the lack of a single authority to carry out reform gave the state a special place in this context. The achievement of independence and partition brought about a crucial change in the situation. The reformist zeal of the state was reserved primarily for the Hindu community, as many of the tallest nationalist leaders also belonged to the majority community. But precisely for these reasons, for the Muslims, it was no longer possible to grant the right to the state to reform their religion—even if the legislatures were elected by universal suffrage. And there are no other representative institutions which can carry on the process. On the official side, the pragmatic argument was put forward by the leadership that there are some communities that are 'not yet ready for reform' so the state should proceed with the reform within the majority community. Therefore, crucial areas like the respective personal laws were left untouched.[33]

It follows from this description that there is from the very beginning, for historical reasons, a way in which 'Indian secularism', has acquired certain distinct marks of identification—the most important being that the state *must intervene in religious reform* precisely to ensure secularization, at least in the self-understanding of the modernizing elite. It also follows that post-partition, for the minorities, this state could not have the legitimacy to reform their religions and personal laws. Nor was there any other space for independent arbitration. Internal reform within communities remained the only possible option. This meant effectively, argues Chatterjee, that the right of communities to be different must be granted. Further, the possibility has to be accepted that they may not justify this right in the language of the modern state. The whole question then, is not that of ensuring some abstract universal principles of secularism. For one thing, such principles are not being challenged by the majoritarian right, and for another, from the perspective of the minorities, it is precisely such principles that are looked at with suspicion, for they seem to be the trojan horse of majoritarianism. There is also no point in simply invoking the resources of toleration in everyday religion without thinking of the institutional bases of ensuring them. The far more difficult question, rather, is one of working out a notion of toleration which can be institutionalized within the framework of a modern democracy.

Clearly, what animates Chatterjee's critique is the realization that the imagined 'archimedean space' of reason, which provided the state with much of its justification as the neutral arbiter between groups is no longer available. It is not simply a question of cultural difference. There are no common grounds, given the context of power, to which recourse can be sought when there are conflicts which themselves originate from different grounds. How must we deal with the question of respect for group cultural rights, especially when it means toleration of illiberal practices within the group concerned, 'if indeed the group chooses not to enter into reasonable dialogue with others on the validity of its practices'?[34]

Chatterjeee caps this discussion with a proposal for a minority representative institution like a separate 'parliament' where the community explains 'in its own chosen forum' its reasons for being different. What he plays on, in making this proposal, is the fact that any community that demands 'toleration' from others (and from the state), can be persuaded or cajoled into satisfying the condition of representativeness. If communities claim a certain representation within the larger structures of the state, they could be compelled at least to satisfy that condition within their group. The question of course is who will persuade or compel them? In a subsequent clarification of this idea, he therefore introduces a fictional character, that is, the advocate of what he calls the 'strategic politics of toleration'. This advocate, Chatterjee suggests, while arguing from within her minority group and *addressing the 'general body of citizens'*, will demand toleration for the beliefs of the group she belongs to. At the same time however, when *addressing her group members*, 'she will demand that the group publicly seek and obtain from its members consent for its practices… She will point out that if the group was to demand and expect toleration from others, it would have to satisfy the condition of representativeness.'[35] She will therefore 'demand an open and democratic debate within her community.'[36] Thus 'by resisting, on the one hand, the normalizing attempt of the national state to define, classify and fix the identity of minorities…and demanding, on the other, that regulative powers within the community be established on a more democratic basis, our protagonist will try to engage in a strategic politics that is neither integrationist nor separatist.'[37] Here he actually proposes then, a possible institutional framework for the handling of intercommunity difference and ensuring toleration. What is striking about this proposal is that there is no singular agency or subject that will act, for it assumes that every citizen could, at the same time, be a member of some community. She will therefore speak simultaneously in two languages: one in which she addresses the citizenry at large and the other in which she addresses her community. She will bring the resources of the one to critique and check the other. Whether we agree with Chatterjee's answer or not, we are still left with his question.

Formulated differently, the question is precisely that of the universalist philosophical-ethical grounds—of liberty, equality, and neutrality—on which secularism stands, and the manner in which these grounds have been problematized by the Indian experience. The question is also of the sources of the authority of secularism in instating itself as the final (neutral?) arbiter between religious communities.

One point that is implicit in the positions of both Nandy and Chatterjee, is that at least part of the problem of secularism has to do with its implication in the history of colonial domination. It also has to do with the fact that according to them, modernity itself or its implication in the colonial encounter and, therefore, the whole body of colonialist knowledge, is the source of much of the problem.

Secularism Defends Itself

These, then, are the broad outlines of the 'anti-secularist' attack. How has secularism responded? What have been the main lines of its defence? A detailed look at the secularist defence seems to say as much about its crisis, as the anti-secularist attack does.

The secularist position has been articulated with equal force and vigour by Sumit Sarkar, Akeel Bilgrami, Rajeev Bhargava, Javeed Alam, and Achin Vanaik. For my purpose in this chapter, I will deal here only with the first three, referring to the latter two occasionally. It is interesting to see however, that if the anti-secularist positions point to the deep problems of secularism, the positions articulated in its defence do nothing to relieve that sense of crisis. Sumit Sarkar alone, among the whole group of secularists most unrepentantly holds the 'strong secularist' position although watered down to some extent. None of the other participants on the side of secularism find it possible to defend the strong, unadulterated version of the creed even though there are powerful ideological reasons for why most of them seem to want to extricate colonialism and modernity from any such responsibility.

Writing in the winter of 1992–93, following the demolition of the Babri Masjid, Sarkar momentarily conceded that 'what is necessary today is the recognition that secularism can and indeed *does have many meanings, that its wide and varied spectrum can extend from the devoutly religious to the free-thinker-atheist* on a common ground of total rejection of communal hatred and a theocratic state.'[38] Notice that this assertion is quite close to Nandy's 'second meaning of secularism'. However, Sarkar went on to add that '(T)his does not mean that non-religious secularists should engage in a breast-beating exercise for having been "alienated" from the "mainstream" and suddenly claim to be more "truly" Hindu or Muslim than the VHP or the Muslim fundamentalists.'[39] He never really makes it clear which of the non-religious secularists have claimed to be more 'truly' religious of any denomination. As our survey of the main positions shows, it is difficult to attribute this position to any of these scholars. Nandy himself only invokes the lived traditions of religious tolerance; he does not claim any kind of religious identity. One must assume that what was in Sarkar's mind probably, was the general atmosphere in *secular political circles*—as, for instance in the CPI (M)'s use of Vivekananda in a pamphlet issued immediately after the demolition, but also more generally among activists who were confronting the campaign of the Hindu right on the ground.[40] This is a point that Sarkar himself recognizes in a subsequent article where he points to the danger of a 'certain complacency *among anti-communal groups*, which may lead us to disregard the quiet shifts in climates of opinion and terms of discourse'[41] that can, in turn, 'weaken the resistance to future Hindutva campaigns'. In other words, this 'breast beating' seems to refer to the strategic shift that certain anti-communal groups were making, rather than to the intellectual trend represented by the anti-secularists. There is an unstated assumption of a correspondence between the anti-secularist intellectual current and the active anti-communal groups that seems to underlie Sarkar's response. Given the fact then, that these strategic shifts were responding to the Hindutva campaigns on the ground of politics, they should have elicited a very different type of response from secular intellectuals. For these responses on the ground cannot really be accused of embracing 'current intellectual fashions like postmodernism'.[42] In fact, most of them would self-consciously disavow any such relationship to postmodernism. Even if some of the anti-secularist intellectuals could be said to have some kind of inclination towards postmodernism/anti-modernism, this is not a charge that can be levelled at the CPI(M), for instance, or on the other anti-communal groups like the Sampradayikta Virodhi Andolan, mentioned earlier. One would imagine then, that the kind of questions a secular intellectual has to face would be different; that s/he would have to ask whether the feeling of 'being alienated from the mainstream' was not a more general condition that secular activists were beginning to have to deal with. There does not seem to be any such moment of self-doubt in Sarkar's discourse. For, it seems to be his fear that to acknowledge this alienation would be to acknowledge a part of the anti-secularist critique: that secularism is a Western/colonial imposition. He notes that the critique of 'colonial discourse' and 'Enlightenment rationalism' is being 'picked up' by Hindutva intellectuals 'in bits and pieces'[43]. In this later essay, he cites BJP MP Uma Bharati's attack on the 'followers of Macaulay' for using the idea of social justice to 'destroy social unity', as an instance of such a 'picking up'. This, he suggests, parallels the way in which 'fascist ideologies had similarly appropriated fragments from the turn-of-the-century philosophical rejections of liberal individualism and rationalism.'[44] In this context, he reminds us of Giovanni's Gentile's description of fascism as 'a revolt against positivism' and Mussolini's denunciation of the 'movement of the 18th century visionaries and Encyclopaedists' and their 'teleological conceptions of history.'[45]

While there may be some justification in the fear, it is probably misplaced in one crucial sense. It seems to me that in this kind of analysis, there is an excessive burden placed on the intellectual and academic world, in terms of its influence on the course of history. While we need not see the world in Hegelian terms where the Owl of Minerva takes wings only at dusk, that is after the event; nevertheless we need to avoid the other tendency that sees the intellectual as a kind of a vanguard/avant-garde. It is not as though the critiques are *first* formulated by philosophers, and *then* appropriated by political activists. Based on our earlier discussion we could, in fact, argue that the sequence was really the other way around: that it was the rapid successes registered by the Hindu right in capturing popular imagination that forced a fresh look at the entire intellectual-theoretical paraphernalia of secularism. There could also be a third line of inquiry. Such an inquiry would start from the premise that specific intellectual constellations and discursive shifts arise in the context of gradually accumulating dissatisfaction with the sterile and oppressive certainties of earlier, hegemonic formations. Such an inquiry would see the discursive shifts themselves as representing deeper practical-political problems with hegemonic discourses. On this way of looking at the problem, the rise of the Hindu right and the rise of anti-communal critiques of secularism would appear to be coeval, though not causally tied to each other; they could be seen as two different responses to a single crisis—that of secular-nationalism. It can also be argued from such a perspective that such large epistemological shifts could carry within them diverse possibilities and it will be fallacious to derive political positions in a straightforward way from them. If that were the case then every epistemological position would yield only one political position, which is clearly not a sustainable position.

To linger on this theme a bit more, we might need to ask why, in certain conjunctures, wholesale shifts in intellectual climate occur? Why is the optimism and confident rationalism of eighteenth-century Europe replaced by the end of the nineteenth century with such a widespread reaction against it? Why, for that matter, do the 1980s and 1990s in India, represent such a widespread interrogation of rationalism and secularism that it is manifested not merely in the rise of the Hindu right, but also in the emergence of major critiques of the whole ideology of Development and Progress in the ecological movements of people displaced by the workings of this ideology? We also might need to question the easy assumption that the entire spectrum of issues that we have discussed in the previous chapter could be simply a creation of certain intellectual fashions imported from Western academies. At the very least, a serious sociology of knowledge will have to answer why such 'fashions' find a ready audience among intellectuals and movements on the ground.

Let us return to Sarkar's argument. Could it be that the intellectual shifts that he refers to, rather than result in the 'weakening of resistance to Hindutva campaigns', might be the consequence of an already weakened resistance, born out of an overwhelming feeling of 'alienation'? Could it be that this 'alienation' in fact had something to do with the abstract rationalism of the earlier epoch and the feeling of loss that widely accompanies the dislocations brought about by rapid modernization? If so, does secular/rationalist discourse not need to address that feeling? One might believe that such 'feelings' are 'irrational' and have no basis in 'fact'; that they represent the nostalgia of those who are waylaid by the 'onward march of historical progress'. And yet, can one ignore its profound desire to recover the lost world? Or, to recreate it? Does not the secular-modernist response, which sees in all these yearnings a reactionary nostalgia for the past, simply vacate the ground to forces like that of the Hindu right? These are issues that might lie behind the wholesale shift in intellectual climate, of which the academic and philosophical world it but a small part. The intellectual world probably merely reflects, in some sense, what goes on in the depths of society. Since Sarkar leaves no room for any self-doubt, he does not consider these questions at all.

He is, on the contrary, deeply perturbed by the anti-secularist appeal to 'authenticity' and 'community'—for its position on these two categories, he believes, reveals the 'shared discursive space' between it and Hindutva. To cite him:

One kind of anticommunal response has been to fling back the charge of inauthenticity, arguing with considerable historical plausibility, that phenomena like organized, countrywide Hindu or Muslim communalism, are primarily modern constructions that have sought to violently displace an earlier catholicity of relatively inchoate, pluralistic traditions [...]Hindutva can then be condemned as a quintessentially late and postcolonial construct, a product of colonial power/knowledge.[46]

It is worth noticing that Sarkar does not deny the 'historical plausibility' of the argument put forward by the anti-secularists, who have demonstrated with considerable persuasiveness that the Hindutva agenda, despite appeals to authenticity, is as modern to the core as is the secularist agenda. What probably troubles him here is that this is accomplished by showing that the roots of the Hindutva project lie in 'colonial power/knowledge'.[47] To press this point further, therefore, he recalls Nandy's comment that the '*khaki* shorts of the RSS unconsciously modelled on the uniform of the colonial police', 'as something that can be interpreted' as the 'final proof that the RSS is an illegitimate child of western colonialism.' It is Sarkar's contention therefore, that the appearance of these types of opinions reveal:

(T)he *common ground* that has unwittingly opened up between Hindutva and its anti-secular critics centres around a similar assumption of secularism being invariably statist, alienated, aggressive and bound up with Enlightenment rationalism.[48]

So he goes on to ask how far it is tenable, historically and conceptually, to regard 'this stereotype of secularism as the innately aggressive product of Enlightenment scepticism, brought into India in the baggage of colonial power-knowledge and embodied subsequently in the repressive modern nation-states?'[49] His response to this argument is that in this construction, a simultaneous double operation is performed on the idea of secularism: in the first place, it is narrowed down into an anti-religious scepticism, virtually atheism, while, at the same time it is broadened into a 'wildly free-floating signifier' to denote everything that goes with the rationality of the modern state. It [secularism] is thus 'uniquely identified with the Enlightenment (which is itself vastly simplified and homogenized in much current 'post-modernist' readings).' In Europe, he argues, the roots of the Enlightenment go back to at least another two hundred years, to the religious wars where 'the first advocates of toleration based on separation of church from state were not rationalist free-thinkers, but sixteenth-century Anabaptists passionately devoted to their own brand of Christianity, who believed that coercion, persecution and any kind of compulsory state religion were contrary to true faith.'[50] Sarkar contends that the fact these

Anabaptists were burnt in their thousands shows, *contra* Nandy what every child should know: that pre-Enlightenment faith was not always pluralistic or non-monolithic.[51]

It seems to me that though it is important to remember that pre-modern and pre-Enlightenment faith was repressive in its own, often inhuman ways, this invocation of pre-Enlightenment repressions does not adequately respond to the anxieties about the modern state. While it is important to remind ourselves of these repressions, they do not provide any comfort about the ways of the modern state, which draws on the Enlightenment promise of emancipation. Nor is it clear from his rendering above why the Anabaptists' claim to 'authenticity' is acceptable as secular, but similar claims in contemporary India are not. Moreover, in relation to Nandy's claim about religious tolerance in non-modern/traditional communities, we might need to remember that it is made in the context of traditional/ non-modern communities in South Asia, and not necessarily for all pre-Enlightenment faith, especially not in contexts where religion is meshed with state power. This is an aspect that Sarkar seems to ignore when he suggests that the fate of the Anabaptists 'proves' Nandy's claim to be wrong. Charges of secularism's statism, alienation, and aggressiveness that Sarkar seeks to counter, also then remain unanswered. In purely logical terms, a critique of the pre-modern/traditional cannot by itself be read as an exoneration of modernity.

The second problem that Sarkar has with the anti-secularists has to do with 'their notion of community'. He argues that they have 'tried to operate with a concept of community and "community consciousness" very different in location and texture: situated in the past rather than the present, marked by "fuzziness" and not precisely "enumerated" through census procedures imposed by colonialism, local and autonomous and not integrated into the modern nation-state.'[52] He calls this the traditionalist critique, which in a different way reproduces the old nationalist argument about Hindu–Muslim amity, 'disrupted only through colonial intrusion.' Nandy's understanding of community is one he shares with others like Sudipta Kaviraj who has persuasively shown how enumeration through censuses transformed the 'fuzziness' of older boundaries. It is a notion of community that underlines some of the crucial ways in which colonial power/knowledge introduces an irreversible transformation in the logic of self-identity. In that sense, Sarkar is right: the anti-secularist notion of community *is* a notion that surely draws upon the past histories of intercommunity relations. But while it is true that there is, in Nandy, a lament, a nostalgia for the lost world, the notion of community he deploys, is not so much a real community of the past. It is more in the nature of a utopian community, one that is necessarily local. This community is invoked mainly in order to interrogate the community in the present. It is the present community, real and with fixed boundaries, that is the object of this critique. However, even in the present, Nandy points to the resistance that these communities offer to the efforts of the modern state to define them with fixed boundaries, as when he refers to the fact that even today there are more than four hundred communities that do not identify themselves as exclusively Hindu or Muslim.[53]

I have mentioned that Sarkar is troubled not only by anti-secularist notions of community but also by what he sees as their implicit claim to authenticity *vis-à-vis* the Hindu right. Even though this is not a claim common to all the anti-secularists, it is worth looking at his argument at greater length. He believes that in the anti-secularist discourse, there remains 'the implicit assumption that to be authentically indigenous is to be more worthy of acceptance'.[54] This is an objection that ties up with our earlier discussion of his position on secularism's 'alienation from the mainstream' for, one way of reading this notion of alienation is to see it as being 'inauthentic'. On that reading, one can see in this statement, a further working out of the logic enunciated earlier. It is not simply his claim that the charge of secularism's alienation is incorrect; he also seems to suggest that rejecting the claim to authenticity itself is a virtue. It is true that the notion of 'authenticity' can acquire very ominous dimensions when articulated within certain kinds of xenophobic and sectarian discourses. But if one were to look at the phenomenon of what we have referred to as the insurrection of little selves, it seems that in a very critical sense, these little selves privilege lived experience as authentic. 'Authenticity' here can take on a meaning that challenges and disrupts the domination of the hegemonic culture. The question here is not one of indigenism, with which Sarkar seems to conflate all claims to authenticity. In my opinion, indigenism is a secondary concern even for Nandy. The real question for everybody is about the growing alienation/marginalization of secularism and the rise of communal sectarian violence.

Sarkar concludes his argument by invoking the century of Dalit and lower caste protests which characteristically have been 'really forthright and "hard" anti-religious, or at least anti-Brahminical Hindu' in their approach. Their strident 'anti-Hinduism' and 'aggressive secularism' and even atheism is of a different order and difficult to dismiss as 'a product of westernization or elite alienation' according to him. This is precisely where I think alternative notions of authenticity, defined in terms of lived experience rather than with reference to elite constructions of national culture, actually come into play. There is no doubt that these currents routinely exploited the presence of the colonial state and notions of rights and equality to negotiate their position *vis-à-vis* the dominant Brahminical Hindu culture, but there remains a crucial difference between them and the secularists. This has to do with the fact that while the Dalit/non-brahmin discourses of Ambedkar and Periyar privileged the authenticity of the lived experience of untouchable existence, secular invocation to the same values occupies a universalist and therefore empty ground, which in better days could only have been filled by the hegemonic culture. It is because of this claim to authenticity that the Hindutva forces find it difficult to attack Dalits on this ground, while secularists have presented no problem. Hindutva has no way of dealing with the Dalits except by trying to include Ambedkar into their pantheon. I have dealt with the entire gamut of issues related to this problem in Chapter 5.

Another protagonist in the debate, standing in defence of secularism is Akeel Bilgrami (1994). Bilgrami has found it particularly difficult to defend Nehruvian secularism *in toto*, arguing that it was 'archimedean' rather than 'emergent'. Thus he agrees partially with the view that this secularism was an imposition, though he hastens to add that the sense in which he considers it to be an imposition is different from both Nandy's and Chatterjee's. It was not a modern intrusion into an essentially traditionalist religious population, he argues, because under an evolving electoral democracy the people have willy-nilly come to understand religion entering politics in a non-traditionalist, modern way. Secularism, he says, was 'an imposition rather in the sense that it (was) assumed that *secularism stood outside the substantive arena of political commitments*...It was not in there with Hinduism and Islam as one among the *substantive* contested political commitments to be *negotiated* as any other contested commitments must be negotiated, one with the other.'[55] Bilgrami explicates this further:

For three decades before independence the Congress under Nehru refused to let a secular policy emerge through negotiation between different communal interests, by denying at every step in the various conferrings with the British, Jinnah's demand that the Muslim League represents the Muslims, a Sikh leader represents the Sikhs, and a harijan (*sic*) leader represents the untouchable community. *And the ground for the denial was simply that as a secular party they could not accept that they* not *represent* all *these communities*... Secularism thus never got a chance to *emerge out of a creative dialogue between* these different communities...This archimedean existence gave secularism procedural priority but in doing so it gave it no abiding authority' (emphasis added).[56]

Sarkar (1994) and Vanaik (1997) have preferred to read Bilgrami's argument above, as an undue concession to the Chatterjee/Nandy kind of argument, but also as an admission that religious communities alone can serve as the basic political unit. Sarkar goes to the extent of implying that this proposal is a mere unoriginal re-hash of the old Congress style opportunism that placated various conservative or communal Hindu and Muslim leaders simultaneously.[57] However, that may not be the only possible negotiation— and neither is it Bilgrami's argument. It is interesting therefore, that in a postscript to a reprint of the same article five years later, Bilgrami seems embarrassed by Sarkar's criticism but unrepentant about his insistence that Nehruvian secularism remained a transcendent and imposed ideal. He explains this notion of its being a transcendent and imposed ideal through a detour. The interesting new addition to the earlier article is a note on the controversy over the Salman Rushdie affair. Bilgrami begins from the premise that now, thanks to immigration, Islam is a world religion and Muslims are no longer 'out there' but right in the midst of the West. There is, therefore, no point in arguing as the liberal press did: 'if you live here you must be like us and accept the primacy of free speech on grounds familiar to us, even in the face of blasphemy against your religion.' There was now no choice but to 'drop the pretensions of standard and familiar liberal theory and engage with Muslims *in an internal argument*, finding reasons within *their* value commitments...'[58]

This means abandoning the attitude that arguments could be carried out within the rhetoric of 'There should be *progress* toward Enlightenment values' or 'If you live here you must be more like us...'[59] He explains how he himself had defended Rushdie by a process of internal reasoning than by expounding liberal theoretical arguments. Of all the secularists, Bilgrami shows an extreme sensitivity to the point at issue: the question is not one of right and wrong but how dialogue must be conditioned so that we can evolve some common ground. In other words, the common ground cannot be simply assumed to exist, as Sarkar notably, often does. Bilgrami therefore, emphasizes that when ideological or political differences arise, unless there is an *internal* argument, the losing side is always likely to perceive its defeat as a result of an alien imposition: whether this is a fact is not important, but the perception is.[60] Of course, Bilgrami ignores the important fact that in most cases arguments are won not on the pure strength of the argument but on the backing of power—for very often, there are no common referents to decide the superiority or inferiority of arguments. Nevertheless, he does see the real hindrance here in that he recognizes the absence of that assumed archimedean ground that is so indispensable to secularism.

What is not so clear in Bilgrami's argument—and here Sarkar's fear may be right—is that if secularism were to be allowed to *emerge* as a value by negotiation between the substantive commitments of different religious communities, how can we be certain *a priori*, that the end result of such negotiation will still be secularism and not any other form of religious toleration? And if any form of toleration is acceptable, does it not reduce the polemic with Nandy and Chatterjee to a mere difference of nomenclature? The logic of an internal argument assumes that a secularist must enter the discursive domain of the community and argue on terms comprehensible to it. Put differently, whether or not she explicitly says that she is a good Hindu or a good Muslim, she must be able to enter into a dialogue with them. Bilgrami does not, in my view, follow the meaning of an internal argument to its logical end.

Rajeev Bhargava discusses the notion of secularism by opening up the possible meanings and possible models of secularism for debate.[61] His concern is primarily with the normative concerns that define secularism, which alone he feels, are important. The models could be many and varied and will need to be formulated differently in different contexts. He begins his exercise by distinguishing between two kinds of secularism—political and ethical, both of which are further differentiated into their weaker and stronger versions. Arguing on the secularist side of the divide, he bases his distinctions on the claims that separation need not be only an exclusion of religion from politics and the state, in the manner of the US 'wall of separation'. In his argument, developed in Bhargava (1998, pp. 486–542) he grounds this classification on a further distinction between what he calls the dominant 'Church—State model' of secularism, which has often been understood as the only model, and the 'religious strife model'. It is the second model that he finds more relevant to the contemporary Indian context. By and large, he casts his vote for *political secularism*, which he distinguishes from *ethical secularism* insofar as the former excludes all *ultimate ideals*, religious and non-religious, from the domain of the state. At the very least, it adopts an attitude of principled distance from all such ideals. Bhargava believes that there is a 'deep, quite irreconcilable conflict between ethical secularism and religion' which is further exacerbated when it seeks 'by state intervention or intellectual fiat, to totally exclude from politics all religious belief.'[62] In his attempt to redefine a possible, reasonable secularism, he further argues that:

(But) secularism can be delinked from ethical conceptions and be given a purely political character. If the state does not take upon itself the task of improving the quality of autonomous living or of making people less and less dependent on what is widely *believed to be cognitively false* or illusory, then it is not unlikely that believers will also put up with it. The philosophy of secularism that grounds such a state accommodates religious orthodoxy, heteronomous interdependence, and tradition because it does not presuppose a high degree of autonomy, full-blooded egalitarianism or mandatory and intense political participation. Thus even believers can accept the separation of religion from politics; *even they can be secular.*[63]

In this rendering Bhargava spells out an interesting notion of the state which will not only shun all ultimate ideals, but will not legislate on what it sees to be 'cognitively false' and seek to 'liberate people' from it. This kind of a state would have to be a state that is different in fundamental ways from what the modern state has historically been. However, Bhargava's argument against the anti-secularist position is that its advocates seem to be barking up the wrong tree: rather than looking for an alternative for secularism, they should be looking for an alternative conception of secularism.[64] There are other aspects of his arguments that are not immediately relevant to our purposes as they are concerned with spelling out in greater detail the alternative conception—the limitations of political secularism and the need for an alternative ethical, rights-based secularism. What is important is to note that this rights-based secularism too, acknowledges a difference between religious communities and between religious and non-religious communities. It does not exclude 'constitutive attachments or religious communities from the political arena' but rather *brings them in*. There is a problem here that he foresees, though—there can be a legitimate fear that the discourse of rights entrenches division rather than allowing for the emergence of the common good. This danger being quite real, Bhargava proposes a modification in the very discourse of rights such that it keeps alive the possibility of reverting to a politics of the common good.[65] How can this possibility be kept alive? Particularly in a situation where we have only two kinds of players: the communities with their divergent, often conflicting rights claims and the state arbitrating between them? And if the legitimacy of the state in assuming that role is already under question, what is the way out? It is true that *that* is not part of Bhargava's immediate concern but it is a question that does concern us here. It is also important to note that in summing up that alternative conception he argues that *this* 'secularism is fully compatible with, indeed even dictates, *a defence of differentiated citizenship* and the rights of religious groups.'[66]

Two things are worthy of notice here in his argument. First, that the secularism of his conception then, is not only compatible with differentiated citizenship, but, in fact, demands abandoning of the idea of abstract citizenship. It is a conception that *must* make room for believers as well to 'be secularist'. Second, that this only workable model of secularism can in fact be made to work only if (a) it is linked to a state that is divested and purged of 'ultimate ideals' and privileges ordinary life; and (b) it be made to desist from the desire to impose its cognitive universe on the believers. Recast thus, it becomes possible to see the emergence of a negotiated or 'emergent' secularism. Delinked from the baggage of high ideals with which it normally comes ('development, megascience and national security', *the package deal for Nandy*), which justifies the violence of the modern nation-state, many anti-secularists would not have very serious problems with this conception.

I have broadly and selectively recounted some of the major positions arrayed on both sides in the debate to highlight the crucial concerns of the participants. What is important here, I believe, is the fact that even as secularism defends itself, the sense of its overall crisis is inescapable. It is certainly possible to accuse the anti-secularists of having overstated their case in many respects, but many of the objections raised by them have forced the secularist response to seriously consider the overall performance as well as the theoretical and philosophical bases of the credo. It is also clear that except for Sarkar, we can already see the commonality of concerns and narrowing down of what seemed widely divergent positions. The secularist defence, we can see, does concede many of the substantive objections in that it either believes secularism to have been archimedean and transcendent (Bilgrami), or in some way implicated in too many other things bearing the burden of high ideals (Bhargava). Both Bhargava and Bilgrami defend secularism but not by simply asserting that the opponents' arguments are wrong-headed, but by first squarely admitting that the crisis does exist. Both, in fact, are acutely aware of the fundamental problem that there seems to be a loss of common ground from where disputes between divergent claims of communities can be addressed: in other words, both these defences are themselves predicated upon a problematization of a certain kind of universalism, whether or not one links it with the legacy of the Enlightenment. In both these important defences there is an acknowledgment that secularism and its emancipatory content can no longer be taken for granted, as something self-evident and *that* is precisely what needs to reworked and rethought. In parenthesis, we may note that even Sarkar accepts—though I believe in an *ideological fashion*[67]—that 'secularism can and does have many meanings' and can embrace anybody from the 'devoutly religious to free-thinkers and atheists'. This acceptance could have fulfilled a theoretical function only if there had been at least an admission alongside that these many meanings are not simply 'there' and in fact, need to be reworked into a rearticulated and retheorized notion of secularism in the manner of Bilgrami and Bhargava.

Secularism and the State

On reviewing the entire debate, it becomes apparent that the secularism/anti-secularism divide is actually predicated on two different conceptions of secularism itself. It is not that there is an object X (secularism) in relation to which some are secularists and some anti-secularists; there are, in fact *two objects*, X1 and X2—not entirely unrelated to but yet distinct from each other. In one case, that of the secularists, secularism stands for a notion of symmetry/principled distance/neutrality between the state and different religions, and between religions and non-religious communities/groups, a notion which is therefore crucially centred on the state. It is the state's symmetry of treatment, neutrality, or principled distance that is in question here. The whole secularist position can only make sense if we consider the question in relation to the state. The question that the secularists seem to be addressing is: if it is true that a denominational state, however tolerant, is not desirable and cannot always be trusted, then a secular state that maintains such symmetry/principled distance is not merely desirable, *it is indispensable*. The question then can at best be one of redefining the nature of this symmetry or distance. But this is a position that, if our reading of Nandy is correct, even he would not have an objection to. What he might argue is that a secular state in itself is utterly insufficient, because in the long run the possibility of living together hinges on intercommunity relations in society. Let us note however, that in the secularist stance, the state alone is the agent of secular transformation while communities—if they ever come into the picture—are locked in sectarian strife.

The object of the second, that is the anti-secularist position, it seems to me, is the question of religious toleration in society at large—in other words, among and between communities. This is so whether we consider Nandy's second meaning of secularism or Chatterjee's more complicated proposal of minority representative institutions. Even though Chatterjee claims that he is looking for political possibilities within the domain of the modern state institutions, his search too is clearly not within the 'state' in

the narrow sense. For, central to his argument is the question: what happens
if a minority refuses to offer reasons for being different and thus refuses to
enter the deliberative/discursive space of precisely such 'stateness'? What
he is looking for therefore, is a way of addressing an impasse in society at
large, of which the state as guarantor of rights is merely a secondary actor.
If Nandy would have nothing to do with the modern nation-state,
Chatterjee too proceeds by keeping the question of the state in suspension.
Take for example his most controversial proposal of something like a
minority parliament, '*its own chosen forum*' where it must explain its reasons.
Here, in this proposal, the state's role is already delimited to that of ensuring
elections based on universal suffrage—the whole question of internal
reforms within communities being predicated on a suspension of the state's
role as activist-modernizer. Here there is an explicit recognition of conflicts
and strivings for democratic transformation *within* communities. In other
words, the agents of secular/democratic transformation are seen to exist
within all communities. This second conception of secularism, by bringing
in the question of communities and of society generally, cannot but widen
the meaning of secularism. In a metaphorical sense, Sarkar's charge that
in their hands, secularism becomes a 'wildly free-floating signifier' may
have some substance here, especially when contrasted to its narrowly state-
centric view. By bringing in the question of society at large one unavoidably
brings in the question of different agendas and different self-perceptions
of the various groups that comprise it. One is then forced to ask what
happens when these social groups do not share the state's modernizing
agenda? One is then forced to abandon the archimedean heights inhabited
by the statist discourse. So while the argument seems to be about one
object, it is really about two different things: (1) about state policy in one
case and about living with the Other in mutual toleration in the second.
(2) Further, it is about *two different roles of the state* perceived as the neutral
arbiter in the secularist case and as the active modernizer in the anti-
secularist case.

In a sense, in this second (anti-secularist) conception secularism *stands
in* for the entire theoretical-epistemological baggage of modernity and of
the technologies of modern power, with which it is coeval. For, the critique
of the activist-modernizer's role of the state here points to the impasse
arising out of the conflict between its modernizing impulses and the non-
modern ways of being of the pre-existing religious communities. This
more serious critique is made explicitly by Nandy in the essays cited above
but is also made by Chatterjee in some of the other essays that we have
discussed in Chapter 1. In those works, as well as in some of Sudipta

Kaviraj's writings, it has been argued that the very possibility of communal or 'fundamentalist' mobilization is opened up only after particular ways of census enumeration and rational history writing came into existence.[68] That census enumerations fixed identities in very large and easily handled categories for the purposes of colonial administration in particular—but also for modern governmental technologies in general—is an argument that has been made by many others. We only need to look at the important work of scholars like Bernard Cohn and Nicholas Dirks among others.[69] The combination of these two very modern secular and rational technologies of power/knowledge produced a qualitatively different set of possibilities.

Two points are worth mentioning in this regard. First, these modern governmental technologies opened up ways of looking at 'our' past in ways fundamentally different and quintessentially modern. Not that there were no sectarian or religious conflicts in earlier times, but they could not possibly have been seen as conflicts that had more than a local resonance— least of all could they have become a conflict between 'Hindus' and 'Muslims' or some such categories. Such mobilizations only became possible at an all-India level, once these large categories were put in place through colonial interventions like censuses. Further, their insertion into the logic of modern nation-states opened up some other possibilities like the imagination of national communities bound in a common past and future destiny. The search for a historical narrative that illuminates the past and future of such a community, therefore, became an important task. This brings us to the second point. There is enough evidence today to show that it was with the introduction of the principles of 'rational scientific' historiography that the beginnings of the search for the 'real Subject' of that history began. As Chatterjee shows through his reading of Mrityunjoy Vidyalankar and Munshi Alimuddin's texts, all these narratives were puranic in their structure and notions of time. None of these narratives were about a national community bound in a common destiny, deriving from an exalted past. More importantly, they understood all acts in the present too, as flowing from Divine Will. Both the coming of the Yavanas as well as their defeat at the hands of the British were a consequence of Divine Will. How could one defy Divine Will? The question of retribution against that Supreme Will simply could not have arisen. The subject of that history, if there ever was one, was always the royal dynasties - the innumerable *Rajabalis* and *Rajataranginis* testify to that. There was no 'Our History' because there was no sense of the 'We': Was it Hindu, Muslim, Indian, Bengali, or Tamil? Even with the early attempts to write 'scientific, rational' history, this part remained unclear for a considerable length of time. I discuss some of these issues in detail in Chapter 4. It is this transformation of the logic of self-identity that makes possible, in the anti-secularist reading, an overarching conflict of identities that is centrally linked to the logic of modernity.

In a crucial sense then, this is where the difference lies: At stake in the debate is modernity itself. To the secularists, communal or sectarian strife represents the non-modern and the irrational; to the anti-secularists on the other, these are eminently modern phenomena and tackling them demands a stepping back and re-examining of modern power and knowledge.

Modernity and Its 'Shame'[70]

At the heart of the question of secularism then, is the problem of our colonial modernity. That modernity everywhere constituted a rupture in the old notions and organizations of time and space, is something that is generally accepted. That secularization or the process of growing marginality of religion in public life was a necessary consequence of this process is equally well accepted. This is now acknowledged even by many who consider themselves modernists, even as they register their sharp disagreements with the antisecularists' view. Javeed Alam for instance argues that 'modernity has a creeping sense of shame as it defends itself'. The entire argument in the first two chapters of his book represent an attempt to extricate himself, secularism, and modernity from the clutches of the Enlightenment legacy whose embodied form he calls 'entrenched modernity'.[71] Elsewhere, he launches on a search for a 'non-foundationalist secularism', for he argues that foundationalism elevates to first principles what are, in fact, historically and culturally specific entities.[72] Achin Vanaik, another unrepentant modernist, claims '(T)he way to counter the advocacy of these false trails [those of the 'anti-modernist, ambiguous modernist and post-modernist' critics of secularism] cannot be a simple argument for the value of an unproblematic modernity. It has to be the defense of a *critical and modest modernity...*'[73]

What scholars like Alam and Vanaik do not accept, however, is that there is a need to distinguish between modernity and secularization *as endogenous processes*, born within particular historical and cultural configurations, and as *processes that come as the concomitants of the colonization* process. It is nevertheless interesting that these defences of modernity and secularism are defences that are acutely aware of the tenuousness of those self-evident universalisms in whose comfort we remained ensconced so far, hoping for deliverance to come. Akeel Bilgrami's gesture towards the need for *internal argument* is also a pointer in that direction.

However, I think not *all critiques of modernity* express a desire for a return to the past. Nor is it entailed in all critiques that we debunk all that modernity brings in its train. What a critique of modernity does entail is a head-on confrontation with its cognitive arrogance—its claim to have discovered, once and for all, the real scientific Truth, the methods of Science which are then elevated to a position from where it can decree all other ways of knowing as false and lowly. What it also entails is a relentless problematization of the entire cognitive baggage that claims a universality across continents, across centuries, and across cultures. In that sense, it does mean, that in our context we at least ask, not necessarily from Nandy's indigenist position, that if categories of thought and knowledge are about reality, how can categories produced in complete oblivion of three-fourths of the world be simply transplantable to those contexts? How do those get translated in the new context, and within what kind of a discourse are they made sense of?

I think this question is of capital importance today, if we are to properly appreciate the meaning of the 'shift in intellectual climate' that Sarkar refers to in his writing. For the critique of modernity and secularism of the 1980s and 90s, cannot be seen merely as the consequence of some fashionable intellectual trends. It is lodged in the experiences of multiple dislocations brought about by modern development. It is lodged, not in the insulated precincts of the academy, but in the pain and agony of those enclaves of the 'non-modern' where the tribals of Narmada or the thrice-displaced communities of Singrauli reside. It is lodged in the angst of the artisans driven to destitution and destruction, their resistance to being sucked into the colonization of capital. Can we afford to see these as a desire to return to the past? And what if they really are a desire for return? How should the secular-modernist understand E.P. Thompson's heroic effort to rescue the eighteenth-century English artisans from the 'enormous condescension of posterity'? How does she make sense of his emphatic claim that though, 'Their hostility to the new industrialism may have been backward-looking, their communitarian ideals may have been fantasies...But they lived through these times of acute social disturbance, and we did not. *Their aspirations were valid in terms of their own experience...*'?[74] That, it seems, is the crux of the matter. Each experience has to be understood in its own terms, there is once again no archimedean space from where right and wrong can be decreed.

If therefore, the 55 million-odd people displaced since independence, some of them twice and even three times from their age-old habitat, in the name of Development and Progress, see modernity as an unmitigated evil, can they be blamed for trying to put the clock back? If the millions who are thus reduced to being 'anti-nationals' because they obstruct the 'Progress of the Nation', construe modernity in entirely negative terms, can they be simply termed reactionary? Do not Science, Development, and Progress here combine—of course with Capital—to disempower and dispossess these old communities? Is there no way to possibly critique this face of modernity without necessarily being seen as pleading for a return? Although for a person displaced, one would imagine, *even that should be justified*. To say that 'my land should be returned to me' surely stands up to the most rigorous standards of liberal notions of justice. And surely to make this critique is not to sanction the violences of the 'past'. And what after all, is 'the past'? To the victims of Progress/Development what is past in secular historical time—homogenous empty time, in Benjamin's celebrated phrase—is very much their living present. By what authority can it be legislated that their present is actually past, a remnant, a survival of some pre-historic social form?

But haven't we strayed away from secularism? In the anti-secularist reading: no. For the simple reason that secularism carries the entire baggage of modernity's cognitive arrogance and of its universalizing/homogenizing drive embodied in the nation-state. It carries the burden of creating the abstract citizen, by practically eliminating tribal or Dalit identity. And it can only be rescued from if this immense historical burden on its shoulders is got rid of.

Notes

1. By institutional framework I mean factors such as the division of powers between the centre and the states, the mechanisms of grievance redressal like the judiciary to settle pending disputes between different regions, states, social groups etc. The disputes could vary from the question of boundaries between states, and sharing of river waters, to issues like reservations in employment and political representative institutions.

2. See Vanaik (1997).

3. There has been an earlier debate in the ealry 1960s but here I will be concerned only with the recent one. For a glimpse of that earlier debate see Bhargava (1998).

4. Nandy (1985).

5. Madan (1987).

6. This is still the case—in fact, the immense misunderstanding of the critique of secularism, as we shall see, can only be attributed to the remaining, though not inconsiderable, influence that the secular discourse still carries, even as it fights its rearguard battles for survival.

7. Nandy (1985), p. 14.

8. By which he presumably means Gandhi.

9. Nandy (1985), p. 14.

10. Ibid., p. 14.

11. Ibid., p. 15.

12. The drive to homogenize, parenthetically, may be noted in the formulation of the Hindu Code Bill in the mid-1950s, where the *shastras* rather than the ways of life of diverse 'Hindu' communities were made the basis of codification. See for instance, Kishwar (1994), pp. 2145–61.

13. Nandy (1990).

14. Ibid., emphasis is Nandy's own.

15. Ibid.

16. Madan (1987).

17. Ibid.

18. Ibid.

19. See the discussion on Sarkar and Alam (1998).

20. Ibid. p. 309.

21. Ibid.

22. Ibid.

23. Madan (1997).

24. Ibid., p. 120.

25. Chatterjee (1994a), note 2.

26. Ibid., p. 1768.

27. Ibid.

28. Ibid., emphasis added.

29. See discussion in this section.

30. Ibid., p. 1769.

31. Ibid., p. 1774.

32. Ibid.

33. The argument here is summarized from the discussion in Chatterjee (1994a), pp. 1770–3.

34. Ibid., p. 1775.

35. See the revised version of 'Secularism and Toleration', published in Bhargava (1998), pp. 375–76.

36. Ibid., p. 376.

37. Ibid. Though Chatterjee does not say so, it will be evident from our brief discussion of the women's movement in Chapter 2, that this strategic politics of location is precisely what it had begun practising in the later period. This is the period, it will be recalled, when instead of the demand for a uniform civil code, the politics of internal reform of personal laws was being seriously discussed and moves towards it were being made. Characteristically, women activists working within communities were already beginning to practise such a politics of simultaneously addressing their community and the 'general body of citizens'.

38. Sarkar (1993), p. 166.

39. Ibid.

40. Another important move in this direction was initiated by the Delhi-based Sampradayikta Virodhi Andolan (Movement Against Communalism) whose slogan 'kan kan mein vyape hain Ram, mat bharkao dange lekar unka naam' gained some measure of popularity in those days. A rough English rendering of this slogan would be: 'Ram is present in every particle of the universe/do not use his name to instigate riots.'

41. Sarkar (1994), p. 101, emphasis added.

42. See Sarkar (1993), p. 165. Here Sarkar talks about how it has already become evident that these 'current academic fashions can reduce the resistance of intellectuals to the ideas of Hindutva'.

43. Ibid., p. 105.

44. Ibid.

45. Ibid.

46. Sarkar (1994), p. 101.

47. Strictly speaking, this is not the anti-secularist case, as it gives the impression of a causal connection. Their argument, in my view, will be that colonial modernity provides the conditions of possibility for the formation of a project like that of Hindutva.

48. Ibid., pp. 102–3.

49. Ibid., p. 103.

50. Ibid.

51. Ibid.

52. Ibid.

53. This is something he has repeated often. For a later reference, see Nandy (1998), p. 297, note 16.

54. Ibid., p. 102.

55. Bilgrami (1994), p. 1753.

56. Ibid., p. 1754.

57. Sarkar (1994), p. 106.

58. Bilgrami (1994) reprinted with postscript in Bhargava (1998), p. 403.

59. Ibid., p. 404.

60. Ibid.

61. Bhargava (1994).

62. Bhargava (1998), p. 495. This essay also incorporates Bhargava (1994).

63. Ibid., pp. 496-7.

64. Ibid., p. 513.

65. Ibid. The argument is developed in pp. 540-2.

66. Ibid., p. 520.

67. I use 'ideological' here in an Althusserian sense where it fulfils a practico-social purpose but not a theoretical function in knowledge. In Althusser's sense, 'Ideology changes...but imperceptibly, conserving its ideological form: it moves but with an *immobile motion* which maintains it *where it is...*', Althusser (1977), p. 142.

68. See Chatterjee (1994b), and Kaviraj (1992).

69. See for instance, Cohn (2001), especially the essay 'The Census, Social Structure and Objectification in South Asia', pp. 224–54. Also see Dirks (2003), especially Chapter 10, 'The Enumeration of Caste: Anthropology as Colonial Rule'.

70. This caption plays on an evocative phrase in Alam (1999b) where he says 'Modernity has a creeping sense of shame as it defends itself.'

71. Alam (1999b). See especially Chapter 1.

72. Alam (1998), 'Indispensability of Secularism', *Social Scientist*, vol. 27, nos. 7–8, July–Aug, p. 3.

73. Vanaik (1997), pp. 13–14.

74. Thompson (1991), p. 12.

4

The Impossible Nation
The Modern 'Indian' Self in Search of History

The nineteenth century in India aspired to political emancipation, social renovation, religious vision and rebirth, but it failed because it adopted Western motives and methods, ignored the spirit, history and destiny of our race and thought that by taking over European education, European machinery, European organization and equipment, we should reproduce European prosperity, energy and progress. *We of the twentieth century reject the aims, ideals and methods of the Anglicized nineteenth century* precisely because we accept its experience. *We refuse to make an idol of the present; we look before and after, backward to the mighty history of our race, forward to the grandiose destiny for which that history has prepared it.*

—Aurobindo Ghose[1]

Introduction

In this chapter, I will discuss the search of the Modern Indian Self—now Hindu, now Muslim, Dalit or Bengali, Tamil or Hindi—for History. I will argue that the very project of Indian nationalism was an impossible one, precisely because it was impossible to have one common history. The project of nationhood/nationalism, as we have discussed earlier, required the idea of a future destiny to be predicated on a common past—a past of common memories and common amnesia. In Aurobindo's eloquent words cited in the epigraph to this chapter, it called for a rejection of the present by 'looking before and after', 'backward to the mighty history of our race and forward to the grandiose destiny that that history has prepared for it.' Aurobindo was of course speaking for the nation as only a Hindu could. The histories of the different modern Selves as they emerge in the landmass called India we will see, belie the common image of different currents of movements merging into a common stream of anticolonialism. By simply privileging the history that the hegemonic construction of nationalism gave to the nation, we will be doing violence to the other aspirations that emerged during the course of the anticolonial struggle. If we have a Dalit or a Muslim history that is opposed to 'national history', the problem cannot be tackled by simply asserting the 'truth' of one history against that of the other. In fact, the residue of historicist notions of history, always in search of 'the truth', can become major obstacles in our understanding.[2] What we need to do therefore, is to problematize the very project of history understood as a search for that elusive Truth. I will indeed, suggest that the 'ground of history' may be an altogether inadequate, rather dangerous ground, for tackling the problems we are confronted with today. Choosing one version or one history over the other does not seem to offer a solution, for that still leaves us within the ground of history, defined as it is by a single linear temporality. If we were to recognize the existential validity of the multifarious experiences of the modern Indian Self—that of colonial subjugation and the civilizational defeat of large sections of the population of the subcontinent (experienced differently by Hindus and Muslims), alongside the simultaneous sense of empowerment that colonialism brings to hitherto enslaved populations *within the colonized, would-be nations*—how do we even begin to talk in terms of *a* historical and objective truth? I will look specifically at the historical imaginations at work among the Dalits and the Muslims in order to argue my case but the argument is in principle extendable to other such aspirations that emerged during the course of the anticolonial struggle. I will primarily look at some contemporary texts from amongst both Dalits and Muslims, that seek to reactivate older imaginations while trying to invest them with a meaning more in tune with contemporary concerns.

I should clarify at the outset that I am not going to be looking at the entire corpus of Dalit and Muslim writings and opinions. I am deeply aware of the fact that there were many different currents within all communities and there was never any single voice that 'represented' any community in its entirety. It is through the present therefore, that I enter the late nineteenth and early twentieth-century discourse in these communities in order to explore precisely what is left unexplored when we begin with the *a priori* assumption of a nation in existence. As I indicated in Chapter 1, my vantage point is to confront the past with the autobiography of not one but *two nations* that emerged at the end of the anticolonial struggle. From that vantage point one cannot treat the voice of the Muslim League simply as an illegitimate voice of a small north Indian elite, as nationalist historiography has tended to do. Even a scholar like Ayesha Jalal takes this position when she contends that 'the overweening idea of the religious community was more a figment of the imagination than a coterminous reality shared by its constituent elements.'[3] For at work in her narrative too, is the idea that 'what happened was a mistake':

'Simply put, the only way of imaginatively cohering two quite different sets of symbolisms in the construction of a single Indian nation was to abandon the dominant discourse on religiously based majority and minority communities derived from colonial categories of enumeration for one based on the ideals of common citizenship.'[4] Rather than assume the vantage point of such an archimedean critique—that of an ideal nation—my purpose will be to understand the logic that was pushing nationalist articulations within the two communities in the direction that they eventually took.

A brief digression may be in order here. There is a problem with a certain kind of deployment of a Foucauldian/Saidian critique of colonial discourse and governmental practices which argues, like Jalal does, that because of colonial enumeration practices, the identities that emerged were 'constructed' and 'invented' and were therefore bad/undesirable. This 'constructed' identity is then posed in opposition to a supposed 'correct identity' that should have undergirded nationalism, that is the ideal of democratic citizenship. Jalal might argue that even this form of nationalism would have to be imagined but that it would be '*the only way* of cohering' the two disparate communities into a single nation. It can be seen that it is the telos of the 'original' impulse of nationalism (that of democratic citizenship) that is at work here. A similar homology between invention/ imagination and falsity or negativity is discernable in Mushirul Hasan's account of Muslim history. So for instance, when he says that it was in the lanes and by-lanes of small towns that the 'myths, memories and divisive religious symbols were invented' to 'heighten communitarian conscious- ness', his reference point is the precolonial past when there had been 'common traditions and common reference points' which had not 'developed into the consolidated solidarities which 'Islam' or 'Hinduism' in the late nineteenth and early twentieth centuries came to signify.'[5] Clearly, both Jalal and Hasan accept some of the points made by historians about the imbrication of communitarian and nationalist politics in the practices of and knowledge produced by the colonial state, but they both seem to suggest identities/politics thus produced they were in some way artificial and certainly undesirable. While I would agree that these were undesirable from a 'secular' point of view, that does not make them any less real. Imagined communities are not unreal communities; rather in a manner of speaking, all communities are imagined, or as Balibar puts it, only imagined communities are real.[6] Hasan's main intellectual question is of course more self-consciously lodged within the Indian secular- nationalist framework that assumes a prior syncretism and then proceeds to ask 'why did a people with a long-standing history of shared living, respond to symbols of discord and disunity at a particular historical juncture?'[7] The implication here is not hard to see: harmony and shared living appear here as timeless features that are only interrupted at 'particular historical junctures'.

My point is not that there was no shared cultural ground between Hindus and Muslims but that it did not comprise the entire arena of intercommunity relations. At a purely theoretical level, a recognition of the absence of communal conflicts in the form they acquired in the nineteenth century, does not justify an assumption of total syncretism. Communities can in fact live together without entering into violent conflicts while at the same time nurturing suspicion and distrust of each other, or at the very least without engaging with each other. Ashis Nandy for instance has made this argument on a number of occasions.[8] Kaviraj has suggested the idea of 'back-to-back' communities as opposed to 'face-to-face' ones, in order to capture this possibility.[9] To that extent, C. A. Bayly's argument that 'the widespread Hindu-Muslim symbiosis of the pre-colonial and early colonial periods did not totally exclude the possibility of riot and disturbance along communal lines' does make sense.[10] I am not sure whether it can still be called 'communalism' in the sense that it came to acquire in the later period. However, the problem with Bayly's argument is that it forms a part of his larger attempt to demonstrate that both communalism and nationalism were continuous with their precolonial past; that colonialism in fact introduced no rupture in the way communities saw themselves. This is not, to my mind, a sustainable position, given the vast body of scholarly work that has been produced in recent decades. Nevertheless, in a limited way, it does make sense to claim that the nineteenth century did not produce communalism and nationalism out of thin air and that it was at least a possibility in the precolonial condition.[11] To that extent, we might argue that it was these different histories of communities and intercommunity relations that provided the ingredients for different imaginations of selfhood, which eventually led to different articulations of nationalism in Hindus and Muslims.

Let us return to the question of 'different voices' within the Muslims that we were discussing earlier. Mushirul Hasan laments that the voice of those who were patronizingly called 'nationalist Muslims' has been relegated to the status of a historian's footnote because of misplaced notions about Islam and nationalism and because of the insistence on projecting a monolithic Muslim community. His longstanding project therefore has been to foreground these 'so-called marginal voices among Muslims' to rewrite the histories of nationalism, communalism, and partition.[12] In a sense, Ayesha Jalal's project is also one of trying to establish that there were serious internal contestations of the Muslim League position and that it is wrong to posit a monolithic Muslim viewpoint. My point however, is that it is precisely the logic of the marginalization of these other voices that we need to focus upon. We need to ask why a voice like that of the Muslim League becomes so overpowering that all others are reduced to mere footnotes. In other words, the claim that 'there were many voices within the Muslims' is not enough; the question of the hegemony of one particular voice will have to be seriously addressed.

The marginalization of the so-called nationalist Muslims is even more significant when we consider the fact that in religious-theological terms they were the ones who stood for the more 'authentic' Islam. Be it the Ulema of Deoband, the Jamiat-Ul-Ulama-I-Hind, or Maulana Abul Kalam Azad, or Zafar Ali Khan of Punjab, the apparent irony has not escaped scholars that it was the 'more culturally exclusive' Muslims, believers in Islamic universalism, who comprised the bulk of nationalist Muslims. This is the paradox that Ziya-ul-Hasan Faruqi, in his study of the Deoband school, also sets out to explore: why did this school which was traditionalist to the core and was 'founded with the express purpose of preserving the "Shari'ah"' throw in its lot with Indian nationalism rather than lead the struggle for achieving Pakistan?[13] Faruqi's answer was that the Deoband Ulema did not trust the modernist Aligarh-followers spearheading the movement for Pakistan as they felt that Islam would not be safe their hands. He also contends that it was their concern for the millions of Muslims who would be left behind, that held them back.[14]

Ayesha Jalal too, remarks on the fact that it was the traditionalists 'who steeped themselves in religious strictures at *madarsas* and *maktabs* only to end up squarely on the side of an inclusionary and "secular" Indian nationalism.'[15] However, despite this sharply posed contradiction Jalal does not follow through the implications of this paradox. I suggest that we cannot understand this apparent paradox except in the context of the modernist investment in the idea of homogeneous nationhood that led to a specific articulation of the Muslim League communitarian discourse culminating in Pakistan.[16] The desire for a homogenous, territorially defined nation itself is at the root of the idea that 'religions had to be territorially specific', as the poet-philosopher Iqbal pointed out.[17] In this passage cited by Jalal, Iqbal criticizes the idea of nationhood and insists that religion must take precedence over nationalism. This assertion is made

presumably in the context of the Hindu nationalist insistence that the
Muslims' territorial loyalties be clearly defined. Writing in early 1938, a
couple of years *before* the Muslim League declaration that henceforth 'all
future constitutional negotiations [have] to proceed on the principle that
Indian Muslims are a nation', Iqbal could possibly retain this distinction
between religion and nationalism.[18] Later his own adherence to religion
would be tied to the territoriality of the new Muslim homeland and he
would have no problem in adopting nationalism as a fundamental creed.
To the theologically inclined Islamic universalist Muslims, on the other
hand, probably the community meant something very different—that of
a territorially unbounded community of believers, not necessarily tied to
the project of nationhood. To many of them this community did not
necessarily stand in sharp opposition to the question of Hindu–Muslim
unity. Of course, it should be remembered that *even this position* is not a
purely theologically derived one but possibly formulated under the pressures
of the anticolonial struggle. For, Islam being a proselytizing religion, it
might have liked to see the whole world turn to its notion of a universal
community.

   In the next section, I will focus primarily on some voices from Pakistan
that seem to me to express an entirely different narrative of the inner
world of early twentieth-century north Indian Muslims. I am aware that
like all narratives, these too cannot be invested with an 'objective' truth
value. However, they do articulate what can be called an 'existential truth'.
What I have said for Muslim voices also holds for Dalit voices in a different
way. In other words, the point is not whether there were more Dalits behind
the Congress than behind Ambedkar, for what Ambedkar was articulating
is what defines the Dalit contemporary today.

   After the section on the Dalit and Muslim relationship with the emerging
nation, I will discuss the question of the subjectivity of the colonized. In
the context of the civilizational defeat of subjugated populations, which
forms a very important part of the experience of colonization, I will
consider some of the writings from Africa, particularly those of Albert
Memmi, Aime Cesaire, and Frantz Fanon. I will do this because their
articulation of the constitution of the colonized subject throws up some
vital insights that also speak to our experience. Finally, through a reading
of the Gandhi-Ambedkar-Savarkar relationship, I will try to focus on the
experience of the previously enslaved populations who found a liberator
in colonialism.

Divergent Histories, Different Selves

Marking the beginning of the new millennium, the *Pioneer* brought out a 12-page supplement titled 'the Dalit Millennium', compiled by some leading Dalit intellectuals.[19] Containing contributions by many non-Dalit intellectuals as well, this supplement carried a remarkable list of what can be called milestone events in the history of Dalit liberation.[20] Among the events of the last five hundred years, the chronology begins with the discovery of the sea route to India and the advent of Vasco da Gama in 1498. This event, it is claimed, opened the way for the eventual contact with the West that led not just to the colonization of the country but exposed it eventually to the ideas of equality and liberty and opened the way for Dalit liberation. Among the other important early events, the raising of the Mahar regiment by the East India Company in 1799 is considered crucial.[21] For many a nationalist this event may be counted among the numerous instances of disunity and betrayal by fellow Indians, that helped usher in the British colonizers. The third event of considerable interest for us is the decree issued by the court of directors of the East India Company, extending education to all castes, including untouchables. A very different reading of the Macaulayan moment of colonial rule, immensely problematic in many other ways, can be seen here.[22]

It is interesting to compare this chronology with the milestones of the 'freedom struggle' as produced by nationalism and nationalist historiography. If the boycott of the Simon Commission is seen as a major landmark and is routinely represented as an occasion where the 'entire nation' rose as one person to oppose the all-white commission's very constitution, we find leaders like Periyar and Ambedkar deposing before it and cooperating in its proceedings. It is remembered as an important aspect of their activity and Ambedkar's testimonies to the commission form a proud part of his collected works. Similarly, if the 1942 Quit India movement is written in the mythology of nationalism in 'letters of gold', it fails to find even a mention in the chronology of Dalit liberation mentioned above. Nor for that matter do events like the non-cooperation movement and the civil disobedience movement. So radical is the difference between the two histories that it is simply not possible to see them as 'different readings' of an otherwise common history—the history of the nation. While it may be possible to see the Congress, the Communist, and the Muslim League versions of history as different interpretations of what were certain common markers of the anticolonial, nationalist struggle, no such reading seems possible here. We cannot but see these as *two different histories*, of two different subjects. The common image of different streams merging into a common anti-imperialist current cannot be sustained here for there are two different histories, moving on different planes, and almost, in opposite directions to each other. Although Ambedkar did refer on occasion to the untouchables as a separate element *in* 'national life', there seems to be little that can make it possible to read the two histories as part of the same 'History of the Nation'.

Reading the passage from Aurobindo in the epigraph to this chapter, in the light of this discussion on the divergent histories of the nation and its repressed, enslaved 'untouchable' people, it is difficult to escape something striking about the relationship of time and Selfhood. If Aurobindo, the voice of the hegemonic twentieth century, rejects the ideas, aims, and methods of the nineteenth century as being entirely derivative of the European, it is because he can see in both the nineteenth and the twentieth centuries, only one singular voice, one single indivisible subject—the Nation. And so he vehemently asserts that 'we refuse to make an idol of the present', for the present is that of colonial subjugation, of humiliating civilizational defeat. The greatness of the nation lies in the hoary past, the past that nationalism must now resurrect so as to claim the future, the 'grandiose destiny' for which that past has prepared it. For Ambedkar and Periyar, on the other hand, as we saw and will discuss at greater length in Chapter 5, it is precisely the present that represents the moment of liberation. And this present, for them, is also the twentieth century—a different twentieth century perhaps, from that of Aurobindo and the nationalists. The past, to them is simply the story of an unmitigated enslavement and repression; the future must not be allowed to lapse back into the past.[23] The present moment must be seized precisely to turn around the direction of history, *away* from that which Aurobindo and the nationalists thought the past had prepared for 'the nation'. In fact, at crucial moments in the history of the anticolonial struggle, Ambedkar privileges the present, refusing steadfastly to defer the question of Dalit liberation to any future that will be called in unnegotiated.

It is interesting that while the history of the Muslims shows no such *apparent* divergence, there are fascinating imaginations at work there, which have been all but subsumed under the deposits of secular and nationalist historiography. After all, it was the Hindu–Muslim question that occupied the secular-nationalist creed most; all attempts were therefore directed at demonstrating a common heritage and a syncretic tradition, as well as a common striving for the independence of the future nation. The Muslim League appears in this kind of narrative as an irritant, best forgotten, because difficult to deal with. How does one square it with the story of syncretism and timeless harmony between the two communities? Therefore, after the arrival of nationalism as a specific ideological configuration in the late nineteenth century, if we go by the canons of secular-nationalist historiography, Hindu–Muslim tensions were mere teething problems of a nation that was growing up. Yet it seems this kind of a reading obscures what was going on in the Muslim mind prior to the nationalist moment, from the early nineteenth century onwards and which continued to find a powerful articulation in the Muslim League subsequently. To get a sense of this Muslim mind, let us briefly look at the following narrative from what is claimed to be a 'first full-length biography of Mohamed Ali in English', written by a Pakistani scholar.[24] Based on painstaking research through government records and private papers, the account is also self-consciously a reconstruction of the 'hope, fears and aspirations of Muslim India from 1778 to 1931.'[25] The biography, it is interesting to note, was written during the Indo-Pakistan War in December 1971, when the author 'was feeling deeply depressed.' The attempt at reconstruction therefore, must have been mediated by innumerable factors, not the least of which would have been an urge to explore the many questions about the Muslim Self that the imminent break-up of Pakistan must have been posing. I use this text by Afzal Iqbal because it seems to offer a coherent narrative of various aspects of a 'history' whose discrete events are, nevertheless, corroborated by other accounts as well. It also affords us a peep into a discursive universe not easily available to the English-speaking secular world, at least in India.

Afzal Iqbal begins his narrative with the assertion that for nearly a thousand years, till the reign of Bahadur Shah Zafar, Muslims had been living in India as rulers. It was only after the 'Mutiny' of 1857, into which Bahadur Shah was dragged against his will, that 'for the first time in their history, Muslims began to live with Hindus as subjects of an alien power.' 'Both Hindus and Muslims had rallied around his person in their last desperate bid to resist the onslaught of the British—the Oudh Taluqdars, the Jhansi Sardars, the Nana, the Mughal Princes, the Maulvi of Fyzabad, *but Muslims alone were held responsible for this revolt and suffered in consequence at the hands of the new rulers.*' He then goes on to catalogue the 'deep differences' that divide the Hindus and the Muslims and adds:

History intensified this sense of difference. The Muslims *remembered that they were once the ruling people.* Never had India been so powerful and prosperous, so well governed, or so famous throughout the world as in the days of Muslim rule, especially that of the Mughals. While Hinduism was confined to the land of its origin, Islam stretched far beyond the bounds of India across the Middle East to the Mediterranean and along its southern shore to the Atlantic, and Muslim civilization in India had been enriched by scholars and artists coming to the Mughal courts from other quarters of the Muslim world and by the cultural traditions of Teheran, Cairo, Baghdad and Granada.[26]

What is striking about this narrative, is of course, the identification of 1857 ('the Mutiny') as marking the 'Fall' from a period when the glory of world Islam was at its peak. Another Pakistani scholar, Muhammad Yusuf Abbasi, observes in a more poetic vein that

The year 1857 runs like a stream of blood, across the chronological landscape of the 19th century, dividing the history of Muslim politics in the South Asian subcontinent into to almost equal segments. The Indian uprising of 1857, in its essence, was the last desperate attempt of the Muslims to redeem their independence from the steady encroachment of the British East India Company...[27]

Thus, the '1857' that was retrospectively produced in the annals of the Nation as the 'First Indian War of Independence', following Marx's celebrated description and Savarkar's use of it, is referred to here by two Muslim scholars, more than a century later, with considerable regret by one (Bahadur Shah Zafar was 'dragged into the mutiny against his will') and despair by the other.[28] In Abbasi's account as in Iqbal's, there is considerable anguish about the fact that though the rebellion was a Hindu–Muslim affair, the British rulers singled out the Muslims for persecution.[29] Iqbal goes on to make laboured efforts to prove that the mutiny was not simply a Muslim affair. This exercise is incomprehensible from the point of view of nationalism. After all, it would have been all too easy to claim the 'First War of Independence' as the proof *par excellence*, of the nationalist credentials of the Muslims. At the very least, it could have been a proud chapter of the history of Pakistan. Iqbal however, does not do that and we shall soon see why. On the other hand, interestingly, we find in the passage from his account above, the gesture to a different history, that of the history of Islam and the glory of its India chapter. The author in fact, later refers to the 'catastrophe of 1857', following which the Muslims found themselves a 'defeated, frustrated and a leaderless community.'[30] It was in this condition, post-1857, that Sir Syed Ahmed found the Indian Muslim community. But why *was* 1857 such a catastrophe? Was it simply because the Muslims were made to pay for the revolt by the new rulers? The narrative of the author provides another view:

From 1830, when the French penetrated North Africa, the Muslims of Morocco, Algeria, Tunisia and Tripolitania had turned their eyes towards Turkey...

In the north-east sector of the Islamic world, the conquest of the Turkish Muslim states was being consummated by Russia. By the 1850s and 1860s, the Khans of these States had begun sending emissaries to the Caliph in search of interest and help ... In the south-east, as Toynbee points out, a sentimental attachment to an idealized conception of the Ottoman Empire began to appear— among the Indian Muslim diaspora—Shia as well as Sunni—as a psychological compensation, for the loss of their former imperial dominion to the British. The Ottoman Empire was, indeed the only political rallying point on which the Muslim victims of Western and Russian imperialism could fall back ... Even in her nineteenth century infirmity, Turkey was by far and away the most powerful, efficient and enlightened Muslim state in existence.[31]

It is in this string of events that the author situates 1857: 'the Crimean War, the Indian 'Mutiny', the conquests of Britain, France, and Russia in Muslim lands...'. Here the event called 1857 appears as *an event in a different history*—that of the worldwide defeat of Islam. In that history, 'the causes of the decline of Islam were to be sought, not in any internal weaknesses or defects, *but in the aggressive imperialism of Christian Europe.*'[32] It is because 1857 is part of this history of defeat, rather than that of the Nation, that it represents such a catastrophe. It was in this rather different historical imagination of the religio-political community of Islam, that the first responses of the north Indian Muslim elites of the colonial period were lodged. This is a question I will return to later in this chapter.

For the present, we may note that what was being understood by the nineteenth-century Muslim intelligentsia as the history of the defeat of Islam, can equally be read as the history of colonialism and imperialism. Islam being a world religion had to confront imperialism in many different countries, in different continents. Unlike Dalit history, however, this history does converge with the history of nationalism and moves alongside thereafter, before fissures finally become unbridgeable and they diverge, once more into two separate nation-states.[33] This story of its coming together and eventual separation has quite often been told in terms of the machinations of the different players on both sides. What is probably not recognized, and what I intend to underline, is that the very form of the nation presents an imperative of having a singular History and that doomed any possibility of coming together. I also wish to argue that the rampant xenophobia or heterophobia that marks anticolonial nationalisms cannot be understood as aberrations, but as inherently constitutive features produced by the experience of colonial subjugation.

The 'discovery' of 'History' as a part of the project of the European Enlightenment, was the 'discovery' of a certain mode of recalling and writing about the past that was supposed to be 'objective and verifiable'. The liberatory dimension of History, however, was as much in its claim to objectivity and verifiability, as it was in the *idea of History as change*: the idea that history was a dynamic process where nothing was eternal and given, nothing was immune to change. The far-reaching consequence of this conception was buttressed by its claim to scientificity as it could claim a counter, scientific truth to its versions as opposed to the theologically sanctioned versions that could only see human society as maintaining the eternal order of God. History then became the battleground where major emancipatory battles were first fought out, before they were translated into political struggles. So it was with Indian nationalism. In Sudipta Kaviraj's words, in nineteenth century discourse, 'history breaks out everywhere' and we see the insistence all round and everywhere, on the need to have a history.[34] Recent developments in thought have however, seriously problematized this idea that history is really a truthful and objective account of the past. It is now generally acknowledged that there is really no 'objective history' that can tell us about the past in an unprejudiced way. It is rather, that at each turn of the present, human collectivities produce narratives of history, meant primarily to serve the present. Accounts of the past are, therefore, continuously re-written with the changing demands of the present. The other, related problem was that the idea of History could not make sense without a subject; it had to have a subject *whose history* had to be written. With the new imperatives of a nation coming-to-be, the subject most suited for the post was this imagined nation. This is precisely where the problem lay. For, the nation did not already exist, but was in the process of being constructed. The possibility, therefore, was open for many candidates to lay claim, *as nations*, to the ground of history. Each produced its own version and what is more, produced it as truth, backed by scientific evidence. Further, its earlier version as a scientific discipline, having arrogated to itself the sole authority of speaking of the past, and having de-legitimized other ways of doing so, set in place a certain mode, in which it becomes possible not merely for emancipatory discourses to be articulated but also for the most xenophobic 'settling-of-past-accounts' kind of discourses to make their appearance. The myriad ways in which this happens is, of course, tied closely to the constitution of the subject under conditions of colonial domination. We therefore need to understand this process of constitution of the colonized subject.

The Constitution of the Subjectivity
of the Colonized

Tunisian writer-theorist Albert Memmi, in his *The Colonizer and the Colonized*, talks of two ways in which the subjectivity of the colonized is negatively marked. These I will call, after him, (i) the *social and historical mutilation* of the colonized; in his words, their denial for centuries, their 'exclusion from history, community and citizenship'[35]—a denial into which is written their difference. (ii) *The cultural schizophrenia* that lies at the heart of the constitution of the colonial/postcolonial subject. This schizophrenia is most marked in the phenomenon of bilingualism—the condition that means living in 'two psychical and cultural realms'.[36]

Memmi says of this colonized subject: 'But who is he? *Surely not man in general, the holder of universal values common to all men.* In fact, he has been excluded from that universality, both in word and in fact. On the contrary, what makes him different from other men has been sought out and hardened to the point of substantiation...To expect the colonized to open his mind to the world and be a humanist and internationalist would seem to be ludicrous thoughtlessness. He is still regaining possession of himself, still examining himself with astonishment, passionately demanding the return of his language.'[37] This, argues Memmi, is at the heart of the xenophobia and racism of the colonized, including all unjust aggressions towards others. In a sense, this is our point of departure.

Memmi delineates two moments of the constitution of this colonized subject, when he talks of two historically possible ways of realization of this subjectivity. The *first moment* of this constitution is mimetic, when the colonized native mimics and emulates the colonial master. The *second moment* of this constitution could be called the moment of epiphany or self-realization. This is the moment when the colonized asserts his/her difference and can be said to coincide with her elaboration of the idea of nationhood.

In a somewhat similar fashion, Frantz Fanon demarcates three phases of this process. In the first phase, he suggests, 'the native intellectual gives proof that he has assimilated the culture of the occupying power...His inspiration is European...' In the second phase, 'the native is disturbed; he *decides to remember what he is.*'[38] But here lies the catch. For, 'since the native is not a part of his people, since he only has exterior relations with his people, he is content to recall their life only. Past happenings of the bygone days of his childhood will be brought up out of the depths of his memory; old legends will be reinterpreted in the light of a borrowed aestheticism and of a conception of the world which was discovered under other skies.'[39] This is why, Chidi Amuta observes, the second 'phase of cultural reaffirmation' is 'characterized by unbridled traditionalism and even ancestor worship.'[40] The third phase described by Fanon, that of a national-revolutionary struggle, is really only the continuation of this second phase.

In a remarkable way, the passage from Aurobindo above sums up these two moments in the Indian context. The Europhile nineteenth century that he has in mind is the moment of mimesis. The twentieth century, when Aurobindo discovers himself and drops his anglicized middle name[41], coincides with the Gandhian return to the sources. The Gandhi who went to England to study law, who tried to learn playing the violin, and dressed like an English gentleman, eventually 'discovers' his roots there. He hears the English translation of the *Bhagwad Gita* in England through his contact with two theosophist brothers; he discovers Hinduism through contact with Madame Blavatsky's Theosphist discourses and vegetarianism through a vegetarian's manual written by an Englishman[42]. If Aurobindo delved into the yogic-spiritual world to discover the great spiritual wealth of ancient India after his return from England, Gandhi shed his Western attire and donned the loin-cloth on his return from South Africa. 'Mohammed Ali, with his excellent Western education and towering personality' according to one scholar, 'grew a beard, figured as a Maulana and became the first Muslim leader of the Muslim masses.'[43] To none of the intellectual leaders of Indian nationalism, did 'tradition' come without a search—even Nehru had to 'discover' his India.

What is remarkable in the proposal of the Memmi–Fanon thesis is that not only is the first moment of mimesis determined by the experience of colonial subjugation, it is precisely the moment when the colonized elite/intellectual 'discovers' him/herself, is s/he constituted by 'conceptions of the world...discovered under other skies.' In a sense, it is what Partha Chatterjee has called the 'moment of departure' of Indian nationalism that represents the most problematic part of its enterprise. Put differently, the reconstitution of Selfhood, the urge for political liberation and of self-determination, was already being defined by the parameters laid out by the colonial encounter. All the responses were irretrievably lodged within them and there was no longer an 'innocent pre-colonial self' in existence any more. And the colonial encounter was no benign dialogue: its terms had already been set by the fact of domination—a relation of domination and power that manifests itself in language, religion, thought, and culture, in the widest sense. In this context, it is worth pursuing Fanon's highly suggestive idea that the 'colonized *decides to* remember what he is'. For here in this predicament of the uprooted native intellectual, is rooted the problem of history and memory. The native actually has no memory of his/her past, except in very different ways, through folklore and myths. When the native actually decides to remember what s/he is, what are the resources s/he draws upon? What are the resources available? If we go through the immense amount of scholarship of recent years, we can see not only that the conceptions with which s/he goes about discovering and re-interpreting her past, as recounted by Fanon, are ones discovered under other skies; more importantly, *the very idea of the past is now different*. Kaviraj suggests that this nineteenth century 'hunger for history'—embodied in Bankim's famous lament that 'unless Bengalis had a history, they would not become human beings', was not for a history in the general ontological sense, which they surely had; 'what they require(d) was an *account*, mortifying and uplifting'. They required a narrative to put some significant order into the disparate facts of their past than they already had.[44] But this was not all. *What they needed to recall of the past*, now differed fundamentally from that of earlier times. One of the crucial differences Kaviraj has suggested is encapsulated in his idea of an enumerated community: 'it might never occur to members of these [non-enumerated, fuzzy] communities to ask how many of them there were...in the world.'[45] For, with enumeration came the fixation of identity and with it the notions of majority and minority. It was this newly-fixed identity that most often required a historical account of itself—and one that distinguished it from others. These new identities were fixed, as we now know, through the processes of colonial censuses and its related anthropology. The very ideas of Selfhood, in other words, were now implicated in the practices of the colonial state.

To recognize that nationalism, and in fact, other constructions of Selfhood, were constituted through this colonial encounter, is not to argue that thereby these different Selves had no agency or are 'robbed of all agency', as Sumit Sarkar puts it. It is rather to open up the possibility of exploring the particular formation of nationalism and its aggressive fear of the Other, that frames these discourses. It is to open up the possibilities of exploration of the complicated ways in which subjectivity comes to be constituted. After all, it is this frame of mind, that of a defeated civilization, that makes it possible for the nationalists to stifle all urges for internal reform, often with the aid of the colonial state. It is this mindset that underlies the mass mobilization on the Age of Consent Bill in the first act of nationalist defiance; it is this again that frames the opposition of the likes of Tilak to the holding of the Social Reform Conference simultaneously with Congress sessions in 1897—instances which Ambedkar commented upon with considerable sarcasm.

However, there is a problem that needs to be explored further, if we take the above description of the constitution of the colonial subject seriously. Clearly, a major transformation that takes place in the conception of selfhood that accounts for the move to the moment of self-realization. What does the transformation consist in? I think the problem can be broken down into two distinct questions. Firstly, what kind of notions of Self make the moment of mimesis possible? Secondly, what is it that makes possible the transition to modern notions of selfhood and national self-respect?

To take the first question first, that is: what notions of Selfhood make this mimesis possible? There are at least two available ways in which this can be understood. One of them can be derived from Michael Taussig's explorations of Western/Swedish ethnologies of healing practices among Cuna Indians in the erstwhile Columbia in Central America. Taussig takes up the problem posed by the discovery of the existence of wooden figurines used by them because 'all these wooden figures represent European types, and to judge by the type of clothes, are from the eighteenth and possibly the seventeenth century.'[46] Taussig observes on the basis of various sources that there are strong reasons to believe that these figurines are the creation of recent times. There are some larger-than-life figures in existence that were used for the exorcism of entire populations and communities. One of these, for instance, 'in the late 1940s was said by an American visitor to be a seven-foot likeness of General Douglas MacArthur.'[47] Taussig draws on Walter Benjamin's idea of the mimetic faculty in order to develop his idea of *mimesis as alterity*. Benjamin argues that mimicry, especially the capacity for producing similarities, is the highest in man and this faculty 'is nothing other than a rudiment of the powerful compulsion in former times to become and behave like something else.'[48] According to Taussig, Benjamin's fascination with mimesis flows from three considerations, namely alterity, primitivism, and the resurgence of mimesis with modernity. Taussig links this idea of the 'rudiment of primitivism', born out of an experience of alterity, with another practice common in non-modern societies: the idea of capturing spirits of such 'others' in inanimate figures and statues as also a means of containing the possible harm they may be able to render. What enhances the mimetic faculty, according to him, 'is a protean self with multiple images...of itself, set in a natural environment whose animals, plants and elements are spiritualized to the point that nature "speaks back" to the humans, every material entity paired with an occasionally visible spirit-double of itself.'[49]

Taussig further links the idea of mimesis with the colonial experience and notes that 'mimesis as fact and as epistemic moment can be understood as redolent with the trace of that *space between*, a colonial space par excellence, a windswept Fuegian[50] space where mankind bottoms out into fairy tale, metamorphoses with children and animals, so mimesis becomes an enactment not merely *of* an original but *by* an original.'[51] What Taussig is interested in here is not the impulse to copy but the power of the copy to actually influence the copied, the represented. That, however, does not concern us here. Two things follow from his discussion: (1) that mimesis can be seen as a way in which many non-modern, 'primitive' peoples deal with otherness and (2) the context of colonialism provides the context of an unprecedented encounter with an unprecedentedly alien Other. Clearly missing from here is any sense of an 'individual' self. And overarchingly present is the conception of a yet-enchanted world of spirits and magic.

The other way of understanding the question of conditions of possibility of mimesis can be extracted from a discussion in Partha Chatterjee on the 'arrival' of modern historiography and earlier modes of recalling the past. Chatterjee presents a detailed reading of an early nineteenth-century text by a Brahmin scholar by the name of Mrityunjay Vidyalankar. This text, *Rajabali* (1808) was commissioned by Fort William College, and was meant to educate company officials and later-day colonial administrators about the land and the people they were to rule. Mrityunjay himself taught Sanskrit at the college. As the name suggests, the account produced by him was a story of the 'Rajas and Badshahs and Nawabs who have occupied the throne in Delhi and Bengal.'[52] According to Chatterjee, Mrityunjay basically drew on existing accounts in circulation at that time among the Brahmin literati. It can therefore be treated as representative 'of the historical memory of elite Bengali society' at the time. Mrityunjay begins his account by demarcating the geographical space of which he is writing, as well as the time period he is going to cover. The temporal sequence begins with the advent of Kaliyuga, during which he claims 4,267 years have elapsed and there have been 119 Hindu kings of different jatis, in this period, to adorn the throne of Delhi. Kshatriyas ruled for 1,812 years followed by the Nandas or the Rajputs, in turn followed by the Buddhist kings ending with the rule of Prithviraj Chauhan.

After this began the *samrajya* of the Musalman. From the beginning of the empire of the Yavanas to the present year 1726 of the Saka era, fifty one kings have ruled for 651 years three months and twenty-eight days.

Chatterjee draws our attention to the notion of time that underlies this narrative, where 'myth, history and the contemporary become part of the same chronological sequence; one is not distinguished from another.' This and the way in which the 'historical value' of Puranic accounts is treated, places Mrityunjay's 'historical allegiances' entirely in the precolonial. And in this historical memory, untouched as yet by modern historiographical practices, it is really interesting to note how the transition from Hindu to Muslim rule is dealt with. On Chatterjee's rendering of Mrityunjay's account, Prithviraj's father had two wives, one of whom was a demoness who ate human flesh and who introduced her husband also to the evil practice. One day she ate the son of the other queen who then fled to take refuge with her brother. There Prthu was born. When he grew up, he killed his father, ostensibly on his father's own request, and fed his flesh to twenty-one women belonging to his jati. 'Because he had killed his father, the story of his infamy spread far and wide. Kings who paid him tribute stopped doing so.' Thus was his rule de-legitimized. And then Shihabuddin Ghuri threatened to attack him. On hearing of the threatening moves of the Yavanas, the king called a number of scholars learned in the Vedas, to perform a sacrifice to 'dissipate the prowess of the threat'. The plan was laid out and the time for it fixed but the scholars realized that it was not going to work. The sacrificial block (*yupa*) that was to be laid could not be moved to its assigned place. At this they told the king:

[W]hat Isvara desires happens. Men cannot override his wishes, but can only act in accordance with them. So, desist in your efforts. It seems this throne will be attacked by the Yavanas.

Nevertheless, Prithviraj, disheartened though he was, fought Shihabuddin, but says Mrityunjay, 'by the grace of Isvara, the Yavana Sahabuddin made a prisoner of Prthuraja.' Mrityunjay repeats the same explanatory logic in relation to the rule of the 'Company Bahadur': 'the Supreme Lord willed that the rule of the Company Bahadur be established.'

This narrative as Chatterjee notes, is based on a notion of divine will and the question of who rules and when is entirely a matter of divine dispensation. Lesser mortals can and must do nothing but obey God's wish. History, in this understanding of the *Puranas* and the *Itihasas*, is about the kings, rajas, and nawabs who rule by carrying out His wish. When they lose His favours, they must make way for others whom He appoints. So, Chatterjee observes that 'if it was ever suggested to Mrityunjay that in the story of the deeds and fortunes of the kings of Delhi might lie the history of the nation, it is doubtful that he would have understood.'

After this text authored by a Brahmin Hindu scholar, Chatterjee offers another, slightly later text by a Bengali Muslim from Barisal, by the name of Munshi Alimuddin, to show how the same explanatory logic governs this narrative derived from presumably different sources. Alimuddin narrates the end of Muslim rule with the last dynasty of 'Shah Alam Bahadur' thus:

Suddenly by a miracle (*daiva*), the English came to this land
And defeated the Nawab in battle.
The English occupied most of the kingdom:
Since then there is the rule of Maharani Victoria.

He continues with a description of that rule:

The people are governed with full justice.
In her reign, the praja have no complaints.
Cowries have been abolished; now
People buy what they need with coins.
People exchange news through mail.
The towns are now lit with gaslights.
The steamer has vanquished the pinnace and the sailboat.
The railway has reduced a week's journey to hours.
In Calcutta they can find out what's happening in England
In a matter of moments—with the help of the wire.

It is interesting that the narrative of Munshi Alimuddin not only makes it possible to understand the rule of 'maharani Victoria' in the light of the idea of divine will; it also shows how the far-reaching transformation of life with the intimations of modernity that come with it, were likewise accepted with wonder: People have justice, the *praja* (the tenants) have no complaint; and the wonders of technology have accelerated pace, reducing the temporal dimension of life in an exhilarating way.

The notions of Selfhood that underlie these narratives and the accompanying ways of looking at the world are those of non-individuated, non-modern selves. They are notions in which the world only makes sense as God's wish. The ordinary folk, the subjects, must not question his designs but rather accept them with grace. If the British conquered India and ruled over it, that too was His wish and the subjects must treat the new rulers as their own. It is within such a worldview that Munshi Alimuddin can sing paeans to 'maharani Victoria' or Mrityunjay welcome the rule of the 'Company Bahadur'. It is in this sense that this notion of Self opens the possibility of mimesis.

It is from this notion of Selfhood, marked by an absence of both notions of individuality and of a collective subject such as the nation, that the transformation to the moment of epiphany or self-discovery takes place. It is this transformation, the 'decision to remember one's past', the hunger for alternative narratives, that underlies the search of the modern 'Indian' Selves' for History. We arrive now at the second question I outlined earlier— what makes possible the transition to modern notions of selfhood.

History, Memory, and Narrative

Let us recall the passage quoted above from the Pakistani scholar, Afzal Iqbal. Talking of Hindu-Muslim differences, he says '*History intensified* this sense of difference. The Muslims *remembered that they were once the ruling people*.' It is almost as if we can read Fanon's description of the second phase, the moment of epiphany, in this description. But what is more, on this account, it is 'history' that inaugurates the self-understanding of loss. It was not 'history' in the sense simply of *the past*, or what Kaviraj calls 'history in the ontological sense', but rather *an account of the past*, a narrative of past greatness and subsequent loss, that intensified this difference. Before this moment, this 'greatness' or its loss did not matter in any significant way; the *intensification* is a function of this newfound 'remembrance'. The melancholia that had gripped the north Indian Muslim elite after 1857 was intensified through further defeats and the collapse of the Ottoman empire. If 1857 was, among other things, a story of the defeat of the Indian Muslim rulers—in a chain of worldwide defeats—the Balkan wars were to put the final seal on the chapter of the end of Islamic glory. Iqbal remarks that the 'shock of the Balkan defeats was intense.' He continues:

The Bulgar, the Serb, the Greek, Turkey's subjects for five centuries, had inflicted an ignominious defeat on it. This reality, the Muslims in Turkey and their brothers in India could not conjure up even in their imagination. Mohamed Ali tried to run away from this reality by attempting to commit suicide.[53]

According to Abbasi, it was the struggle in defence of the Khilafat that 'enlivened the Muslim mind' at this juncture: '(T)he awareness of a common destiny enlivened the Muslim mind and constituted a defence mechanism which buoyed them up amidst the disasters that engulfed them in the aftermath of 1857.'[54] However, the claim of the Ottoman Sultan 'to be the Caliph of all Muslims', according to Iqbal, was relatively new.

Since the end of the classical Caliphate in the first century of Islam, there had been no single universally recognized head of the Islamic community. Each monarch was a Caliph in his own realm. The assertion of such authority beyond a Sultan's frontier was a departure for the first time since the fall of the Abbasids, to establish a universal Islamic leadership and to claim it for the house of Usman.[55]

This status, according to him, was conferred by the Treaty of Kucuk Kaynarca, as late as July 1774. In other words, this was neither ancient tradition, nor actually had a religious sanction. Yet, the imagination of a world community of Islam became centred on this Caliphate and was to become the rallying point of the highly charged creed of pan-Islamism. So much so that Abadi Bano Abdul Ali Begum, the mother of the Ali brothers, writing to Annie Besant in December 1917, on the eve of the Khilafat Movement, stated that the 'spiritual allegiance to their ruler [i.e. of the Moslems of Turkey] is not a political creed that each of us is free to hold or to discard without prejudice to his salvation hereafter...' She was clear that '*it is a religious doctrine that is the essence of our faith...*'[56]

The point here is that these were the mental pre-occupations of the Muslim elite in northern India in the nineteenth and early twentieth centuries. It is the erstwhile ruling elite with its identification with the ruling elites elsewhere in the Muslim world, that becomes the vehicle of this new imagination. Such ideas were not available to 'Muslims' in general, especially not to Muslims who were yet untouched by 'history' and historical consciousness. Among these too, through the nineteenth century, there are Islamic reform movements, the two most important being the Wahhabi movement with influence in large parts of the country, and the Faraizi movement, concentrated in the districts of East Bengal.[57] These movements too, were clearly sectarian in their theological insistence on the purity of Islamic faith and on the need to overcome the 'bad influence' of Hindus and Europeans on their faith. However, what is absent in all these is a sense of an 'all-India' community of Muslims, not to speak of the historical consciousness of being part of a worldwide pan-Islamic one. Also absent in them was any sense of having once been a ruling elite.

The concerns of most of these movements were rooted in the conditions of the peasantry under the regime of the East India Company.[58] The Wahhabi movement at the all-India level, initiated by Sayyid Ahmad Barelvi (1786–1831), viewed India under British rule as a *Daru'l Harb*, or the land of the enemy and therefore advocated emigration or self-exile (*hijrat*), in order to be able to conduct war (*jehad*) against the British. This section of the Wahhabis had acted as the precursors of the so-called Mutiny, and they participated in the rising of 1857 in a significant way.[59] Noted historian K.M. Ashraf sums up the contradictory impulses of the movement saying 'the Wahhabi outlook on politics and religious life embodied the century-old hostility of the Muslim ruling classes to the growing encroachments of the British, as also the urgings of the working masses for better and happier conditions of life.'[60] Both the Wahhabi and the Faraizi movements responded to the complicated class conflict with the mainly Hindu landlords in almost religious-fanatic terms. For instance, groups of Wahhabi Muslim *raiyats* retaliating against a tax on beards imposed by a Hindu zamindar, went around killing cows and desecrating Hindu temples with their blood.[61] The issues here were, however, not even remotely connected to that other history we see in the elite imagination of north Indian Muslims. Similarly, consider the Mappila (Moplah) revolts in the Malabar region of what is now Kerala. From 1836–85 there were revolts against rack-renting and evictions by Hindu *jenmis*, articulated within a universe of religious discourse. There were, therefore, many instances here too, of attacks on temples, the Hindu landlords and their families (and of course, Europeans), and even of large-scale forcible conversions. What is remarkable by its absence was once again the imagination of the world community of Islam, in which the north Indian elite participated.[62] Sectarian conflicts these certainly were, but as Gyanendra Pandey has argued, these were almost always local conflicts and always overdetermined by numerous other factors like 'land wars'. There was a palpable absence of the idea of all-India Muslim or Hindu communities with their discrete histories.[63] Even in the northern region, as late as in 1921, during the full bloom of the Khilafat non-cooperation movement, the Muslim peasantry moved in unison with the Hindu peasantry in the outbursts, seen for instance, in Chauri Chaura. In fact, as Shahid Amin's fascinating study shows, it was the 'Mahatma' all the way, and the Khilafat had no separate meaning for the peasants of Chauri Chaura; nor did the movement leave 'any separate space for Shaukat Ali and Mohammad Ali' when they visited the area along with Gandhi.[64] Nehru too, mentions that in many villages he found that Khilafat was actually understood to mean 'opposition' to the raj–*khilaf* being the common spoken word for opposition.[65]

I should emphasize here that my point is not the simple nationalist one that it was the Muslim elite that was anti-national and that the bulk of the Muslim peasantry was either fighting class battles or joining in nationalist mobilizations. For such a rendering suggests that the peasants displayed a conscious affiliation to either class or nationalist politics. This is something that the scholarship of the last two decades has shown to be part of nationalist mythology. My point, on the contrary, is that precisely because these peasant masses were still untouched by modern historical consciousness, they were responding to what were essentially local questions. Islam here became the medium through which they attempted to make sense of their local conflicts rather than identify with a world community.

In passing, it is also useful to keep in mind that modern historical consciousness did not always yield only one kind of pan-Islamism among the north Indian elite. It is interesting to consider the figure of Maulana Abul Kalam Azad, whose pan-Islamism was different from that of say, Syed Ahmed Khan. Azad hailed from a family that had migrated to Mecca after the defeat of 1857, and who was born there, becoming a key figure among those who came to be known as 'nationalist Muslims'. Azad's Urdu paper, *Al-Hilal*, selling 26,000 copies a week, combined a Khilafatist stance with a nationalist one, and he himself remained an active part of the Khilafat Committee. However, what moved people like Azad was not a simple nostalgia for the lost Kingdom, but a strong desire to combine Muslim identity with an Indian one. Azad narrates how his contact with the Arab and Turk revolutionaries, during his trip to Egypt, Iraq, Syria, and Turkey—especially his contact with the followers of Mustafa Kemal Pasha—reinforced his nationalist political beliefs. 'They expressed surprise' says Azad, 'that Indian Muslims were either indifferent to or against nationalist demands.'[66] To a large extent, therefore, the pro-Turkey stance of leaders like Azad stood in sharp contrast to the loyalist stance of the Ali brothers, who turned against the British much later, when the Caliphate was threatened by the Treaty of Sevres.[67] Azad probably represented that section of the north Indian elite that was trying to articulate a different conception of nationalism from both the Muslim League and the Nehruvian secular-nationalist, which Ayesha Jalal calls composite nationalism. Similarly we can discern an anti-imperialist defence of the Khilafat rather than a pro-Islamist one in the position of a die-hard secularist like Professor Mohammed Habib. Habib recalls the 'shudder that went through Muslim minds' at the terrible provisions of the Treaty of Sevres, even though he finds no reason to mourn the demise of the Caliphate at the hands of Kemal Pasha.[68]

Sir Syed Ahmed Khan, the pioneer of Muslim modernity, the relentless campaigner for Western education and for harmony between Islam and modern science, ostracized by the ulema as an infidel, can be taken as a typical representative of the community to whom the modern business of identity mattered in the way it did not for, say, Munshi Alimuddin or even Titu Mir, or the Faraizi leaders. So, even while being a harbinger of modernity in Muslim society, Syed Ahmed Khan was therefore, 'perhaps the first Indian' to don a Turkish Fez cap and 'made it a part of the students' uniform in Aligarh.'[69] It was this symbolic move (and others like these) that established a sense of a wider international community, not only among the despondent and defeated Muslim elites of northern India, but also among the larger Muslim society, that then gradually became instituted as 'a memory'. This symbolic move connected the history of Indian Muslims with the international history of Islam at a popular level. The historical account that Afzal Iqbal produces more than a century later, of the worldwide defeat of Islam, is hardly imaginable in that sense, in earlier times.

As anxieties for identity increase, with nationalism also acquiring a distinctly Hindu colour, and with the Khilafat issue acquiring importance, there is a coming together of two strands of elite Muslim politics—a section of the ulemas and the modernists represented by Syed Ahmed Khan. The newly united elite was united by a project that Mushirul Hasan describes as follows:

Their main pre-occupation, if not their sole concern, was to define the *community* afresh...

Once the ulama and the erstwhile *bete noire*, the western-trained professional politicians, put their heads together they came up with a definition that was developed in the context of colonial institutions and their own scriptural rhetoric. This definition sought to create a corporate identity and set Muslims apart form their own class, region and linguistic unit.[70]

These elites had, according to Hasan, a three-fold project: 'to trace the historical evolution of an imaginary community as an anti-thesis to the Congress theory of "unity in diversity"; to emphasize distinct identity and separateness of this community...; and to invoke Islamic symbols of unity that would, in its essential thrust delink specific 'Muslim aspirations' from the broader concerns of the countrywide nationalist struggle.'[71]

It is by now well documented and widely accepted that as 'history breaks out everywhere', there is what can be called a veritable 'scramble for history' in the late nineteenth and early twentieth centuries—among the various elites. Everywhere there is an intense search for the past and almost invariably, the various constructions of different histories is fuelled by one or the other strand of Orientalist scholarship. If mainstream Hindu nationalism harked back to the Vedic or Vedantic religion and its glory, presenting the entire thousand-year period of Muslim rule as the period of decline, we have already seen how the dominant Muslim imagination saw the period of Muslim rule as precisely the period of the flowering of Indian culture and civilization. On the other hand, most lower caste movements, with the exception of Ambedkar, seized on the Aryan invasion theory then gaining currency, to claim that they were the real and original inhabitants of India. For the leaders of these movements, 'the golden age of the sub-continent was the pre-Aryan epoch when social equality was presumed to have flourished and society on the whole was organized along fraternal and democratic lines. In the south and the west, the pre-Aryan era was conceptualized as the Dravidian, Adi-Dravidian civilization.'[72] The ideology of Adi-Dravida extended throughout the entire southern peninsula. In the north, this imagination took the form Adi-Hinduism and Ad-Dharma in the united provinces and the Punjab, and likewise insisted on the egalitarianism of pre-Aryan times.[73] There were also attempts by some lower caste groups, particularly untouchable castes to claim a kshatriya status in the past.

At this stage, it may be useful to take a glance at some of these Dalit/ Pariah constructions of the past. Right from the time when the Non-Brahmin Manifesto was issued in 1916, it was clear that a very different imagination from the nationalist one was at work here too. The manifesto's assertion of a distinctly non-Brahmin identity was accompanied by the political distance from nationalism that it marked. 'What proved most enabling to these new imaginings of the self and the community' remark Geetha and Rajadurai, ' was the discovery of history by the non-Brahmin intellectuals towards the last quarter of the nineteenth century.'[74] As M.S.S. Pandian puts it, it was 'a strand of Orientalist scholarship, which constructed a hoary Tamil past and invested the Tamil language with a distinct superior identity [that] came in as the basis for an empowering discourse for the relatively disempowered non-Brahmin Vellala elite.'[75] In fact, one might say, extending Pandian's as well as Geetha and Rajadurai's arguments, that it was through the scholarship of writers like Peter Percival, G.U. Pope, and Robert Caldwell, that the formation of 'Dravidian ideology' became possible. In the writings of Iyothee Thass on Pariah history, there is already a construction of 'Indian' history as one of conflict between Buddhism and Brahminism and of the Pariahs as the original Tamils who were Buddhists. They were the real (*yathartha*) Brahmins, 'whose fame, learning and wisdom were (mis)appropriated by Aryan mlechchas or Persians'.[76] Geetha and Rajadurai comment that:

The works of the adi dravida intellectuals centred around *Tamizhan* [the non-Brahmin newspaper] reveal a vivid and creative historiographical imagination at work. It is clear that these men reaped to advantage the information and insights proffered by the new colonialist knowledges of the time: philology, linguistics, anthropology and a universal philosophy of history derived from Enlightenment notions of time. Such knowledges made available to the bilingual and literate natives everywhere the necessary interpretative means to grapple with and make sense of a complex and distant past. Further, the findings of these new knowledges were available, from at least the mid-nineteenth century onwards, in a modular form: the Aryan theory of race—and the refutation of its premises and findings by Bishop Caldwell in 1856—provided Brahmin, non-Brahmin and Adi Dravida intellectuals with a stock of arguments they could deploy at will in their semantic and political quarrels with each other.[77]

It is also true that while much of what followed was the work of imagination, rather than strictly speaking, 'scientific history', it can be legitimately argued that even the most rigorous scientific history is no less an imaginative account, as recent interrogations of nationalist scientific history have shown.[78]

Ambedkar, who disagreed with the Aryan invasion thesis and held the so-called Hindu religion entirely responsible for the status and oppression of the untouchable castes, also laboured hard to produce a narrative of Indian history as the history of perennial struggle between Buddhism and Brahminism. He proposed that 'the Untouchables were Broken Men' who because they were poor and 'could not give up beef-eating and Buddhism, were treated as untouchables'. Ambedkar's biographer mentions Colonel Alcott's thesis in his book, *The Poor Pariah*, as a kind of 'original work' which put forward the idea that the untouchables were Buddhists.[79] The important point about most of these different constructions of their respective pasts was their constant reference to the Orientalist scholarship of that period and their reference to the canons of modern, rationalist history for legitimation. It is certainly true that most of these constructions of Selfhood were based on a certain experiential core but the overall historical narratives within which they were now cast had really very little to do with any *pre-existing* memory. At best there were collective memories of humiliating untouchable existence, for example, but the larger historical narratives they produced were already constituted by colonial knowledge and administrative technologies—and above all, by modern notions of subjectivity. That some of these historical narratives were still rudimentary and just about taking shape is evident from the fact that the very subject of these histories was not very clearly defined in these cases. So for example, in his Preface to *What Congress and Gandhi Have Done to the Untouchables*, Ambedkar writes:

The reader will find that I have used quite promiscuously in the course of this book a variety of nomenclature (sic) such as Depressed Classes, Scheduled Castes, Harijans, and Servile Classes, to designate the Untouchables. I am aware that this is likely to cause confusion [...]The fault is not altogether mine. All these names have been used officially and unofficially at one time or other [...]In a flowing situation like that it is not possible to fix upon one name...

What is striking about this statement is that apart from negative and often purely administrative categories, as late as in 1945 when this Preface was written, Ambedkar had no name with which to refer to his community. It was still a community in the making. Each section of it, for example the Mahars, presumably had their own fragmented 'memories' and identity. In fact the early attempts by most pariah communities were to claim a higher status in the past, much like Iyothee Thass' yathartha Brahmins. What we see in all these cases, in the course of these diverse imaginings of Selfhood, is that 'history' comes to stand for the authorized narrative of the past that is then *instituted as memory*. It *becomes* common memory of the community, or the nation.

Much of the critical work done by the Subaltern School historians and political theorists in this respect, draws attention to the impact of the modern regime of power and the new forms of governmentality introduced in the wake of colonization. More specifically, this body of work draws on the work of Michel Foucault and Edward Said and points to the implication of colonial knowledge in the mechanisms of power and domination. Important among the themes explored in this body of work was the impact of colonial censuses in the whole process of identity fixation, as well as the role of Orientalist knowledge in the production of the first histories of India.[80] Gyanendra Pandey has shown how not only were identities fixed, but how, often, sectarian conflicts between Hindus and Muslims routinely got written as 'communal' in the observations and accounts of colonial administrators, thus produced within the larger narrative of 'an unenlightened population in continuous strife'. He also shows that the consciousness of all-India Muslim and Hindu communities was hardly possible before that time. This was a specific feature of the enumerated communities of the later part of the nineteenth century. More work since, has established that the major sources of inspiration of nationalist accounts of the 'nation's' own history were drawn from different strands of Orientalist knowledge produced by Western scholars.[81] It is against this background that the impossibility of the project of Indian nationhood needs to be understood. The last section that follows will discuss in detail

Ambedkar's tract on Pakistan and three biographies, those of Ambedkar, Gandhi, and Savarkar by a single biographer of Savarkarite persuasion.

Gandhi, Ambedkar, and the Emergent Nation/s

The impossible project of Indian nationhood can probably be best understood through the fate of its 'father'. The assassination of Mahatma Gandhi, at the hands of a fiery young Hindu nationalist, represents probably the greatest and most tragic irony of modern Indian history. For the forces behind the assassination, it was Gandhi's 'anti-national appeasement' of the Muslims that led to the partition of the country and represented the 'emasculation' of the nation's virility.[82] Gandhi, who had almost become an atheist and then, having 'discovered' his 'Hinduism', had consistently insisted on being a Sanatani, was considered by many Hindus of his time to be an 'anti-national Muslim-lover'. By the Muslim League and its followers, however, he continued to be seen as a representative of the 'Hindu' Congress. Gandhi alone among the top leaders of the Indian National Congress and the anticolonial struggle, was continuously tormented by the fact that the untouchables were not able to join the common struggle. He was tormented by the fact that Hindu society continued its 'sinful practice' of untouchability and made, in his own way, the abolition of untouchability his central pre-occupation. And yet, in the end, he remained unacceptable to the enlightened leaders of the Depressed Classes. In July 1946, he wrote to Sardar Patel that 'things seem to be slipping out of the hands of the Congress'. 'The postmen [referring to the postal strike in Bombay] do not listen to it, nor does Ahmedabad [a reference to the communal riots there], nor do Harijans, nor Muslims.'[83] This was barely four months after the Congress swept the provincial elections in March, 'completely annihilating the Roy, Savarkar and Ambedkar parties'.[84] In a word, he stood isolated and 'misunderstood' by every section of the nation that he fathered.

An equally great and interesting irony can be read, I suggest, in the amazing reversal of fates of the two personalities most relevant today, namely Gandhi and Ambedkar: One, the supposed father of the nation, ending up as a tragic figure in the very moment of its birth; the other, the nation's outcaste, maligned ever so often as traitor by Gandhi's followers, presiding over the Constitution-making process of the new nation-state. The irony is highlighted even further by Periyar's interrogations of the constituent assembly proceedings and his eventual rejection of the Constitution and of the 'promises held out by 15 August 1947'—in a way, a rejection of Ambedkar's attempt to negotiate a place within the emergent nation.[85]

The very opening of the constituent assembly proceedings in December 1946 was marked by the absence of the Grand Old Man of the freedom struggle, along with two other absences: the Muslim League and the representatives of five hundred and sixty-odd princely states. While moving the *Aims and Objectives* resolution, Jawaharlal Nehru certainly mentioned being 'haunted by' these three absences, but the mood that he reflected was in stark contrast to the mood that had taken hold of Gandhi. While Gandhi was away on a trek for communal amity in Calcutta and Bihar, thoroughly disgusted and disillusioned with the arrival of the much-awaited freedom, Nehru began his speech in almost poetic terms. He described his feeling as a 'sense of standing on the swords-edge' between a past ('the great past of India, to the 5000 years of India's history') and an uncertain future. It is a strange moment in India's history, he said, 'but I do feel that there is some magic in this moment of transition from the old to the new...'[86]

Thus we have on the one hand Gandhi, reconciled to the vivisection of the country, rapidly losing grip over the developments, increasingly under attack—including attempts to physically eliminate him—from his own countrymen.[87] And on the other hand, we have Dr B.R. Ambedkar, Gandhi's most trenchant critic, in his final hour of glory. How do we understand this reversal of roles? In the remaining part of this chapter, I want to explore this dynamic and suggest that in the tragedy and final assassination of Gandhi, we can actually read the broad contours of the narrative of the impossible project of Indian nationhood.

It may be interesting to begin this discussion by looking at a text that encapsulates both the 'problems' we are discussing—Ambedkar's fate as well as the logic of Muslim politics—and through them read the other absent text, namely Gandhi. This text is Ambedkar's book *Pakistan or The Partition of India*. Written shortly after the Muslim League formally adopted what came to be known as the 'Pakistan resolution', Ambedkar unequivocally supports the demand for a separate Muslim homeland on the basis of a recognition of the idea that the Hindus and the Muslims constitute two separate nations. He argues that it is also necessary to take the demand seriously because it has behind it 'the sentiment, if not the passionate support, of 90 per cent of the Muslims of India.'[88] He castigates the Hindu nationalist who forgets that

the right of nationalism to freedom from an aggressive foreign imperialism and the right of a minority to freedom from an aggressive majority's nationalism are not two different things [...] They are merely two aspects of the struggle for freedom, and as such, equal in their moral import.[89]

In the first chapter of the book, Ambedkar goes into a detailed and sympathetic rendering of the Muslim League argument for a separate homeland. He does this through an extensive reading of Ernest Renan's celebrated essay on nationalism. Two principles are crucial, he says, quoting Renan, for the nation form to come into being: the possession of a heritage of common memories and the will to live together. Both these are missing in the case of the Hindus and the Muslims. They have past histories of intense conflict and no desire to live together. Notice that having no investment in either secular-nationalism or Muslim nationalism, and deeply distrustful of the Hindu nationalists, Ambedkar can acknowledge the past histories of conflict without hesitation. In fact, throughout the tract he presents his argument in a perfectly 'even-handed' way.

This circumstance of past conflict and the lack of will to live together, he argues, could still be overcome, if the two communities were prepared to 'forget their past', and here he once again invokes the authority of Renan. The passage that he quotes deserves to be reproduced, as it is crucial to the understanding of our problem also:

Forgetfulness, and I shall even say historical error, form *an essential factor in the creation of the nation*; and thus it is that the progress of historical studies may often be dangerous to the nationality. *Historical research, in fact, brings back to light the deeds of violence that have taken place at the commencement of all political formations, even of those the consequences of which have been most beneficial.* Unity is ever achieved by brutality. The union of Northern and Southern France was the result of an extermination, and of a reign of terror that lasted for nearly a hundred years.[90]

Ambedkar then goes on to argue that it is futile to say that the Muslim claim to separate nationhood is 'an afterthought of their leaders', for even though this is true, that does not really refute the thesis of Muslim constituting a separate nation. Clearly, the nation in this rendering, is an imagined construct and not a given, eternal entity. The will to live together and therefore, to forget their past quarrels, so crucial for this imagined community to take shape, is clearly absent, thereby undercutting both principles of nationhood.[91] More importantly, Ambedkar quotes from Lord Acton to buttress his argument, that 'the demand by a nationality for a national state does not require to be supported by any list of grievances' and that 'the will of the people is enough to justify it.'[92] 'Are the Hindus to be a ruling race and the Muslims and other minorities to be subject races under Swaraj?' he asks, establishing what seems to be a relationship with the predicament faced by the Dalit/untouchable communities themselves.

Ambedkar is vitriolic in his attack on the Hindu upper caste leadership. Quoting from Lala Hardayal's political testament which was published in the *Pratap* of Lahore, where he had advocated Hindu Raj and the '*Shuddhi* [reconversion] of the Moslems' not only in the present India but also the 'conquest and shuddhi of Afghanistan and the Frontiers', he attacked the very idea of Hindu proselytization. If Hindu religion is not a missionary religion like Islam and Christianity, it is not because of any inherent greatness of the religion itself. It is so, he argued, because 'caste is incompatible with conversion'. 'To be able to convert a stranger to its religion, it is not enough for a community to offer its creed. It must be in a position to admit the convert to its social life and to absorb and assimilate him among the kindred.'[93] According to the Hindus, for a person to belong to a caste he must be born into it, and a convert, he goes on to say, is not born into a caste. He therefore, belongs to no caste.

In a subsequent section, he discusses what he calls the 'Savarkarite alternative to Pakistan'. Quoting chapter and verse from Savarkar, he shows that Savarkar 'admits that the Muslims are a separate nation.' Savarkar, according to Ambedkar, 'concedes that they [Muslims] have a right to cultural autonomy' and 'allows them to have a national flag'. Yet he opposes their demand for a separate homeland. This Ambedkar finds *dangerous* in the extreme, for the 'safety and security of India'. In a peculiar twist, here Ambedkar falls back on history, to buttress his argument. According to him, history records only two ways that are open to a major nation to deal with a minor one when they are citizens of the same country and subject to the same constitution: either destroy the nationality of the minor nation and assimilate it into the major one, or divide the country and allow the minor nation autonomous and sovereign existence. Savarkar's proposal is dangerous because he takes neither of the historically sanctioned paths. He wants Hindus and Muslims to live as two separate nations in one country and that too, in a mutually hostile relationship to each other.[94] This is like having an enemy within. He quotes the example of Austria, Czechoslovakia, and Turkey which 'came to ruination' for insisting upon the kind of scheme Savarkar is proposing. The destruction of Czechoslovakia was brought about, says Ambedkar, 'by an enemy within her own borders' and this enemy was the 'intransigent nationalism of the Slovaks'. The 'true and principal cause' of the decline of Turkey was the growth of the nationalist spirit of its subject peoples.[95] Ambedkar goes on to say:

The Turks were by no means as illiberal as they are painted. They allowed their minorities a large measure of autonomy. The Turks had gone far towards solving the problem of how people of different communities with different social heritages are to live together in harmony. The Ottoman Empire had accorded...to the non-Muslim and non-Turkish communities within its frontiers a degree of territorial as well as cultural autonomy which had never been dreamt of in the political philosophy of the West.[96]

Yet this could not prevent the rise of nationalism among the minorities, who were not satisfied with local autonomy. The lesson from these experiences then, he argues is to recognize the nationalist aspirations of the minorities and grant them their separate homeland. What is interesting about this part of Ambedkar's argument is that it is lodged entirely within the perspective of the nation-state and the logic of modern nation-states. The over-riding desire that keeps cropping up is that of achieving a homogeneity of national culture. The reason he finds the existence of a separate Muslim nation within the proposed Indian nation-state to be 'dangerous to the safety and security' of India, is precisely this desire, and as we shall see, in this respect his concept of 'nationhood' was not very different from the nationalist.

We may note here that unlike him, Gandhi on the other hand, refuses both the ground of history and that of the nation-state. Gandhi's nation is *ahistorical*; it is not a really existing entity but a spiritual 'soul force'. In a well-known formulation, therefore, Gandhi talks of history as merely recording conflicts and breaks in harmony: if two brothers fight, go to court over property, or kill each other, then it is recorded as history; if on the other hand they resolve their dispute among themselves, it is not worthy of recording as history. The Truth, for Gandhi, is love and harmony— eternal and transcendent. If Hindus and Muslims fight today, that for Gandhi is unreal and untrue. His solution then is to refer to that transcendent truth—*the essence of all religions*—that alone will make it possible to restore peace. Gandhi's denial of history is his attempt to forget. Ambedkar, on the other hand, despite his invocation of Renan on the 'dangers of history', can only take recourse to the history of endless strife among the Hindus and the Muslims, and come up thereby, with a highly essentialized understanding of communities. The failure of Hindu-Muslim unity lies, in his opinion, in causes that 'take their origin in historical, religious, cultural and social antipathy'.[97] If Gandhi's refusal of history is also the rejection of the idea that the actual, empirical Hindu–Muslim relations represent the truth, for Ambedkar, they represent the unalterable truth. Gandhi's refusal to come to terms with the partition then, and identify with the new nation-state founded on massacres on both sides, is an extension of this belief, while for Ambedkar, the pragmatic modernist, this was the only realistic option left. He shares, in a sense, this pragmatism of the other modernists like Jawaharlal Nehru and Sardar Patel, who took over the reins of power of the new nation-state. This difference between the two, then, already sets the stage for the eventual reversal of fortunes.

While Ambedkar does seem at times to essentialize difference and fall prey to the stereotypes of Islam and the Muslims, derived generally from Western/Christian scholarship, in many ways he is also aware of and rejects them. For instance, he refutes Renan's assertions to the effect that 'what is essentially distinctive of the Mussalman is his hatred of science' his persuasion that 'research is useless, frivolous, almost impious' and that 'to the human reason Islamism has only been injurious.' If this were true, he argues, then 'how are we to account for the stir and ferment that is going on in all Muslim countries outside India, where the spirit of inquiry, the spirit of change and the desire to reform are noticeable in every walk of life?'[98] Islam clearly, cannot be the reason for the Indian Muslims' resistance to change. He offers a possible explanation:

It seems to me that the reason for the absence of the spirit of change in the Indian Musalman is to be sought in the peculiar position he occupies in India. He is placed in a social environment which is predominantly Hindu. That Hindu environment is always silently but surely encroaching upon him. He feels that it is de-musalmanazing (sic) him. As a protection against this gradual weaning away he is led to insist on preserving everything that is Islamic [...]Secondly, the Muslims in India are placed in a political environment which is also predominantly Hindu [...]Their energies are directed to maintaining a constant struggle against the Hindus for seats and posts in which there is no time, no thought and no room for questions relating to social reform.[99]

Yet, Ambedkar is unsparing in his critique of the social conservatism of the 'Indian Muslims', as well as of what he calls their politically 'extravagant demands', especially as they appeared around the 1940s in the Muslim League claim for 50 per cent share in legislatures and the demand for Urdu as the national language.[100] However, the absence of any distinction between the Muslim League and 'the Muslims' in general (not to mention the different strands within the Muslims themselves), makes his position often very close to that of the Hindu Mahasabha. To Gandhi, on the other hand, because he sees himself as the leader of the Congress, claiming to represent the entire nation, the distinction comes automatically. He cannot relinquish the claim to represent the Muslims entirely to the Muslim

League. For Ambedkar, primarily because he cannot allow the Congress and Gandhi to represent the Depressed Classes, he must recognize the complete, organic connection between the Muslim masses and the Muslim League leadership. This cannot but lead to the inability to see the distinction between communities and their self-appointed leaders. He, therefore, argues that there is an increasing tendency among 'them' to 'exploit the weaknesses of the Hindus', which he illustrates with reference to their 'insistence upon cow slaughter and the stoppage of music before mosques.' These are neither entailed by Islamic law nor practised in other Islamic countries, he says, but here they insist upon them simply because 'Hindus claim a right to it'. He also refers to the 'adoption by the Muslims of the gangster's methods in politics'. He at one point seems to suggest that riots are primarily a Muslim affair. 'The riots are a sufficient indication that gangsterism has become a settled part of their strategy in politics.'[101]

It is only when we recognize Ambedkar's belief in the organicity of community identity that we can begin to make sense of his repeatedly falling back on the essentialist stereotypes which he otherwise seems to reject. In examining the Hindu case against Pakistan, for instance, and in order to establish that there was never any unity in the past, he recounts from various Western/Christian sources the history of the successive Muslim invasions of India and the fact that they were mostly inspired by the desire to proselytize and extend the Islamic dominion. While the Afghans, the Tartars, and the Mongols 'were deadly rivals of one another', they were all united, he argues, with the common objective 'to destroy the Hindu faith'.[102] While there may be some truth in many of these recountings, it is amazing to find Ambedkar uncritically accept the various accounts as 'history' almost in the positivist sense, unadulterated by prejudice and value judgement. His entire discussion on Indian Islam then, is based on the work of a certain Dr Titus, about whom we are told nothing—not even the full name. It transpires, however, that this gentleman was Dr Murray Titus, whose book *Indian Islam*, was a version of his doctoral thesis, written for the Faculty of the Kennedy School of Missions of the Hartford Seminary Foundation, USA.[103] While the book does try to maintain a certain objectivity, it seems to be coloured by the innumerable Christian prejudices about Islam at that time. For instance, Titus refers to an incident that goes without any footnote, in an otherwise meticulously documented book. This incident, quoted by Ambedkar too, is of 'Mohd bin Qasim's first act of religious zeal' that is said to have been the 'forcible circumcision' of the Brahmins of the captured city of Debul. When they objected, they were put to death and all the women and children were 'led into slavery'.[104]

How to deal with this politics of 'Muslim aggression' is the question that Ambedkar finally poses. And here he not only dismisses the Hindu Mahasabha solution as 'arrant nonsense', he also mounts a trenchant critique of the Congress way of handling the issue. Here, in this critique of the Congress policy in relation to the 'Muslim question', we find a fuller exposition of the abovementioned trends in his thought. For Ambedkar believes, like many Hindus of his time, that under Gandhi's leadership the Congress attitude to the Muslims was one of *appeasement*. He distinguishes between 'appeasement' and what he calls a 'settlement', as two different possible ways of dealing with the problem. Appeasement, he argues, 'means buying off the aggressor by conniving at his acts of murder, rape, arson and loot against innocent persons who happen for the moment to be victims of his displeasure', while a settlement means laying down the bounds that neither party can transgress.[105] The former then, 'sets no limits to the demands and the aspirations of the aggressor' while the latter does. It is Ambedkar's reading of the situation that it is this policy of appeasement that has not only increased Muslim aggressiveness but worse, that it has come to be interpreted it as a sign of Hindu weakness. He sees the proposal for Pakistan as an issue for a possible settlement.[106]

It may be relevant to bring in here another element in the Ambedkar–Gandhi relationship, through a reading of another set of texts. This element relates to the question of modernity and the internal reforms within communities. The most authoritative biography of Ambedkar is one by Dhananjay Keer. A little noticed but intriguing fact about this biography is that Keer happens to be a Savarkarite by conviction and, going by the fact that he was awarded the Padma Bhushan by the Government of India in 1971, in recognition of his contribution as a biographer, his work is important enough to merit some discussion.[107] Keer has written biographies of many important leaders but the most interesting to read in conjunction, are his biographies of Ambedkar, Savarkar, and Gandhi. Keer's account of Ambedkar's life is highly laudatory and sympathetic in the extreme. He even enthrones Ambedkar, in his narrative, as the Modern Manu, in appreciation of his role in the making of the Constitution.[108] And this is not done with the simple intention of appropriation. There is a certain logic that underlies Keer's reading of the three personalities and their ideological positions. This logic, I may add, is not an idiosyncratic one, peculiar to Keer, but represents the more sophisticated strand of thought within the ideology of Hindutva itself.

Central to Keer's understanding of the three personalities are two concerns: the decay of Hindu society and the challenge of modernity on

the one hand and on the other, the problem posed by the constant presence
of the dissonant Muslim Other as the main obstacle to the emergence of
the homogeneous Nation.[109] In his account of Savarkar, therefore, he
underlines the rot that had set into Hindu society and the urgent need for
it to modernize. Savarkar's Sanghathanist ideology, that sought to eliminate
the caste system and unite the Hindus into a single community with a
single will, is therefore seen as the fulcrum of his thought in his exposition.
'It was inevitable,' he says, 'that such an unadulterated Hindu movement
should upset the mental balance of the Gandhian pro-Muslim zealots' for
the Hindu Sabha of Ratnagiri, that Savarkar led, concentrated its fire
against the 'fads and fashions' of Gandhianism. 'Worship of strength and
love for the machine age were taboos to the Gandhian faddists.'[110] And
these were necessary attributes if the Hindus were to be welded into a
single, homogeneous nation. 'Like all positive and powerful reformers',
therefore, 'Savarkar wielded the force, construction and hammer of
Luther...[His] one aim was to purge Hinduism of its most baneful
superstitions and orthodox bigotry.' After all, a Luther, says Keer, 'is not
born for laurels'[111] . In a remarkable passage, he then says:

So he raised his mighty pen against superstition from which flowed Voltaire's
satire and emanated the force of Luther. Voltaire venerated nothing while Savarkar,
like Swift, did his job with remarkable candour. Voltaire smashed ancient idols;
Savarkar swept them into a corner as historical and cultural monuments for record
and research. Voltaire disfigured the idols, Savarkar dethroned them.
    Savarkar's outlook was absolutely modern, scientific and secular. He showed
the fallacy of time-worn and scripture-born arguments. He denounced religious
ideologies that described the machine as a device of the devil...[112]

Establishing a direction kinship with the entire Enlightenment tradition,
Keer goes on to add that Savarkar 'was to Maharashtra what the eighteenth
century great European reformers were to Europe.'[113]
    The problem however, is that like the *philosophes* developed their critiques
within a Christian universe, Savarkar, likewise was situated within a Hindu
world. What is more, he was a Chitpavan Brahmin. His concern was with
the modernization of this world. But what *was* this Hindu world? Was it
the world of *varnashrama dharma* that he so hated and that Gandhi
passionately upheld with all his superstitions and orthodox beliefs? Savarkar
was seized with this problem and with defining afresh what being Hindu
meant. And he was agonizing over this problem in the context of Gandhi's
emergence as the patriarch of the anticolonial struggle. It was in this
situation that Savarkar wrote his now well-known book *Hindutva*, while he

was lodged in Ratnagiri jail. According to Keer, this book was 'a result of Savarkar's deep reflection and intense reaction to Gandhism which had surrendered to the antinational demands of the Muslim reactionaries...'[114] Savarkar's much quoted definition of Hindutva, as formulated in this book and taken over by his later day legatees, was basically an ingenious attempt to deal with the idea of being Hindu in a modern and secular world. That was possible only when 'Hinduness' (which is what *hindutva* literally means) was defined as *nationhood rather than as religion*. It had to be defined in such a way that not only made internal caste divisions within Hindu society irrelevant, but that also could incorporate the Buddhist, Sikh, and Jain faiths, along with all other autochthonous peoples. His insistence then, on defining Hindus as those who considered India (*Bharat Bhumi*) as both, their Fatherland (*Pitribhumi*) and Holyland (*Punyabhumi*) clearly served both these aims. It identified the Muslims (and Christians) as the Other, their Holyland being elsewhere, while providing Hindu society with a more inclusive and modern self-definition.

In this context, the movement launched by Savarkar combined two elements. The internal, that is, the complete elimination of the caste system, was the precondition of the struggle for a homogeneous nation; and the external, that followed from the internal, was that of the 'Indianization' of the Muslims and Christians. As we saw, Ambedkar had astutely noted that as long as the caste system remains, Lala Hardayal's dream of Hindu consolidation and the shuddhi of the Muslims would remain a wild fantasy. So Keer observes: 'The reconversion movement was a war. And *a war with the Hindu orthodoxy was a war indirectly with the maulvies and missionaries.*'[115]

In the Hindutva worldview, it is in this inseparable connection between the two elements that the importance of Ambedkar lies. It is for this reason that Savarkar not only supported Ambedkar's struggle for the elimination of caste but in the early phase of the movement for temple-entry, he even invited Ambedkar to preside over the function for temple-entry organized by him in Ratnagiri. Also interesting here is Keer's account of the reactions to Ambedkar's famous Yeola declaration, where he announced that though he was born as a Hindu, he would certainly not die as one. The threat to quit the Hindu fold and adopt another religion, had unleashed a flurry of activity among Hindu nationalist leaders like B.S. Moonje, who tried to ensure that if Ambedkar must convert, he should either become a Sikh or a Buddhist but on no account a Muslim or a Christian. Keer notes that the 'ruthless and misanthropic orthodox Hindus were unmoved by the decision' and they even rejoiced and 'heaved a sigh of relief'. It was the 'enlightened and political-minded opinion in the country who deplored the Untouchables' decision.[116] They were after all, the leaders of the new, enumerated, Hindu community, aspiring to nationhood.

How does Gandhi appear then in this narrative?

Gandhi thus came forward to put back the hand of progress made by the Hindu leaders. Indeed he hampered the past and the contemporary work of the galaxy of social reformers and evolutionaries (sic) like Ram Mohan Roy, Mahatma Jotirao Phule, Swami Dayanand Saraswati, Swami Shraddhanand, Acharya P.C. Ray, R.C. Dutta, B.C. Pal, Jadunath Sarkar, Aurobindo Ghose, Ramanand Chatterjee, Bhai Parmanand, Hardayal, Shahu Chhatrapati, Veer Savarkar and Dr. Ambedkar who raised their hammer against the caste system *which deprived the Hindus of a strong feeling of patriotism and nationality, of social equality and solidarity* and denied opportunity to develop fully and freely.[117]

Not only was Gandhi turning the clock back in terms of the struggle against the institution of caste, but worse, he was an inveterate enemy of modern civilization. Modernity, in this reading, unlike in the case of Gandhi and many others, was not something to cope with, but to be celebrated. Gandhi's 'wholesale condemnation of Western civilization is hardly justifiable'. 'The history of civilization is itself the history of secularization. When Europe had seen the twilight of God, Gandhi was dealing in God, religion and hope. He ennobles asceticism (sic), poverty and ignorance rather than material welfare, culture and knowledge. Modern education has an ennobling influence on morality and religion.'[118] Keer goes on: 'When religion prevailed and ruled, there were wars, poverty and injustice. Gandhi's diatribes against railways, doctors, hospitals, machines and lawyers are equally strange and faddish.'[119]

It was this reactionary content of Gandhi's thought that was also responsible for his political blunders. Himself a 'religious-minded man', Gandhi 'took up the cry of the Muslims [regarding Khilafat] without understanding its implications and significance and the conditions in Turkey.' After all, it was Turkey's 'revolutionary leader, Gazi Mustafa Kemal Pasha' who had declared that 'Islam, this theology of an immortal Arab is a dead thing'. He wanted to tear out religion 'from the body politic of Turkey.'[120]

On Keer's account, contrary to the spirit of the age, Gandhi was committing the Indian nationalist movement to a reactionary, religious, and socially outdated outlook. 'It inspired loyalty to the traditions of a dead past and advocated return to some old position [...] it was a counter-revolutionary movement [...] to preserve the established social order and to revive older institutions, although politically it aimed at a revolution.'[121]

Keer is unsparing in his critique of Gandhi's entire worldview: Not only did Gandhi know nothing of Indian history, his use of anecdotes and instances from the *Puranas* and history were opportunistically meant to buttress his standpoint.[122] A study of Indian history hardly supports Gandhi's view of non-violence. It is simply a perversion of Indian history to say that its course has not run through war and bloodshed.[123] But that is hardly surprising for a mystic like Gandhi who believed that history is merely a record of wars; who believed that 'a nation that has no history is a happy nation'.[124] And equally unsurprisingly, Keer sympathizes with those critics of Gandhi who accuse him of 'fathering Pakistan', and of being a pro-Muslim zealot. Even though he condemns his assassination, Keer hardly conceals his sympathy for the assassin's viewpoint and his admiration for him.[125]

The assassin's viewpoint, according to Keer, *reflected the general mood and opinion of the Hindus* who were increasingly coming to hold Gandhi's 'policy of appeasement' responsible for 'Muslim riots' and attacks on the Hindus. It is at this point that Gandhi becomes the common object of hate for both the Hindu nationalist and for Ambedkar. The interesting thing of course, is that Keer's anti-Muslim position is itself a consequence of his modern outlook: Muslims represent obscurantism and bigotry, and the religious-minded Gandhi can only pander to them because of his own obscurantism.

It is also interesting to see here how all these formulations regarding the 'backward feudal Muslims,' 'advanced bourgeois Hindus', and 'the fads of Gandhi', appear *in almost identical terms in Nehru,* as we have already seen in our discussion of secular-nationalism in Chapter 1.

We get a final clue to the reversal of fortunes of Gandhi and Ambedkar in the proposal made by Sardar Patel to Gandhi, to 'negotiate with Ambedkar out of fear of the [Muslim] League'. Gandhi, of course considered this to be a risky proposition as it involved 'dealing with a man who would become Christian, Muslim or Sikh and then be reconverted according to his convenience.'[126]

In the event, as things were shaping up, the 'reactionary and backward looking' Gandhi, who cared little for the logic of modern politics, and was bent upon chasing the 'chimera of Hindu-Muslim unity', turned out to be the really risky proposition. Ambedkar, for all his attacks on Hinduism, was a man of the times and understood the logic of the modern nation-state and its imperatives much more clearly. He knew better than Gandhi that the idea of Hindu–Muslim unity was a battle already lost and discretion dictated that one look forward to the tasks ahead, rather than be bogged down in sentimentality.

The discourse of secular-nationalism, however, was premised on a blindness to the various currents working at cross purposes to each other. At the most, it could uneasily relate to the Mahatma, for his consistent, if naïve and religiously inspired, stance in support of Hindu–Muslim unity. All others, including the Depressed Classes were irritants, somehow lacking in their nationalism and always talking the backward and reactionary language of 'caste'. In the happy mythology of secular-nationalism, all these were retrograde currents that would die a natural death with the advance of a modern, scientific education and a scientific temper. That was the task the newly born nation-state was to accomplish. Ambedkar, despite his subaltern location, understood this logic of the nation-state quite well and could adjust to the new dispensation, despite occasional problems.

Notes

1. Paranjape (1999), p. 30. All emphasis added.

2. I use the term 'historicist' here in relation to the notion of historical time discussed in the introductory chapter, where history is understood as being defined by a single, linear temporality. In such an understanding, it is evident, any moment in history is, or can be, characterized by a single 'present' and therefore represented in the self-consciousness of the dominant presence.

3. Jalal (2001), p. 142.

4. Ibid., p. 240. This statement however does not represent her position fully. In fact, there is a clear tension that runs through this work—that of trying to reconcile this position with an equally vehement critique of Nehruvian secular-nationalism which she says, 'avoids the problem of difference by projecting a singular narrative construction of Indian identity' (Ibid., p. 573). The tension is never quite resolved and all too often in this book, Jalal seems to slip into equating the Muslim League position with the 'Muslim' position.

5. Hasan (2000), pp. 8–9.

6. Balibar (1991), p. 93.

7. Ibid., p. 10.

8. For a recent statement of this argument, see Nandy (2001), 'Time Travel to a Possible Self', pp. 157–209.

9. For one rendering of this idea see Kaviraj (1995c).

216 The Insurrection of Little Selves

10. Bayly (1998). See his essay 'The Pre-history of 'Communalism'? Religious Conflict in India, 1700–1860' , p. 214.

11. Ibid. See especially, Chapter 7. Of course, it needs to be stated right away that the opponent that Bayly seems to be attacking is a straw man, for no one to my knowledge has seriously argued that colonialism concocted religious identities out of nothing. The whole point of those who have focused on this aspect of colonial discourse is to say that such identities were not inevitable and that had colonialism adopted different criteria of classification, the nature of nationalist politics too might have been different. In other words, this reference to colonial governmentality must not be read as a complete explanatory theory about communalism and nationalism. As Gyanendra Pandey, one of the key proponents of the 'colonial construction of communalism' argument himself suggests, it is not as if conflicts and violence between communities did not take place in precolonial times, it was the nature of conflicts that changed as communities became more clearly defined, and 'historically more self-conscious, and very much more aware of the differences between "Us" and "Them".' See Pandey (1992), p. 159. Also see Chakrabarty (1995), 'Modernity and Ethnicity in India—A History for the Present' in *Economic and Political Weekly*, vol. 30, no. 52, 30 Dec. 1995, for a similar argument. It is also worth noticing that Bayly's account itself shows that religious conflicts of the eighteenth century were not quite 'communal' conflicts in the sense they came to acquire later.

12. Hasan (2000), p. 15.

13. Faruqi (1963), p. vii.

14. Ibid., p. 124.

15. See Jalal (2001), pp. 78–9.

16. I need hardly say that of course I am not arguing that 'Pakistan' was an inevitability; on the contrary, the role played by the Hindu nationalists and the Congress at large played a crucial part in pushing the Muslim League towards this position. But this is not the issue here.

17. Cited by Jalal (2001), p. 577.

18. The citation is from Jalal's description of the rally in Lahore, following the adoption of the Pakistan resolution, Jalal (2001), p. 397.

19. The *Pioneer*, 30 January 2000.

20. The chronology referred to appears on p. 9 and was compiled a team of eight intellectuals from the movement, seven of them Dalits.

21. The Mahars are an untouchable caste in the Deccan plateau—the caste to which Ambedkar belonged. The raising of the Mahar regiment is also seen by Ambedkar as a landmark event in opening out educational avenues to the untouchables and as an index of their martial capacities. Ambedkar (1991), p. 188.

22. I use the term in the more general sense to denote the colonial educational programme articulated by Macaulay, even though he may not necessarily be associated with every decision. I was told in a personal interview by one of the editors, Chandra Bhan Prasad, that Macaulay is considered among the leading twenty figures of the past two centuries, responsible for making the liberation of Dalits possible.

23. However, as we shall soon see, even here, there is an attempt to construct an even more ancient and pristine past. The difference then lies in which past one identifies with.

24. Iqbal (1978).

25. This is, in fact, the sub-title of the book.

26. Ibid. p.3. Emphasis added. Other accounts also corroborate that 1857 is indeed the year of the Fall. See, for instance, Hasan(1995), p. 2996.

27. Abbasi (1987), p. 1.

28. Savarkar published his tract with the title *The Volcano or the First War of Indian Independence*. There are other historians like R.C. Majumdar and Tarachand, of course, who saw the event as 'not the birth-pangs of a freedom movement in India, but the dying groans of an obsolete aristocracy.' For details see, Roy (1994).

29. Abbasi (1987), p. 2.

30. Iqbal (1978), p. 4.

31. Ibid., p. 13.

32. Ibid., p. 15.

33. Ambedkar, it is interesting to note, uses the same metaphor of 'the common stream' to comment on this history: 'The Hindus and Muslims have trodden parallel paths. No doubt, they went in the same direction. But they never travelled the same road.' Or, 'The point is, they have never merged. Only during the Khilafat agitation did the waters of the two channels leave their appointed course and flow as one stream in one channel' (vol. 8, p. 337).

34. Kaviraj (1998), and Chatterjee (1994 b).

35. Memmi (1974), p. 92.

36. Ibid., p. 107.

37. Ibid., p. 132.

38. Fanon (1971), pp. 178–9.

39. Ibid., p. 179.

40. Amuta (1999), p. 159.

41. His name was Aurobindo Ackroyd Ghose. For a fascinating discussion, see Nandy (1983).

42. See Gandhi (1927).

43. Habib (1970), p. xiv.

44. Kaviraj (1998), p. 125.

45. Kaviraj (1992), p. 25.

46. Taussig (1993), p. 3.

47. Ibid., p. 10.

48. Quoted in Ibid., p. 19.

49. Ibid., p. 97.

50. The referrence is to Terra del Fuega, the place of this colonial confrontation.

51. Ibid., p. 79, emphasis in original.

52. Chatterjee (1994b), p. 77. All references in this section are from the same work, pp. 76–94.

53. Iqbal (1978), p. 68.

54. Abbasi (1987), p. 48.

55. Iqbal (1978), p. 14.

56. Muhammad (1979), p. 127. The reading of the Khilafat movement as the unifying and elevating role, symbolic for the Muslim community as a whole, is also corroborated by others like Ayesha Jalal. She suggests that even to those who might have had misgivings about the legitimacy of the Turkish Khilafat, this became a common symbol, and it was 'arguably the more powerful reason Indian Muslims rallied behind the symbol of the crescent.' Jalal (2001), p. 193.

57. According to Ahmed (1981), the movement generally referred to 'erroneously' as Wahhabism was actually the *Tariqah-I-Muhammadiya* movement. However, the general genealogy of the movement that he provides, going back to Sayyid Ahmed Barelvi, remains the same.

58. For details of the Wahabi and Faraizi Movements in Bengal, see Ahmed (1901), Kaviraj (1982). For an overview of the Wahabi movement at the all-India level, see Ahmad (1984).

59. See Ahmad (1984).

60. Ibid., p. 282.

61. Kaviraj (1982), pp. 37–43.

62. For a detailed account, see Panikkar (1992).

63. Pandey (1992), p. 16. The term 'land wars' here is from Chris Bayly's essay against whose position Pandey is arguing.

64. Amin (1996), p. 170.

65. Nehru (1998), p. 69.

66. For details, see Azad (1988) and May (1970).

67. See Habib (1970).

68. Ibid., pp. xiv–xv.

69. Iqbal (1978), p. 15.

70. Hasan (1995), p. 2997.

71. Ibid.

72. Aloysius (1997), p. 164.

73. Ibid., pp. 164–5. See also Gooptu (1993).

74. Geetha and Rajadurai (1998), p. 9.

75. Pandian (1994), p. 88.

76. Geetha and Rajadurai (1998), pp. 96–7.

77. Ibid., pp. 108–9.

78. Interestingly, in the case of Madras, Geetha and Rajadurai argue, official history departments, that is the discipline proper, were still in the hands of the Brahmins, who looked down upon these untrained novices dabbling in history, p. 120.

79. Keer (1997), p. 407.

80. See for instance, Kaviraj (1992) and Pandey (1992).

81. See Chatterjee (1986) and Kaviraj (1992, 1998).

82. See Ghosh (1973) for the statement of Nathu Ram Godse. An erstwhile Gandhian, K. M. Munshi, for instance said this in a somewhat moderated way while addressing an RSS gathering, when he explained that he had left the Congress because he could not 'reconcile himself to the principle of abjuring violence in matters of self-defence'. See Munshi (1942).

83. *Collected Works of Mahatma Gandhi* (1982), vol. LXXXV, The Publications Division, Ministry of Information and Broadcasting, Govt. of India, p. 35.

84. Keer (1973), p. 743.

85. Geetha and Rajadurai (1998), p. 323.

86. *Constituent Assembly Debates*, Official Report, reprinted by the Lok Sabha Secretariat, New Delhi, vol. I, p. 6.

87. See Keer (1973).

88. Moon (1990), p. 9.

89. Ibid., pp. 10–11.

90. Ibid., quoted on page 36. All emphasis added.

91. We need to remember however, that Renan is an advocate of nationalism and the forgetting that he insists upon is directed at the minority cultures that have been assimilated in the creation of the French nation. It is doubtful whether he will ask the majority culture to forget violence inflicted upon it. However, that is not relevant for our present discussion as through this passage, Ambedkar addresses both communities.

92. Ibid., pp. 41–2.

93. Ibid., pp. 130–1.

94. Ibid., pp. 132–45. I have merely paraphrased Ambedkar's argument here, often using his own words, though not always within inverted commas.

95. Ibid., p. 211.

96. Ibid., p. 216.

97. Ibid., p. 329.

98. Quoted in ibid., p. 234.

99. Ibid., p. 235.

100. Ibid., p. 264.

101. Ibid., pp. 268–9. Ambedkar's reading of the Mappila uprising too, is very close to that of conventional Hindu accounts which represent it as a fanatical, anti-Hindu outburst. He talks of the bloodcurdling atrocities committed by the Mappilas against the Hindus, pp. 157–60.

102. Ibid., pp. 56–7.

103. Titus (1936).

104. Ibid., p. 19, quoted by Ambedkar (1991), p. 57.

105. Ambedkar actually echoes all the major Hindu criticisms of Gandhi in this respect. 'Can any sane man go so far, for the sake of Hindu-Muslim unity?', he asks at one point. Ibid., p. 155.

106. Ibid., p. 270.

107. See the author's introduction in his biography of Ambedkar, Keer (1997). The details of the three biographies are: *Veer Savarkar*, Popular Prakashan, Bombay (1950/1966); *Dr Ambedkar—Life and Mission*, Popular Prakashan, Bombay (1954/1997); *Mahatma Gandhi—Political Saint and Unarmed Prophet*, Popular Prakashan, Bombay (1973).

108. 'The Modern Manu' is in fact the title of one of his chapters in Ambedkar's biography.

109. Even the second problem is a derivative of the first, that is, of the challenge of modernity, for the problem of the Muslim other only becomes important in the context of forging a modern nation. So central is the rational-modern to him that Keer believes that there have been only three 'Indian political leaders of the day' who stood on the ground of a firm and well-defined political philosophy, namely M.N. Roy, Ambedkar, and Savarkar. See Keer (1950/66), pp. 161–2.

110. Ibid., p. 172.

111. Ibid., p. 194.

112. Ibid., pp. 203–4.

113. Ibid., p. 204. Keer goes on to argue that Savarkar believed in absolute science and that the best 'man' could do was to learn the laws of science and use in them the best way possible. According to him, Savarkar asked the Hindus to follow the 'cause and effect theory that is never disturbed by the thought of Divine pleasure or displeasure', where water always boils at a certain temperature, and fixed proportions of hydrogen and oxygen always give water, 'whether God wills it or not'. See pp. 204–6.

114. Ibid., p. 162.

115. Ibid., p. 180.

116. Keer (1997), p. 257.

117. Keer (1973), p. 362. Emphasis added.

118. Ibid., p. 174.

119. Ibid., p. 175.

120. Ibid., p. 302.

121. Ibid., p. 313.

122. Ibid., p. 240.

123. Ibid., p. 241.

124. Ibid., p. 172.

125. Ibid., pp. 780–1.

126. *Collected Works of Mahatma Gandhi*, vol. LXXXV, p. 102.

5

Secularism, Modernity, Nation
An Epistemology of the Dalit Critique

Introduction

This chapter will explore the existential dilemmas of Dalit politics and the theoretical implications of the questions raised by Dalit politics, for secularism in general. A few clarifications regarding the title of this chapter need to be made at the very outset. What do I mean by the 'Dalit Critique' of modernity? Is there a body of writings by the Dalits that we may call 'a critique of modernity'? The answer is no, not at least in the manifest sense. However, it is the argument of this chapter that such a critique does exist—although without a name, or in a different name. A critique of modernity is an 'absent presence' in a large body of Dalit writings, which we need to extricate in order to be able to appreciate many of the more problematic aspects of the Dalit relationship to secular-nationalist or radical-secular politics.

The second clarification concerns the use of the term 'modernity'. In a sense, it may be incorrect, strictly speaking, to talk of a Dalit critique of *modernity*, if by that term we simply mean modern development, science, and reason. However, as I will argue, these implicit critiques do interrogate the two great artefacts of political modernity in India—secularism and the nation. Dalit politics embodies a serious resistance to the binaries set up by modern politics in the era of nationalist struggle and subsequently in the contemporary moment. It refuses to get incorporated into either term of the binary of nationalism/colonialism and secularism/ communalism. It represents in its very existence, the problematic 'third term' that continuously challenges the common sense of the secular-modern. This resistance to these categories of modern politics is, at its core, a resistance to the very universalisms that characterize the emancipatory discourses of modernity. These discourses placed at their centre, the abstract, unmarked citizen—Universal Man—or the equally abstract 'working class', as *the subject* of history. Dalit politics in my reading, is deeply resistant to both the ideas—that of the abstract citizen and the privileged class. In parentheses, we may note that the 'neglect of minority cultures' inherent in these ideas, as Vernon Van Dyke and Will Kymlicka argue, 'has deep roots in the Western political tradition' and was the dominant common sense of both liberal and Marxist traditions throughout the nineteenth and early twentieth centuries. To be sure, there were 'countervailing' arguments in favour of minority rights too, but they were the marginalized tendencies; hegemonic traditions continued to stand in favour of such abstract notions of citizenship that recognized only *national identity*. Democratic constitutions too, when they did stipulate against discrimination on grounds of race, community, religion, and so on, did so with the individual citizen in mind. It is also worth pointing out here that a critique of *abstract unmarked citizenship* does not entail a rejection of the notion of universal citizenship as such. In fact, I would argue, it is precisely to make the latter more meaningful that the idea of a citizenship that is limited to the 'bilateral relationship between state and individual', is sought to be critiqued. Such a critique enables a recognition of a third party, the community, as a rights-bearing subject.[1]

The third clarification relates to the use of the term 'epistemology'. I use the term here to suggest that what we can extricate as the Dalit critique represents a resistance to some of the key political and theoretical *categories* of modern political discourse. It is not merely a political difference of opinion on strategy or tactics. In a larger and deeper sense, the term also indicates that in its emergence—both during the anticolonial struggle and now—the Dalit critique presents a challenge to the central diremption instituted by modernity, that between *the subject and the object*. Dalit histories, Dalit accounts of the past, like feminist ones in an earlier era, raise a fundamental question about the very possibility of the 'knowing subject' who stands outside the so-called object whose history she writes and about whom she 'produces knowledge'. The centrality Dalit discourse accords to the experience of caste oppression and the insistence that 'authentic' knowledge about the Dalit can only be produced by a Dalit, breaks down the subject-object dualism in a profound way. That no Dalit histories could be produced till Dalits themselves started writing their own history—much like the feminists—points to a deeper problem with academic histories written from the distance of a scientist, ever unable to share the experience of oppression or even see the existence of certain experiences.[2] In what follows, I will talk not about the Dalit experience but about what the knowledge produced by Dalit scholars has to say to (unmarked) 'academic scholars', and what it might have to say to the believers and practitioners of radical-secular politics.

We have seen in Chapter 2, how in the last two decades, more specifically since the anti-Mandal agitation, upper-caste discourse successfully repressed the category of caste by speaking the language of 'merit', 'efficiency' and even 'class' and 'economic deprivation'. We have also seen that this particular use of language has a much longer history that is embedded in the very structure of nationalist discourse—both secular and Hindu. The unspeakability of caste, I will argue, was not simply a matter of the casteism of the upper castes; it was also a result of the modernist discomfort with non-secular and 'retrograde' categories and really provided the overarching rationale within which the modern discourse of the upper castes took shape. In the recent past, however, especially in the post-Mandal commission period, the secularist has discovered the 'secularity' of 'caste', particularly of the Dalit movement. The fact that it was the irreducibility of caste divisions that actually turned out to be the rock against which the project of Hindutva seemed to repeatedly founder, made the category of caste respectable among secularists. The problem, however, is that while gestures towards the 'radical and secular' potential of caste are routinely made by the secularists, there has been little attempt to theorize the question of caste and its possible 'secularity'. It was backward and retrograde when the hegemony of secular-nationalism was unchallenged; it is radical and secular, now that bad days are here and the need for all kinds of allies is pressing. In the process, the politics of the Dalit movement is never sought to be understood on its own terms.

Caste and Secular-Nationalism

I will begin by posing the problem with reference to two recent essays by Sumit Sarkar. In his book, *Writing Social History*, Sarkar devotes an entire chapter, 'Identity and Difference: Caste in the Formation of the Ideologies of Nationalism and Hindutva' to the question of 'caste'. Here, as in the earlier paper, 'Indian Nationalism and the Politics of Hindutva', he confronts the problem of what he calls the 'historiographical silencing' and 'elisions of the category of caste'[3] and the *very obvious links* between such silencing and the priorities of mainstream nationalist history writing'.[4] In 'Identity and Difference', Sarkar takes the instance of the 'text-book understanding' of 'late colonial history' which in his view, is still largely *grounded on the assumption that the entire meaningful world of political action and discourse can be comprehended through the categories of imperialism, nationalism and colonialism...*'[5] In other words, Sarkar suggests that the elision of the category of caste, in historiography, is not merely an oversight: it is a *silencing* that is entailed by the illegitimacy bestowed on it by the very structure of historiographical discourse and the categories that it deploys. It is, or has been, illegitimate to talk of caste *as a category* in the writing of nationalist history precisely because in it the only legitimate actors were the forces of imperialism and nationalism. In the world of political action, one could only be either a nationalist or an imperialist stooge. In arguing thus, Sarkar points to an aspect of the politics of knowledge that will concern us in this chapter: the way in which the categories of thought and knowledge shape the very possibilities of political action. However, Sarkar only points in that direction; he does not lead us there. For he does not unpack the 'very obvious reasons' that he refers to, and so fails to uncover the *structure and assumptions of nationalist thought which rendered caste silent*. The thrust of his argument on the contrary, pushes in a very different direction, which is best understood by following him part of the way through his polemic with the historians of the Subaltern School. We need not go into the details of that debate here but it is instructive, for the purpose of posing our problem, to follow the main lines of his argument.

Sarkar says:

Less obvious, and therefore more worrying, are some recent tendencies that seem to be *reproducing that silence* precisely through what is accepted by many as the most radical and chic critique of all such nation-state projects. The burden of this critique is no longer class or even elite domination, but the alleged root of the modern or postcolonial nation-state in Western, Enlightenment rationalism, successfully imposed on the Third World by colonial cultural domination. *The logical corollary* of this total concentration on the critique of colonial discourse is that *only movements or aspects of life demonstrably free of such Western or rationalist taint can be given the status of authentic, properly indigenous, protest, resistance and culture.*[6]

Sarkar does not demonstrate the *logical* connection between the critique of colonial discourse and the search for authentic/indigenous traditions; he merely asserts it. As a matter of fact, it can be argued that the two are logically distinct questions: the object of the critiques of colonial discourse is colonialism, while protests and resistances whether supposedly 'tainted' by 'rationalism' or not, form the objects of very different histories which need not be affected by the former. However, to proceed with Sarkar's argument: The result of this connection, he says, is that '(I)t then becomes difficult to study with any marked sympathy, not only the history of the traditional Marxist left, but also figures like Phule or Ambedkar or the many movements that have tried to extend the rights of lower castes and women by selectively appropriating elements from Western discourses and even on using colonial state policies as resources'.[7] Sarkar goes on to characterize this 'deafening silence' of the 'bulk of subaltern studies historiography' in these areas as symptomatic of a general disease.

However, as Sarkar himself indirectly admits, this is certainly not an elision that is peculiar to the hardcore of nationalist historiography and *simply reproduced* by the Subaltern historians due to their 'obsession with colonial discourse'. Let me quote a long footnote from 'Identity and Difference', where he makes a kind of self-interrogation:

My own writings can provide some telling examples. *Modern India* (Delhi, 1983) probably gave more space to caste movements than did most other surveys of late colonial history. *I notice now,* however, that I had kept on using phrases like 'false consciousness of caste solidarity' and 'sectional forms' of expressing 'lower class' discontent, even while presenting sympathetic accounts of movements like Phule's Satyashodhak Samaj. *I have been going back recently to some of the early twentieth century Bengal material which I must have had a look at while writing my* Swadeshi Movement in Bengal (New Delhi, 1973). *Caste seems now to have been quite a central theme: it had figured only marginally in my doctoral dissertation and subsequent work.*[8]

Interesting here, is the suggestion that not only was nationalist historiography guilty of eliding caste, the only other serious alternative to it in India, namely, Marxist historiography too, suffered from the same distorted vision. Caste, which *seems now* to Sarkar, to *have been then* 'quite a central theme' had appeared only marginally, if sympathetically, in his own writings of that time. Despite having given more space to caste than many others, his work too continued to see it as the 'false consciousness' of a 'sectional' form (a *section*? Of the nation? The class?) Isn't the delegitimization of caste already accomplished in this understanding? If the thing called caste had occasionally been given space in any kind of history writing, it was simply because it kept irrupting onto the political stage. It appeared therefore as a matter of deep embarrassment—when it did. If that be the case, can we really avoid the suggestion that the 'elision of caste' may have stemmed from reasons not really all that 'obvious', such as the upper-caste character of nationalists (as Sarkar seems to suggest).[9] Perhaps the reasons lie deeper, and have something to do with the modernist-universalist desire to 'transcend' narrow 'sectional' identities?

I will just add two more instances here to buttress my point, before I go on to elaborate it. Nehru mentions in his autobiography, his reaction to Gandhi's announcement of his fast from Yervada prison, protesting against

Ramsay Macdonald's grant of a separate electorate to the 'Depressed Classes'. Reacting from Dehra Dun jail, Nehru expressed his great annoyance with Gandhi,

for choosing a side-issue for his final sacrifice - just a question of electorate. What would be the result on our freedom movement? Would not the larger issues fade into the background, for the time being at least? [...]And was not his action a recognition, and in part an acceptance, of the Communal Award [...]After so much sacrifice and brave endeavour, was our movement to tail off into something insignificant?[10]

Nehru's deep embarrassment is evident in his expressions like 'a side-issue', or 'something insignificant'. Nehru in fact, describes the 'emotional crisis' and the bouts of 'anger and hopelessness' that Gandhi's decision threw him into. In the same passage, Nehru then goes on to say that he felt angry with Gandhi for 'his religious and sentimental approach to a political question', leaving us in no doubt that what irked him was the 'irrationality' of Gandhian discourse. We now know that from the Dalit/Depressed Classes' point of view Gandhi stood then on the wrong side of the divide; that it was his stubborn Hindu upper-caste self that resisted their attempt to find separate representation. Yet it was to his credit that he alone, among the nationalist leaders of the Congress, grappled with the question of bringing Dalits into the anticolonial movement all his life, though all his moves were quite insensitive to the lived experience of the Dalits.

My second example: E.M.S. Namboodiripad in his *History of the Indian Freedom Struggle* comments on the Poona Pact and the great clash of the titans, Gandhi and Ambedkar thus:

However, this was a great blow to the freedom movement. For this led to the diversion of the people's attention from the objective of full independence *to the mundane cause of the upliftment of the Harijans* (emphasis added).[11]

What finds expression in both Nehru and Namboodiripad here is precisely a *modernist discomfort* with the category of caste and, as I will try to demonstrate later in this chapter, their argument is clearly drawn from the perspective of a modernist anti-imperialist nationalism rather than from that of their upper-caste position.

To return to Sarkar's passage cited above: why is it that today caste has suddenly become visible and more importantly, a legitimate object of both secular-nationalist and left-radical discourse, including that of historiography? In other words, why is it that when, after a gap of twenty years, the same historian confronts the same material, s/he discovers the centrality of a theme that had, on the first visit, seemed so marginal? Can we read this as a result of the other larger transformations that have taken place in recent years, transformations that mark the present conjuncture? To be more specific, I read in Sarkar's footnote the idea that the relationship of the historian/scholar to the 'material' or archive is always mediated by the external world *of the present*, forcing her into endless re-readings, reinterpretation of 'facts', and restructuring of her vision to be able to 'see' those 'facts'. That many of us today can see what was hitherto invisible, has been enabled by a fundamental restructuring of our vision in the last decade or more. And this restructuring of our cherished intellectual frameworks has been forced by developments from the outside. One of these developments is what I have called the *insurrection of little selves*. For this insurrection of little selves, we have seen, marks a global crisis of modernity and its great project of realizing the emancipation of Universal Man, embodied in the abstract citizen, unmarked by any identity. This project, we realize today, was meant to be achieved by erasing and repressing particular identities. In India, this crisis has been coeval with the crisis of the nationalist imaginary and the nation-state. With this 'insurrection of little selves', the Dalit has emerged—not merely as the *object* whose history 'we' secular historians and scholars can now write, but as the *subject* who writes her own history. It is this emergence of the Dalit as the subject-object of another history, one that falls outside the reckoning of secular/nationalist historians that we must now deal with. In other words, we must begin to deal with Dalit history *not as an adjunct to, or a part of, a history of nationalism and secularism*, merely reiterating its supposed 'secularity', but as the voice that demands recognition in its own right. As I will argue later in this chapter, if the early Dalitbahujan assertions in the personalities of Ambedkar, Periyar, Iyothee Thass, and such others, resists the incorporation into the nationalist narratives, so does the present Dalit movement resist the bid to assimilate its voice into that of secularism. If we listen attentively to the voices from within, we can hear precisely their refusal—despite heavy investments in the modern—to be willing parts of the two great artefacts of our modernity, namely, secularism and the nation. I will therefore argue that, belonging as it does to this instance of crisis, both the manner and the moment of the emergence of the new Dalit assertion direct us to read it as a critique of modernity.

This may sound strange because in the entire manifest discourse of the leaders of the Dalit and more generally, non-Brahmin leaders, modernity appears as the liberator from the tyranny of the past Brahminical order. The task that I seek to undertake in the rest of this chapter then, is to read the Dalit movement and its discourse as a text, *against its own self-perception*, in order to extricate the elements of its critique of modernity.

The Insurrection of Little Selves: Dalits and Others

The decade of the 1980s, we have already seen, saw the appearance of the first ruptures in the secular-nationalist discourse that had emerged from the freedom struggle. For the first time, the overarching 'Indian' identity gives way during this period, to innumerable smaller, 'fragmented' identities. These developments represented the unravelling of the structure of nationhood that had been laboriously built over the years of the national movement and given further shape in the constituent assembly.

From the Dalit or the Dalitbahujan standpoint, this moment of rupture has been seen as unprecedentedly liberatory. I am aware of the reservations expressed by certain sections of Dalit activists and scholars about the attempt to unite all the disparate groups into a single entity called the 'Dalitbahujan'. However, for the purposes of this chapter and the book, I will not dwell on these different strands within the movement and, instead, treat the Dalitbahujan discourse as one. In these articulations, the period since the 1980s but more specifically, the post-Mandal (1990) phase has been seen as the 'turning point'. Before I go into the critique, it may be necessary to recall the common sense about the Dalit relationship to modernity (and colonial rule), as well as Dalit self-perception on this issue, in order to make my point clearer.

It is by now common sense that there has been a considerable investment in modernity and its emancipatory promise among the Dalits and more generally, among the many non-Brahmin castes. To the extent that modernity in India is historically a product of the colonial encounter, this extends to a positive assessment of colonial rule. As V. Geetha and S.V. Rajadurai note, it was the availability of the language of rights and the secularization of public space, thanks to Western education and the modern processes unleashed by British rule, that provided the main ingredients for the emancipatory struggle of the non-Brahmin and the *adi-dravidas* (the Dalits).

If the declaration of certain spaces as public rendered them open and free in terms of approach and use to subaltern groups, a language of rights, which Western education and an acquaintance with political liberalism had provoked into existence, came to structure and direct subaltern aspirations for equality and justice.[12]

In fact, British presence meant something more. It was seen as a kind of Bonapartist regime that could balance different interests and provide the much needed space to non-Brahmin and Dalit assertions for dignity. As the Non-Brahmin Manifesto issued in December 1916 observed, it was the British alone who could 'hold the scales even between creed and class and ... develop that sense of solidarity and unity without which India will continue to be a group of mutually exclusive warring groups without common purpose and common patriotism.'[13]

Industrialization and modern education continue to be seen as liberators of the oppressed Dalit communities, and the social space of the city as the place of freedom. Chandra Bhan Prasad, a leading Dalit intellectual, in a highly symptomatic series of articles, also assesses the coming of the British as 'having made a difference' in this respect, in the following words:

British arrival coincided with the particular era when societies world over were emancipating themselves from the medieval social systems. The *emergence of urban civilization was a great phenomenon*, which made medieval institutions redundant worldwide. Emergence of urban civilization was intrinsically interwoven with *inventions of modern tools, scientific discoveries, spread of modern education*, in other words, industrial revolution, with which were associated *the notions of liberty, freedom and democracy.*[14]

How strong this aversion to 'medieval social institutions', in particular to the village, is can be seen clearly from the way D.R. Nagaraj relates the conflict between the militant farmers' movement in Karnataka and the Dalits.

The Farmers' Movement notice board at the very entrance of the village, declaring that no government official could enter it without the permission of the Raita Sangha is only a symbolic act... And this naturally means that the Farmers' Movement has intentions to establish administrative control also over the village. Dalits are wary of such moves since it smacks of the caste Hindu hegemony of the past.[15]

The motifs are all present and clear. The language of rights, the spread of modern scientific education, the emergence of a secular urban space, the ideas of liberty, freedom, equality—all situated in the city. These are recurring themes.

Yet, there is something amiss in this eulogy to the modern. A relentless resistance to the idea of abstract citizenship, through the insistence on what was called 'communal proportional representation' is inscribed in the very heart of Dalit and non-Brahmin politics from its very inception.

The life-and-death contestations that took place around this issue, which unrepentant modernists like Nehru and Namboodiripad found so embarrassing, and which eventually found their embodiment in the Indian Constitution, points to the need to examine afresh the various layers of this relationship between the Dalits and modernity. There are other compelling reasons why this exercise needs to be undertaken. Two hundred years of modern development and four decades of independence later, the struggle of the Dalits began anew in very different circumstances. It would be interesting to take a look at this new critique now. For the purposes of this chapter, I take one of the best articulated of these, *Towards the Dalitization of the Nation*, by Kancha Ilaiah.[16] I will occasionally refer to some others, to emphasize that his is not an isolated, idiosyncratic position. I will also refer, as and when necessary, to some other writings by him.

The New Dalit Critique

In the above mentioned essay, as well as in what can be called a companion piece,[17] Ilaiah distinguishes between three schools of thought in the anti-colonial struggle, namely: 1) Dalitbahujan nationalism represented by Jotirao Phule, B.R. Ambedkar, and Periyar. 2) Hindu nationalism represented by Tilak and Mahatma Gandhi (and in the second essay, he includes in this 'epistemological current', characters as diverse as Rammohun Roy, Nehru, Golwalkar, and S.P Mookerjee). 3) The Brahminical communist nationalism represented by P.C. Joshi and S.A Dange (in the second essay this list includes M.N. Roy, R.P. Dutt, T. Nagi Reddy and E.M.S. Namboodiripad and is referred to as the 'secular socialist nationalism that was caste-blind').[18] A footnote in the latter essay further comments on the secular communist stream, saying: 'All of them came from upper-caste and upper class backgrounds. In all their writings, Hinduism and Brahminism were never critiqued.'[19] This threefold distinction is important for it reveals some of the inner tensions of nationalism, even though it presents nationalism as a singular entity, subsuming the Dalitbahujan current as just another 'nationalism', and omits other currents such as that of Muslims.

According to Ilaiah, with the dawn of independence,

(T)he adoption of a republican, parliamentarian, constitutional democracy gave notional rights to the Dalitbahujans. *Gandhi's Hindu nationalist agenda was subtly given effect to by Nehru,* who strengthened the tendency to recruit *bhadralok* brahminical forces to control the state structures.

He then elaborates this point:

The Gandhian Harijanization process was also carried out through the state apparatus. *The Nehruvian state did this through the process of brahminization of the state* structures which ensured that *the so-called secular state became the private property of the brahminical castes.* The recruitment boards, educational centres, judicial structures, the military and police agencies *were consciously handed over to the brahminical forces.* To appear to be secular, some marginalized institutions were allowed to be headed by the Muslim elite, but they were coerced into accepting brahminical hegemony. The Nehruvian state structure *resisted the entry of the Dalitbahujans even through reservations,* their entry being described as the degeneration of the system.[20]

The interesting thing about this perception is that it sees the Gandhian Hindu-religious discourse as flowing seamlessly into what took shape as the Nehruvian state, Nehru's own discomfort and embarrassment with Gandhian 'sentimentality and religiosity' notwithstanding. It is also interesting that Ilaiah sees the process of the secular state becoming the 'private property of the brahminical castes' as a *conscious act* of the Nehruvian state elite, not as an unintended by-product of its working. Finally, his perception that the entry of the Dalitbahujans even through reservations, was seen as the degeneration of the system, points to the continuing embarrassment of the Nehruvian/modern elites with the idea of recognizing caste.

How do we understand this critique? One possible way of reading it would be to do so straight off, in its most manifest sense. But for such a reading to make sense, one would have to fall back on an essentialization of caste identity that remains unchanged through the great changes that modernity was expected to, and did, bring in its train. Alternatively, we would have to resort to a conspiracy theory of history and see the entire story of our modernity and of postcolonial India as the outcome of such a conspiracy. D. R. Nagaraj for instance, refers to it as 'the treacherous deal that was struck between the forces of modernity and the caste system.'[21] His is of course a very sophisticated rendering of the idea and he comes very close to anticipating what I think is the crux of the problem. So, he goes on to suggest that 'the Shudra thinkers were accurate and insightful in laying bare the strategies of oppression practiced by traditional society, but they were naive in their optimistic support to agents and practices of modernity.'[22] His reference to the 'naivete' in investing their 'optimistic support' in modernity actually points to the need for an investigation into the discourses and processes of modernity. However, here Nagaraj disappoints us and notwithstanding his own suggestion, still continues to see the problem as one of upper-caste conspiracy alone.

Before exploring the meaning of this critique, let us delve a bit more into what Ilaiah has to say. He goes on to argue that the 'Nehruvian state was not a secular agency because in its everyday practices in the offices, brahminism alone was constructed as meritorious, and it alone was shown to be India's salvation.'[23] He then makes the most amazing move of distinguishing between *two different modernities* in India: the Hindu nationalist—or what we may understand as official— modernity and the 'indigenous modernity' of the proto-scientific practices of the Dalitbahujans and women, always ever innovating in the course of their productive work.[24] This operation of bifurcating modernity and separating 'high' from 'low' already problematizes modernity, which has involved the erasure and silencing of such low cultures in order to homogenize, and standardize cultures/knowledges. Ilaiah then goes on to elaborate that this high 'official' modernity came to its own with the 'feudal Brahmins' selling away their landed properties and coming to occupy the position of the urban middle class. Through its control over the English language, this class came to control the state sector and finally, 'it was in the cities that the nexus between the twice-born castes (Brahmins and Banias) was consolidated.'[25] Thus was shattered the 'dream of the city' that was the fulcrum of the Dalit's attachment to modernity.

Politically, what is most galling however, is that with the emergence of the Hindutva challenge, came the re-imposition of the kind of binarism that was reminiscent of the national movement. 'The Dalitbahujan school *looked at the secularism vs. communalism opposition with suspicion* because Brahminism in whatever form cannot be secular.'[26] Many Dalit and Dalitbahujan scholars would agree with Ilaiah and clearly the BSP's alliance with the BJP in Uttar Pradesh would suggest that this argument against an absolute prioritizing of the secular-communal divide, has wider purchase. However, I am not very sure they would all agree with Ilaiah's reasons for regarding it with suspicion. Ilaiah gives the impression that the Dalitbahujan critique was that the so-called secularists were insufficiently secular because they were 'Brahmin'. More likely, the suspicion is because the imposition of the secular-communal binary model de-legitimized all other aspirations that were now coming to the fore, including that of the Dalits. Once the opposition was set in place, any political stance could only be understood if it made sense in the terms set by this discourse. Often the struggle between the Dalits and the neo-Brahmins in the countryside—or the neo-Kshatriyas as Ilaiah calls them, namely the dominant OBCs—forced a different kind of logic of alliances. Seen in the dichotomous world of 'secularism versus communalism', the BSP's alliance with the BJP in UP could *only be understood as opportunism*. Later in the essay, Ilaiah comes closer to spelling this out:

The so-called secular upper-castes, again in order to undermine the Mandalization process, organized a discourse around secularism vs. communalism. In this, the 'upper' castes working under various shades of ideologies—the socialist, Communist, liberal-democratic forces of the Congress variety...were very active...The leading role was, however, taken by the brahminical communists.[27]

Lest this be seen as idiosyncratic, let us quote from the article by Chandra Bhan Prasad mentioned above: 'Once again when the question of social transformation is being raised, we are being told we must join the "secular brigade" to defeat "communal fascism", and *probably they mean that the social questions can be tackled later.*'[28]

A Fissured Modernity and the Protean[29] Self

Let us try to make sense of Ilaiah's analysis (which, as I have indicated, is shared by some other important Dalitbahujan writers) of the seamless flow of Gandhian anti-modern Hindu-religious nationalism into the structuring of Nehruvian modernity. How do we understand this transformation or explain this perception without taking recourse to either option—that of cultural essentialism or that of a conspiracy theory of history?

Here I wish to refer to a slippage in Ilaiah's reading of the situation. What he attributes to the Nehruvian postcolonial state was in fact an already inherited condition. Yet I think this is not simply a factual error. I suspect that something else is at work here. If one were to argue that the Brahmin control over modern institutions had already become entrenched during colonial rule itself, then how does one reconcile this with the claim that it was colonialism and modernity that brought in possibilities of Dalit liberation? Laying the blame on the Nehruvian state on the other hand, does not raise such a problem given the Dalit experience with Nehruvian secular-nationalism. I am not suggesting that Ilaiah is dissembling; rather, my point is that just as caste constitutes a blind spot for secular-nationalist discourse, so colonialism and modernity constitute a blind spot for Dalit discourse. Chandra Bhan Prasad for instance, has often remarked in the past few years that the Dalit critique of colonialists is that 'they came too late and left too early.' Ilaiah does not go so far but where he criticizes 'official modernity' by positing a different modernity, he somehow seems to avoid implicating colonial rule in it.

Let us briefly look at the writings of some of the Dalitbahujan leaders during the course of colonial rule to understand this better. In his important work, *What Congress and Gandhi Have Done to the Untouchables* (1945), Ambedkar discusses the nature of what he calls the governing class, clearly in the colonial context. He has no doubt that the Brahmins are the governing class. He adduces two reasons for believing this. The first is their *cultural hegemony* or what he calls the 'sentiment of the people'. He explains this through several instances such as that of Malabar, 'where Sambandham marriages prevail' among the 'the servile classes such as the Nairs' who 'regard it an honour to have their females kept as mistresses by Brahmins to deflower their queens (sic) on *prima noctis*.'[30] The second reason, more relevant for us 'is the *control of the administration*.' He then goes on to provide statistical data of the community-wise distribution of gazetted posts in the year 1943 in Madras presidency to show the preponderance of Brahmins— especially in the more highly paid ones. He claims that similar data from other provinces can also be adduced in support of this conclusion but that would be unnecessary because it is so patently obvious.[31] Ambedkar went further and compiled the information on Congress victories in the 1937 elections and the representation of communities among Congress members of provincial assemblies, cabinets, and parliamentary secretaries to buttress his argument. 'In all the Hindu Provinces, the Prime Ministers were Brahmins. In all Hindu Provinces if the Non-Hindu ministers were excluded, the Cabinets were wholly composed of Brahmins.'[32] It may be noted that Iyothee Thass' frontal attack on the swadeshi activities indeed reflected the same anxieties. He 'located the power of the modern secular Brahmin in the control he wielded over public opinion'. The nationalist press, especially, was the butt of his attacks.[33]

Like Ambedkar, E.V. Ramasamy Naicker 'Periyar' too was concerned with the new power being acquired by the Brahmin in the modern secular realm. 'As far the Self-Respecters were concerned, the single-most secular index of Brahmin power in these modern times was the newspaper [...]The Self-Respecters were so convinced of the links between the power of the written (newspaper) word that they began newspapers of their own'[34] Geetha and Rajadurai draw attention to what they call Periyar's reading of the protean Brahmin sensibility. 'He remarked on several occasions that the Brahmins retained their privileges by remaining open to change and by adopting a winning flexibility.'[35] One of his statements in this regard is particularly striking:

Rajaji will eat at a panchama's house; Shankaracharya will bathe on seeing a panchama; some others will bathe if a panchama's shadow falls on them, others if a panchama touches them. Yet others will marry a panchama man or woman— but all of them will still remain brahmanas...Brahmin orthodoxy in 1940 was of a different kind than what obtained in 1900. After 1940 this orthodoxy changed form again.[36]

It is remarkable that Periyar is constantly alert to the extreme flexibility of the Brahmin self. He is also alluding here to the two different realms—one occupied and represented by Rajaji, the modern Congress politician and the other by the orthodox Shankaracharya. In Rajaji's realm the changes taking place, I believe, were such that the Brahmin was not only negotiating the challenges brought in by the processes of the modern but also *recasting the Brahmin self* in crucial ways. Many Brahmins remained Brahmins but many of them had seriously started believing that Hindu society needed to be modernized and freed of caste distinctions. The route taken for this was nationalism—the new imagination of a homogenous Hindu society as the centre-piece of the emergent Indian nation. The problem was that even they wanted this change on their own terms, that is, *without relinquishing their power, merely transforming it to suit the new and emerging secular realm.*

This is incidentally one of the points on which some of the historians of the Cambridge school seem to have built their argument against the non-Brahmin movement. David Washbrook for instance, notes that:

They [Justice Party leaders] argued that their challenge was solely towards the secular, political position which the Brahmins had attained. Yet, once the Brahmin's spiritual role has been stripped from him, how can he remain a Brahmin in any meaningful sense? What the Justice party really objected to was the political position of certain individuals *who happened to be Brahmins.*"[37]

The point raised by Washbrook touches the key issue involved—if in a somewhat *mala fide* manner. For Washbrook does point to the fact that it was not Brahminism in the old 'non-secular' ('spiritual') sense that was at issue. From there, however, he moves to asserting that therefore, it was a 'wholly secular' conflict (with individuals who merely 'happened to be Brahmins'). It seems to me that this is precisely where we need to uncover the layers of meaning associated with the transformation of Brahmin power in the secular realm—in the realm of civil society and institutions of modern representative democracy. Washbrook's simple conclusion that if this struggle was not against 'spiritual' brahminism, then it *could only have been against the secular power* of 'individuals who happened to be Brahmins' should alert us to the pitfalls of using such dichotomized categories. The modern/non-modern or modern/traditonal dichotomy often seems to blind us to the complexity of the very processes of articulation of the traditional and the modern.

Seen thus, what laid the foundations for the domination of the modern Nehruvian state institutions by the brahminical upper castes was probably not the kinship between Gandhian traditionalism and Nehruvian modernity, as Kancha Ilaiah suggests, but the very forms of articulation of the modern with the traditional, which was already taking shape during colonial rule. It is probably more likely that by the turn of the century neither sector was purely 'traditional' or 'modern'. I wish to suggest that what we identify as 'tradition' and 'modernity' in our context, actually represent *different articulations or combinations* of the traditional and the modern. And in between these two poles lie other variations of such differential articulations. It may be more useful to see what appear to be two separate aspects—the breakdown of the old order and the insertion into the new, necessarily hybrid, modernity—as *constituting a single moment.*[38] Thus it was not that the processes of modernity ushered in by the colonial encounter *first* destroyed the hold of caste hierarchies and *then* brought in the new world of modern development, industrialization and, a regime of rights and citizenship. Rather, the old was 'always already' present in the new but no longer in the old form. At one level this can sound like a moth-eaten truism. After all, a Marxist dialectician can always claim that the notion of *auhfebung* is *at once* the preservation of the old in the new *and* its transcendence. What I am suggesting here is not simply the play of the 'thesis' and the 'anti-thesis' that leads in the Hegelian-Marxist understanding to the new 'synthesis', for at the root of this understanding lies the singularity of the contradiction and the singularity of the synthesis. My suggestion, rather is that there are multiple articulations of the traditional and the modern, neither of which actually speaks with a single voice. Moreover, modernity does not begin writing its script on a *tabula rasa*; the traditional is constitutive of the form that modernity takes as much as the modern becomes the condition of the existence of the traditional. However, Marxist historiography and scholarship on India has seen this process in dichotomous terms as the 'dual role' of colonialism—the destruction of the traditional and the initiation of the modern. The categories thus have remained as dichotomized as in the writings of the modernization theorists.

In suggesting that the 'two aspects' be considered as a single moment, I wish to draw attention to the fact that the very process by which the political category of the 'Brahmin' became available to the non-Brahmin movement, thanks to the discourse of equality and rights, was simultaneously the process by which Brahmin power was re-instituted in the secular-modern realm.[39] Thus, by the time it thus became possible to challenge the Brahmin's oppression he had already mutated into something else. This new Brahmin's power accrued to him not because of his ritual superiority but because he had the advantages of English education.

There were at least two faces to this new Brahminism. If it is true that the Brahmin in colonial India was already a different being, we can see one face of his existence, as Periyar did, in the Brahmin whose infinitely malleable and 'protean' self saw the opportunities offered by colonial rule and quickly adapted itself to the new dispensation. This Brahmin deftly appropriated the public/private distinction to his convenience and 'privatized' caste identity by becoming secular in the public realm and a believer in the private.[40] Within his 'inner' domain, he continued to be a casteist, even to the extent of continuing to practise untouchability. But there was another face—that of the mutated 'nationalist' whose nationalism, like Savarkar's, was modern to the core, and which demanded the subordination of all questions of internal reform of the Hindu society to the fight for independence, or to the consolidation of the Nation.[41] This is what we see also with the Brahmins of secular anti-imperialist nationalist persuasion, such as Nehru and the Communists, though unlike Savarkar, Tilak, or Sardar Patel, theirs was a more inclusive nationalism. In a different way from the first then, this mutated upper-caste self too became, willy-nilly, a party to suppression of the urge of Dalits for liberation.

The problem with the pervasive sociologistic understanding of the category of the 'upper caste' (or caste in general) is that it can only fall back on the formal nomenclature, thus misrecognizing the function it begins to perform in the changed context. Let me make this more explicit by trying to break down the category of the 'urban upper-caste self' by interrogating the most problematic aspect of it—the notion of the 'Brahminical Marxist'. We may begin with Kanshi Ram's colourful metaphor regarding the communists: that they are 'green snakes in green grass'.[42] This metaphor leads us straight to the deep-rooted anti-communism within one important strand of the Dalit movement, right from the days of Ambedkar. Why this anti-communism came to be so strong among the most oppressed sections of Indian society is a question that has never been sufficiently posed by secular, radical, or communist scholars. From the side of the Dalits too, at best there has been a gesturing towards the upper-caste character of the Indian communists, but that is precisely the kind of sociologism that has become an uninterrogated common sense, which falls back on the essentialism that I seek to question.

The second part of Kanshi Ram's metaphor regarding the upper castes in other parties like the BJP, provides a cue that can be productively followed up. These upper castes are, according to him like 'white snakes in green grass'. In other words, the difference between the upper castes in other parties and those in the communist parties is that the latter are more difficult to identify. The radicalism of the communists makes 'them' indistinguishable from 'us'. This indistinguishability in itself may not have been a problem and the entire Dalit movement could have moved over to Marxism if it had seen its liberation as being possible there. 'Indigenism' did not carry weight for them and with the Marxists' celebration of modern civilization and technology, there should have been even less of a distance. What actually prevented such a possibility was the fact that already Indian Marxism had exposed itself as being insensitive and blind to Dalit oppression, operating within a framework that was most comfortable for the brahminical mind. Why this was so is precisely the issue that concerns us here and calls for further investigation.

In the first bursts of Dalitbahujan assertion, in the early years of this century, there was probably an important factor at work: what was at issue was a radical definition of the Self, an assertion of Dalit subjectivity. This Self *had to be, of necessity*, defined in radical alterity to its brahminical Other. This represents another, rather different articulation of the traditional and the modern since for the Dalit to be able to speak his/her lived experience, she had to speak in terms of brahminism and of caste in general. Marxism, on the other hand, in its reduction of all oppressions to class, tended to do violence to that enterprise of self-definition. The absolute prioritization of 'class' made caste oppression unspeakable. Further, the Dalit enterprise of self-definition was predicated on another, quintessentially modern project, a search for Dalit history. Marxism's rendering of history, its claim to be the sole agent of that history and its privileging of the anti-imperialist struggle over all others (in the name of History) was problematic, given the fact that, in effect, it proposed what the 'brahminical' Hindu nationalists wanted, although in a language that was irritatingly close to that of the Dalitbahujan leaders. In fact, Ambedkar's turn towards Buddhism and his introduction of a whole new narrative of Indian history as one of struggle between Buddhism and Brahminism was, I believe, an ingenious attempt at instituting a new historical discourse *as cultural memory*. By doing this Ambedkar was producing a modernist, rational-historical narrative while at the same time filling up what had been a major blank, an absence, the denial of a past to the Dalit. To be able to speak of the past in the language of history and modern subjectivity was the task at hand. If this was the magnitude of the task being undertaken by Ambedkar, he could scarcely afford to resort to abstract universal history. And abstract universal history may have seemed to him to be a means of *forgetting rather than recalling* because it dissolved the specificity of Dalit experience into a grand narrative of history. I would, in fact, suggest that the reason why many individuals from the privileged upper castes took shelter in 'universal history' was that by dissolving the specificities of particular experiences, it probably helped him/her to forget his/her 'shameful past' as oppressor or person of privilege. Class oppression was universal and we also had it—there was nothing shameful about it. But to accept that 'untouchability' was also a heritage of our past, was something the modern mind found difficult to deal with.[43]

Yet, anybody even remotely familiar with the history of Indian Marxism and Marxists would be aware that the generations of youth who came to the movement *did so through a rejection of their traditional identities, in search of a modern one*. The majority were youth from upper-caste backgrounds, though there were Muslims in fairly large numbers, and there were some from the lower castes too, who joined the communists. Their coming to Marxism was for them the acquisition of a new identity. They could thenceforth talk about their society and the struggle to change it in terms that belonged to the lexicon of modernity. To most of them, even the suggestion that they carried their upper caste socialization still within them would have seemed scandalous. Marxism was a means of forgetting the specific past for many, in the name of a larger universal one ('the history of all hitherto existing societies is a history of class struggles'). Here in this transformation, in the 'overdetermined' constitution of our modern self lies its protean character. *This* modern Self is not simply a traditional casteist in disguise. It is modern and in its self-perception, thoroughly purged of its traditional caste socialization. Often, it sincerely believes that the best way to be modern is to erase all thought of caste and religion from its mind. It is thus the truly liberated Self that in looking beyond the narrow confines of sectarian particularisms actually becomes blind to their continuing salience in a myriad new ways. It is this modern Self that appears upper caste in all the ways that the modern Self in the West appears routinely as white, upper class, male. If there is any trace in its consciousness of any of these privileges, there is always a rational and modern explanation for it. I will illustrate this with the example of E.M.S. Namboodiripad's text on the *National Question in India*. In this text, Namboodiripad summons the tools of historical materialism to explain Kerala's history. He understands the historical role of brahminism in terms of the institution of the caste system that 'ushered in *a superior economic organization of society*'. Dilip Menon's fascinating but troubling study quotes from the earlier Malayalam version of the text:

The greatest advantage of the caste system was that it paved the way for a major economic revolution. What the transfer of the rights over land from the hands of those who cleared the forests and cultivated the land, to those who lived off a portion of the produce without engaging in cultivation, actually meant was the emergence of a new sense of private property.[44]

Namboodiripad goes on to mobilize the most modern of the available arguments, thus:

...the well-known American anthropologist Lewis Henry Morgan, has conclusively shown that the matriarchal family is of a lower order than the patriarchal family. So have Marxist historians...(beginning with Engels himself) shown that the changeover from matriarchy to patriarchy takes place at a time when the hoe is replaced by the plough as the instrument of production in agriculture.[45]

Notice that this defence of the caste system and patriarchy follows an altogether modern logic rather than that of his erstwhile Brahmin Self. One can add with a fair degree of confidence that many of the communist leaders and activists, at least at a conscious level, made serious efforts to purge aspects of casteist practices that they had inherited from their early socialization. And yet they remained caught within the mesh of caste (and of gender) privilege and therefore, of discriminatory practices. To recognize this phenomenon as modern is to problematize the universalisms of modernity; it is also to realize the formidable challenge that this mutated 'upper-caste-ness' presents. I therefore, find it difficult to agree with Dilip Menon or many of the Dalitbahujan critics who would prefer to read this as a straightforward attempt by E.M.S. at negotiating 'his Namboodiri identity at a time when Brahmins were under siege in south India...'[46]

In this context, it is interesting that this problem of sociologistic essentialization of caste identity seems to have presented itself before both Ambedkar and Periyar and they grappled with it in their own ways. Ambedkar, in fact, at one stage made this explicit: 'By Brahminism, I do not mean the power, privileges and interests of the Brahmins as a community. That is not the sense in which I am using the word. By Brahminism I mean the negation of the spirit of liberty, equality and fraternity [...]In that sense, *it is rampant in all classes*'.[47] He then goes on to say that the effects of this Brahminism were evident not merely in the social sphere but also in the denial of civic rights to untouchables as well as in the field of economic opportunities.[48] Periyar even coined a term for this new form of Brahminism—'political brahminism'. He often noted that the Brahmin's resistance to social reform was grounded less in religious orthodoxy and faith and more in their political proclivities, intents, and ambitions.[49]

To understand this upper-caste-ness as mere Brahminism in a sociologistic fashion is to imply that they are incomplete moderns. It is to imply that this lack can be overcome by more and better modernization. On the other hand, to understand this phenomenon as the way the universalism of modernity took root in our specific conditions—as in the West, where too, it has constructed the dominant culture there as the norm—is to problematize the specific trajectory of modernity in our context and thus open up the possibility of emancipation and the recovery of lost voices in the new dispensation. We need to recognize that notwithstanding this feature of the universal modern, it remained a 'secular' modernity. In fact this is precisely what the contemporary crisis of modernity seems to be all about. The insurrection of little selves, globally, is precisely a challenge to that universalizing aspiration of modernity that, in its bid to standardize and homogenize and to create the 'Universal Man' (the abstract citizen) actually ended up presenting European culture as the norm. Universalism is the privilege of the dominant in the contemporary world. For it to be able to see what is not dominant, it has to be fissured. Only then does it become possible for us to see this protean modern Self—the Self which is a mutant of the old but is still irreducibly new. The 'treacherous deal' that Nagaraj talks of cannot, therefore, be understood as a mere conspiracy between the upper castes and modernity. It is a problem of the universalizing tendency of modernity that it is destined to run up against the subversive deployments of its own discourses of rights and equality, thus opening up such fissures and breaches on its front.

Ambedkar, Periyar, and Modernity

It seems to me that one of the persons to see this problematic aspect of modernity—though he did not articulate his discomfort in these terms—was Ambedkar. His alertness to the question arises out of his subaltern social location and becomes apparent in relation to what Gail Omvedt has described as the 'problem of entry'. What she means by the 'problem of entry' is basically that of 'getting jobs and getting land'[50] in the case of workers and the peasants respectively. She argues that 'Dalits *were* workers; they *were* peasants; but as workers they were invariably in the lowest paid and most unskilled industrial jobs and as peasants they were likely to be landless or poor peasants'.[51] It was this that concerned Ambedkar more than anything else. Consequently, he saw how the 'basic problems of the untouchables being excluded from the higher paid weaving jobs' was also being reflected in their being less represented in leading and organizing the struggles of textile workers. In the course of the 'historic textile strike' of 1928, Ambedkar told the Simon Commission, he had brought up this matter repeatedly before union leaders. 'I said to the members of the union that if they did not recognize the right of the depressed classes to work in all the departments, *I would rather dissuade the depressed classes from taking part in the strike*[52] .

As we shall see below, there are two important senses in which Ambedkar resists the universalizing urge. First, by refusing to privilege the 'nation', 'anti-imperialism', and 'class', over the question of caste, he is resisting the idea of the part being represented in an *essential section* of the whole.[53] In other words, he is resisting the prevalent common sense, that if the whole is free, the part will be free; if India is free so will all its constituent parts. The part—Dalit Being—is not part of any whole and cannot be represented in any essence of the whole. The irreducibility of the part is also its declaration of autonomy. Second, he is also questioning *the very given-ness of the working class*. The 'problem of entry' then, is the problem of the very 'making' of the working class. The working class was no transcendent entity in whose abstract embodiment, as the Subject of History, the Dalits could invest their future. It was a real, 'actually existing' class, which, like everything else, could be and had to be shaped. It had to be transformed from its upper-caste blindness to the Dalit experience. This, by the way, is part of a larger sensibility shared by many Dalit leaders of the time and the instance of the 1921 strike in the Buckingham and Carnatic Mills in Madras city brought out the conflicts equally clearly. It also exposed the fissures *within* the larger non-Brahmin identity that was being constructed by the Justice Party. We need not go into the circumstances of the strike called by the Congress-supported union but it is important to note that the adi-dravida (Dalit) workers of Binny Mills refused to participate in the strike. Amidst accusations that they were blacklegs, M.C. Raja, one of the important political leaders of the adi-dravidas, commented that the 'adi-dravidas had exercised their right to give or withhold their labour as they thought best in their own interests. Previous experience had taught the adi-dravidas that participation in strikes proved detrimental to their interests and they had often been forced to sell their property and pledge their jewels in the past.'[54] The interesting account of the long fall-out of the strike and the disturbances that followed as violence erupted in Pulianthope in north Madras, between the adi-dravidas and the strikers, is described in detail by Geetha and Rajadurai. This description throws into sharp relief, the background that may have shaped Ambedkar's later stance on the matter.

The above statement of Ambedkar's is not an isolated instance. He was clearly continuously troubled by the problem of the 'making' of the working class. Even when he got involved with the task of organizing the 'actually existing' working class, he remained alive to this problem. It is well-known that when he formed his first political party in 1936, he called it the Independent *Labour* Party. From then on, till the Cripps proposals forced the question of constitution-making on the agenda, bringing alive the spectre of an imminent Hindu rule, and he had to re-position himself as the leader of the Depressed Classes, he continued to be keenly involved with the questions of labour and the making of the working class. Dhananjay Keer highlights this role of his in a fairly detailed manner. This was the time that he concerned himself also with the general struggles of the working class, resisting the infamous Industrial Disputes Bill, and organizing strikes and public meetings jointly with the communists. Even during this period, however, his concern in this direction can be seen, for instance, in his organizing of the Untouchable Railway Workers Conference and attempts to address their issues separately as well. 'He asked his critics how they would consolidate the working classes when they did not remove such glaring injustice and partiality which was wrong in principle and injurious to the principle of solidarity.'[55]

While resigning from Gandhi's Harijan Sevak Sangh, Ambedkar wrote a long letter to A.V. Thakkar, secretary of the Sangh, stating: 'Like the Negro in America, he [the Untouchable] is the last to be employed in days of prosperity and the first to be fired in days of adversity. And even when he gets a foothold, he is confined to the lowest paid department...'[56]

As I mentioned, not only does Ambedkar refuse to take the working class as given, he equally vehemently refuses to accept the givenness of the nation, such as was sought to be constructed by the Congress.

...(I)f the Untouchables have not joined the 'Fight for Freedom', he contended, 'it is not because they are the tools of British Imperialism but because they fear that the freedom of India will establish Hindu domination which is sure to close to them, and forever, the prospect of life, liberty and pursuit of happiness...The Congress, on the other hand regards the freedom of India from British imperialism to be the be-all and end-all of Indian nationalism. [57]

It is important to note too, that Ambedkar not only argued against the Congress idea of nationhood; he problematized the very category itself. In the text I have quoted above, which he intended the 'foreigner' [rather Westerner] to also read, Ambedkar deals at length with the category of 'nation'. For he believes that the foreigner is allowing himself to be deceived by the Congress brand of nationalism. Thus Ambedkar: 'words such as society, nation, and country are just amorphous, if not ambiguous terms. There is no gainsaying that "Nation" though one word means many classes. Philosophically, it may be possible to consider a nation as a unit but sociologically it cannot but be regarded as consisting of many classes.' The reason why the foreigner allows himself to be misled into supporting the Congress, he says, 'is to be found in the wrong notions of self-government and democracy which are prevalent in the West.'[58]

He goes on to argue:

Western writers on democracy believe that what is necessary for the realization of the ideal of democracy, namely, government by the people, of the people, and for the people, is the establishment of universal adult suffrage. Other means have been suggested such as recall, plebiscite, and short parliaments...I have no hesitation saying that both these notions are fallacious and grossly misleading.[59]

Ambedkar then goes on to comment that democracy and self-government have failed everywhere and the reason is their inability to deal with the question of 'classes'.[60] The idea that he holds responsible for this failure is that of abstract citizenship. In many countries, 'the governing class may be so well entrenched that the servile classes will need other safeguards besides adult suffrage to achieve the same end [i.e. self-government].'[61] This is a failure of understanding that is irritating to him because it afflicts even the 'leaders of the British Labour Party, heads of radical and leftist groups in Europe and America represented by men like Laski, Kingsley Martin, Brailsford, and editors of journals like the *Nation* in America and the *New Statesman* in England...'[62] I suggest that this desperate bid to deal with the political categories of liberal democracy, born out of Ambedkar's social location, must be read as an attempt at negotiating the manner of their reception in our specific context. A tension runs throughout his life-work between the attempt to occupy an unmarked, universalist ground and his being forced to repeatedly abandon it. It is certainly as a modernist that Ambedkar acts, but all the same he refuses to take modernity and its theoretical and political categories as a package deal, questioning and resisting the very mode of its articulation with the non-modern.

The refusal to take the nation as given is evident also in the writings of all the major leaders of the Dalits/non-Brahmins. I have already mentioned Iyothee Thass. E.V. Ramasamy (Periyar), too was involved in continuously interrogating the nationalist project. As has been argued forcefully by M.S.S. Pandian, Periyar's concept of nation 'denied its origin in the classical Indian/Tamil past and envisaged it wholly in the anticipatory.'[63] Periyar's trajectory is interesting for, unlike Ambedkar after him, he did have a brief five-year spell of political life as a committed Gandhian and Congressman. In this phase, Ramasamy was fiercely nationalist and it was with his gradual disenchantment with Congress that he re-evaluated his understanding of British rule. It was then that he came to the conclusion that 'if we had remained the slaves of *north Indians*, we would have remained 'sudran', 'rakshashan', 'asuran', 'kundakan', 'kolakan', 'pratikolan', 'narakan'...'[64] His final break with the Congress came in November 1925, with the Kancheepuram Conference of the Tamil Nadu Congress, when two of his resolutions in support of 'communal representation' were disallowed.[65] In his interventions at the Kancheepuram conference he candidly stated that, '(I)n our present situation many fear that Swaraj if granted will only usher in Brahmana Raj. If, in these days of British rule, it is possible for some to prevent others from walking down certain streets and to prevent them from having access to water from the village wells and ponds [...]what would they [...] not do if they came to wield [political] authority? What horrors would they not perpetrate?'[66] There are many different phases through which his critiques of nationalism pass but all through them what remains more or less constant is the attack on the many faces of Brahminism as the centre-piece of that critique. It finally led, despite Ambedkar, to his 'painstaking...interrogations of the proceedings of the Constituent Assembly ...It culminated...[in his] rejection of the Constitution of India...'[67]

Unlike Ambedkar, Periyar actually remained a strong votary of socialism—what he called *samadharma*—and an admirer of the Soviet

Union. He also remained firm in his rejection of religion and his strong advocacy of rationalism, science, and progress. And yet, his subject is neither the industrial proletariat nor the abstract unmarked citizen produced within a discourse of universal history. His search for the Self leads him to an exercise analogous to that of Ambedkar's. He therefore produces a narrative of Indian history as one of the perennial struggle between the subjugated Dravidas and the subjugating Aryans.[68] His search leads him to the discovery of the Dravida Self, which he occasionally expands to include the Sudras and the ati-Sudras of the north—an untenable exercise in terms of the canons of history in whose name the fight was being conducted. But then, that is precisely the point. History, in this struggle, was not a scientific, objective reading of the past. It was a narrative already constituted by and therefore subordinate to the political demands of the present. Often, this history was not 'memory'; it was instituted as memory to fill in the big absence produced by the denial of the adi-dravida and Sudra past. But this mode of 'modern scientific history', as against the Vedas, Itihasas, and the Puranas which he relentlessly critiqued as 'irrational' and 'unscientific', was a necessary condition of emancipation, for it framed the entire constitution of the non-Brahmin, Dravida Self.

Despite E.V. Ramasamy's great appreciation of socialism, he, like Ambedkar came into conflict with the communists and socialists. He argued that class divisions in Hindu society were inscribed within caste divisions. '(B)rahmins lived of their intellectual capital and spiritual surplus while the non-brahmins, denied easy access to either, had to labour to live. The division of labour into intellectual and manual labour and the elaborate religious and cultural codes devised to validate this division were considered by the Self-Respecters to be fundamental to the problems of justice and equality in caste society.'[69] The modern category of class was thus constituted by the very nature of modernity's articulation with the non-modern, by the existence of caste.

In concluding this discussion then, I wish to suggest that the very existence of Dalit politics, both during the anticolonial struggle as well as in the present, continuously disturbs and challenges the binaries of nationalism/imperialism and secularism/communalism, refusing incorporation into either term of the binaries. Its very existence therefore challenges the complicity of the two terms which effectively serve to *prevent the emergence of the Dalit as subject*. It keeps erupting as the *problematic third term* repressed by the modern discourses of secularism, nationalism, and secular-nationalism. In fact, as our discussion shows, the argument is that precisely at the moments when the Dalit begins to find her voice, it is the binary mode of conceptualizing politics that seeks to stifle it. What continuously pits the Dalit against these categories framing thought and political action, therefore, is the *experience of subaltern location*, which sees modernity as simultaneously liberating and as denial of voice and agency. This is what gives centrality to the category of *experience* in Dalit scholarship and lies at the root of the widespread distrust of non-Dalit accounts of Dalit history. However, what appears as the essentialization of Dalit identity in this insistence on Dalit accounts of their own history, seems to be in fact, an attempt to reclaim the Dalit voice from the hegemonic practices of historiography.

To go back to Sumit Sarkar then, the 'deafening silence of historiography', I would suggest, needs to be understood as the effect of what can be called, with apologies to Kant, the 'categorical imperative' of modern politics as it historically came to be.

Caste and Political Society: The Other Face of the Modern Self

It is necessary at this stage to underline that the discussion so far deals explicitly with *only one aspect* of caste in modern society. This is exemplified by the existence of 'caste' in the modern Self that is, the committed secularist-liberal/Marxist individual. I have tried to break down the category of the 'brahminical Marxist' in Dalitbahujan discourse, in order to understand the existence of this self. The modern individuated self inhabits the ground of high modernity in India—the ground of civil society, governed by modern notions of citizenship and defined by contractual relations and rules of free entry and exit. Equality, autonomy, and deliberative procedures of decision-making are the values that underlie the functioning of the institutions that constitute it.[70]

On the other hand, there are vast domains of life that are differentially incorporated into this arena of citizenship. The history of the modern Self in India—and indeed in many non-Western, postcolonial societies—is marked by the existence of a very large domain where very different, often contradictory processes are at work. The advent of modernity has transformed the overall context and provided a kind of institutional set-up within which the so-called traditional has to negotiate its daily existence. In this domain of daily transactions between the traditional and the modern, we see the continued existence and salience of caste, religion, or ethnicity as it struggles to adjust itself to the new languages and practices of a modern democratic polity. I have referred to this domain, after Partha Chatterjee, as the domain of political society. The kind of secularized self discussed earlier, represented by the liberal/Marxist individual, actually consists only of a small, if crucial dimension of 'our modernity'. In this other vast domain of political society there are people who could even be described as say, 'full-blooded casteists'. If we look at the ways in which routinely, everyday discourse is marked even in the cities, by the languages of caste, religion, and the like, we would be compelled to acknowledge that there is a great deal of truth in the Dalit critique that the brahminical castes have taken over our public institutions and colonized the public sphere. And yet these too are *neither traditional nor modern*. These modes of existence represent attempts at negotiating the new world in languages that inflect the languages of political modernity with a distinctly 'traditional' flavour.

To understand the dynamic of what I am referring to, let us look at the phenomenon of caste associations. In the late 1960s, Lloyd and Susanne Rudolph described this politics of the caste associations as *the modernity of tradition*.[71] In this pioneering study, the Rudolphs described caste associations as 'paracommunities' 'that enable members of castes to pursue social mobility, political power, and economic advantage.' They argued that '(t)he characteristics of the paracommunity resemble in many ways those of the voluntary association or the interest group familiar to European and American politics.'[72] This was so in the sense that membership in the association was not purely ascriptive. Birth in a particular caste was a necessary but not a sufficient condition of membership in the association. More importantly, they argue:

When caste associations turned to the state for furthering their purposes, their initial claims were aimed at raising caste status in terms of the values and structure of the caste order. But as liberal democratic ideas penetrated to wider sections of the population, *the aims of caste association began to shift from sacred to secular goals.* Instead of demanding entry into temples, prestigious caste names, and 'honorable' occupations and histories in the Census, the associations began to press for places in the new administrative and educational institutions and for political representation. Independence and the realization of political democracy intensified these new concerns. Caste associations attempted to have their members nominated for elective office, working through existing parties or forming their own; to maximize caste representation and influence in state cabinets and lesser governing bodies... Perhaps the most significant aspect of the caste association in the contemporary era, however, *has been its capacity to organize what appears to be a politically illiterate mass electorate.* Doing so enabled it to realize in some measure its new formed aspirations *and to educate its members in the methods and values of political democracy.* [73]

There is a lot of empirical work that has been done since, in more recent times, that has made us alert to the more complicated dimensions of the developments that the Rudolphs refer to. In the first place, it can be argued that even the early attempts at recognition of their status by the state, which the Rudolphs think are in terms of the values of the caste order are, in fact, not so. Once the technologies of colonial governmentality were in place and the operations of enumeration and state recognition introduced the new dimensions in the recognition of status, the desire to get that recognition was *already* located outside the framework of the caste system. Sanction of status by the ritual authorities was subverted at the very instance the caste associations came into being. This continued well into the post-independence period. In one early study by Rajni Kothari and Rushikesh Maru, for instance, the authors showed how the formation of the Kshatriya Sabha of Gujarat brought together a marginal peasant and landless labourer caste called Bariyas, and the Bhils (a depressed tribal community) under the leadership of twice-born Rajputs. Kothari and Maru argued that the socially and politically democratic character of the Kshatriya Sabha was evident in the motivation behind its formation. 'Caste consciousness played a part, but not for the purpose of preserving caste traditions and customs but rather of transforming them through political power.'[74] In a study conducted around the same time by Myron Weiner, this secularization of caste became more evident. For instance one of the respondents told Weiner that being a Rajput 'is not a question of blood but of spirit and action'. Another told him that '(t)he Kshatriyas are a class, not a caste', while yet another told him that if the Bhils are brave enough, we will call them Kshatriyas'.[75] The change in status, notes the study, is not 'merely rhetorical', and that, at least within the sabha, 'Bariyas now sit on charpoys...on an equal level with Rajputs.'[76]

The more important point, however, is the suggestion that these associations have turned out to be paracommunities, implying that they have become detached in some way from ritual hierarchy and are emerging as equal to other communities or paracommunities, playing a mediatory role between the 'illiterate mass' and the political system. It is here, in this articulation of the new caste-community interests in relation to the state and at the same time, in making the new languages more intelligible to the masses they seek to represent, that the caste association (and by extension, communities in general) open up a new domain of political transactions between the two worlds. The Rudolphs correctly observe that the leadership in the caste association is no longer in the hands of those qualified by heredity. 'The availability of association leaders is conditioned by their ability to articulate and represent the purposes of the caste association and for this purpose they must be literate in the ways of modern administration and the new democratic politics.'[77] The very organization of the association then acquires the structure of modern voluntary associations: 'It has offices, membership, incipient bureaucratization, publications and a quasi-legislative process expressed through conferences, delegates and resolutions.'[78]

The Rudolphs also refer to a study by Willaim L. Rowe who reviewed 'the doctrinal orientations' of the *Kayastha Samachar* of Allahabad between 1873 and 1915. The interesting thing about this journal of the All-India Kayastha Association is that mid-way through its existence, it underwent a change of nomenclature and became the *Hindustan Review*. Rowe also found that by 1905, 'the specifically "caste" matters have been relegated to the rear section...with an increasing number of articles on national and political questions...(sometimes) by Parsi, Muslim and foreign writers.' He also quotes an editorial in the June 1901 issue entitled 'Caste Conferences and National Progress' that argued that caste feeling hindered 'true national feeling'.[79]

And yet, if were to conclude from this evidence that caste has become thoroughly modernized, we would be making a mistake. In order to understand the existence of caste in this wider domain, we need to refer to what Harold Gould calls 'compartmentalization'. In his study of the Lucknow rickshawallas, Gould found that all the persons in his sample adhered fairly strictly to the norms of endogamy. They dined too with members of their own caste groups 'under domestic conditions despite the fact that during working hours they constantly violated the rule enjoining commensal exclusiveness.' 'Respondents saw no inconsistency in this', according to him, as 'they held that their work is part of one domain with its specific necessities respecting social interaction while their domestic or non-work life is quite part of another.'[80] This compartment-alization of the domain of the home and the family from that of the workplace—and in a larger sense the entire public domain—is a crucial mechanism by which I believe, this other self negotiates modernity and its processes. The Rudolphs call this 'the Indian dilemma' and describe it as the 'contradiction between public ideology and private commitment'.[81] They go on to argue, along with Gould, that '(p)rivate commitment to tradition, to ascriptive communities and their values, however, not only is compatible with continued modernization but also, as long as it remains private, facilitates it by providing adaptive institutions.'[82] It is not difficult to understand that the continuance of the practices of untouchability in the private domain, along with other less abhorrent caste practices, can also be quite compatible with modernization. In the other domain of political society, at least, it continues to be so.

In more recent days, D.L. Sheth has also pointed to the continuance of similar trends of secularization of caste. On the basis of the CSDS election survey data, he has argued that caste has ceased to 'reproduce' itself as an institution of ritual hierarchy. His description tends to come close to that of the Rudolphs', that caste has in fact become a kind of 'paracommunity'.[83]

There is one problem, however, with this reading presented by the above studies. Despite obvious merits, they produce these descriptions within an overall narrative of modernization. All these studies conducted in the 1960s, carry the stamp of the times and the imprint of the modernization theory is writ large all over them. These studies then, can only see these developments as different stations on the high road to modernization of the peripheries of the non-Western world. The idea of compartment-alization or the 'Indian dilemma' appears then, to be of major significance, as the assumption is that as long as commitment to ascriptive identities *can be kept at a private level* they can *facilitate modernization*. And like the West, where religion has been consigned to the private realm, these commitments here too can ultimately become and remain private matters. Continued adherence to them therefore need present no problem to the modernizing project. A considerable amount of scholarship interrogating this kind of understanding of the modernization process has now made all the problems with it manifest. Without going into the details of such a critique, we can simply note that the modernization theory eventually ends up overlooking the specificity of different, alternative modernities. From such an understanding, it is only possible to see these hybrid formations as incompletely modern, but nevertheless, on the way to becoming fully modern ones.

It is necessary to underline that this simple story needs to be complicated today in order to properly grasp the trajectory of modernity in postcolonial societies like India's. The problem with this trajectory of postcolonial modernity is not only that it was an elite project as indeed, it was in the West too. Its problem rather, was that it was the project of an elite that discovered its Self in the humiliating experience of colonial domination. It wanted to be modern, for it understood that that was the very condition of its liberation from foreign domination, but it wanted to do so on what it considered to be its own terms. Undoubtedly, this elite was a brahminical Hindu elite and the terms on which it imagined its national liberation to be possible was therefore, by declaring its sovereignty in the spiritual/cultural domain.[84] This was what led, from the early years of the formation of nationalist discourse, in its moment of epiphany, to the stifling of all the impulses of internal social reform within communities and effected a closure that has been at the heart of the problem of our modernity. The critical point is therefore, that 'the search for a postcolonial modernity has been tied, from its very birth, *with its struggle against modernity*'.[85] The specific context of our colonial encounter and the way in which nationalism took shape then could not but lead to other such closures—as for instance among the Muslims.[86] The modernizing project, in our context then, is likely to always carry the trace of this past.

In some of his recent writings, Partha Chatterjee has also suggested that there is lodged, in the very constitution of postcolonial democracies, a contradiction that he describes as one between modernity and democracy. If by democracy we mean, not merely a set of institutions and practices, but more importantly, the 'entry of the masses into politics', then the ways in which this entry materialized in the first place, is further likely to pose a constant challenge to the project of modernization. I would, therefore, argue, with Chatterjee, and in the light of our discussion so far, that the contradiction is what ensures that the very character of our modernity is fraught with all these contradictory impulses. For this reason, even though caste remains but a trace of itself, and may thus have ceased to reproduce itself it is, like the religious community and communalism, bound to acquire a new life within the logic of the modern regime of power.

The new Dalit critique of caste then is really not so much about untouchability and the ritual practices associated with caste in the private sphere, but needs to be understood as a continuing struggle against the modern incarnations of 'casteism'. In this sphere, the point I wish to underline in conclusion, is that these modern incarnations of upper-caste privilege continue to have a powerful afterlife, precisely because they are no more articulated in the old language of caste. Their new resilience depends entirely on the modern discourses of 'efficiency', 'merit', and even 'hygiene'—when for instance, questions of purity and pollution come to be articulated within a modern universe. To that extent, the language of our secular discourse provides Brahminism with its most effective political weapon and language.

Notes

1. See Kymlicka (1997). See also Heater (1999). The term 'bilateral relationship', in this context has been used by Heater, p. 115.

2. I must clarify, that in arguing thus, I do not wish to essentialize 'experience'—which can itself be understood in different ways, in different contexts, by the subject of that experience. The question is too complicated to be discussed here. However, I do want to argue for a certain irreducibility of experience in its relationship to the subject. Else, these new histories would have been produced without women or Dalits ever having to speak for themselves.

3. 'Indian Nationalism and the Politics of Hindutva' in Ludden (1996), pp. 292–3; and Sarkar (1997), Chapter 9.

4. Sarkar (1996), pp. 292–3.

5. Sarkar (1997), p. 358, emphasis added.

6. Sarkar (1996), p. 292, emphasis added.

7. Ibid., pp. 292–3.

8. Sarkar (1997), fn. 3, p. 359. All emphasis added.

9. Later in his book, he does suggest precisely such a sociologistic explanation when referring to how nationalists of all hues resort to a lost glorious past (now Hindu, now 'secular') as the civilizational foundation of nationalism. He says that, on such occasions, 'it becomes difficult, even for a Nehru writing his *Discovery of India*, to resist the further slide towards assuming that that unity, after all, has been primarily Hindu' and adds: 'The slide was made easier by the undeniable fact that the bulk of the leading cadres of the nationalist and even the Left movements have come from Hindu upper caste backgrounds' (1997, p. 363).

10. Nehru (1936/98), p. 370.

11. Quoted in Omvedt (1994), p. 177. It is worth noticing that for reasons just the opposite, the Dalits too see the Poona Pact as a disaster—not of course to the 'freedom movement' but to their own 'freedom struggle'.

12. V. Geetha and Rajadurai (1998), p. 56.

13. Ibid., pp. 2–3.

14. Prasad (1999). I have quoted from an unpublished version of the same article.

15. Nagaraj (1993).

16. Ilaiah (1998).

17. Ilaiah (1999).

18. Ilaiah (1998), pp. 268–9 and (1999), p. 19.

19. Ilaiah (1999), fn 4, p. 39.

20. Ilaiah (1998), p. 272. All emphasis added.

21. Nagaraj (1993), p. 56.

22. Ibid., p. 56.

23. Ilaiah (1998), p. 275.

24. Ibid., p. 276.

25. Ibid., p. 280.

26. Ibid., p. 283, emphasis added.

27. Ibid., p. 285.

28. Prasad (1999).

29. This expression is suggestively used by Geetha and Rajadurai (1998).

30. Moon (1991), vol. 9, p. 205.

31. Ibid., pp. 206–07.

32. Ibid., p. 218. The figures in the tables accompanying this statement show a fairly high number of non-Brahmins too as an aggregate category but from the argument it seems that Ambedkar seemed to include the Banias and often, Kshatriyas as being part of the brahminical governing class.

33. Geetha and Rajadurai (1998), p. 63.

34. Ibid., pp. 314–5.

35. Ibid., p. 316.

36. Quoted in Geetha and Rajadurai (1998), p. 317. 'Panchama' is another name for the Dalit, the fifth, that is outcaste, in the four-fold system of *chaturvarna*. The rest of the discussion in this section is based on this work and on Pandian (1993), (1995).

37. Quoted in Pandian (1995), p. 387

38. I owe this point to a discussion with Nivedita Menon. Further discussion with M.S.S. Pandian helped me sharpen the understanding in the context of non-Brahminism.

39. I owe the point about the emergence of the 'Brahmin' as a political category to M.S.S. Pandian, made in a personal communication to me.

40. For a more detailed consideration of this category, see the last section of this chapter.

41. See the discussion in the last section of Chapter 4.

42. Ilaiah (1999), p. 41, fn. 31.

43. Some commentators in a recent volume, *Dalit Jan-Ubhar*, point out that enthusiasts of class-struggle considered caste an 'unnecessary complication', better ignored, and preferred to look ahead. See Rathor et al. (n.d.), p. 284.

44. Menon (1999), p. 76.

45. Namboodiripad (1952), p. 7.

46. Menon (1999), p. 61.

47. Keer (1954/1997), p. 303.

48. Ibid., p. 304.

49. Geetha and Rajadurai (1998), p. 319.

50. Omvedt (1994), p. 154.

51. Ibid.

52. Ibid, emphasis added.

53. Here I am slightly misusing Althusser's notion of the 'essential section' or *coup d'essence*. See *Reading Capital*, p. 94.

54. Geetha and Rajadurai (1998), pp. 181–3.

55. Keer, Op. Cit. p. 304

56. Ambedkar (1991) Op. Cit. P. 187

57. Ibid. Pp. 168, 169

58. Ibid., pp. 201–2.

59. Ibid., pp. 202–3.

60. One may note that Ambedkar often uses the terms 'governing' and 'servile classes' to denote castes.

61. Ibid., p. 204.

62. Ibid., p. 235.

63. Pandian (1993), p. 2282.

64. Ibid., p. 2283. These are different names for 'demons' or demonic people.

65. Ibid., p. 2282.

66. Geetha and Rajadurai (1998), p. 291.

67. Ibid., p. 323.

68. It may be mentioned that Ambedkar had rejected this Aryan domination theory, though others like Jyotiba Phule upheld it. It has since been revived by Kanshi Ram and the BSP. See Dube (1997) for details.

69. Ibid., p. 439.

70. For a quick definition, see Chatterjee (1998), p. 10.

71. Rudolph and Rudolph (1967).

72. Ibid., p. 29.

73. Ibid., pp. 32–3. Emphasis added.

74. Kothari and Maru (1965), quoted in Rudolph and Rudolph (1967), pp. 99–100.

75. Weiner (1967), quoted in ibid., pp. 100–1. There are any number of historical and sociological studies available now to illustrate this point. I am only indicating the ones quoted by the Rudolphs.

76. Ibid., p. 101.

77. Ibid., p. 34.

78. Ibid., p. 35.

79. Quoted in ibid., p. 125.

80. Gould, 'Lucknow Rickshawallas: The Social Organization of an Occupational Category', *International Journal of Comparative Sociology*, quoted in ibid., p. 121.

81. Ibid., p. 130.

82. Ibid., p. 130.

83. Sheth (1999).

84. Chatterjee (1993), p. 6.

85. Ibid., p. 75.

86. See discussion in Chapter 4, especially Ambedkar's discussion of this question.

6

Secularism the Marxist Way
'High' Theory and 'Low' Practice

Introduction

In Chapter 3, through a reading of the secularism debate, we discussed
the fate of state secularism in the face of increasing challenges from the
various assertions of identity. In the previous chapter, I have discussed the
implications for secular politics in general of the Dalit critique of secularism
and of the nation. There was however, another kind of secularist project
that was distinct from state-secularism. This was the left/radical secularist
project. In this chapter, I will discuss the fate of that project through an
examination of the experience of one of the most important left-wing
formations, namely the CPI(M) in recent years. As this experience has a
direct lineage linking it to the international communist movement, some
of the issues arising out of that experience and its relation to the early
experience of Marxism in India will also come up for discussion.

Our review of the secularism debate of the 1980s and 90s, in Chapter
3, revealed two kinds of problems. First, that the crisis of secularism has a
lot to do with its being a state-centric discourse that occupied a kind of
archimedean space, as the neutral arbiter between communities, that the
creed referred to universalist values of rights, equality, autonomy, and liberty
for its legitimation, which provided it a neutral, but abstract ground. This
ideology continued to enjoy a hegemonic position with the emergence of
the new nation-state. With the partition accomplished, the Muslim League
out of the picture, and the other sections willing to give freedom and the
Nehruvian elite a chance, this elite established its hegemony alongside the
hegemony of the secularist creed. With the hegemony of this elite coming
under challenge, the hegemonic position of the secular creed also came to
be questioned. As new conflicts developed, it became clear that the old
archimedean ideal was no longer commonly acceptable. There was a
breakdown of communication, or in Partha Chatterjee's terms, a 'refusal

to engage in reasonable discourse', the possibilities of deliberating within a common frame of value commitments and resolving tensions within them, became thin.

Second, we also saw in our discussion that the universalist language of secular-nationalism had not only rendered it incapable of dealing with the non-secular oppressions like caste but also, on the contrary, facilitated the preservation of the old relations of power within the new dispensation. While the notions of equality, liberty, and the discourse of rights provided the oppressed sections with a language of struggle and resistance, the fact that this new language became available to these sections within a context of colonial domination, led to a series of complications. As our discussion of the constitution of the colonized's subjectivity showed, the self-realization of the modern elites was not only framed by the experience of a civilizational defeat; it was already conditioned by colonial practices. Notions of selfhood that took root were framed within the practices of colonial governmentality; more importantly, they were also lodged within the epistemological criteria established by the West. New historical imaginations were set in motion, which built upon fragments of 'memories' of past experiences and reproduced them within narratives that were lodged within a field already structured by these governmental practices and the Orientalist scholarship from which these constructions invariably drew. The fact of being subjugated by a foreign power, we also saw, effected certain closures in the processes of reform within communities that had begun in the early part of the nineteenth century. It was this context of 'self-realization' that mediated the reception of the ideas of the secular-modern imaginary by the elites, thus leading to the ideas of equality and liberty themselves undergoing a silent transformation of meaning. Referring to the 'vernacularization' of these ideas, Sudipta Kaviraj has shown how notions like the individual right to autonomy were 'simply transferred' 'to the national community'.[1] Liberalism thus played a crucial role, not in implanting liberal ideas but nationalist ones. 'The democratic language largely bypassed liberalism.'[2] I would extend this argument, in the light of our preceding discussion, to say that this conceptual paraphernalia was transferred not merely to the national community, but to each social group or community that entered the fray and thereby appropriated it to its own vocabulary in the struggle with other communities. What our discussion suggests is that this circumstance led to the democratic language instituting a fundamentally different logic in the relations between these different communities: *they became one another's adversaries*; equality and autonomy became their attributes in the unfolding struggle for power. This was so not only in the case of the lower castes, but also for instance, between the Hindus and Muslims, and wherever power was unequally shared. Secularism and democracy, in other words, appeared very different here from the sense in which we know them from Western history. Secularism either remained the creed of a high modernist elite, always ill at ease with the way the contest between communities was playing itself out, or was appropriated to serve the purposes of an upper-caste hegemony.

It is scarcely surprising therefore, that the Indian debate on secularism and modernity has been framed largely in terms of the state/community and tradition/modernity dichotomies. While the Indian debate reveals rich insights into the questions at issue, it seems that it also remains caught within its own terms. So for instance, for critics and supporters alike, secularism (and modernity) are engaged with as being colonial impositions and therefore state-centric. The question then really hinges on evaluating the nature of colonial interventions in Indian society. Many critics of secularism would argue that the fact of colonial imposition should alert us to its inherent limitations, while many secularists hold that as the colonial state merely built on processes (and resources) within precolonial society, it did not really introduce a fundamental rupture. Still others would acknowledge the rupture but invest it with an entirely positive meaning, the past/tradition being only worthy of rejection.

However, there was at least one more route through which the secular-modern imaginary entered societies like India's: this was the route of Marxism, which had neither the burden of the state nor the colonial legacy to shoulder and which should therefore have been different in its approach from that other secularism, namely state-secularism. As it happens, the fate of left-secularism and state-secularism actually converged as the crisis grew. This, I will argue, had something to do with the profound epistemic rupture introduced by the canonized versions of Marxism. This rupture, I will argue, was not merely a function of colonial rule; nonetheless, it shared a common epistemological ground with colonial modernity. These modern ideas did not begin writing their script on a clean slate; nor were they always received by passive colonized elites as readymade recipes. The emerging new elites often saw them as resources to be put to use in their own way, inflecting them with their own specific meanings. This is what Kaviraj attempts to capture in his notion of 'vernacularization' of the categories of Western political thought. But it will be a mistake to think that 'vernacularization' was the only way these categories made their way in these new habitats. There was among a section of elites, an equally strong impetus to uncritically accept some of these categories and modes of thought. They could not, as a consequence, really enter into a conversation with the situation existing in the postcolonial world. Many communists would belong to this latter category. I would emphasize however, that there is no neat separation possible between these two kinds of responses to Western modes of thought and all too often we find differential combinations of these two within the same individuals or discourses. What we probably need to bear in mind is Fanon's suggestion that the native intellectual who becomes the vehicle of nationalism, is an already uprooted colonial product. This condition becomes both his strength and his weakness as s/he stands at the confluence of two worlds and can bring in the resources of the one to critique the other. It is such an intellectual, caught in this fascinating dialectic of universality and difference, who becomes the vanguard of the Marxist movement as well. It is this dialectic of the universality and difference that I shall be concerned with in this chapter.

Marxism and the Postcolonial World

Since the problem of Marxism concerns the entire postcolonial world, let me pose the question by quoting a passage from an Egyptian Marxist scholar, Anouar Abdel-Malek. In the introductory chapter we discussed Engels' remarks on the Slav nationalities. Here Abdel-Malek cites instances from Argentine historian Gustavo Beyhaut on the problem of race in Latin America where Beyhaut cites 'a number of interesting references to Engels' where he discusses nineteenth-century European colonial wars:

In an article published on 23 January 1848 in the *Deutsche Zeitung* and another published in February 1849 in the *New Zeitung*, Engels discusses the war of 1847 between the United States and Mexico. He refers quite unambiguously, to the positive character of American expansion in Mexico, in so far as it represents the expansion of an advanced civilization...This could be extended even, let us say, to cover Vietnam a century later.[3]

Note Abdel-Malek's ironic remark that draws attention to the fact that a century later the story of civilizational advance could no longer be read into the American aggression in Vietnam. In a very stark fashion, this passage says something about the profound change, the radical alteration of the terms of discourse, that had already taken place in Marxism during the intervening century. Was this simply because the nature of capitalism's expansion underwent a qualitative change with the appearance of imperialism? Or, was it the case that with the appearance of Lenin's

Imperialism, The Highest Stage of Capitalism, the basis was laid for the complete transformation of Marxist discourse? Any number of quotations can be marshalled from the writings of the founders of Marxism to show how nineteenth-century Marxism shared a common ground with Orientalist, colonialist discourse, in fact, was largely located within it. However, the transformation referred to above, remains relatively uninvestigated.

To recall what the founders of Marxism said in 1848, let us also look at the following, well-known passage from *The Communist Manifesto*:

The bourgeoisie has subjected the country to the rule of the towns. It has created enormous cities, has greatly increased urban population as compared with the rural, and has thus rescued a considerable part of the population from the idiocy of rural life. *Just as it made the country dependent on the towns, so it has made barbarian and semi-barbarian countries dependent on the civilized ones, nations of peasants on the nations of bourgeois, the East on the West.*[4]

Notice that the terms 'rural population', 'country' 'barbarian and semi-barbarian countries', and the 'East' are all analogous categories—repositories of idiocy (the *lack* of Reason?), embodiments of a past that was unproblematically and unadulteratedly 'barbarian'. Since then, things have changed significantly, so that today, if at all Marxism survives it does so in the continents of Asia Africa and Latin America. Its long march has traversed not merely one and a half centuries, it has moved from the West where it was born, to the East which it saw as the habitat of the barbarians and the irrational, and where it found its most enduring home.

Taking the cue from Abdel-Malek, I will suggest that what happened in this period to Marxist theory, crucially, was the displacement of the historical/economic determinist problematic by the centrality acquired by the 'specificity of the political'. If the celebratory tone of the *Manifesto* was predicated upon the 'higher technological and cultural/civilizational levels' of capitalism (that made it the 'unconscious tool of history'), the Leninist-Maoist moment of Marxism's development *privileged the political*—the revolutionary potential of the oppressed peoples and the peasantry of the colonial world and, in its later form, of the 'Third World'. There are major tensions on this point in the writings of Lenin, whose initial faith rested on the West and subsequent to the October revolution, specifically on the European proletariat, which was to be the standard-bearer of world revolution. The Maoist moment, on the other hand, in the enunciation of the contradiction between 'national liberation struggles and imperialism' as the central and focal contradiction of the epoch, (at the time of the Great Proletarian Cultural Revolution), represents the complete displacement of the economistic problematic. The fact that the Chinese people were 'poor and blank' became the virtue, the source of their revolutionary energy. The subsequent, completely bizarre form in which this expressed itself in the so-called three worlds theory, also represents to an extent the extension of the same dynamic.[5] This emphasis on the political rather than the economic, in my opinion, had to do with the aspect that Kaviraj highlights in the context of liberalism, namely the vernacularization of Marxism.

In 1848, when the *Manifesto* was published, the West was the centre of the world and the world revolution, and the East figured in the document, as in many other pronouncements of the founders of Marxism, as a mere remnant of the past. I have already quoted some of the relevant passages above. Not only are they steeped in Orientalist common sense, they are also fully in line with the metaphor of darkness and light that is the central organizing principle of the Enlightenment. What were different societies, different cultural configurations located outside the physical space of the Enlightenment, became transformed and constituted as temporally prior— as relics of the past whose dissolution had to be welcomed as they represented backwardness. And for this, colonial wars of expansion could be justified in the name of History. The East was backward because of its superstitious beliefs in religion, magic, sorcery, and the like. It had to wait for the West to civilize it, to bring it to light.

I had argued elsewhere that Marx's resort to such Orientalism only showed that even for a revolutionary like him it was not possible to transcend the discursive horizon of his times.[6] Andre Gunder Frank has responded to this suggestion, arguing quite forcefully that far from being simply limited by the discursive horizon of his times, Marx is in fact constitutive of that moment in Western thought that relegated the Orient to the position it came to occupy. He also draws attention to Western scholarship till as late as Adam Smith which recognized the immense contributions of Oriental societies like the Arab world, China and India.[7] This is a legacy that continues through a large part of the history of the communist movement. The 'East' continues to appear as a problematic object: Almost all the questions of identity, religion and community keep appearing here, throwing the secular universalism of Marxism into repeated crises.

Fernando Claudin, in his studied and extremely well-documented account of the Communist movement, shows how the problematic category of the 'East' appeared as a crucial one through successive struggles within the Comintern. He shows that Lenin himself was till as late as

1912, a European at heart.[8] In his article on the 'Awakening of Asia', written in the wake of Sun Yatsen's revolution in China, Lenin wrote welcoming the revolution:

Does that mean...that the materialist West has hopelessly decayed and that the light shines only from the mystic, religious East? No, quite the opposite. *It means that the East has definitely taken the Western path, that new hundreds of millions of people will from now on share in the struggle for the ideals which the West has already worked out for itself.*[9]

There is a long history of the way in which Lenin came to reappraise the situation and theorize the rise of imperialism, especially after the Russian revolution and the formation of the Comintern, when he actually had to deal with the question of the 'backward nationalities' within Soviet Union and in the world at large. Much of that history is well documented and need not be recounted here. I shall merely relate some of the telling instances below. Claudin's account clearly maps the changes in the position of the Comintern. He claims that the First Congress almost completely ignored the question of the colonies and

expressed very clearly the traditional ideas that were strongly rooted in the minds of the Marxists: 'The emancipation of the colonies is possible only in conjunction with the emancipation of the metropolitan working class. The workers and peasants not only of Annam, Algiers and Bengal, but also of Persia and Armenia, will gain the opportunity of independent existence *only when the workers of England and France have overthrown Lloyd George and Clemenceau...*[10]

Claudin argues that three things happened between the First and the Second Congresses that put the 'national and colonial question' on the agenda. First, the ebbing of the proletarian revolutionary tide in the West. Second, the upsurge in the colonies and third, the sharp rise of the national and colonial question inside the Soviet Union.[11]

The Second Congress, which was attended by many delegates from the colonies, saw the almost complete reversal of the position quoted above, through the stand taken by delegates like M.N. Roy. Claudin quotes the report of the Congress Commission on the National and Colonial Question, which said that 'Comrade Roy defends the idea that *the fate of the revolutionary movement in Europe depends entirely on the course of the revolution in the East.*'[12] Roy was, of course, basing his argument on the idea that as long as the imperialist powers continued to extract super-profits from the colonies, they would never enter into a terminal crisis of capitalism. Lenin countered Roy by referring to the fact that '(I)n spite of the fact that the proletariat in India numbers five million and there are 37 million landless peasants, the Indian communists have not succeeded in creating a communist party...*This fact alone shows that Com. Roy's views are to a large extent unfounded.*'[13] Clearly Lenin was hitting below the belt by putting forward this entirely non-theoretical argument. This fact really showed nothing so far as the question at issue was concerned.

The Third Congress, held a year later, completely bypassed the issue due to certain strategic requirements of the USSR. I will not go into the details of these requirements but suffice it to note that Roy had to protest against it while making his report on India, where the mass movement was reaching unprecedented heights. I quote: 'I have been allowed five minutes for my report. As this theme cannot be dealt with adequately even in an hour, I wish to employ these five minutes for an energetic protest.' He went on to remark that the way in which the Eastern question has been dealt with at this Congress is purely opportunist and is worthy rather of a Congress of the Second International.'[14] In the Fifth Congress, the issue was raised forcefully by the Japanese Communist Party delegate Sen Katayama and Ho Chi Minh (then Nguyen Ai Quoc).

It is interesting in this context, to note that at the Fourth Congress, Tan Malaka of the Indonesian Communist Party narrated the story of the party's collaboration with an organization called the Sarekat Islam. He said:

...We collaborate with the Islamists...Between 1912 and 1916, this union had one million members, perhaps it had three or even four million. It was a very large proletarian union which sprang up spontaneously and was very revolutionary. Until 1920 we collaborated with this union...In 1921 we succeeded in making Sarekat Islam adopt our programme and it went into the villages agitating for control of production and for the watchword: 'All power to the poor peasants and to the proletariat'. However, a split occurred in 1921, owing to the tactless criticism of the leaders of the Sarekat Islam. The government and its agents made use of this split, and also of the decisions of the Second Congress of the Comintern, to fight against Pan-Islamism.

Amidst interruptions from the Chair, Malaka went on to add, 'I have come from India (sic), it took me forty days to come here' and expressed amidst applause, what can only be described as the most crucial existential crisis of a communist of the colonial world: '*they (the Sarekat Islamists) are with us "with their stomach" (to use a popular expression) but with their hearts they remain with the Sarekat Islam— with their heaven which we cannot give them.*'[15]

If this was the situation in the colonies in the rest of the world, the situation inside the Soviet Union was no different. If anything, it was more complicated. Claudin writes of the Muslim peoples of Central Asia: 'Tsarist colonization had taken in these regions...an "Algerian" form: settlement by Russian colonists [peasants and also some workers], who inevitably acquired a colonialist mentality. When Bolshevik power was established in the heartland of Russia, this Russian minority at once became "Soviet" and from its ranks were recruited many of the "Bolsheviks" who were to take over the leading functions in the new institutions.' In 1920, Lenin sent one of his closest collaborators, Safarov, to study the problem and Claudin remarks that Safarov was to write some years later that,

It was inevitable that the Russian revolution should have a colonialist character in Turkestan. The Turkestani working class, numerically small, had neither leader, programme, party nor revolutionary tradition...Under Tsarist colonialism, it was the privilege of the Russians to belong to the industrial proletariat. For this reason, *the dictatorship of the proletariat took on a typically colonialist character.*[16]

We may also remind ourselves of the heroic efforts of the Tartar communist, Sultan Galiev, to make Marxism relate to the specific conditions of Tartar society, in the immediate aftermath of the Bolshevik revolution. Galiev came to believe that Muslim society as a whole had been oppressed by the Russians in the Tsarist empire. There was therefore no point in creating artificial differences based on class, within it.[17] Himself an atheist, Sultan Galiev nevertheless recommended 'that Islam be handled gently, through a gradual 'de-fanaticization' and secularization.'[18] In this task, he proposed to seek the cooperation of the 'petty-bourgeois intellectuals and the reformist clergy' who were positively inclined towards the revolution. Faced with massive opposition from the Russian communists and the central government, Galiev was later arrested and expelled from the communist party. According to Maxime Rodinson, as Galiev saw it towards the later part of his life, 'the Bolshevik programme amounted to replacing oppression by the European bourgeoisie with oppression by the European proletariat.'

At the famous Baku Congress of the Peoples of the East, Narbutabekov from Turkestan made the following impassioned plea:

We...have faith in our...leaders of the world proletariat—comrades Lenin, Trotsky, Zinoviev and others, but all the same we must state...what we want, and the voice of the Muslim workers and the peoples of the East must be heard...Everyone knows that the East is utterly different from the West and its interests are different - thus, rigid application of the ideas of Communism will meet with resistance in the East...They [the leaders] should come and see for themselves what is happening in *our country*, what exactly the local authorities, whose policies drive the working masses away from the Soviet power, are up to...(I)n shedding our blood on the Turkestan fronts against the enemies of Soviet power, we bound up our lives closely with the working masses of the whole of Russia and *the accusations of chauvinist tendencies made against Turkestani leaders must be dropped*...I tell you comrades, that our Turkestani masses have to fight on two fronts. On the one hand, against the evil mullahs at home, and *on the other against the narrow nationalist inclinations of local Europeans*.[19]

It is worth noticing here the use of terms like 'our country' and 'local Europeans'. We also need to register the fact that already the complexity of conflict between local cultures and high theory was being played out, the latter talking the language of universalism while the former were asserting their ineradicable difference. In fact, Narbutabekov's speech shows how their idea of universalism was predicated precisely on the recognition of difference—otherwise the fear was that in the name of universalism, *local European nationalism* would ride roughshod over them. Hence the fight on two fronts. The long history of Marxism's sojourn in the East, in fact, can be seen as one of continuous struggle between these two imperatives— between the dictates of a theory which posited abstract categories but was steeped in European traditions and the imperatives of cultures making their own revolution. They could not afford to adopt an instrumentalist attitude towards their own cultures or be deprecatory about them.

Most of the time however, as Abdel-Malek observes, the communists from the colonies 'were less concerned to expound theses than to say: we exist.'[20] To some extent, Roy did try to theorize but then, in his theoretical predilections he was more European than most other colonial Marxists. His theorizations therefore, were mainly confined to asserting the importance of the Eastern question and to demonstrate that it could not be made politically subordinate to the tasks of the communists in the West. Of all the colonial Marxists, it was Mao Tsetung who went furthest in his effort to theorize though, as we shall see, these efforts too fell far short of the requirements. It may be useful at this point to look at some of his forays into theory.

Three concepts seem to be of crucial importance in Mao Tsetung's attempt at dealing with the application of Marxism's predominantly European theoretical paraphernalia and the rigid imposition of the Comintern's code. First, the positing of the '*law of uneven development*' as an absolute law. 'Nothing in the world develops absolutely evenly,' he proclaims.[21] Through this assertion, Mao in an almost instinctive fashion subverts the metaphysical positivist desire of finding laws and regularities governing human societies—a baggage Marxism had itself inherited through the Second International and continued by the Third, that is, the Comintern. Second, he makes what is his central conceptual move through his enunciation of the 'particularity and universality of contradiction'. The universality of the contradiction is simply the idea that 'contradiction exists in the development of all things' but *it is precisely in the particularity of the contradiction that the universality resides.*[22] Universality, says Mao, is easier to understand because 'it has been widely recognized' since Marx, Engels, Lenin, and Stalin, but 'the particularity of contradiction is still not clearly understood by many comrades, especially the dogmatists.'[23]

Here is Mao's second major subversion: if universality of contradiction was to a certain Marxism, the Universal appearing, *a la* a certain Marxist Hegel, in each particular, and each particular representing a mere moment of the Universal, Mao in one stroke, completely reverses its meaning. The particular now becomes the only way in which the Universal can appear. This is Mao's famous *law of contradiction*. This notion is the second universal truth. The two statements together constitute what Mao calls 'the universal truths' of Marxism, thus holding on to the idea in words but interpreting it in a way that practically denies its universality. In his rendering then, this is universality, but *one which has no attribute of its own*; it acquires everywhere the attributes of the particularity. That is why Mao can ask: 'Why is it that the Chinese revolution can avoid a capitalist future and be directly linked with socialism, without taking the old historical road of Western countries...?' and answer: 'The sole reason is the concrete conditions of the time.'[24]

By making these moves, Mao is further able to complicate notions of subjectivity and agency handed down by the Internationals. Contradictions exist, according to him, not only between the exploiters and the exploited, but equally importantly, 'among the people'. In the concrete conditions of China, he refers to 'contradictions *within the working class, contradictions within the peasantry*, the contradictions within the intelligentsia, the contradictions *between the working class and the peasantry*'.[25]

It is true that Mao never theoretically follows through and works out the ideas of subjectivity and agency in the light of these formulations but all through his practice we can see that he is acutely aware of the implications of the above. It is easy to see that, put this way, simplistic notions like a 'class-in-itself' turning into a 'class-for-itself'—another specifically nineteenth-century Europeanism—become impossible to conceive. For, having already posited the contradiction within the class, it is neither possible to simply derive class consciousness from class position, nor think of a single unified will of a class, expressed through a single party. Needless to say, attributing a *telos* of History to it is well-nigh impossible.

In case we had any doubts, Mao goes further. True, he does put 'contradictions among the people' in the category of 'non-antagonistic contradictions' as opposed to 'antagonistic' ones among the exploiters and the exploited. Yet, these are not fixed categories which can only be resolved only in one particular way, consonant with the larger *telos*. So he argues that one can easily turn into the other. '(T)his contradiction between the two classes (the national bourgeoisie and the working class), *if properly handled* can be transformed into a nonantagonistic one and be resolved by peaceful methods.'[26] On the other hand, '(I)n ordinary circumstances, contradictions among the people are not antagonistic...but *if they are not handled properly*...antagonism may arise.'[27]

The phrase 'if handled properly' then leads us to the *third concept* of Mao's: politics in command. The economy and the logic of production provide nothing but the limiting conditions. The rest depends upon politics, upon how forces are rallied, how alliances are struck, how struggles are conducted, and what organizational forms mediate each of these—how things are 'handled', in short.

We must however, be cautious while understanding the use to which Mao puts these concepts. He wanted to puncture the rigidly structured and codified canon of the Comintern and create the space for his own activity. The *political task* of accomplishing the Chinese revolution demanded a partial rejection of that canon but in the balance of world forces then existing, he could not afford to become another Tito, excommunicated by the communist world. It was to create this space that he conceives of the idea of a particularity that does not just express the essence of the Universal but is an entity in its own right! The *theoretical/philosophical* task that followed from Mao's initiative, at once bolder and more conservative than Lenin's, was never undertaken, either by him or by his successors. In many ways therefore, Mao remained a believer in 'the universal truths of Marxism-Leninism' even though he chose to define them in a manner that strips them of their universality. Today, we surely can read these conceptual moves made by him in a more radical way.

This caution is necessary in order to understand that because the theoretical/philosophical implications were never followed through into an alternative theorization of the specificities of the colonial world/East. Marxism even its Maoist incarnation, remained within the larger framework of post-Enlightenment, even positivist, thought. It was therefore easy for it to slip back into the canon and in the case of China, into the high modernist paradigm that rules it in the post-Mao phase.

It is important, therefore, to underline here that to create a space for a different practice and an alternative theorization is no substitute for an alternative theory. In order to accomplish that latter task, a further step is required: it is not enough to say that 'our history' is different from theirs; we must move towards a reconstruction of this history on its own terms. In saying this, I do not wish to suggest a search for the pristine, precolonial histories. Nor am I suggesting that all responses of the nationalist leaders and intelligentsia, in India for instance, to colonial modernity that were based on some sort of dialogue with colonialism, were *a priori* illegitimate. The search, on the contrary, must be based on an effort to understand why they related to colonialism in the way that they did.

Early Marxism and India

It needs to be underlined that by the time Marxism came to India, it had already undergone its first major metamorphosis. To the hundreds of youth who joined the communist movement in the country in the second and third decades of this century, Marxism was an anti-imperialist doctrine of liberation from colonialism. That much was *already self-evident*. Its hostility to colonialism was a logical extension of its hostility to capitalism as such, in its imperialist phase. On this issue, Eastern Marxism did not seem to suffer from any internal contradiction. Many of the youth who felt attracted towards the communist movement were *nationalists to begin with*, driven by a passion for a new, free India. Others were believers in Islam and were anti-British; they wanted to fight for the Khilafat. For many of the Khilafatists though, their religiosity does not seem to have been articulated with their nationalism. These are points that are often overlooked when Indian Marxism is understood to have been the carrier of an alienated, Western-oriented way of thinking. There seem to be many more layers of complication than are visible at first sight, as we shall see later. There was certainly something internal to communism too, which happened in later years and also transformed Indian communism to its subsequent alienated form.

The first generation of Muslim youth who joined M.N. Roy and became, according to his account, co-founders of the communist party in Tashkent, were in fact *muhajirs*—self-exiled or on *hijrat*.[28] Roy writes of them that 'they were not even nationalists'. He says of them:

My preliminary efforts with the educated minority produced *greater results than I expected and wanted*. Most of them *transferred their fanatical allegiance from Islam to Communism*. I had not spoken to them at all about Communism. I had only told them that driving the British out of India would be no revolution, if it was succeeded by replacing foreign exploiters by native ones. I had to explain the social significance of a revolution: that, to be worthwhile, a revolution should liberate the toiling masses of India from their present economic position. Instinctively idealists, they readily agreed with my opinion and jumped to the conclusion that if the revolution had to liberate the toiling masses, it would have to be a Communist revolution.[29]

The significant statement here is this: The *mohajirs* 'transferred their fanatical allegiance from Islam to communism'. How did this happen? Their being idealists does not fully explain their conversion. For, as we have seen, religion was a central concern to the Muslim youth who joined the Khilafat agitation. Could it be that to these early youth, conversion to communism did not stand in contradiction to their religion? If this is so, could it be that they saw in communism primarily a political imaginary that did not demand a subordination of their spiritual world to the political? The idea of a communist revolution was in the air; it was already there in the stories that were told in hushed tones that narrated how the hated landowners and rulers had been overthrown in Russia, led by a larger-than-life messiah called Lenin. Only further scholarship can reveal the extent to which the story of the revolution was acquiring, or had acquired, a mythological character. One thing seems certain: the stories of these early years did not yet reveal communism to be a godless, irreligious creed. And for the believers of Islam, to whom the world, the Creation, was greater than any nation, the idea of a revolution that sought to transcend national boundaries may have seemed very attractive. How else do we make sense of the wholesale transfer of allegiance that Roy talks of? The story of Tan Malaka, of the initial collaboration between the Sarekat Islam and the communists, the tale of Narbutabekov—all of them point in the direction of a conclusion that at least in the early years, conversion to communism did not involve anything more than the adoption of a new political vision of how to recast the world. It certainly did not entail the epistemological rupture, the abandonment of old ways of making sense of the world and the adoption of the standpoint of High Rationalism.

If this was the frame of mind of the muhajir-turned-communists, the situation of those at home was no different. Muzaffar Ahmed, one of the founders of the CPI at home, has described his own situation in his pre-communist days, in his autobiography:

I would be suppressing the truth if I were to say that I was never involved in anything communal. I used to participate in meetings and organizations raising the specific demands of Muslims. I was also a religious Muslim at that time. Even if I did not offer *namaz* five times a day, I did fast throughout the entire month of *Ramzan*.[30]

Muzaffar Ahmed further explains that later, during the 1920s, given his 'the state of mind... and the thrill that was associated with the terrorist movement' it was not entirely impossible that he joined a terrorist revolutionary group.

But there were major hurdles in the way. The terrorist revolutionaries drew their inspiration from Bankimchandra's *Anandamath*. This book was full of communal hatred from the beginning to the end. Its basic *mantra* was the song *Bandemataram*... How could a monotheistic Islamic youth recite this *mantra*?[31]

It is interesting that even though the monotheistic Muslim youth found it difficult to chant the Hindu mantra, he did eventually become a communist; Islam did not stand in the way. I suspect that for leaders and political activists like him, communism would have been the first station on the route to rationalism and atheism. They did not in the first instance feel compelled to shed their religious-spiritual beliefs.

Saroj Mukhopadhyay, one of the stalwarts of the Bengal communists who joined the CPI in the thirties, also begins his autobiography with the concerns that animated some of the youth who joined the communist movement at that time.

We wanted the freedom of the country. We wanted to usher in an arrangement wherein the people could live in happiness after driving out the British rulers. In what misery do the workers, peasants, the people of the villages and industrial areas live! We wanted an end to that state of affairs and to build a happy and prosperous country...This was the thought that we were obsessed with.[32]

Autobiographies of other Marxist stalwarts like E.M.S. Namboodiripad and A.K. Gopalan also show how their early attraction to Marxism and socialism went side by side with their work in the Congress and later, the Congress Socialist Party. It was the disillusionment with the Gandhian methods and the consequent search for a different path for liberation that stirred them. In Namboodiripad's case, it was in fact, the programme of reform *within the Namboothiri community* that occupied his attention for a long time—even after he became a full-fledged nationalist. One of the reformist papers, *Unni Namboothiri*, was later to become a voice of 'Kerala's socio-cultural revolutionary movements', but retained its Namboothiri name.[33] In fact, Namboodiripad's reminiscences were first serialized in the *Unni Namboothiri*.[34]

The concerns that brought these youth of diverse persuasions to the communist movement were similar in many respects. They were nationalists in a different way, in the sense that they wanted the well-being of the people who constituted the majority of the 'nation', namely the poor, toiling people.[35] Their nationalism had nothing to with any prior 'Indian essence'. And a precondition to this well-being was freedom from foreign rule. Alternatively, they were religiously inclined 'internationalists' such as the Khilafatists, who once again wanted the 'revolution of the toiling masses' and therefore managed to free themselves of their narrow religious concerns for the sake of the larger cause.[36] In other words, to them also, their Islamic allegiance presented no barrier in the transition to communism. The case of the Hindus who became communists was particularly striking in at least one way. There was a strong desire to transcend the identity of the community they were born into—the desire to forget. In most cases, there was a near-complete absence of any experience of subalternity and of the kind of search therefore that leaders of the lower castes were engaged in. Even in the case of Namboodiripad, where the agenda of Namboothiri social reform was crucial to his politicization, the move to an identification with the nationalist cause was rapid and smooth. This is something that contrasts in a stark manner with the painful transitions and reversals that marked the leaders of the lower castes like Periyar, who had to leave the Congress after a five-year stint as a staunch Gandhian, or Ambedkar who could not till the end, identify with the Congress or its nationalism. So, if A.K. Gopalan could simply decide that instead of 'the welfare of one village' he should think of '7 lakh villages' and so 'cast his eyes over the whole of India', it was also because that path was open for him.[37] To Namboodiripad too, it was so unproblematically self-evident that 'the non-cooperation movement which attracted the progressive Namboothiris, at once attracted such progressive sections of other communities also.' It seemed so to him not only when it happened, but decades later when he was writing his autobiography: 'It was a movement that united all people irrespective of religious or communal differences.'[38] Talking of his privileged location in relation to temple satyagrahas, E.M.S. says that in those circumstances, 'if he did not feel anything intolerable in the atmosphere obtaining in Guruvayoor temple, I should not be accused.' That was after all his socialization. And 'only such things as securing some social reform in the Namboothiri community' formed the horizon of his progressive thinking.[39] When he did break free from the narrow confines of that progressivism, he claims, 'a feeling grew in me that not only the communal system [here, the reference is to caste] but even belief in God was a hindrance to the material development of human beings. I too joined the ranks of the revolutionary movement sprouted under the leadership of E.V. Ramaswami Naicker in Tamil Nadu and Sahodaran Ayyappan in Kerala against the communal system and for a rational thinking.'[40] Significantly however, he did not join either of them but joined the nationalist Congress.

M.N. Roy's own involvement with the revolutionary terrorist groups of Bengal, it seems, was facilitated by his Brahmin upbringing, since most of them were permeated with a profoundly Hindu inspiration. To them, as to Aurobindo Ghosh, nationalism came easily. This was a path that was clearly not available to Muzaffar Ahmed, as we have seen. In fact, this may explain why so many of the progressive Muslims in Bengal, like Ahmed, Abdul Halim, Nazrul Islam, Abdul Momin, and Qutubudin Ahmed, moved straight to the Communist Party and were instrumental in organizing it. For many later-day communists who hailed from a Hindu background, the most natural route, at least in Bengal, was through the terrorist groups. There were others who came through the Congress, especially in states like present-day Kerala. For both these groups, this journey was facilitated by the fact that all of them came from socially privileged backgrounds. It is hardly surprising then that all of them identified with the core beliefs of nationalism with great ease. Writing his reminiscences in the 1980s, Saroj Mukhopadhyay narrates this move of the 'revolutionary youth' towards socialism against the background of the intensified movement against the Simon Commission. It is interesting that he describes the movement in what would now appear to be naïve terms. 'All organizations in India—people of different persuasions and different political parties decided to boycott this Commission.'[41] Jyoti Basu's memoirs too mention how in his early youth, he experienced a romantic attraction towards the revolutionary terrorist youth who were fighting for the freedom of the country. His real politicization took place in England where he came in contact with British communists. The context there was the growing political tension in Europe with the rise of fascism.[42] This virtual absence of a prior experience of subalternity, which made them feel at home in nationalist politics, stands in sharp contrast to both Muslims and Dalits who, as we have seen, were continuously forced into carving out their own separate spaces.

I have already argued that Marxism came to India after its meta-morphosis into an anti-imperialist doctrine. Now it may be possible to see how that relentlessly militant anti-imperialist doctrine became so attractive to the nationalist youth who were looking for a way out of the inexplicable ways of Gandhian politics and its often compromising tone. To the elite sensibilities of most of these youth, the sanitized and modern language of Marxism provided an alternative to the Hindu inspiration of their past affiliations as well as to the 'embarrassing religious sentimentality' of the Gandhian idiom. Around the advent of the thirties, the experience of the Great Depression and the fact that the Soviet Union came out of it untouched, provided an additional impetus to the move towards socialism.

However, as we have seen, the first move towards socialism and com-munism was, to all these youth of different persuasions and backgrounds, merely a move towards a different political ideal. It was still possible for the early socialists/communists to participate in the ongoing dialogue with 'tradition' and retain their links with their filiative worlds. Their relationship to nationalism and religiosity was predicated upon their dialogue with tradition and the past. In a manner of speaking, they represented attempts to cope with colonial modernity from within the ground of a tradition that was already ineradicably lodged within it and, therefore, conditioned by it. Their critiques of precolonial Indian society, especially Hindu society, were no more or less aggressive than those of the nationalists. Their strident anticolonialism sat perfectly well with the nationalist vision of 'unity of all castes and communities' and the concomitant stifling of all urge for internal reform, deferring it to an indeterminate future. Sanjay Seth has recently suggested that Lenin's description of the nationalist movements in the colonies as 'bourgeois-democratic' did not really leave any possibility of considering that there might be something 'reactionary' too, about these nationalisms. Their representation as 'anti-theses of imperialism' meant that 'no particular conclusions' as to their political content 'necessarily followed.'[43] This has a complex set of implications, the consideration of which I will take up in the last section of this chapter.

Marxist Practice and the Activist Voice

In the discussion of the unravelling of the secular-nationalism discourse, particularly in Chapter 2, I have pointed to the emergence of the politics of 'identity'—especially that of caste and community. How has Marxist practice dealt with it? I will discuss this question here with reference to the perceptions within—as articulated by activists of the CPI(M) in Bengal and elsewhere—in order to highlight the tensions between high theory and day-to-day practice.

Before I go into the intricacies of the actual practice and its relationship with the 'high theory' of secularism, let me quote a couple of extracts from an official document of the Communist Party of India (Marxist), to underline how the impact of the unravelling of the 'nation' was likewise affecting the other secular category of 'class' and how it was being perceived by the party. In September 1983, the party central committee adopted a document on the work in the trade unions, where it dealt with the problems of inculcating 'class consciousness' among the workers. In this document it noted how, two years ago, the working class in the textile industry of Gujarat had 'split into two hostile camps' on the issue of 'reservations of jobs for harijans'(sic). 'Twenty-five thousand harijan workers came out on a strike to defend reservation. Next day, nearly a lakh of workers came on strike to oppose reservations. Class unity was completely shattered...' This recognition in itself was not important. What was important was that the document went on to observe that,

The working class and trade union movement must understand that *these are not just an expression of casteism*. Behind them stand feudal wrongs, lack of equality and inhuman treatment.

It went on further to underline that the 'harijan (sic) workers' need to be drawn into the common class struggle. However the problem as perceived by it was:

This cannot be done unless the trade unions recognize that the muslims, the tribals, the harijans have a separate and genuine grievance of their own *which does not arise out of the worker-capitalist relationship*. The fight against this must be shared by all sections of the workers if these discriminated sections are to join the trade union battle.[44]

A belated, though welcome recognition. This we may recall, was Ambedkar's most serious problem with the communists. The recognition, moreover, that there are problems specific not just to the Dalits but also the Muslims and the tribals, that do not have their roots in the capital-labour relationship, is significant, because it actually points to precisely the points at which the discourse of secular-nationalism was most under pressure and where its blind spots were being revealed, so to speak. That this recognition did not really lead to any distinct change in the party's trade union practice, however, is another matter. That it *could not* lead to any corresponding change in its practice is related to the fact that theoretically, there was no way of accounting for this situation and a mere recognition of it was unlikely to convince the mass of the party activists. For the sheer force of the old ways of thinking are difficult to break, unless there is a concerted effort to re-examine the theoretical premises that informed past practices and to rethink that theory.

However, the interesting thing about political movements is that they do not always adhere to the rigours of high theory when they become mass phenomena. Such is also the case with communist practice, at least in the states where it has grown as a mass movement. In my study of communist practice in India, I have found that there is a regular tension between the rigours imposed by high theory and the actual practice at the lower levels. In a sense, it is a tension that also expresses itself as a tension between the leaders and activists and between the elite and the popular. This is particularly so in the case of parties and movements that are highly 'ideological' in nature.[45] One of the interesting statements of this tension is evident in A.K. Gopalan's autobiographical narrative. Since this is a problem that I will be exploring in the rest of the chapter, this being a crucial part of the argument of this book, let me also quote from Gopalan:

I am not an intellectual. Intellectuals do not particularly like my speeches. They say they are devoid of politics. This is true in a way. I have not learnt the 'theories' they have learnt from books and the theories they cherish. Even if I learn them, I do not vomit them undigested. But the people like my speeches. With great care, I have studied the life of the people, their ways of dress, their habitations and their surroundings. I describe their travails in a language they can understand.[46]

It is difficult to miss the bitterness and the sarcasm here. The term 'intellectuals' here does not refer merely to the pure unattached intellectual but to the leaders who spout 'theory'. This becomes clear from a later elaboration, when Gopalan quotes a conversation between two cotton mill workers, returning after a meeting: ' all others speak only about China and Spain. Only Gopalettan [a term for elder brother] speaks about our *maistry* and timekeeper.'[47] The contrasts are sharp: they talk about international matters, I talk about peoples' lives; they have read books, I have studied the way people live; they talk the language of the elite, I talk the peoples' language. And for anyone familiar with the history of the communist movement, this was certainly not an exercise in self-glorification. Gopalan *was* among the very few communists who were always open to what 'the people' had to say. Not surprisingly, when he started picketing as Congress volunteer, during the civil disobedience movement, and heard

people talk, he realized that the 'common man felt that picketing was
against his interests.' 'The leadership of these [pickets] was in the hands
of the middle class and educated youth. There was amongst the poor a
sort of hostility towards this programme.'[48] Gopalan realized that the
lower castes and the Muslims distrusted the movement and that nationalism
was an elitist creed—a conclusion that he, of course, fights shy of explicitly
drawing.

It is this dynamic that reveals itself in the course of the real politics of
communist practice wherever it managed to become a mass movement.
The conflict between mass leaders and the apparatchiks, between the elite
and the popular levels of politics, becomes manifest at every level. In what
follows, I discuss this issue in relation to West Bengal, especially in the
context of the Durga Puja and the party activists' involvement in it but
also in relation to religion more generally. While the high discourse of the
party continues to fight shy of any association with the Puja festivities, the
organization is also forced to overlook the unstated relationship that its
activists maintain with it. On occasion though, it does intervene to prevent
this 'mixing of religion and politics' as was evident in the course of my
discussions with party activists. I will first try to present the gist of my
conversations with some activists and leaders of the party, before I draw
some theoretical conclusions from them.

The Durga Puja, as is well known, is a festival that is central to Bengali
life. A Hindu festival, it has now become a kind of 'national event' of
Bengali life, involving Muslims and other minorities also, though to varying
degrees. As Chandan Sinha, a CPI(M) 'sympathizer' and secretary of the
pro-Left Front Nagarik Committee in Taltola, central Calcutta, put it, 'it
is the national festival of the *Bangali jati* [jati is generally used for 'nation'
or 'nationality'] and it evolved in its present form of a *sarbojaneen* puja
during the freedom struggle.'[49] Two other companions of Sinha, Tarun
Majumdar and Deepak Roychoudhury, both belonging to the Taltola local
committee of the Nagarik Committee, a citizen's organization, were
involved in the preparations for the Puja that was to begin in another ten
days. Sinha spoke of the anti-imperialist tradition of Durga Puja. 'It was
begun as a *sarbojaneen* [literally, open to all] puja as a front for anti-
imperialist, anti-British activities, providing a cover for all types of people
from Gandhian, terrorist to communists', he said. Later, in the 1960s and
1970s however, said Sinha, its character changed and it degenerated into
an opportunity for self-aggrandisement of certain individuals who
patronized it—a clear reference to the doings of certain Congress-affiliated
anti-socials.[50] 'Hindu religion' according to Sinha, 'never had a code of

conduct unlike many other religions, and whenever there has been an attempt to impose, it has broken and failed.' He mentioned that Muslims also participate in the Durga Puja, like for instance 'we Bengalis (*amra Bangaalira*)'[51] observe festivities on Christmas. On being asked about Id, he was less categorical. He said that sometimes 'we' do participate and 'they, that is the Muslims, often send a part of the sacrificed animal meat 'which we accept with due respect'. Sinha also asserted that the interpretation of 'dharma nirapekshata' varies from person to person.

In the words of Pradeep Bakshi, a freelance Marxist intellectual, the communist movement remained a purely upper class/caste *bhadralok* affair in terms of leadership.[52] He explained the defeat of the CPI(M) in the prestigious Dum Dum constituency in the 1999 elections in terms of the long-term fall-out of the left's failure to come to grips with the problems of consciousness, politically and theoretically speaking. He felt that while the left's 'solid base' among the 'refugee' population was a result of its struggles for their rehabilitation, at the level of ideas, it was merely the anti-Congress thrust that held them to the left. They were told that the Congress was responsible for the partition of the country, or for their continuing neglect. In an interesting reference, he recalls the well-known editorials in the Bengali daily *Basumati*, written by the veteran journalist, Vivekananda Mukhopadhyay in the 1960s and 1970s. These represent a kind of 'Hindu Congress' or 'Hindu socialist' orientation, according to him. 'They combined a strident Hindu communalism with the praise of socialism and the Soviet Union', he adds. There was a peculiar way in which a certain kind of 'Hindu communalism' could peaceably exist within a leftist political universe, without feeling unduly threatened, primarily because of this upper caste/class character of the communists and the communist movement. 'You can pick up any ten families of communists and pose them random questions on issues propagated by the BJP regarding the stereotypical Muslim: they are dirty, they reproduce at a high rate etc., and you will find that invariably they will share these stereotypes. This is how women inside families talk. Men also talk but outside, in public, they are more discreet.' There has also been the dominant understanding, he feels, that 'it is only after political power is captured, that there will be a cultural revolution. It is thought therefore that such issues are better deferred.' These issues are thus never confronted. About the Muslims, Bakshi felt that there had in fact been a strong section of liberal Muslims emerging in the early years of the century, but Gandhi by supporting the Khilafat, actually helped the more orthodox and sectarian sections to develop.

According to Nepal Deb Bhattacharya, former member of the West
Bengal state committee and of the powerful North 24 Parganas district
secretariat (now expelled from the party), 'we have conceded a lot of ground
among the believers to the *Hindutvapanthis* by not understanding the
ordinary religious-minded people. They do not necessarily believe in or
observe religious injunctions, they are simply God-fearing (*dharma bhiru*).
In trying to oppose communalism, we have often failed to make this
distinction.' Bhattacharya also feels that the secularism of the leaders in
Alimuddin Street [the West Bengal CPI(M)'s headquarters] has often left
enough scope for it to be interpreted as being anti-Hindu. 'The problem
of modernization of communities' he feels, 'is a matter of consciousness.
It cannot be brought about through a legislative imposition.'[53]

It is interesting that both Sinha and Bhattacharya refer to the processes
of internal struggles that have contributed to 'make Hinduism liberal'.
They especially refer to the contributions of Ramakrishna Paramhansa,
encapsulated in his adage '*jato mot, tato poth*' [there are as many ways to
reach God, as there are opinions/beliefs]. Sinha underlined the fact that
Ramakrishna went to the mosque and offered *namaz*. Both underplayed
the dimension introduced by Ramakrishna's illustrious follower,
Vivekananda, whose project was to form a mission and centralize the
religion. On the contrary, Bhattacharya emphasized the humanist rather
than religious aspect of Vivekananda, by quoting his famous statement, 'I
am not with those whose father is hanuman and mother is the cow (*hanuman
jader baba aar goru jader ma, ami tader shongey nei*)' and '*shabar oporey manush
satya, tahar oporey nai*' [man is the ultimate truth; there is no truth bigger
than him]. Bhattacharya recalled the struggle of Ram Mohun Roy and
others to emphasize his point about internal struggles for reform. 'The
important thing is to respect others' beliefs. If I do not give them respect,
how can I expect to get theirs?' He differentiates between 'secularism' and
'dharma nirapekshata' in his own way. The idea of respect for others is
inherent in the idea of 'secularism', while dharma nirapekshata only means
neutrality—it is a doctrine of state neutrality. Secularism then, for him, is
a wider creed.

Bhattacharya talked of the process of the democratization of the puja
when it came out of the zamindar's precincts. The emergence of the
thakurtala (the public space in the village where the first community pujas
were held) as opposed to the *thakurdalan* (the landlord's puja house), was
the sign of the democratization of the religion, of its becoming available
to the common people. This signified among other things, the beginning
of the breakdown of the monopoly of the zamindars and the Brahmin

priests they supported, over the conduct of the puja. He explains the process as it happened in Bhatpara, an area inhabited by the high Vedic Brahmin castes. Bhatpara is situated in the middle, surrounded by many lower caste localities on all sides—the Kumorpara, Jelepara, and Sadgopepara. When the puja became *baaroaari* [i.e. a community affair], the great division was over whether everybody would sit together to eat in the traditional fashion, now that all castes were present. Bhattacharya mentions the early Marxists in Bhatpara, who were involved in the process; they were at once pandits and Marxists. He particularly mentioned Janakiballabh Bhattacharya, the first 'Brahmin communist' of the area in 1936, who was a product of this liberal-Hindu struggle. It was under his leadership that the struggle to make Saraswati Puja a baaroaari *puja* was carried on. 'Even in our time, when we were kids, this struggle was on to make this puja open to all. I also participated in it in Bhatpara. I feel that if I had been a Sheikh Alam or a Mohd. Salim I could not have done it. Being a Bhattacharjee, I could fight other Bhattacharjees who were orthodox.'

Prabhat Mukhopadhyay and Pradeep Dutta, both from the CPI(M) local committee in Konnagar, in Hooghly district, began the conversation in the usual style of party activists and leaders, underlining the importance of separation of religion and politics. However, as the discussion proceeded, I began to get a glimpse of the 'messiness' of the real world they lived in, where the rigours of theory had to be continuously diluted in favour of more common sense versions of it. 'In no book of the communist party is it written that you have to believe, or not believe in God. What is written is that people have to be brought out of their blind faith. Now to speak to those who do believe, we have to enter their world in the name of God and religion. It is true that often we do not participate in organising puja programmes, but often we do; *we have to*, as a matter of fact.'[54] This 'have to' is explained by Mukhopadhyay with reference to 'maintaining the sarbojaneen character' of the puja. Often, according to him, some exclusivity develops 'due to various personal or political reasons, or maybe some people are not allowed to touch things'. In such situations, we have to be more involved to ensure that the open character of the puja is maintained. 'Often when our party comrades do become secretaries of puja committees, we are questioned by our opponents as to why we do this when we do not believe in religion. Still we have to.' And it is not just Hindu festivals like the Durga puja, he adds. 'I also participate in Muslim festivals. I have also offered *namaz* and observed *roza*.' I asked him if there had been any objections from the Muslims. No, he said and explained: 'It was not that suddenly one day, I decided to offer namaz. I have stayed with these people and stood by them. In the aftermath of the demolition of the Babri Masjid, in 1992, when they were feeling terrified, we kept vigil all night for many days. They began to trust me. I observed the roza fasts, along with them.' This was also necessary, he said, because it is more difficult to draw Muslims into the mainstream, into more liberal ways of thinking. 'We don't ask them to give up their religion. As a consequence, we have been able to draw some of them towards us. They also participate in "our" pujas.' Mukhopadhyay mentioned the high tension in the area in the immediate aftermath of the demolition of the mosque. However, it did not take any violent form. Incidentally, there are different ways in which party members reacted to the event, in different places in West Bengal itself. In parts of North 24 Parganas, the party was virtually divided within between the Hindus and the Muslims. According to the report of senior leaders, one of whom is a minister, the Bashirhat local committee had organized a protest demonstration. It was one of the largest ever organized by a local committee, with over 2000 people participating. Not more than ten to fifteen Hindu party members participated in it.[55] That the division did not express itself openly was presumably because of the overall authority of the party. Later, the tensions built up in the area which was thick with rumours while mobilization and counter-mobilization went on in the two communities.

Durga Puja, according to Tapas Basu, former President of the CPI(M)-affiliated Students' Federation of India and Calcutta district secretariat member of the party, is a major festival of Bengalis all right, but is much more. In terms of the involvement of all kinds of people, from different castes and communities, in the simple economic sense, it has a crucial significance.[56]

Puja is the time for Bengalis to buy new clothes, for instance, and a very large proportion of the tailors here are Muslims. It provides a kind of lifeline in the immense amount of commercial-economic activity that goes on in the state. Ever since we came to power, there has been of course, an additional responsibility upon us to see that things go smoothly and order is maintained. But that apart, in terms of a providing a medium of social intercourse, it is important for us to be linked to the festivities. We have all through maintained such links for example, by putting up our bookstalls in the puja pandals.

Basu mentioned an occasion when as SFI President, he had gone to Cooch Behar district in north Bengal. The SFI district secretary in Cooch Behar was Reazul Haq, a Muslim by birth. 'I was wandering around in the localities with him and heard people tell him that 'without you there cannnot be a puja here'. I was a bit puzzled and so I asked him what it was all about. He then told me that for the past three years he had been the secretary of the puja committee there.' Reazul then told Basu that 'thereafter, the party had instructed him not to be directly involved in the conduct of puja, so he withdrew.' The interesting thing here is not simply that Reazul Haq was a Muslim and a communist, and also the puja committee secretary, but rather, the fact that this was widely acceptable to the people of the area. Indeed, his involvement was seen as crucial to the conduct of the puja. Also interesting in this little account is that tension between the sense of ideological purity of 'the party', and the normal, unselfconscious way in which the local populace related to the whole matter. Basu further mentioned that this was a feature that was still in existence in many places and in two or three puja committees in the Kidderpore area, the secretaries are Muslims. 'To that extent, we do not see this as a mere religious occasion, but more as a social occasion.' When asked about the decision of the party to stop Reazul Haq from associating with puja festivities, Basu said that 'actually, often this does happen in the case of comrades in leading positions, but often enough we do continue to maintain an attitude of support and cooperation from outside—without being members or key organizers of these puja committees.'

Basu seemed to think that much of the involvement of the party in many religious occasions had been necessitated by the fact that it has been in power for such a long time and there is a responsibility that devolves on it by virtue of that fact. He mentioned the Ganga Sagar Mela, held at the time of *poush sankranti* when lakhs and lakhs of pilgrims go to Ganga Sagar from all over India. For that entire period, one of the major tasks of the South 24-Parganas district committee of the party is to arrange, through its various mass fronts and peoples' organizations, drinking water, medical camps, resting camps, and so on.

Basu accepts that there was a kind of suspicion of Muslims even among Hindu party activists, especially in the aftermath of the demolition of the Babri Masjid. There was always what he called a *supta abeg* (a slumbering emotion) which had never manifested itself openly in public. Among the refugee sections, along with support for the left because of its struggle for their rehabilitation, there was always also an anti-Muslim sentiment because of the partition experience. 'In fact, the main areas where we have lost in recent elections, have been these refugee areas. This had now clearly become more evident'.

Basu also accepted that in recent years, activists of left parties have had to take recourse more and more to traditional resources and to invoking the contribution of figures like Ramakrishna and Vivekananda. But he is quick to add that while this is undoubtedly a defensive move, it is also necessitated by the fact that the BJP is seeking to 'portray our entire heritage as communal'. 'This is a complete distortion of history. It is not as if we have been aggressive about the devotion (*bhakti*) of the common person in the past, for often enough that devotion has also been transferred to the communist movement, alongside the gods and goddesses.' He mentions instances he has heard from others in the party, where in interior villages, alongside the *shivlingas*, people plant the red flag. Often, he believes, it was this uncritical bhakti that expressed itself in the support for the communists. The BJP therefore, has to be countered by trying to disprove that they are the inheritors of the legacy of people like Vivekananda or Ramakrishna. 'So, the battle today is no longer what Marx or Lenin said about religion, or what we personally believe, but to bring out the fact that from within our soil itself we can find the resources of *dharma nirapekshata*, in the work of these great figures who came forward to reform Hinduism and as representatives of Hinduism', adds Basu. In an interesting aside, Basu referred to the 'historic debate that we had with the "naxals" in the student movement in the 1970s', when they were breaking the idols of precisely these figures, of figures like Vidyasagar, Rabindranath Tagore, Vivekananda and others. 'We had to underline that we cannot decry and completely disown the contribution of these people' whose efforts, he also seemed to believe along with many others, in a way laid the ground for the positive reception of leftist ideas. However, Basu also seemed to feel that the debate with 'left-sectarianism' was also probably lacking in depth for 'we were also often afflicted with a certain sectarianism'; history has not been properly debated and assessed by the left, and it is a crying need today.

The most outspoken and hard-hitting statement however, came from one of the dissident leaders of the state CPI(M), and at the time of writing, Transport Minister in the government, Subhash Chakravarty. Chakravarty has been a kind of cult figure among the youth and student leaders in the difficult years of the late 1960s and 1970s, when the party was under intense physical attack from the government as well as the ruling Congress-affiliated anti-socials.

Secularism, says Chakravarty, in his own idiosyncratic style, 'as I have understood it, is *meney neyoa*' (literally, to accept, or we could say, tolerance).[57] 'It is to accept life, to accept Indian society as it has emerged and is with us. In this landmass called India, where there was a kind of unprecedented diversity not only of beliefs and communities, but of political units. There

were over two thousand five hundred "kingdoms" starting with the raja of
Cooch Behar to Chittor of Rajasthan. In Rajasthan alone there were
over 700 such "kingdoms"'. The anticolonial nationalist struggle marks
for Chakravarty, as for others, the coming together of 'all castes and
communities into a common struggle, irrespective of differences.' 'This
was the basis of our tolerance. This "acceptance" is crucial to our
secularism. And this is something that we have to deal with daily. We have
puja festivities by cordoning off the roads. Some people enjoy, while it
causes inconvenience for others. We have political meetings dislocating
the traffic and causing inconvenience to many, while for many others,
these are important. But we all "accept" this situation, despite
inconveniences. This is crucial to our secularism. This is how the makers
of our constitution understood it, in my view. "Secularism" as a term
expresses, in our particular context, a counter to fundamentalism and
aggressive chauvinism—particularly in the affairs of running the state.'

Chakravarty went on: 'But for the Left movement, or any movement,
the first task is to understand the society it wants to change. The problem
of the Left movement and of its failure is precisely its failure to understand
the society it functions in. It has completely failed to understand India. In
thirteen elections, it has not managed to get more than 10 percent votes.'
This has to do, among other things, with the inability to strike roots.
Chakravarty narrated that on that very day (this was the *mahalay* day, the
first day of puja) he had gone to the Ganga to see the phenomenon of
'*pitri tarpan*', to see lakhs and lakhs of people assemble on the ghats of the
Ganga river to offer prayers for their departed ancestors, to understand
what made them come there. 'I was fascinated by the immense kind of
expectations and dreams, the various states of mind with which they come
there. I was trying to understand why people came there; what they were
thinking. I have been to Ganga Sagar Mela also twenty-seven times. The
first time I went there was to accompany my mother in 1961. It is a strange
feeling simply trying to gauge what was going on in peoples' minds. We
have to understand this. Very few leaders, least of all the communists,
have understood India. Only Gandhi understood this country. Among
others who understood India to some extent were Nehru, Indira Gandhi
and V.P. Singh.' The ideological influence of the left movement, he said,
was very weak, or else, how does one explain the sudden shift of so many
voters to the BJP (in Bengal) in recent years. 'What was understood as the
strength of the Left movement was actually the strength of an anti-
establishment current at a particular time in our history. An anti-
establishment movement could be led as easily by the rightists as by the

leftists. In fact, the rightists can do so more effectively; they can be more virulent, more violent. The leftists have to often work within certain norms.'

In the decade of the 1950s and earlier, says Chakravarty, in the formative stages of the communist movement, the communists were part of the local peoples' lives, their festivities and their pujas. 'The moment they started thinking of themselves as leaders of a political party, not only did they themselves sever connections within the lives of common people, they ensured that others did likewise'. He mentions a circular issued by the party a few years ago, prohibiting the association of party members with puja organizing, and said, 'some of us believe that this is increasing our isolation.' Chakravarty, however, seemed to be unmoved by all these circulars and mandates and said, 'I am linked to about a hundred puja committees in Calcutta. I consider it not merely a puja; to my mind it is the biggest event of Bengali society. If you look at it closely, you will see it has traditions of patriotism, of anti-caste struggles, of nationalism.' Chakravarty explained how the puja was a purely private affair held in zamindar households, which has now become a central event of Bengali society and its culture. He explained the origin of the baaroaari puja, the first step towards its becoming a community affair. The term 'baaroaari', he said, is a derivative from '*baaro iyaar*' (twelve friends) who first broke away from the Mallik *rajbari* (royal home) in Joynagar, in the early nineteenth century, when the Sudras were not allowed to enter the puja performed in royal homes. The next landmark event was 1905, the year of the division of Bengal. From then it became transformed gradually into the *sarbojanin Durgotsav*, under the leadership and initiative of people like Suren Banerjea and Ashwini Kumar Dutta. Thus it increased its scope and spread, acquiring nationalist overtones. The first step in its becoming a public event was anti-casteism, and the second was anti-imperialism.[58]

The communists considered Durga Puja a purely religious event.

In 1964, '65, '66, I had to fight with Promode Dasgupta [then secretary of the state CPI(M)]. I personally started the campaign within [for participating] and then he came out with this formula that has now become a permanent feature— that of setting up bookstalls in puja pandals. Now they think this is revolutionary activity. This was only a mid-way solution. I was given a mandate to leave the secretary-ship of the puja committee that I used to hold. One senior and respected leader asked me to quit the committee. I told him I would after the puja. He insisted that I do it right away. I said then I will leave the party right away. If anybody tries to study the phenomenon one will see that, for example a poet tries to write his/her best poems to be published in the Puja special issues of magazines. A good singer tries to record his/her best songs to sell them during puja. The artisan who creates the images of Durga puts in his best to produce the best possible image. A sari designer or a shoe designer—all have their eyes glued on to the coming puja. The entire year's planning centres around the puja. For two months around this period, not one room is available in any hotel in Calcutta. People come to buy, sell, strike deals, enjoy and celebrate. The communists have no idea of what happens in Bengal around the event called puja.

Chakravarty is also critical of the use of the sanitized term '*sharadotsav*' instead of Durga Puja. 'They think they are becoming secular', he says. He is scathing in his criticism of the practice of giving the wholetimers working in party presses or doing other party work, an allowance at the time of the October revolution anniversary on 7 November, when everybody else gets it during the pujas. 'The need for money is at that time which is barely a few weeks before November 7. But they fear that it will be marked as puja allowance. This way they think they are being revolutionary.'

Referring to struggles for internal reforms, Chakravarty is highly optimistic. 'Whether the communists want it or not, these struggles will continue. There are many such progressive people who are consciously carrying on this fight within their respective communities. I believe that the more one underlines the quotidian [*dainondin*] aspects of life without getting too worked up about religious matters, the more these things will get secularized. The more you 'fight' communalism in the way it is being fought (by the party), the more it tends to get strengthened.'

Certain issues emerge from the discussions with CPI(M) activists and leaders above. The first thing to be noted is the immense variation of the meanings assigned to the term 'secular'. What this points to, in my opinion, is not that secularism like everything else has 'many meanings' but on the contrary, that there is an attempt in the present conjuncture, to try to negotiate the rapidly changing situation. It cannot be said with any degree of certainty that these would have been the responses if the interviews had been conducted twenty years ago. Chances are, that the responses would have been more closely aligned to the 'party line'. The responses seem to be attempts to redefine and come to a minimalist understanding of religious toleration. But beyond the express level of *defining* the category of secularism, there is something else that calls for attention. What kind of practices have been articulated around the notion of a secular politics in the past? Here the ground is more 'messy', that is, not easily amenable to a theoretical articulation within received understandings of theory. We have a kind of overriding understanding that the 'liberal content' of contemporary Bengali society was a result of long years of struggle *within*

Hindu bhadralok society. In a way, the mantle of progressiveness is assumed by this *bhadralok* common sense, to be its heritage in a way that is often uninformed by what has been going on in Bengali Muslim society at large, for the last two hundred years. Nor is the sense of the agency of the *Sudras* or the lower castes in evidence anywhere.

I may be permitted a small diversion here. Regarding the character of the bhadralok elite, Muzaffar Ahmed has a few interesting observations. This is a 'class' apart in Bengal, according to him. Composed of primarily the Brahmins, Vaidyas, and Kayasthas, this section of society was marked by its complete distance from any kind of manual labour. When the British came to rule and English became the language of the offices and courts, this section seized upon the opportunity and started learning English. They quickly took control of most jobs in the administration and courts. Ahmed is of the opinion that it was the despair of this bhadralok elite when others started coming into these professions, thus challenging their monopoly, that was responsible for their move towards terrorism in the early years of the twentieth century. Ahmed also believes, significantly, that the division of Bengal (*Banga bhanga*) by Lord Curzon stirred this elite in such a big way because they found their territory was reduced immensely and the part that was called 'East Bengal and Assam' now had a Muslim majority and 'consequently, Muslims started getting more jobs there'. 'This was one of the reasons of the despair of this educated bhadralok youth.'[59] That this is the perception of a Bengali Muslim communist leader is significant and says a lot about the domination of this Hindu elite in the 'radical politics' of that time. Parenthetically, we may also note that Ambedkar too had made a similar point about the Hindu opposition to the division of Bengal. That such an awareness of the character of nationalist and radical politics is completely missing from the accounts of all my interviewees (all Hindus), except Pradeep Bakshi's, is revealing. My feeling is that many communists today may, in fact, feel embarrassed at Ahmed's statement and tend to overlook it as a residual sign of the minority communities' communal perceptions. The struggle against *Banga bhanga*, after all is a golden chapter in the history of nationalism and, as we saw in Subhash Chakravarty's account, of the Durga Puja.

It is with this caveat about the nature of radical common sense that I would begin to read the accounts of the interviews above. For this prevalent common sense frames the responses and the attempts at articulating the understanding of secular politics that we find in these interviews. The most important issue that I believe emerges from the discussions above, however, relates at a more theoretical level, to the question of modernization of communities and the location of the radical activist in relation to that process. What Chakravarty, Bhattacharya, and Basu believe to be true of Bengali society as a whole, must be read as a question of the relationship of the radical activists to the specifically Hindu bhadralok society. There is something to the idea that an anti-establishment sentiment, with a slumbering Hindu consciousness ensconced within it, was misrecognized as ideological support for the left and that this points to the fragility of this radical hegemony. But I think it points to an even more imperceptible continuation of a largely Hindu bhadralok common sense within the left-secular discourse—a common sense that was by virtue of its 'norming', incapable, despite its own self-conscious radicalism, of understanding the condition of the marginalized and subaltern communities. The discourse of secular 'high theory' remained completely confined to the top leadership of the party, but more significant is the fact that, as we have seen in earlier chapters, the high theory of secular discourse itself was caught within the Hindu norm. The dissidents and the activists at the lower levels too, although directly in touch with the people, remained unable to break out of this norm.

However, as I argue in this book, this is probably inevitable. There is no archimedean space available from where all experiences can be understood and reforms conducted. The failure of state-sponsored reforms in our conditions is only too evident, for unless they are backed, and I would venture to add, *preceded by*, prolonged internal struggles within the communities, they can only lead to further alienation and distance between the community and the modernizing and/or radical elites. The struggle for modernization and liberalization of community life must be situated necessarily within the discursive universe of the community. What *is* problematic, in my view then, is not that these activists operate within the discursive universe of their community but that within official party discourse this recognition is not possible. It might be more fruitful to accept that activists within each community will have to function within different universes and allow such expressions to come up as legitimate experiences within the organizational forums.

The Radical Elite and The 'Masses'

The discussion so far leads us to the main question that I wish to raise in the context of Marxist or left-secular practice. This is the question of the relationship between the modernizing impulses of radical political elites and the 'masses'. I should qualify that here I am not discussing *all kinds of modernizing elites* nor all kinds of modern politics. The politics of nationalism, too, as we have seen, was an elite intervention—as much as communal politics of all kinds has been. These kinds of politics somehow have not faced the dilemma that a radical secularist might have to face. The modernizing agenda of both nationalism and communal/communitarian politics was always a programme of modernizing the given community and what is more, in ways that emphasize rather than try to overcome difference. Their agendas, by simply valorizing the space of *their particular community*, in opposition to others, occupy a ground that is for that reason secure in its location. We now know that many peasant and mass struggles of pre-nationalist vintage were quite oblivious to the kinds of cultural difference introduced by elite interventions in politics[60]. Such has been evident from our own discussion of the revolts of the Mappilas or the Wahhabis and Faraizis in Bengal. Javeed Alam has recently discussed this phenomenon in relation to the Pabna and Deccan riots and has underlined three features of these struggles, in terms of their relationship with the elite intelligentsia. First, Alam argues that they involved both Hindu and Muslim masses, without any consciousness of their respective 'communal selves'. This feature is related to the second, that 'the entire leadership came from the ranks of the peasantry' and were therefore, 'free of any command from the outside world'. Finally, they were routinely viewed with suspicion by the emerging intelligentsia.[61] Alam however, seems to argue that this non-recognition or condemnation of peasant militancy '*created a rupture* between the intelligentsia and the peasant world' and locates the reasons of this distrust of the peasantry to the 'rentier class location' of the intelligentsia. In my view, that rupture was the initial condition of elite intervention in politics and was intrinsic to the character of the colonial middle class. Its later move towards the masses, including Gandhi's, was an *act of affiliation*, in order to provide the mass basis for the nationalist struggle in one case, and to carve out respective communal constituencies in others.

The difference between elite interventions represented by such political trends and those of the radical secular kinds lies, in my opinion, at two levels. Firstly, while radical-secular politics aimed at transcending the boundaries of community identity and investing its nationalism with a universalist content, the nationalist/communalist kinds of interventions found their *raison d'etre* in the assertion of difference. As a corollary, while the latter 'borrowed their poetry from the past'[62], the former sought it in the future. Secondly, while the emancipatory vision of the secular-radical imaginary was predicated upon the idea of an individuated, *gesellschaft-*

like society and a dissolution of particularistic identities, nationalist/
communalist politics aimed at the creation of a new kind of *gemeinschaft-
in-gesellschaft* political community and probably represented, as I have
suggested in the introductory chapter, an attempt to negotiate the process
of individuation precisely, in the creation of this national society. For both
these reasons, the nationalist/communalist modernizers had available to
them the resources of tradition, in whose name they appealed and which
they also transformed, in accordance with their vision. No such possibility
was open to the radical secularists. The agenda of cultural transformation
presents, in that sense, one of the most complex and difficult problems for
any serious radical politics, since it demands *dialogue and transformation at the
same time*. That is something that seemed to elude Left-wing radicals.

The radical-secularists, that is the Marxists, in making their move from
communism as a political imaginary, to Communism (with a Capital C)
as a *weltanschauung*, effected a closure of the kind of dialogue that was
possible in the early years. A move to the high Rationalism of this
weltanschauung was related to another metamorphosis that had taken place
within Marxism. The first metamorphosis, we have noted, had transformed
Marxism into an anti-imperialist doctrine. The second one was not really
a metamorphosis in that sense. It was basically a closure effected by the
canonization of the doctrine that made illegitimate the attempts of people
like Sultan Galiev, Tan Malaka, and Narbutabekov, to negotiate the distance
of high theory from their real worlds. It 'resolved' the dialectic of theory
and practice in favour of high theory, thus appending Marxist practice
ever more firmly to the epistemological world of Western, post-
Enlightenment rationalism. The communists in India, did not encounter
this 'shift' in the Comintern's position that Tan Malaka had experienced
with all his being because by the time they espoused Marxism as a new
worldview, it was already a canonized doctrine. To them the exciting story
of the workers' revolution in Russia presented a picture of the new world
where all markers of difference were being erased. This was a picture of
Marxism and socialism that was very different from the one that the
'backward peoples' of Turkestan and Soviet Central Asia were beginning
to experience through a rapid marginalization of their own cultures. The
meaning of the revolution was clearly felt differently, within and without.
I am not suggesting that the revolution brought only disaster to the people
of Soviet Central Asia. I am only suggesting that the different story that
was beginning to unfold there was at that time not accessible to those who
later became communists in India. To them the dream of a happy,
prosperous, and exploitation-free nation was at hand and the Soviet Union

showed them the way to it. Since the question of pan-Islamism had already been 'resolved' by the Comintern, for the Indian communists, it—and the religious question in general—was already handed down as received wisdom, unlike Malaka, for whom it remained an open question with the backing of a different experience. The leap for the Indian communists therefore, was one into *this* worldview, not the one being defended by Malaka or Narbutabekov.

What further complicated the situation in the context of the Indian communist movement was that it became totally unreflexive by virtue of its complete dependence on the Comintern and the Soviet Union, not merely for its ideological-theoretical nourishment but also its organizational coordination. The problem is not simply that the idea of Marxism was born on alien soil, but that it completely lost the capability to adapt to different conditions, thanks to its canonization.

Symptomatic of the control of the .Comintern over the Indian Communist Party was the first *Manifesto* of the Party titled 'Manifesto to The Delegates of the XXXVI Indian National Congress'. The document was written and printed in Moscow by M.N. Roy and approved by Lenin and Stalin. It is significant that the people who drafted and approved the document had no day-to-day touch with the movement in the country. Mikhail Borodin had gone to Madrid to attend a conference and brought with him a pile of Indian papers for Roy, who then submerged himself in them and then eventually produced the document. The Manifesto is full of unsought advice to the Congress. It further displays the most elementary lack of political sense in that it shows no appreciation of the dynamics of political dialogue: why should the delegates to the Congress session have taken this unasked for bit of advice seriously when they did not even know, let alone trust those who were handing it out? The tone of the advice is often derisive in the extreme. For instance, it says: 'Several thousand of noisy, irresponsible students and a number of middle class intellectuals followed by an ignorant mob momentarily incited by fanaticism, cannot be the social basis of the political organ of a nation.'[63]

On the positive side, the document does try to expose the 'freedom first' argument by emphasizing that there can be no genuine freedom without the toiling people and their demands figuring centrally in the movement. The document also provides some interesting insights into the dialectic of the elite and the masses and how the early communists saw and understood it. It therefore proceeds:

How can the Congress expect to arouse lasting popular enthusiasm in the name of the Khilafat and by demanding the revision of the treaty of Sivres (sic)? *The high politics behind such slogans may be easy for the learned intellectuals...but it is beyond the comprehension of the masses of the Indian people who have been steeped in ignorance* not only by the foreign ruler, but by our own religious and social institutions...Their consciousness must be aroused first of all. They must know what they are fighting for.

The entire reference in the preceding quote and in the above passage, it is clear, is to the Khilafat movement and Gandhi's support to it. We have discussed earlier how the Khilafat movement was quite clearly the result of an elite intervention. Yet, it did move the Muslim masses into action and, coupled with Gandhi's non-cooperation movement, became the vehicle of an unprecedented mass mobilization in the history of the anti-colonial struggle. We have also seen how it was often understood simply as 'opposition' [from 'khilaf'], indicating that both Gandhian and Khilafatist slogans were understood in many different ways. Contrary to what communists like Roy expected, it did not prove to be 'beyond the comprehension of the ignorant masses'; they merely comprehended it in ways that made sense to them. In any event, 'they' understood *this* appeal to 'high politics' more easily than they did the high politics of the communists. The document continues in the same vein and castigates the Gandhian-Khilafatist leadership for this 'high politics' and what it called its 'abstract idealism':

The programme of the Congress has to be denuded of all sentimental trimmings; it has to be dragged down from the height of abstract idealism; *it must talk of the things indispensable for mortal life* of the common human being...the object for which the Indian people will fight should not be looked for somewhere in the unknown regions of Mesopotamia or Arabia or Constantinople...

Recall Malaka's lament that 'with their hearts they [the people] remain with the Sarekat Islam—with their heaven which *we cannot give them*'. There is a deep and fundamental divide here in relation to spirituality, between what communists thought was 'high' politics but was probably understood by ordinary people as something close to them, even in their this-worldly existence. This *inability to understand* the meaning of the 'peoples' heaven', this construing of all spirituality/religiosity as ignorance, is centrally linked to the epistemological leap into the world of post-enlightenment rationalism, effected by the second metamorphosis. It is possible to argue, though it is by no means evident, that the mass mobilization on the Khilafat issue and Gandhi's wholehearted support to it strengthened the more reactionary voices within the Muslims. Even if one assumes that it did, I am not sure whether a purely external critique of the Khilafat movement, such as the one offered by the communists, has any relevance for ordinary Muslims. Such a critique, if it had to have any efficacy would have had to come from within the community. The presence of a large number of motivated Muslim *muhajir* youth among the communists, it seems from hindsight, did open up a possibility of the kind that Tan Malaka had been arguing for. Such a possibility, however, was ruled out from the beginning for two further related reasons. By the time the communists started getting down to business in India, pan-Islamism had already been declared dangerous and a force to be fought. Secondly, the Comintern had already embarked on its programme of the 'Bolshevization' of all communist parties. Henceforth, no space would be left for individual communist parties to decide how they wished to fight pan-Islamism and by extension, all other such tendencies. After all, our discussion with the communist activists above indicates that the struggle for the liberalization of the Hindu community became possible from precisely such an internal location.

It should be clear that I am not arguing that communists should themselves have 'been religious' but simply that they were unable to understand the world of those who are religious; to understand what gives meaning to their lives. In that sense they had lost the resources of conducting any meaningful dialogue with 'the masses' who had already been constituted as Hindus, Muslims, non-Brahmins etc. In other words, I am talking of the closure of dialogue, the diremption entailed in this leap. If the communists could not understand the religious mind, nor could they understand the force of nationalism. Argentinean Marxist sociologist Ronaldo Munck has traced the history of the continuous tension between Marxism and nationalism and suggested that some of the twentieth-century successes of Marxism lie in the attempts to synthesize the two—especially in unconventional experiments like those of Amilcar Cabral, Che Guevara, and Mao Tsetung.[64] However, if we leave aside these somewhat later attempts, formulated either in defiance of the Comintern or in the phase of the decentring of the communist movement, we can see that the problem of relating to nationalism has remained equally crucial. This inability to understand the force of both religion and nationalism arises out the communists' inability to deal with tradition and their desire, therefore, to simply wish it away as 'ignorance' and 'sentimentality'. Neither nationalism nor religion in contemporary times can be said to be a 'traditional' set of beliefs or ideologies, but they do reproduce themselves as modern entities within a discursive world that relates to and appropriates the traditional.

However, as our discussion with communist activists shows, this split or closure can never be complete. It is always mediated by the figure of the activist. It is the activist or what Gramsci called the organic intellectual, who stands at the confluence of these two worlds and speaks the languages of both with equal facility, who emerges as the critical figure here. It is upon the activist that the task of continuous translation and retranslation rests if a radical agenda of cultural transformation has to take shape. It is with a brief discussion of political location of this figure that I will conclude this discussion.

Bilingual Politics and the Radical Activist

One theme that runs through the various statements from A.K. Gopalan to Subhash Chakravarty and other activists is that of the deep divide between the 'intellectual world' of the party leadership and the 'life of the masses'. As Prabhat Mukhopadhyay and Pradeep Dutta put it, despite party injunctions to the contrary, 'we have to' participate in the life of the community. The contrast is brought out more starkly in Subhash Chakravarty's claim that in the formative years of the party, there was some attempt to relate to the lives of communities but 'once they started seeing themselves as the leaders of a political party, they became detached' and withdrew into their rarified worlds. The divide however can become a hermetically sealed one if the party in question is overtaken by a death wish. For any living organization this is not an option. Precisely for this reason, if we look at the ways in which the Marxists have grown in places where they became a mass force, it seems that this growth has been made possible by allowing for deviations from the injunctions and rigours of high theory. This is not to say that the major class-based struggles, especially of the peasantry, did not contribute to that growth. As a matter of fact these were precisely the kinds of struggles that made the communists a force to reckon with in Andhra Pradesh in the early 1950s, following the Telengana struggle. The movements of tenants and agricultural labourers in Kerala, and the Tebhaga movement involving the sharecroppers of Bengal, certainly played a crucial role in making the communists a big force in these two states. And yet, it is a recorded but underplayed fact that in all these states the growth of the party was closely tied to the party's link with an incipient subnationalism. In Andhra the party was in the forefront of the Visalandhra movement, playing a key role in the Andhra Mahasabha, while in Kerala its existence has been deeply meshed with the very formation of Malayali nationality. In Bengal too, we have seen how the narratives of the communist activists establish a direct continuity with the legacy of the Bengal Renaissance on the one hand and that of Ramakrishna Paramhans and Vivekananda, on the other. Bengali identity is in fact quite central to the existence of the communist movement in West Bengal. We have also seen how the life of the activist is closely meshed with the social and cultural life of ordinary people.

This however, is a slippery terrain. Being part of a cultural universe also carries with it the danger of always making peace with the conservatism that defines these worlds and which the given cultures encode. Often radical engagement with such cultural worlds has been of this kind, as it seeks not to disturb given power relations, as its own interest is simply in 'using culture' for political mobilization. It should not be difficult to see that such an approach is completely at variance with the sort of engagement that was exhibited by the great nineteenth century social reformers who were upsetting the apple-cart in various ways and did not have the imperative of immediate political and electoral mobilization to account for. If the struggle for secularism is, first and foremost, a battle for cultural transformation of communities, it cannot be simply fought at the level of ensuring the state's neutrality between communities. If that is the agenda, the key figure on whom the spotlight must move, is the figure of the bilingual activist or the bilingual intellectual.

The modern organism of the political party, especially a communist party, operates at two levels. This is particularly so in the postcolonial context. Invoking our earlier distinctions, we may say that these are the domains of civil and political society. At one level, within the domain of civil society, its functioning is conditioned by the high discourse of modernity, in which it itself participates. Here, where the party has to participate in parliamentary and legislative forums of the state, it is entirely governed by the framework of constitutional norms. In its self-projection before the media or in international relations, it operates within the overall framework of modern institutions. Yet, at the other level, from where it draws its activists, members and mass following, it operates in those vast sectors of society that lie beyond the individuated citizens of civil society— the world of communities and community existence.[65] These activist individuals represent the liberal-democratic elements *within* communities. They are the 'bilingual' organic intellectuals who speak both the language of civil society and that of the community. These individuals actually mediate between the two worlds and the organism of the political party provides the forum where the regular business of translation between the two worlds takes place through them. And it takes place despite the injunctions of theory. It is here, in this domain, that it becomes necessary to spell out the relationship of the party/ies to the independent strivings that are always active within communities. And it is here that the Leninist notion of a 'vanguard' turns out to be most problematic, for it demands the strengthening of the 'vanguard', that is, the party, by admitting the 'militants' and the 'most advanced sections' from the masses *into its apparatus*. This admission into the vanguard is actually an admission into the world of high-theory discourse that demands a severance of all ties with all 'backward ideas'—in other words a severance of ties with the other discursive world of the community. This vanguardist notion thus reproduces the rupture effected by the canonization of the doctrine on a regular and continuing basis. Thus, even when it is under pressure and it grudgingly recognizes the need for 'talking in two languages', it cannot do so. For, it has lost the capacity to speak the other language; it can only do it in an externalist fashion, as an outsider.

In the recent past, there has also been a different kind of experiment within the left. In this case there has been an attempt at theoretically recognizing the problems of bilingualism and of simultaneously operating in two discursive universes. I am referring to the formation of the Inquilabi Muslim Conference and the Dalit Mahasabha by the largest of the far left formations—the CPI(ML) Liberation. These two organizations were formed by the party in the early 1990s—the former in 1991 and the latter, in the face of the challenge from the BSP, in 1993. However, the problem was that the party continued to treat these organizations as the 'front organizations' of the vanguard. Vinod Mishra, the charismatic general secretary of the party would often be the main speaker in their conferences, leaving no doubt that the agenda was less the internal reform within the communities, more that of drawing the Dalit and Muslim masses into the party's fold. According to Vinod Mishra, the Dalit Mahasabha was started 'in order to actively intervene in the Dalit discourse vis-à-vis BSP'. However, he conceded that it 'remained a non-starter and subsequently we decided to abandon this project.'[66] This business of 'intervening in Dalit discourse' was doomed to failure because it assumed the vanguardist monopoly of truth and still defined an externalist relationship to the Dalits. However, it was to the credit of the party that it was able to see the problem. It therefore decided on what seems to be a more fruitful and less vanguardist perspective. 'The correct policy', says Mishra, 'would be to unite with radical Dalit organizations and interact with progressive intellectual circles such as proponents of "Dalit literature".' However, in the same breath, Mishra warned of the 'infiltration of dalitist ideas' in our organization.[67] This reaction underlines one of the crucial problems of bilingualism. Bilingual politics can only make sense if the so-called vanguard gives up its claim to the monopoly of truth and recognizes that there might be something that it might also have to learn. In such a situation, the desire to protect the purity of the creed can be counter-productive.

In relation to the Muslim community too, the party took some important steps outside of and beyond the formation of the Inquilabi Muslim Conference. In this case, the attitude seemed to be one of developing a relationship with the internal strivings for reform. Speaking at a convention organized by a liberal Muslim outfit called the All India Muslim Forum, Mishra exhorted Indian Muslims to align themselves with the left. The crisis posed by Hindutva, he says, 'also brings a historic opportunity before the Muslim masses to reassert their identity' on which 'a lot of discussion is going on among [the] Muslim intelligentsia'. While categorically opposing state-imposed reforms, he refers to the questions of polygamy and divorce as being crucial to any reform agenda. 'In Muslim countries like Turkey and Tunisia polygamy has been banned and even in Pakistan and Bangladesh lots of restrictions are placed. So this is a question which I think enlightened sections among the Muslims must seriously ponder over.'[68]

Regarding the experience of the Inquilabi Muslim Conference in Bihar, Mishra's assessment is more positive but he notes that 'by itself it could not advance much and failed to intervene in the debates within the community on the question of women, reservations for Dalit Muslims etc.' However, it helped in understanding the problems of the Muslims and in 'formulating our responses'.[69] This intervention points to a different way of relating to communities where the party does not step in with a ready-made set of externalist readings of 'what ails Indian Muslims' but, on the contrary, is prepared to understand what in the community's view is the problem. Also, the decision to strike a relationship with internal strivings for reforms and with radical organizations representing them, it seems, is one that has more than a merely tactical significance. For, it means a recognition that the space of a secular politics and a secular intelligentsia is not simply outside communities, in an archimedean 'nowhere', *but everywhere, within* all communities *and* outside them. If that be the case, then the conclusion is inescapable that we are no longer left with *a secular intelligentsia* but with so many 'secular' intelligentsias marked by their community identities, striving for a liberalization or democratization of their respective communities.

The Right to Exit

Finally, in conclusion, I would like to suggest that the 'right to exit' that has been talked of in recent times, makes sense only within the context of such a notion of radical politics.[70] But before I go into this question, let me state a problem in relation to the idea of internal reform. Much of the resistance to the idea arises out of the often bland binary opposition that is set up between 'state-sponsored reform' and 'internal reform' which is then translated quite unproblematically into a 'modernity versus tradition' opposition. Opposition to state-sponsored or state-initiated reform does not by itself imply support for either the total autonomy of the community or the absence of individual rights within communities. At least, one can say that it need not. The dichotomy between state-led reforms and community autonomy often seems insurmountable because somewhere behind this is the understanding that any internalist position can only mean that we are perennially trapped within the oppressive 'traditional' discourse of the community. We live in modern societies and in such kinds of societies, communities do not lead a hermetically sealed existence. In modern democratic societies they must constantly engage in some kind of dialogue, however minimal, not only with other communities but also with political parties and the logic of the state. The very fact that an individual is not ever *a singular subject* but is always located at nodes occupying multiple subject positions, implies that there is always a way in which the perspective of the one has the potential of destabilizing the other be it caste, gender, community, race, or class. What the idea of internal reform does is to seize upon this instability to raise either questions of gender or caste or language to interrogate the hegemonic constructs of community. Such has been the position of feminists working within the Muslims, for example. I therefore, take Partha Chatterjee's idea of the 'right' of communities 'not to offer reasons for being different' to be a recognition of the limits that must be placed on the state or on any secular-modern elite bent upon pushing reforms upon an unwilling community. I also understand it to refer to a condition where the possibilities of dialogue between communities are seriously impaired. In such a situation, it may be important, as suggested by Chatterjee, to ensure a minimum democratic representation within communities, especially since that is something they ask for in their external relationships, from other communities and the state. Such democratic representation, (not necessarily a state institution like the parliament) that will provide the community with the opportunity to 'justify itself in its own chosen forum', it seems, can facilitate the struggle for internal reform.

However, as we know from experience, this process need not always be easy. Powerful groups and vested interests within communities enjoying traditional hegemony can always subvert the processes by targeting key individuals. It is in this context that the idea of a 'right to exit' suggested by Javeed Alam needs to be considered, as the limit to the community's control over the individual.[71]

Alam's discussion of the right to exit, however, is predicated on the idea of individuation. In his rendering, 'an individuated person demands dignity of person' for 'individuation at its minimum, creates a distance between one's self and one's community' based on a sense of egalitarianism and freedom.[72] Alam believes that 'the growth of industry, the pervasive commercialization of agriculture and rural economy, increasing urban residence, the expansion of democracy and especially of the impact of electoral politics, and increasing exposure to mass media' render the process 'almost inevitable'. This process, he argues, 'represents a threat to the community', because as a consequence, individuals tend to make 'individually conceived choices and options' which 'is anathema to those who preside over the fate of communities'.[73] The process described by him leave us in no doubt that the individual emerging out of it might be simply the bourgeois self-maximizing individual. Such an individual, much as s/he acts on the basis of her own choices, I believe, represents no threat to the community or its leaders. Indeed in contexts like India's such an individual can be easily interpellated into the discourse of community politics and is quite open to the possibility of using it to his/her own advantage.[74] Alternatively, s/he can lead a purely anonymous individual urban life. The telos of individuation does not in my opinion, lead to internal reform. Alam is aware of this second possibility at least, insofar as he talks of the 'passive exit' effected by 'emancipated individuals' and keeps them out of his discussion of the 'right to exit'.[75] It seems to me that the threat to dominant powers within the community comes not from such bourgeois individuals but from those who either reject that 'individuation' and like Gandhi (Alam's example) make the reverse move towards community, or have not become 'fully individuated' in the first instance. In other words, it is the political activist of whatever description, who has made the choice of being within the community and transforming it, who represents the threat to 'those who preside over the fate of the community'. The question of a right to exit, I suggest, makes most sense only in the case of this missing subject, who is neither the state nor the community—nor even the individual. For a radical secular politics with the agenda of cultural transformation then, this is the subject that must be made visible.

Notes

1. Kaviraj (1995b), p. 93.

2. Ibid., pp. 93–7.

3. Abdel-Malek (1981), p. 81.

4. Marx and Engels (1982), p. 39.

5. At the height of the Cultural Revolution, it will be recalled, the Chinese Communist Party propounded the theory that the 'villages of the world' would encircle and liberate the 'cities'. This was one specific aspect of the three world theory that was subsequently attributed to Lin Piao.

6. Nigam (1999).

7. Frank (n.d.).

8. Claudin (1975).

9. Ibid., vol. I, p. 50, emphasis added.

10. Ibid., p. 246, emphasis added.

11. Ibid.

12. Ibid., p. 247.

13. Ibid., p. 248, emphasis added.

14. One of the best documented sources for these debates is d'Encausse and Schram (1965). I have used both this text and that of Claudin, though the references are mostly to the latter.

15. See note 87, Chapter 4. Emphasis added.

16. Claudin (1975), pp. 256–7.

17. For this account I have relied mainly on Rodinson (1980), pp. 133–40.

18. Ibid., p. 134.

19. Claudin (1975), note 85, Chapter 4. Emphasis added.

20. Abdel-Malek (1981), p. 86.

21. Mao Tsetung (1977), 'On Contradiction', vol. I, p. 336.

22. Ibid., p. 316.

23. Ibid., pp. 315–6. The reference to dogmatists is to those in the Chinese Cummunist Party who wanted to mechanically replicate the Comintern's line.

24. Ibid., p. 341.

25. Mao Tsetung (1977), 'On the Correct Handling of Contradictions Among the People', vol. V, p. 385.

26. Ibid., p. 386.

27. Ibid., p. 391.

28. We have seen in Chapter 4, that many Muslims who considered British India to be a *Dar ul-harb*, found it necessary to go on such self-exile, in order to wage war against the colonialists. They were the *mohajirs*.

29. Roy (1984), p. 464. Emphasis added.

30. Ahmed (1981), p. 7.

31. Ibid., p. 9.

32. Mukhopadhyay (1985), vol. I, p. 7.

33. Namboodiripad (1976), p. 94.

34. See Namboodiripad (1976) and Gopalan (1976).

35. Seth (1995), p. 108.

36. It is worth mentioning that while the muhajir youth did become communists, organized under the name of 'Association of Indian Revolutionaries', contrary to Roy's claim, they did not join the communist party when it was formed in Tashkent. Muzaffar Ahmed points out in his memoirs that none of their names appear in the minutes of the formation meetings, found in the Tashkent archives. Probably this may have been due to a personality conflict between Roy and the mohajir leaders. However, that is not really relevant to our discussion.

37. Gopalan (1976), pp. 11–2.

38. Namboodiripad (1976), p. 34.

39. Ibid., p. 69.

40. Ibid., p. 70.

41. Mukhopadhyay (1985), p. 17. I say 'naive' because, as discussed in Chapters 4 and 5, the lower caste/Dalit groups stood on the other side.

42. See Basu (1998).

43. Sanjay Seth, Op. Cit. p. 49

44. CPI(M), *Tasks on the Trade Union Front*, Document adopted by the Central Committee, New Delhi, September 10–16, 1983. Emphasis added, pp. 28–9.

45. My use of the term 'ideological' here requires clarification. I do not believe that there are any 'non-ideological' movements. I use this term here as a shorthand expression to distinguish such movements from those that draw on the given resources of 'tradition' like the various movements of the right, or in a different way, on repressed traditions, like the Dalit and other such movements where the lived experience of social groups mediates their 'ideology'. 'Ideological' here then refers more to the more explicitly modernist and radical political movements that seek to transcend those categories handed over by tradition.

46. Gopalan (1976), p. 22.

47. Ibid., p. 23.

48. Ibid., pp. 23–5.

49. Personal interview on 8 October 1999 at Chandan Sinha's small restaurant near the party's Calcutta district committee office.

50. In the 1960s and 1970s, under the rule of the Congress-patronized hoodlums, the puja was transformed into an extortionist enterprise. Its use of personal aggrandisement was rampant and could only be gradually eliminated after the Left Front came to power. Such tendencies however, seem to have reappeared lately, though to a lesser extent.

51. It is a common slippage to identify 'Bengali' with 'Hindu'. There is a constant 'othering' of not just the Muslims but also of Hindi-speaking Hindus that routinely takes place in the bhadralok mind.

52. Personal interview, 9 October 1999.

53. Personal interview, 10 October 1999.

54. Ibid.

55. This information was given to me by Nepal Bhattacharya.

56. Personal interview, 11 October 1999.

57. Personal interview, 10 October 1999.

58. I must add that here I am merely reproducing the narrative of the interviewees and am not concerned with the factual accuracy of their narrative.

59. Ahmed (1981), pp. 396–7.

60. To say that they were oblivious to cultural difference is merely to underline that while they lived their culture, they probably did not feel called upon to define it in terms that foreground difference.

61. Alam (1999b), pp. 86–8.

62. The reference here is to Marx's celebrated comment that the 'social revolution of the proletariat cannot borrow its poetry from the past' in *The Eighteenth Brumaire of Louis Bonaparte.*

63. The document is reproduced in Ahmed (1981). All references and quotations are from this text.

64. Munck (1986) provides a comprehensive and fascinating review of Marxism's relationship with nationalism.

65. For a discussion of the distinction between civil and political society, see the Conclusion of this book.

66. Mishra (1999), p. 194.

67. Ibid.

68. Ibid., p. 199.

69. Ibid., 201.

70. For a detailed discussion in the Indian context, see Alam (1999b), parts III and IV.

71.   Ibid. I however, do not agree with Alam that the *right* to exit makes available the *initial conditions* of internal reforms (p. 217). In my opinion, it can only be considered a limiting device to the power of the community.

72.   Ibid., p. 221.

73.   Ibid., pp. 218–9.

74.   In the postcolonial context, we have many instances of such individuated middle class people affiliatively attaching themselves to 'their' community. In recent years, such individuals who have lost earlier forms of sociality and face-to-face communication, have been known to reactivate such affiliations through electronic communication. This is, of course, too new and complex an area for us to enter into here.

75.   I believe Alam is right that there is a way in which individuals *in the process of individuating*, especially those living in rural communities and exercising choice in matters of love and choice of marriage partners, can destabilize the logic of both family and community, leading to severe reprisals from community leaders. Such cases may also be considered as a case where the right to exit needs to be made available—even though these are clearly not cases of 'internal reform'. I therefore do not bring them into the discussion here.

Conclusion

In conclusion, a brief recapitulation of the main lines of the argument of this book will be in order. This book has been mainly concerned with understanding the relationship of secularism and the Indian 'nation'. The specific context of this exploration has been what I have called the insurrection of little selves since the 1980s, which I see as part of a global conjuncture of a crisis of modernity. I have also argued that this insurrection of little selves in our context has been linked to the specific manner in which the project of Indian nationhood came to be shaped and how it dealt with identity questions generally. In this context, the specific ideological configuration called secular-nationalism has been the focus of my inquiry, for in the post-independence period, it was this configuration that constituted the dominant discourse framing basic assumptions of Indian politics and nationhood.

In order to understand the constitution of Indian nationhood, I have explored a range of issues related to nationalism in general in the introductory chapter. First, I have discussed the more problematic aspects of modern subjectivity that emerge with the process of large-scale dislocations that modernity initiates. I have argued that the subject that emerges from these processes is not always the individuated modern self that is assumed to be the basis of all democratic citizenship but also a new kind of subject/agent that Hannah Arendt has called the 'mass man'. Contrary to the common assumption that all individuals desire autonomy, this kind of an individual presents a fundamental problem for democratic theory in so far as s/he embodies what Erich Fromm calls the 'fear of freedom'—a fear of the alienation and loneliness of modern life. He therefore seeks community and tradition and therefore invests his/her agential role in some external figure of authority, says Fromm. This 'mass man' produced by modern societies is therefore, available for all kinds of contradictory mobilizations, particularly of the nationalist or fascist kind, which are generally articulated around some rhetoric of tradition. In these developments, I have argued, lies the ever-present possibility of the subversion of the democratic project that nationalism sets out to realize. In this context, I have referred to the deep chasm that divides the 'enlightened' elite and the 'backward' masses in all modern societies. This chasm, I have also suggested, has to do vitally with the largely ignored question of power relations between these elites and the masses. We have seen in our discussion that it is always the power-wielding elite that comes forth as the carrier of new ideas, of 'enlightenment', while the masses are 'steeped in tradition'. It is this elite that wants to destroy tradition, the sole support of this conservative man.

The introductory chapter also focuses on the project of nationalism to forge homogeneous national cultures and its extremely problematic relationship to minority cultures. I consider this question in relation to another aspect that many scholars like Hans Kohn and Benedict Anderson have drawn attention to—nationalism's link with the emergence of Universal History (Kohn) and a new notion of simultaneity (Anderson)—implicit in which is the new consciousness of time that comes with modernity. Anderson calls this, after Walter Benjamin, 'homogeneous empty time'. While these notions make it possible to understand the coexistence of different societies and cultures 'in the same time', I have drawn on more recent scholarship that suggests that there is an implicit violence in this notion that reduces 'Other cultures' (that is, non-Western cultures) to the status of mere survivals of the past, through a kind of temporalization of space. Important in this context, in interrogating this time-conception of modernity have been the writings of Reinhart Koselleck, Louis Althusser, and Etienne Balibar. Drawing on Althusser's notion of time, linked to the nature of social totality, I have further argued in this chapter that the recognition of different temporalities and their articulation must be seen as the precondition of the totality. The 'social totality' cannot be simply assumed to be a pre-given whole governed by a singular logic, but must be seen as an articulation of different elements, each driven by a different dynamic. In a sense, this idea forms the basis of my discussion of anticolonial nationalisms. I have found it useful to see the 'nation' as such a totality—formed *ex post facto*, with the coming together of different cultures, rather than existing prior to all discrete cultures as some eternal entity. It is specifically in the context of minority cultures and their always-problematic relationship to the nation, that this idea seems to provide the most useful insights. I have discussed the experience of South Africa and India in terms of such an articulation of different histories later in the book.

In Chapter 1, I discuss more specifically, the existing literature on nationalism. While looking at the phenomenon, I have however, tried to use the present focus of my inquiry as my entry point. That is to say, I have avoided a simple recapitulation of all the earlier debates on nationalism, and referred only to those aspects which relate directly to the focus of this book. Debates that have their origins in the specific histories of European nationalism and have therefore addressed a different set of questions, did not always seem immediately relevant to my inquiry. However, there are at least three issues that seemed to me to be of critical relevance for my purposes. First the idea, common to most theorists and scholars, is that nationalism is a modern phenomenon, linked to the rise of either industrial or capitalist societies, both of which call for a certain homogenization of cultures. There seems to be a broad agreement among theorists I have studied—with the exception of Elie Kedourie—that the creation of a single national culture out of the pre-existing disparate and scattered cultural and linguistic social groups, was the precondition to the most important emancipatory aspect of the nationalist project, namely, the institution of democratic citizenship. Second, again common to most scholars, the idea that this initial link with democratic citizenship seemed to have given way, somewhere along the line, to the link with a more problematic notion of an organic community. Third, the idea that in a crucial sense, nationalism marks the 'entry of the masses' into history. This is a point that is more specifically made by Tom Nairn and followed up by Anderson, but shared by others implicitly, in the link that they establish between nationalism and the advent of democracy and citizenship.

There is also a fourth idea, implicit in the first two, but not clearly spelt out in most cases: that nationalism, because it was coeval with industrial/capitalist development, was also coeval with a large-scale dislocation in social terms leading to uprooting of communities and their insertion into a different logic of modern community-identity formation. I have also drawn my major assumption, that nations are primarily imagined communities, from Benedict Anderson's path-breaking work in this field. From my reading of the process of social dislocation and the advent of mass society, along with Anderson's insight, I have argued that it appears that nationalism defies the received understanding of societies moving in any straightforward way, from *gemeinschaft* to *gesellschaft* formations. Nationalism, I have therefore suggested, is simultaneously a phenomenon that has to do critically with the attempt to deal with these dislocations. Individuation, that is supposed to mark the emergence of *gesellschaft* formations, and consequently the rational citizen, does not seem to be a necessary outcome of these dislocations, bringing forth the other kind of subject I have mentioned above. Nationalism, on this reading, seems to me to represent an attempt, simultaneously, to deal with these dislocations and create new *gemeinschaft-in-gesellschaft* formations: new communities that are composed of individuals, but bound together with notions of common tradition and affect.

I have also separately discussed the phenomenon of anticolonial nationalisms as I believe the experience of colonial subjugation does something to that entire enterprise, by making it open to all kinds of xenophobic articulations. The centrality of the experience of subjugation accounts for a peculiar 'inwardness' that marks the consciousness of these nationalisms, which I seek to explore. For this, I have particularly relied on a reading of Edward Said, Partha Chatterjee, and Benedict Anderson. In a manner of speaking, the rest of the book explores this aspect of anti-colonial nationalisms in the context of Indian nationalism.

In Chapter 2, I have tried to map the developments of the 1980s and 1990s, in order to understand the changes and shifts in the terms of political discourse that mark this period. I have suggested that this period marks the unravelling of the structure of nationhood that was inherited from the nationalist struggle and consolidated over the early decades of the post-independence period. The emergence of the numerous little selves on the political stage, I have suggested, should be seen as, in crucial ways, demands for the redrawing of the cultural boundaries of the nation. I locate two moments here. The first, beginning around 1978, when the nation's boundaries begin to be challenged from different directions and in different ways. The second, around the turn of the decade and the advent of the 1990s, when the 'nation strikes back'. It is in this conjuncture, when secular-nationalism is thoroughly beleaguered and battered, that the alternative Hindu nationalist discourse moves in to occupy the ground being vacated by it.

In Chapter 3, I have looked at the recent debates in India on secularism. In reading the positions of the various protagonists in the debate, I have tried to understand the central question thrown up by the developments discussed in Chapter 2, namely, the rapid disappearance of the neutral ground of arbitration between different communities, represented by the nation-state. I have argued that despite sharp disagreements and divergences, the different positions point towards some common elements, especially with regard to redefinition of the secularist project. There is, by and large, an agreement about the need to find a different ground, that is negotiated and 'emergent' rather than imposed and archimedean.

Chapter 4 discusses the different histories in conflict and articulation, that intersect in the process of the formation of the Indian nation. I especially focus on the Muslim and Dalit histories and their relationship to the history of the nation. This chapter also focuses on the notions of time and selfhood that underlie these different imaginations of Selfhood, not all of which enjoy a smooth and easy relationship with hegemonic imaginations of the nation. Also crucial to the discussions here and in Chapter 5 is the relationship of history and memory, where I have argued that once the principles of 'rational scientific history' became common, history became instituted as memory. The modern Indian Self's search for History led it to draw on various strands of Orientalist writings in order to tell its history. The different Selves, narrating different histories, come into very problematic relationships with the nation's history. Gandhi responds by refusing the ground of history and the nation-state, arguing that 'truth resides outside history'. In the final section, this chapter discusses the reversal of fates of Gandhi and Ambedkar on the eve of independence—Gandhi, marginalized in the nation he fathered and Ambedkar, enjoying his final moment of glory as one of the key drafters of the Constitution. In this discussion, I focus on the question of the relation between the Hindus and the Muslims and the future of the incipient nation-state, as the ground on which this reversal takes place.

In Chapter 5, I discuss the Dalit relationship to secularism, modernity, and the nation. It has come to be common sense that the Dalit relationship to modernity is quite unproblematic because it opened up possibilities of their liberation. I suggest in this chapter that this is probably only one part of the story, for in certain other crucial respects, Dalit politics represents a deep resistance to the two great political artefacts of our modernity, secularism and the nation. By privileging lived experience, as for instance feminism does, it also represents a resistance to the fundamental epistemic diremption instituted by modernity, that between the subject and the object.

Finally, Chapter 6 discusses the experience of the other secularism—left-radical secularism. Unlike state secularism, it neither had to shoulder the legacy of colonialism nor that of the postcolonial state. Yet, when secularism was under attack, this secularism seemed to share the same fate as state-secularism. In this chapter, I discuss in detail the wide gap between the high theory of secularism and the actual practice of activists on the ground. This chapter is based on detailed interviews and discussions with CPI(M) activists in West Bengal. In the face of increasing challenge from the discourse of the Hindu right, the activists seem to be rethinking and reformulating their notions of secularism in line with their practice of maintaining a different relationship with people of different communities. The activists on the ground have, I suggest on the basis of my reading of these different interviews, a double existence—one within civil society dominated by the high discourse of secularism, and another within the community where a very different language dominates. I discuss this domain, which I have called political society, after Partha Chatterjee, below.

One of the conclusions that suggests itself from my exploration of the crisis and the unravelling of the secular-nationalist discourse, is that it was undergirded by a Hindu ethos and helped to preserve the power of the upper-caste Hindu elite. The second conclusion that emerges from this exploration is that like other nationalisms, Indian nationalism too remained a homogenizing project. While the second conclusion has been discussed at length throughout, the first needs to be considered here at some length. The question is: if secular-nationalism was Hindu in many ways, how is/was it different from Hindu nationalism?

Secular-Nationalism: The Crisis of Universalisms

I have argued in the preceding chapters that politics in India in the 1980s and 1990s, has been marked by an explosion of what is generally referred to as 'identity politics'. I have avoided using the term 'identity politics', which is often counter-posed to 'class politics', because I believe even class politics at one level, is a question of identity. For, even though class exists as a structural feature, it only becomes the subject of political action and mobilization when members of the class begin to imagine themselves as a class. In other words, only when members of a class see their selfhood as being defined by class existence and class oppression, does the class become available for mobilization.[1] I have therefore, chosen to describe the politics of this period as an 'insurrection of little selves'. I have also argued that this insurrection of little selves should be seen as a consequence of the global crisis of certain emancipatory visions of modern politics—visions that sought to erase all difference so that the unmarked abstract citizen may emerge, standing above parochial loyalties, or visions that sought deliverance through the agency of the proletariat as the universal class. In the course of the discussion we have seen how both these ideas have turned out to be counter-productive. My argument about why they are counter-productive, focuses on the character of *modern universalisms*, which have only ended up universalizing dominant cultures. In fact, it can be put in terms of a much stronger claim, that there is a *constitutive* relationship between modern univeralisms and dominant cultures. So far, I have suggested only a strong connection between the two. The fundamental reason why this historical connection assumes a necessary character, I suggest, is related to modernity's consciousness of time. Dominant cultures are dominant because they are 'advanced' and carriers of 'progress'; they are historical cultures, and therefore, 'unconscious tools of History'. Modern universalisms, predicated as they are upon the notion of a singular World-History, often with a common Past and a common Future, tended to see the world as a single entity. This is a vision that could not hold out in the context of the historical encounter between the West and the world it colonized. The different pasts of the colonized were somehow recognized, but the telos of the Future remained: either in the form of abstract universal citizenship, or in the form of an equally abstract classless society. The argument generally then took a different form: it is true that different societies—not human society, in the abstract singular—have different histories; however, with the integration of the world into a single entity in modern times, they must all from now on move towards the same goal. The Present, in this understanding of time, now became the present of the more advanced societies. Other societies were reduced to the status of 'remnants' and 'survivals' of the past.

In suggesting this constitutive link between modern universalisms and the universalization of dominant cultures, I am not suggesting that modernity itself is thereby 'incorrigible'. While these universalisms constituted the dominant tendencies in modern thought, modern thought exceeds them. There are many traditions of modern thought that offer a critique of these tendencies, but they are traditions that were rapidly marginalized and reduced to silence. One of the possibilities that opens up with the current conjuncture of the global crisis of modernity, is that of recasting and reworking our notions of emancipation. By making visible the relationship of these universalisms with a certain ethnocentrism, this crisis forces us to re-think our notions of freedom.

I have also argued in this book, that nationalism was the mode through which cultures were, and are, homogenized in order to produce the modern abstract citizen. I have mentioned above that it is this language of abstract, unmarked citizenship, cast within the narrative of Progress and World-History, that by delegitimizing other narratives of Selfhood produces mainstream and majority cultures as the secular norm. In this context, I have argued that the fate of secular-nationalism in India has not been very different from the fate of all such universalisms. It has, *despite itself,* produced a Hindu ethos as the norm, and has helped in the preservation of the power of the erstwhile dominant Hindu upper castes. Precisely for this reason, there has been a close kinship between secular-nationalism and Hindu-nationalism, the latter representing the nationalism of the dominant culture. It may, in fact, be argued that the emergence of Hindu nationalism in the form of the Sangh Parivar,[2] in the moment of secular-nationalism's crisis, in the moment of the emergence of the myriad repressed voices, was the response of the upper caste Hindu elite to the perceived 'threat to the nation'. In the heyday of secular-nationalism's hegemony, upper-caste privileges in the modern institutions of Indian society were preserved intact; their control over productive and other assets and resources remained unchallenged. The 'threat to the nation' therefore did not exist.

As Nehru had understood very well, the Indian bourgeoisie, harbinger of its modernity, was essentially Hindu, and it was this class that consolidated its rule under the Nehruvian 'passive revolution'. In this dispensation both the secular upper-caste Hindu and the 'real' Hindu, cohabited in close kinship. In immaculately secular terms, these elites continued to dominate institutions and assets of society, keeping marginalized groups like the Muslims, Dalits, tribals, and others in perpetual deprivation. 'Merit', 'efficiency', and 'productivity' were its new slogans. In trying to understand the intricate character of secular-nationalism, however, we need to underline one complexity here. I have discussed the discourse of secular-nationalism through a reading of Nehru in Chapter 1. But we need to add further, that the Hindu-ness of secular-nationalist practice also exceeded what Nehru himself wanted or propounded. There were secular-nationalists who were more unabashedly Hindu than Nehru would allow for. They, nevertheless, lived a full life as Congress leaders under Nehru's benign leadership. This will be particularly clear if we go back to the early years of independence. Let us return to the time when the constituent assembly was in the process of formulating the secular-democratic Constitution of India. Precisely when Congress leaders like Sardar Patel, K.M. Munshi, Rajendra Prasad, Govind Ballabh Pant, and the like were pushing through their modernizing agenda in the assembly, their conduct outside revealed their ill-concealed Hindu face. Mushirul Hasan writes of the 1948 by-elections in Faizabad, where Congress candidate Baba Raghav Das was facing Acharya Narendra Dev, the Marxist socialist. G.B. Pant, campaigning for the Congress candidate, declared that 'the Acharya did not believe in the divinity of Lord Ram' which was evident from the fact that he did not sport a *choti*, like devout

Brahmins. Das, on the other hand, campaigned distributing *tulsi* leaves to the people.[3] Hasan further catalogues some of the other instances:

Acharya Kripalani, as Congress President, felt uneasy with Nehru's policy towards Pakistan and wanted an immediate blockade of Kashmir, a complete break in economic relations with Pakistan, strong measures on evacuee property.

His successor, Pattabhi Sitaramayya, whose defeat once Gandhi had considered his defeat, spoke at the All India Hindu Code Bill Conference, chaired by Jagadguru Shankaracharya, at which opposition was voiced to efforts to reform the Hindu Personal Law.[4]

The country's President, Rajendra Prasad, presided over a Cow Welfare Workers' Conference, along with the Agriculture minister, Jairamdas Doulatram.

Rajendra Prasad also insisted, against Nehru's advice, on inaugurating the rebuilt Somnath temple, and came out strongly against the Hindu Code Bill, for which, he found powerful support in the Congress.[5]

Senior Congress leaders like Purushottam Das Tandon, and K.M. Munshi, Sampurnanand, and Seth Govind Das, are known to have been passionate Hindu nationalists and their role in communalizing the Hindi/Urdu controversy is also quite well-documented.

If we look at the entire evidence together, we cannot avoid facing the conclusion that the Congress at its secular-nationalist best was a 'Hindu' organization. I have put the word Hindu within quotation marks, because these leaders were not Hindu in the religious, traditionalist sense. Their Hindu-ness, at least in part, was a function of their nationalism. In fact their speeches and their role in the constituent assembly reveal very different persona. To illustrate, take the following comment from Rajendra Prasad briefly referred to earlier, made in the inaugural session of the assembly:

It is also to be remembered and we, who are present in the House, cannot forget it even for a moment that many of the seats are vacant at this meeting. Our brethren of the Muslim League are not with us and their absence increases our responsibility. We shall have to think at each step, what they would have done if they had been here? We hope they will soon come and take their places...But if unfortunately these seats continue to remain unoccupied, it will be our duty to frame a constitution which will leave no room for complaint from anybody.[6]

Or, take the following from Purushottam Das Tandon, who spoke of Indian tradition's 'respect for other rights' and of considering the whole world one family:

We shall do justice to all communities and give them full freedom in their social and religious affairs...

The differences which the British harp upon have been created by them. They were not in existence before their advent. Hindus and Muslims had a common civilization and lived amicably [...]Those who are opposing us under the instigation of the British, are our brethren and we certainly desire their cooperation; but in order to have them on our side we cannot sacrifice our principles [...]Congress has always tried to unite all sections of the population to fight for the freedom of their country. Our leaders have never indulged in communal bickerings. Congress is the only body in which Hindus, Muslims, Parsees, Jains and Buddhists can unite. In politics it refuses to recognize any difference on account of religion.'[7]

Leaders like Seth Govind Das argued in the Constituent Assembly, that India's constitution 'could only be socialist'.[8] Algurai Shastri spoke of how the 'Aims and Objects' resolution moved by Nehru, 'embodied the ideals of equality and fraternity of Rg Veda and scientific socialism', namely, 'to each according to one's needs and from each according to one's capacity'. He also spoke of how Vedic ideals had been 'held high during Muslim rule from Hazrat Umar to Bahadur Shah, Akbar and Humayun'.[9] Pandit Govind Ballabh Pant spoke of the 'individual citizen, who is really the backbone of the state, the cardinal centre of all social activity', who 'has been lost here in the indiscriminate body known as the community.'[10]

It will be wrong in my view, to see these professions of secularism by 'Hindu' nationalists in the Congress, as signs of mere hypocrisy. The desire for instituting the individual citizen, of ensuring non-discrimination between communities, of a vague 'socialism', was real, not a mere posture meant to satisfy Nehru, who was in any case, in a hopeless minority. These were the essential premises of secular-nationalism that all of them shared. Nehru may or may not have personally agreed with all the utterances and actions of his colleagues but how can it be denied that in the overall discourse of secular-nationalism that he espoused, there was room for different shades of Hindu nationalism, that there was, in fact a close kinship between the two? Nehru chose to understand this paradox between the desire for abstract citizenship and the Hinduness of nationalism in terms of the logic of World-History as we have seen earlier, and thus make peace with himself. There is, however, one more point that this account of the role of leading Congress leaders brings out—the bilingualism of the activist inhabiting two worlds, both civil and political society. What kinds of pressures does it place upon the bilingual intellectual? How are these negotiated? I have discussed this issue in relation to communist activists in Chapter 6 but I will return to it in the final section of this conclusion.

The hegemonic status acquired by the discourse of secular-nationalism and the great expectations of it from the postcolonial state elite, ensured for almost four decades that the Congress remained at the helm of affairs. It was the character acquired by the Congress in the immediate aftermath of independence, which enabled it to function as the instrument of the Hindu upper caste bourgeoisie, even while drawing its social base from the Muslim and Dalit masses. For many decades, this was the winning electoral combination which made the emergence of the Congress as 'a system' possible—the 'Congress system' as Rajni Kothari and Morris-Jones have aptly described it.

And yet, it is necessary to underline that secular-nationalism *was* secular; it *was* different from Hindu nationalism of the Savarkar and the Hindu right variety. Where did this difference lie? It seems to me that the most fundamental difference lay in its understanding of the nation, its attitude to history and its relevance for the present. It differed sharply from the Hindu nationalist view of India as Hindu, and posited instead a 'unity-in-diversity' of different cultures. This is also what made it different from European nationalisms. Its understanding of Indian tradition and history was essentially that it was syncretic. That this diversity was undergirded by a Hindu ethos and culture was more a consequence of its universalism than a religiously inspired position. It also sharply contested the Hindu nationalist version of medieval Indian history as a simple oppression of Hindus by sectarian *Muslims*. Its narrative of that history was cast in terms of a composite or syncretic culture, that drew on secular ideas of conflicts around class, rather than community, as we have seen in our discussion of Nehru in Chapter 1. Its claim was that it was the Muslim *rulers*, who like any other rulers, used various means to preserve their power.[11] The popular level, in its understanding, was one marked by dialogue and exchange between cultures. Whatever the blind spots of such a vision—and that only became apparent retrospectively—it was a vision of history that posited a syncretic unity and held colonial rule responsible for breaking that unity of Hindus and Muslims, as Purushottam Das Tandon's quote above so vividly demonstrates. Naturally then, secular-nationalism was also sharply opposed, despite failings of individual leaders, to the Hindu nationalist attempts to correct the 'wrongs of history' in the present. In a sense, we could say, it was Hindu only by default, as most modern universalisms turned out to be representatives of dominant cultures. Its 'modernity', while delegitimizing all talk of community and caste matters, also delegitimized the justified urges of the hitherto marginalized groups, the specificity of whose experiences could hardly be represented in abstract and secular terms.

Those who were marginalized in this dispensation, could not really make their claims without drawing attention to their continued exclusion by the very upper-caste Hindus, whom they now saw dominating over the affairs of the postcolonial secular state. To these excluded/marginalized sections, secular-nationalism appeared therefore, as the 'ideological maneuvre' of the brahminical upper castes, who as Periyar had astutely remarked, had acquired a kind of 'winning flexibility' and begun dominating the modern institutions. Many contemporary Dalit writers, I have shown in Chapter 5, therefore see little difference between Nehru's secular-nationalism and the Gandhian defence of Hindu tradition and caste-system. Muslims, of course, could not afford to articulate their critiques as stridently as the Dalits, for the simple reason that they were seen as the 'threatening' Other, whose loyalties to the 'nation' were always suspect. In some ways, their predicament differed from that of the Dalits, precisely for this reason. The Congress under Nehru, especially as it came to be in the post-independence phase, was their best bet. For, lurking in the wings was the Hindu right, and communists and others were too weak to provide them any security. It was only in the course of the build-up to the Babri Masjid crisis in the late 1980s, that sections of the Muslims started moving away from the Congress. The episode of the Shah Bano judgement and the subsequent surrender to 'fundamentalist' Muslim pressure by Rajiv Gandhi, went hand in hand with the *shilanyas*, or the foundation-stone-laying ceremony at Ayodhya, that was accomplished under the Congress. We have seen how, in those days of the final coming apart of secular-nationalism, it was the same Congress that, under Rajiv Gandhi's leadership, accelerated the drift towards a Hindu-oriented practice that had been inaugurated by Indira Gandhi in an explicit sense. If pandering to 'majority Hindu' sentiments in dealing with the Akalis in Punjab had led Indira Gandhi to practically stigmatize the entire Sikh community, Rajiv Gandhi managed to do so with the Muslims, when he began his 1989 election campaign from Ayodhya with the slogan of *Ram-rajya*. It is also well-known that this dispute, long forgotten, was brought out into the open with the connivance of the government. The crowning event came with the demolition of Babri Masjid, under the watchful eyes of the Congress government under Narasimha Rao. All day long the dance of destruction went unchallenged, leaving little doubt where the Congress government's sympathies lay. At the very least, it can be said that the

Congress knew by then whom it could afford to do without and whom it must try to woo.

And yet, we may ask: Was this Congress the same Congress as the one Nehru had bequeathed? The answer must be simultaneously 'yes' and 'no'. Nehru's own Congress, we have seen, was not the same that led the anticolonial struggle. Once Pakistan was formed and the Muslim League was out of the way, the rapid transformations that it underwent were important in this respect.[12] Similarly, the split in the Congress in 1969, with a large part of the Old Guard under Morarji Desai and Nijalingappa parting ways, also changed it in significant ways. Ironically though, with the right wing Old Guard out of the way and the sharp 'left turn' accomplished under Indira Gandhi, the foundations of secularism within the organization weakened, rather than strengthened. For the left-ward shift was a political manoeuvre adopted in order to outflank the Old Guard, at a time when the crisis of the Congress' legitimacy was already becoming evident. The rapid erosion of its mass support, it loss of nine state governments in 1967, the distinct atmosphere of radicalism that was building up by feeding on widespread mass discontent—all these were signs of increasing instability that the political system was to experience as endemic in later decades. Increasingly, the Congress, now shorn of the Old Guard, became an organization centred on a single individual. Politics now increasingly became a question of retaining by any and every means, the ground that was slipping from under its feet. Nothing would prevent Indira Gandhi and subsequent Congress leaders from using all kinds of sectarian appeals and forces in order to do this. So, it may be possible to argue that it was this shift of the late-1960s that was responsible for the degeneration of Congress secularism, and not its Nehruvian legacy. And yet, it is not possible to understand the ease with which all this happened, without comprehending the nature of Nehruvian secularism itself. Its degeneration into a soft Hindu platform was an always-present possibility in the very structure of its secular discourse.

It was when this hegemony of the upper-caste Hindu bourgeoisie was threatened that this class, so accustomed to seeing its own interests as being coterminus with 'the nation', began perceiving it as a threat to the nation. There is no doubt that when the unravelling and redrawing of the cultural boundaries of the nation began, many tendencies came to the fore that expressed a strident, sectarian xenophobia. In making the critique of secular-nationalism, therefore, I do not propose a simple celebration of the 'insurrection of little selves'. However, I think it is only by trying to understand the anxieties expressed through these assertions that we can even begin to interrogate the practice of secular-nationalism and examine its most serious problems. For, in order to realise the secular ideal of non-discrimination between communities, faiths, and beliefs, actually existing secular practice needs to be thoroughly examined. This examination must also address the problem of the state-centric model of secularism, where the state is expected to act as the archimedean ground, arbitrating between communities. It will be evident from the discussion in the preceding chapters that it is precisely the rapid disappearance of this ground that has made the crisis of secularism manifest. It is through such an examination that the ideal of secularism itself can be effectively reconstructed.

This reconstruction of secular practice may eventually lead to a very different practice that may not even be recognizable as 'secular' in our existing ways of thinking it. Such for instance, is the model suggested by Charles Taylor. He argues for a model of secularism that he calls, after Rawls, 'the overlapping consensus' model. Unlike the 'old post-Enlightenment independent ethic' model that ascribes to the state the role of arbitrator between communities, which in turn represents an independent ethical standpoint, he considers this model superior because it does not prescribe any prior justification. It is 'susceptible to conflicts of a new kind—or perhaps to a multiplication of these conflicts... It will be hard to manage. It will require a change of our mindset which will only settle for the single right answer generated from unchallenged foundational principles.'[13]

Now, there might be an apparent contradiction in the way I have posed the question of the crisis of secularism. On the one hand, I have claimed that the crisis manifests itself in its being Hindu. On the other hand, I have argued that secularism as an archimedean ideal was essentially state-centric in its conception, and therefore, alienated from the mass of the people. This appears to be a contradiction only as long as we see this Hinduness of its norms as a religious factor. What I am suggesting is that secular-nationalism's Hinduness was a consequence of the fact that it was born within a Hindu universe and therefore, carried traces of its culture *even in its secular form*. This Hinduness is as far removed from a religious Hinduism as say, Christian religion is from Western secularism that unproblematically adopts the Christian calendar and the Christian Sabbath as the norm. None of these really prevent it from being rationalist and secular. In our context, the persona of Jawaharlal Nehru embodies these two sides and he could be described as the archetypal secularist in India. And precisely because secular-nationalism never recognized community and caste identity, it refused to consider the question of the continuing control of upper caste Hindus over state and civil institutions and the exclusion of the minorities. The distribution of power in the Nehruvian dispensation remained skewed in favour of a secular modern elite that was largely Hindu. It was never recognized by the minorities as 'their own'. Yet it was not necessarily a Hindu elite in religious/community terms.

There can be no denying the fact that Hindu nationalism in the form of the Hindu Mahasabha and the RSS diverged in significant ways from secular-nationalism and that they were always hostile to each other. In the colonial period though, the presence of a large number of Hindu Mahasabha and Arya Samaj leaders within the fold of the Congress occasionally blurred the boundaries substantially. It is relevant for our purposes that one of the points where Hindu nationalism and secular-nationalism were at odds during the colonial period, concerns the legacy of Gandhi. Although both saw Gandhi as irrational and backward-looking, Nehru was more tolerant of him because of his magical effect as a mass leader and his role in promoting Hindu–Muslim unity. The Hindu nationalists, on the other hand, always considered him to be too soft and accommodating of 'Muslim separatism'—too 'effeminate' for facing the challenges of the modern world. It is noteworthy that the entire doctrine of the 'appeasement of Muslims' that was to be later transferred wholesale onto Nehruvian secularism, was in fact, originally elaborated against Gandhi, right from the days of the non-cooperation/Khilafat movement. In the post-independence period, however, with the assassination of Gandhi and the widespread anger and remorse that followed, the Hindu nationalists actually became marginal in political life. As Nehru moved ahead to consolidate his hegemony over the new nation-state, new correlations came into being. For the Muslims the Congress was the best bet and they threw in their lot with it. For the Dalits and the lower castes too, this seemed the best option. At any rate, with Dr Ambedkar playing a key role in the formulation of the Constitution and also becoming part of Nehru's cabinet, a new relation was struck with the Congress itself that survived Ambedkar. Within a short time, the Nehruvian elite had coopted all other streams within it and had reduced the RSS and other Hindu nationalists to marginality and incoherence.

With the onset of the postcolonial nation-building phase in the public realm, in what are generally known as the institutions of civil society, the hegemony of Nehruvian secular-nationalist discourse was firmly established. From the press, mass media, radio, and the films produced by the films division, educational institutions, universities and schools, and even the privately run film industry—everywhere it was this discourse that set the terms of public discourse and produced the common sense of the era. This was the so-called 'Nehruvian consensus'. Other tendencies, including the Hindu right and the Muslim orthodoxy, seen as illegitimate and as obstructing the cause of nation-building, were rendered invisible in this domain. It seems with hindsight though, that the 'Nehruvian consensus' and this hegemony of secular-nationalism had merely pushed these discourses 'underground'. They were never defeated in open battle in society at large. Over the decades, they continued to carry out their separate activity—through their own counter institutions. A wide network of schools, hospitals, libraries, propaganda journals, and publishing houses retailed the viewpoint of these organizations within the respective communities on a daily and hourly basis. This was a particularly inwardly addressed discourse, one that therefore operated on a different set of assumptions from those of civil society. So while the institutions of 'civil society' operated on the logic of bourgeois society, with rules of contract, free entry and exit, and within a discourse of individual rights, there was a simultaneous sphere of non-modern existence, where discourses of specific communities circulated and reproduced themselves daily. It is in this sphere, that the existence of the different tendencies now rendered illegitimate elsewhere, continued unhindered.

Political Society: The Underground

At this stage, it is necessary to pause and take a deeper look at this domain, especially of postcolonial polities, which constitutes, in my view, the 'underground' of civil society. What is this domain that exists in the depths of our social world, where neither the rules of reasonable, rational-secular discourse, nor the institutions of modern democracy have the resonance that we are accustomed to in civil society? If we have to understand the breakdown of the 'Nehruvian consensus', we must be clear, in the first place that it was a consensus *within civil society*; we must be clear that in these depths of the underground, the common sense of secular-nationalist discourse *was never hegemonic*. We know how through a series of parallel institutions, the Hindu right carried on its own propaganda, manufacturing its own common sense. We also have some idea of how through a similar set of parallel institutions, the Muslims and Dalits too, as many others carried on similar activities, each elaborating a discourse of 'community rights'. Institutions like the press, educational institutions, hospitals, libraries, and so on, that we know from Western political theory to be inseparable parts of civil society, at least theoretically open to all, performed a different function in this realm of the underground.

In the preceding chapters we have repeatedly encountered the existence of this domain of politics that is neither the domain of the state, nor strictly speaking, that of civil society. Especially in Chapters 5 and 6, we have seen how this domain, of political mobilization, also functions as the arena for transactions between the modern discourse of the state, rights and sovereignty, and of community existence. It is here, in this process of continuous translation of the languages of the two worlds, that notions of rights and equality undergo a *decalage*, transferred from the individual citizen to the community. The very institutions identified by Western political theory as institutions of civil society, governed by voluntary entry and exit and by rules of contract, function here then, on a completely different logic.

In order to understand this better, let me elaborate a highly suggestive and useful notion proposed by Partha Chatterjee—the notion of political society. But before I go into his notion and my rendering of it, let me elaborate the problem that I wish to address by invoking this idea. I had mentioned in the introductory chapter, the pervasive fear of the masses that lay at the founding moment of liberal democracy. Writers like Gustav Le Bon and many others, of primarily aristocratic persuasion, had written extensively on the matter even at the time of the French revolution. More relevant and important from our point of view is the crisis of liberal democracies in the late nineteenth and early twentieth centuries. It was however, in the early twentieth century, when *the majority* literally entered the hallowed portals of parliamentary democracy, when the masses gained their right to vote, that this crisis really came to the fore. The crisis of parliamentary democracy was not merely coeval with the entry of the masses, but it has been argued forcefully, constitutively linked to it. We have discussed the other writers on this subject in the introduction, but by far the most far-reaching critique of liberal democracy was made by Carl Schmitt in *The Crisis of Parliamentary Democracy*. Schmitt argued that the crisis of democracy was really the crisis of liberal parliamentary institutions. Its crisis was the result of the rise of mass democracy, which liberal institutions were singularly incapable of handling. Schmitt mounts his attack by pointing to the most astounding absence in all of liberal democratic theory: the invisibility of that organism of modern society without which democracy would be impossible to imagine—the political party. Neither modern constitutions nor liberal theory recognize the existence of this all-important organism. The institutions of the parliamentary system, he argues, are based on the idea that free and reasoned deliberations are the only way to sort things out—as if it were simply a matter of right and wrong opinions that had to be sorted out. Crucially, this edifice of parliamentary institutions is built on the assumption of individual citizens entering into reasoned deliberations. With the emergence of parties and party-majorities, positions of individuals in the parliamentary arena are determined not by what they think is right and wrong but by party policy. Schmitt points out that politics is about friend-enemy relations, and political parties mobilize on the basis of interests and passion. There is an irreducible split, in his reading, at the very heart of democracy—between the supposed sphere of reasonable discourse embodied in the parliamentary institutions and the sphere of passions and interests embodied in the mobilizational technologies of political parties. Needless to say, historically, this text of Schmitt's is situated within the frightening scenario that developed around this split in the early decades of twentieth-century Europe, namely, the rise of fascism. The massive erosion of the legitimacy of the parliamentary institutions was closely linked to the distance this faith in a rational public sphere marked from the 'irrational masses' who suddenly entered them.[14] That the 'entry of the masses into history' should spell doom for democracy is a paradox (or is it?) that stands in crying need of serious theorization, especially for us today in India.

In some of his recent writings, Partha Chatterjee has suggested that in the very heart of postcolonial democracies, lies a contradiction—that between 'modernity' and 'democracy'.[15] Democracy, understood as the 'entry of the masses' into politics, has been pitted against the search for modernity.[16] The problem as Chatterjee poses it, is that the sphere of civil society as understood in its classical sense by Hegel and Marx as bourgeois society as the sphere of modern civil institutions governed by contractual relations of entry and exit, of rights, sovereignty and citizenship—is in societies like India, a very limited domain. It constitutes the high ground of modernity. The state, with its welfare functions, targets the majority of people as 'population', and dispenses welfare to those who in practice can hardly be considered rights-bearing citizens of civil society. These people, the majority, live often in different degrees of illegality and negotiate with the state, through the various mobilizational avenues provided to them by democracy. Chatterjee elaborates this idea through a discussion of a squatters' settlement in Calcutta on government land, which they cannot 'rightfully' occupy. Yet, the government must, in discharging its governmental functions, take cognisance of its responsibility to the population at large. It is on this terrain of a moral claim on a government, rather than that of rights, that this dispute is then negotiated. In another instance taken from West Bengal, he discusses this notion in the context of the political negotiation of the death of a leader of a religious sect, whose followers believed that he had merely gone into *samadhi*, and therefore, refused to let his body be removed. As the body lay rotting, threatening to become a health hazard, the rationalist press and public raised a big hue and cry about the government surrendering before obscurantist and reactionary elements. The resolution of the dispute and the forcible removal of the body eventually took place after a long round of strategic manoeuvres by the Left Front, which sought to get public opinion to its side. This negotiation too, says Chatterjee, was a negotiation that was accomplished on a terrain distinct from that of rights and sovereignty, once again that of the responsibility of the government as government. Strictly speaking, the government would have been well within its legal rights to remove the body but the compulsion of not antagonising the followers had to lead to prolonged rounds of negotiations. It is this domain—the domain of the daily negotiations of the majority with the state—that he calls political society. The logic of this sphere is such that it does not always obey the rules of civil society, governed as it still is by 'the imaginative power of a traditional structure of community', even though it is 'wedded to the modern emancipatory rhetoric of autonomy and equal rights.'[17] This political society, in his opinion, 'is built around the framework of *modern political associations such as the political party*.' The political party, of course represents here a paradigmatic instance, but as Chatterjee himself elaborates at different points, these associational forms include non-party political formations, movements, and such other institutions.[18] The need to demarcate this separate sphere of political society I believe, arises also because we need to grapple with some of the points raised in the discussion above.[19] I am not so much persuaded by Chatterjee's insistence on governmentality as the defining reference point for political society but am more specifically interested in the three suggestions referred to above: (1) the contradiction between the logic of mass democracy and the normative ideals of modernity, institutionalized in civil bodies. (2) The continuing hold of the idea of community in the imagination of those who are by now equally wedded to 'the rhetoric of rights and autonomy'. (3) The institution of the political party as paradigmatic of the associations in political society—in other words, the arena of political mobilization.

It is by now also widely acknowledged that in the last two decades or so Indian democracy has seen an unprecedented entry of the masses into the

democratic-political arena. Much of the discomfort of the formerly
dominant, sophisticated liberal elites with the entry of these 'untutored
masses', and the general cynicism about politics among them can be
understood in this perspective. It is also worthwhile noticing that the crisis
of institutions of democracy has to do precisely with this inability to take
the strains of the new developments. It has been pointed out by Yogendra
Yadav and other analysts of recent elections, especially at the CSDS, Delhi,
that the entry of these masses has brought into the democratic
parliamentary arena, languages and idioms that do not sit easily with the
refined tastes of upper class liberals.[20] So, if they decry the endemic political
instability of the electoral system as petty factionalism of the corrupt,
uncouth masses and their new breed of representatives, someone like
Kanshi Ram routinely celebrates this instability. The stability of yore is
seen by him and the Dalits as that of brahminical control.

While I think there is much to celebrate in these developments, the
matter cannot end there. For it must draw our attention to the circumstance
that it is not merely the breakdown of old elitist norms that has taken
place as a consequence; there are no commonly acceptable norms any
more. Once legislative bodies are invaded by the logic of political society,
the incommensurablities that define the latter become more pervasive.
Different communities, which have their own ways of understanding their
situation, now send their representatives into these forums. Much of the
conflict around the Babri Masjid/Ayodhya issue, for example, can be read
as an instance of this incommensurability. So, when the VHP or the
Bajrang Dal say that they will not abide by the decision of the Supreme
Court because matters of faith cannot be decided in any court, we are
faced with a real problem. It is true that the political arm of the Sangh
family, comprising the more sophisticated parliamentary leaders, is more
accustomed to and trained in the ways of parliamentary functioning, but
they seem to have evolved a neat division of labour among themselves.
Active Bajrang Dal and VHP leaders are now important office bearers
and parliamentary/legislative representatives on the BJP ticket. What this
means is that while the important government leaders like Atal Behari
Vajpayee or L.K. Advani always present the parliamentary face of the
movement, and occasionally adopt misleadingly conciliatory tones, the
activities of the other wings continues without any restraint. The most
telling instance of this circumstance can of course, be seen in the Gujarat
carnages in March–April 2002. Here, it was the democratically elected
government that took the lead in actively sponsoring the carnages. Many
ministers were reported to have posted themselves in police stations and

directed the police not to act in defence of the Muslims. Here we have the complete Schmittian invasion of the parliamentary domain by the logic of political mobilization. It is here that other dangerous possibilities in political society become manifest. The instances used by Chatterjee to illustrate the logic of political society seem too benign in relation to these. Notice that here no abstract governmental responsibility towards its population is in evidence. If there is, it is not to a descriptive Foucauldian category of 'population' but to a putative community at the cost of others.

By bringing out these examples, I wish to underline the problematic nature of political society as such. It is this that we must address and thus find new and different modes of dealing with difference. Let us once more recall that liberal democracy cannot handle this rise of mass democracy because its very project is *predicated upon an assumption of a prior pedagogical exercise* of unprecedented proportions—that of 'training the masses' in the ways of parliamentary democracy. This democracy can function only when the vast majority has been taught to function within the etiquette of liberal rational discourse. The *demos* of a democracy is not an untutored mass. The assumption is that at least this sphere of public discourse must be framed by certain rules of deliberation that must be accepted by all. In a sense, this was achieved in the institutions of civil society in the heyday of the Nehruvian consensus. With its breakdown, however, different tendencies that had so far been 'outlawed' now made their appearance on the political stage and in parliament. They did not share in the rules that were framed by the liberal-democratic elite.

The problem as I now see it therefore, is as follows: If the ways of liberal parliamentary democracy were too elitist and archimedean; if the Nehruvian consensus was merely a consensus within a certain secular-nationalist elite, then its pedagogical solution is certainly no more worthy of emulation. Nevertheless, we are still left with the problem that that lies at the very centre of the democratic project and which the Nehruvian consensus tried to overcome in its own particular way. It seems to me that the only way is to shift the ground of struggle and take it to the realm of political society. Now, this is easier said than done, for it precisely when we begin to think in these terms that we are brought face to face with the utter inadequacy of our language. The modern constitutionalist language of civil society cannot be the language of conversation in political society. Here the key figure, as I have suggested, is the bilingual intellectual/activist who speaks at once the language of community and that of civil society. In other words, the privileged position of the enlightened intelligentsia has to be abandoned.

As I argued in Chapter 6, this terrain is a slippery terrain but nevertheless the only one left where the struggle for a new imagination of emancipation must be fought. As our discussion of the secularism debate also showed, once we abandon the archimedean heights inhabited by secular discourse, the only way in which we can continue conversation is through the medium of an internal argument. This in turn means that alongside a secular secularist, we will have to think of a Hindu secularist and a Muslim secularist or a Christian secularist.

To reiterate then, what the above discussion shows, in my view, is that the place of the secularist or the democrat is no more in an archimedean 'nowhere'. Now the place for such politics must be seen to be everywhere. This means that we need to think in terms of more dispersed political subjectivities, rather than those which were attached in the modernist conception to the agency of a privileged elite.

Notes

1. This is a complex question and it can be seen with a little reflection that such self-representations (identity) are in turn created through mobilizations. Since the question is not really relevant to our discussion here, I shall not probe this further.

2. Sangh Parivar or the 'Sangh family' is the self-description of the group of Hindu right organizations allied to the Rashtriya Swayamsevak Sangh, whose parliamentary wing, the BJP, was the leading partner in their ruling coalition.

3. Hasan (1997), pp. 145–6. 'Choti' refers to the pigtail sported by Brahmins in more orthodox settings even now, while 'tulsi' refers to a plant considered sacred by the Hindus.

4. Each of the four big 'muths' or religious centres of the Hindus is headed by a Shankaracharya.

5. Ibid., pp. 146–7.

6. *Constituent Assembly Debates*, Official Report, reprinted by the Lok Sabha Secretariat, New Delhi, vol. 1, 9/12/1946 to 23/12/1946, p. 50.

7. Ibid., pp. 67–8.

8. Ibid., p. 108.

9. Ibid., vol. 2, pp. 287–8.

10. Ibid., vol. 2, p. 332.

11. Nehru in fact refuses to refer to them as *Muslim* rulers and all through his writings calls them either Turkish or Afghan rulers.

12. Actually these transformations began before independence, as the formation of Pakistan became imminent.

13. Charles Taylor, 'Modes of Secularism' in Rajeev Bhargava (1999), ed., *Secularism and its Critics*, Oxford University Press, New Delhi, pp. 52–3.

14. It is also necessary to recall here our discussion in the introductory chapter about the deep chasm between the enlightened elite and the 'backward' masses. The split between the two domains it seems is much more pervasive than we imagine.

15. I have paraphrased his argument in the discussion that follows, from three recent texts by Chatterjee, where he has elaborated this notion: Chatterjee (1997) 'Beyond the Nation? Or Within?', *Economic and Political Weekly*, 4–11 Jan.; Chatterjee (1998a) 'Community in the East', *EPW*, 7 Feb.; and Chatterjee (1998b), 'Introduction', *Wages of Freedom: Fifty Years of the Indian Nation-State*, Oxford University Press, New Delhi.

16. This particular construction about democracy is mine.

17. Chatterjee (1998a), p. 282.

18. Chatterjee (1997), p. 32.

19. I have explored this idea of political society at greater length elsewhere, elaborating my own disagreements with Chatterjee's explication of the concept and will not go into all its aspects here. See Nigam (2005).

20. See for example, Yadav (1996), pp. 120–45.

Bibliography

Documents, Newspapers, and Periodicals

Anandpur Sahib Resolution, Society for Integration, Kindness and Humanity (SIKH), New Delhi, December 1984.

Constituent Assembly Debates, Official Report, reprinted by the Lok Sabha Secretariat, New Delhi, vols 1–13.

BJP National Executive Resolutions and other Documents, New Delhi, 1980–5.

CPI(M), *Tasks on the Trade Union Front*, Document adopted by the Central Committee, New Delhi, 10–16 September 1983.

CPI(M), 'Resolution on Andhra Elections', adopted in the Central Committee meeting held in Calcutta, 25–8 January 1983. Politburo circular no. 3/1983 (upto district committees).

'The Freedom Charter' of the South African Peoples reprinted in *New International*, no. 5, Fall 1985.

Umrabulo—Let's Talk Politically, no. 8, Special edition of the ANC document for the National General Council to be held in Port Elizabeth from 11–15 July 2000. (Document prepared by the Political Education and Training Unit of the ANC).

Lok Sabha Debates, Sixth, Seventh, and Eighth Series, Lok Sabha Secretariat, New Delhi.

The *Sunday Independent*, June 2000, Johannesburg.

The *Statesman*, Delhi, 1978–91.

The *Times of India*, Bombay, 1978–91

Business India, New Delhi, 1985 91.

India Today, New Delhi, 1989–92.

Link, New Delhi, 1980–88.

Books and Articles

Abbasi, Muhammad Yusuf (1987), *The Genesis of Muslim Fundamentalism in British India*, Publication Deptt, Indian Institute of Applied Political Research.

Abdel-Malek, Anouar (1981), *Nation and Revolution: vol. 2 of Social Dialectics*, The Macmillan Press, London and Basingstoke.

Adedeji, Adebayo (ed.) (1993), *Africa Within the World—Beyond Dispossession and Dependence*, Zed Books, London and New Jersey.

Ahir, D.C. (1990), *The Legacy of Dr Ambedkar*, B.R. Publishing Corporation, Delhi.

Ahmad, Qeyamuddin (1984), 'Wahabi Movement in India', in Nitish Ranjan Ray (ed.), *Challenge: A Saga of India's Struggle for Freedom*, People's Publishing House, New Delhi.

Ahmed, Aijaz (1996), *Lineages of the Present*, Tulika, New Delhi.

Ahmed, Muzaffar (1981), *Amar Jibon O Bharater Communist Party*, National Book Agency, Calcutta.

Rafiuddin, Ahmed (1981), *The Bengal Muslims, 1871–1906—A Quest for Identity*, Oxford University Press, New Delhi.

Alam, Jayeed (1987), 'Class, Political and National Dimensions of the State Autonomy Movements in India' in TDSS.

————— (1989), 'Political Articulation of Mass Consciousness in Present-Day India', in Zoya Hasan, S.N. Jha, and Rasheeduddin Khan (eds), *State, Political Processes and Identity*, Sage Publications, New Delhi.

————— (1998), 'The Indispensability of Secularism', *Social Scientist*, vol. 27, nos. 7–8, July–August.

————— (1999a), 'Public Sphere and Democratic Governance' in Amiya Bagchi and Rajeev Bhargava (eds), *Multiculturalism and Problems of Democratic Governance*, Oxford University Press, New Delhi.

————— (1999b), *India: Living with Modernity*, Oxford University Press, New Delhi.

————— (Unpublished), 'Right to Exit: Problems of Individual and Community Rights'.

Altbeker, Antony and Jonny Steinberg (1998), 'Race, Reason and Representation in National Party Disourse, 1990–92', in David R. Howarth and Aletta J. Norval (eds), *South Africa in Transition*, Macmillan Press, Great Britain, and St Martin Press Inc.

Althusser, Louis and Balibar Etienne (1977), *Reading Capital*, New Left Books, London.

Ambedkar, Dr Babasaheb (1991), *Writings and Speeches*, Vasant Moon (ed.), vol. 9, Education Department, Government of Maharashtra.

Amin, Shahid (1996), *Event, Metaphor, Memory—Chauri Chaura 1922–92*, Oxford University Press, New Delhi.

————— (2002), 'Retelling the Muslim Conquest of North India' in Partha Chatterjee and Anjan Ghosh (eds) *History and the Present*, Permanent Black, New Delhi.

Amuta, Chidi (1999), 'Fanon, Cabral and Ngugi on National Liberation', in Bill Ashcroft, Gareth Griffiths, and Helen Tiffin (eds), *The Post-colonial Studies Reader*, Routledge, New York.

Anderson, Benedict (1991), *Imagined Communities*, Verso, London and New York.

————— (1998), *The Spectre of Comparisons: Nationalism, Southeast Asia and the World*, Verso, London and New York.

Ansari, Nasim (1999), *Choosing to Stay—Memoirs of an Indian Muslim*, City Press, Karachi.

Arendt, Hannah (1968), *Totalitarianism*, (part three of *The Origins of Totalitarianism*) A Harvest/HBJ Book, San Diego, New York, and London.

Ashraf, Mujeeb (1982), *Muslim Attitudes Towards British Rule and Western Culture in India*, Idarah-I-Adabiyat-I-Delli, Delhi.

Azad, Maulana Abul Kalam (1988), *India Wins Freedom*, Orient Longman, Hyderabad and Madras.

Balibar, Etiene (1991), 'The Nation Form', in Etiene Balibar and Immanuel Wallerstein (1991), *Race, Nation and Class—Ambiguous Identities*, Verso, London and New York.

———— (1994), *Masses, Classes and Ideas—Studies on Politics and Philosophy After Marx*, Routledge, New York and London.

Baruah, Sanjib (1999), *India Against Itself—Assam and the Politics of Nationality*, Oxford University Press, New Delhi.

Basavapunnaiah, M. (1985), 'On Para 112 of Our Party Programme', *The Marxist*, vol. III, no. 1, January–March.

Basu, Jyoti (1998), *Jato Door Money Porey*, National Book Agency, Calcutta.

Basu, Tapan, Pradip Datta, Sumit Sarkar, Tanika Sarkar, and Sambuddha Sen (1993), *Khaki Shorts Saffron Flags*, Orient Longman, Delhi and Hyderabad.

Baxi, Upendra and Bhikhu Parekh (eds) (1995), *Crisis and Change in Contemporary India*, Sage Publications, New Delhi.

Bayly, C.A. (1998), *Origins of Nationality in South Asia—Patriotism and Ethical Government in the Making of Modern India*, Oxford University Press, New Delhi.

Bhabha, Homi (ed.) (1995), *Nation and Narration*, Routledge, London and New York.

Bharati, Kanwal *et al.* (ed.) (n.d., probably 1999) *Dalit Jan-Ubhar*, BM Prakashan, Lucknow

Bhargava, Rajeev (1990) 'The Right to Culture' reprinted in K.N. Panikkar (ed.) (1995) *Communalism in India: History, Politics and Culture*, Manohar, New Delhi.

———— (1994), 'Giving Secularism its Due', *Economic and Political Weekly*, vol. XXIX, no. 28, 9 July.

———— (ed.) (1998), *Secularism and its Critics*, Oxford University Press, New Delhi.

Biko, Steve (1996), *I Write What I Like*, Ravan Press, South Africa.

Bilgrami, Akeel (1994), 'Two Concepts of Secularism: Reason, Modernity and the Archimedean Ideal' *Economic and Political Weekly*, vol. XXIX, no. 28, 9 July.

Bourdieu, Pierre (1991), *The Political Ontology of Martin Heidegger*, Polity Press, Cambridge and Oxford (in collaboration with Basil Blackwell).

———— (1992), *Language and Symbolic Power*, Polity Press, Cambridge and Oxford.

Breuilly, John (1992), *Nationalism and the State*, Manchester University Press, Manchester.

Chakrabarty, Dipesh (1995), 'Modernity and Ethnicity in India – A History for the Present', *Economic and Political Weekly*, vol. 30, no. 52, 30 December.

Chakravarti, Uma (2000), *Rewriting History: The Life and Times of Pandita Ramabai*, Kali for Women, New Delhi.

Chandra, Sudhir (1994), *The Oppressive Present—Literature and Social Consciousness in Colonial India*, Oxford University Press, New Delhi.

Carr'e re d'Encausse, He'l'ene and Schram Stuart (1965), *Marxism and Asia*, Allen Lane, The Penguin Press, London.

Chatterjee, Partha (1975), 'Bengal: Rise and Growth of a Nationality', *Social Scientist* no. 37, (vol. 4, no. 1) August 1975.

———— (1986), *Nationalist Thought and the Colonial World—A Derivative Discourse?* Zed Books and United Nations University, UK.

———— (1994a), 'Secularism and Toleration', *Economic and Political Weekly*, vol. XXIX, no. 28, 9 July.

———— (1994b), *Nation and its Fragments*, Oxford University Press, New Delhi.

———— (1994c), 'Claims on The Past: The Genealogy of Modern Historiography in Bengal', in *Subaltern Studies VIII—Essays in Honour of Ranajit Guha*, Oxford University Press, New Delhi.

———— (1997), 'Beyond the Nation? Or Within?', *Economic and Political Weekly*, 4–11 January.

———— (ed.) (1998a), *Wages of Freedom—Fifty Years of the Nation-State*, Oxford University Press, New Delhi.

———— (1998b), 'Community in the East', *Economic and Political Weekly*, 7 February, pp. 277–82.

Claudin, Fernando (1975), *The Communist Movement: From Comintern to Cominform*, two volumes, Monthly Review Press, New York and London.

Cohn, Bernard S. (2001), *An Anthropologist Among Historians and Other Essays*, Oxford University Press, New Delhi.

Dallmayr, Fred (1996), 'The Discourse of Modernity: Hegel, Nietzche, Heidegger and Habermas' in Maurizio Passerin D'Entreves and Seyla Benhabib (eds), *Habermas and the Unfinished Project of Modernity*, Polity Press, Cambridge and Oxford.

Dang, Satyapal (1998), *Genesis of Terrorism—An Analytical Study of Punjab Terrorists*, Patriot Publishers, New Delhi.

Datar, Chhaya (1983), 'The Women's Movement: A Feminist Perspective' in Harsh Sethi and Smitu Kothari, *The Non-Party Political Process—Uncertain Alternatives*, Mimeograph, UNRISD/Lokayanj, Delhi.

Davenport, T.R.H. (1992), *South Africa—A Modern History*, Macmillan Press, Great Britain.

Deleuze, Gilles and Felix Guattari (1984), *Anti-Oedipus: Capitalism and Schizophrenia*, The Athlone Press, London.

D'Entreves, Maurizio Passerin and Seyla Benhabib (1996), *Habermas and the Unfinished Project of Modernity*. Polity Press, Cambridge and Oxford.

Deshpande, Satish (1993), 'Imagined Economies—Styles of Nation-Building in Twentieth Century India', *Journal of Arts and Ideas*, nos 25–6, December.

Dhareshwar, Vivek (1993), 'Caste and the Secular Self', *Journal of Arts and Ideas*, nos 25–6, December.

Dietrich, Gabriele (1992), *Reflections on the Women's Movement in India—Religion, Ecology and Development*, Horizon India Books, New Delhi.

Dirks, Nicholas B. (2003), *Castes of Mind—Colonialism and the Making of Modern India*, Permanent Black, Delhi.

Dube, Abhay Kumar (1997), *Kanshi Ram* [*Aaj Ke Neta/Alochnatmak Adhayaynmala* Series] Rajkamal Prakashan, Delhi.

Eley, Geoff and Ronald Grigor Suny (1996), *Becoming National*, Oxford University Press, New York and Oxford.

Esack, Farid (1997), *Quran, Liberation and Pluralism—An Islamic Perspective of Inter-religious Solidarity Against Oppression*, Oneworld, Oxford.

Fabian, Johannes (1983), *Time and the Other—How Anthropology Makes Its Object*, Columbia University Press, New York.

Fanon, Frantz (1971), *The Wretched of the Earth*, Penguin Books, England and Australia.

Faruqi, Zia-ul-Hasan (1963), *The Deoband School and the Demand for Pakistan*, Asia Publishing House, Bombay.

Fernandes, Walter and Samaydip Chatterjee (1995), 'A Critique of the Draft National Policy', *Lokayan Bulletin*, vol. 11, no. 5, March–April.

Foucault, Michel (1977), *Power/Knowledge: Selected Interviews and Other Writings, 1972–77*, by Colin Cordon (ed.), Harvester Press, Sussex.

Frank, Andre Gunder (n.d.), 'The Communist Manifesto: A 150 Year Tardy Re-examination of the Historical Evidence That Marx Swept Under the Ideological Rug', http://www.geocities.com/zed_chaotics/english/tcm/htm downloaded on 25 June 2002.

Frankel, Francine, Zoya Hasan, Rajeev Bhargava, and Balveer Arora (eds) (2001), *Transforming India – Social and Political Dynamics of Democracy*, Oxford University Press, New Delhi.

Fraser, Nancy (2000), 'Rethinking Recognition', *New Left Review*, May–June, pp. 107–19.

Fromm, Erich (1942/2001), *The Fear of Freedom*, Routledge, London and New York.

Gandhi, M.K. (1927), *An Autobiography or The Story of My Experiments With Truth*, Navajivan Publishing House, Ahmedabad.

——————— (1982), *Collected Works of Mahatma Gandhi*, The Publications Division, Ministry of Information and Broadcasting, Govt of India.

Gandhi, Nandita and Nandita Shah (1992), *The Issues At Stake – Theory and Practice in Contemporary Women's Movement in India*, Kali for Women, Delhi.

Gasset, Jose Ortega y (1932), *The Revolt of the Masses*, W.W. Norton and Co. Inc., New York.

Geetha, V. and S.V. Rajadurai (1998), *Towards a Non-Brahmin Millennium: From Iyothee Thass to Periyar*, Samya, Calcutta.

Gellner, Ernest (1983), *Nations and Nationalism*, Basil Blackwell, Oxford.

Gellner, Ernest (1994), *Encounters with Nationalism*, Blackwell Publishers, Oxford and Cambridge.

Ghosh, Tapan (1973), *Gandhi Murder Trial*, Asia Publishing House, Bombay.

Giner, Salvador (1976), *Mass Society*, Academic Press, Inc., New York and San Francisco.

Gohain, Hiren (1980a), 'Count-Down in Assam', *Economic and Political Weekly*, vol. XV, no. 21, 24 May.

———— (1980b), 'Tangle Jargonized', *Economic and Political Weekly*, vol. XV, no. 32, 9 August.

Gordon, David C. (197), *Self-Determination and History in the Third World*, Princeton University Press, Princeton.

Gooptu, Nandini (1993), 'Caste and Labour: Untouchable Social Movements in Urban Uttar Pradesh in the Early Twentieth Century', in Peter Robb (ed.), *Dalit Movements and the Meanings of Labour in India*, Oxford University Press, New Delhi.

Gramsci, Antonio (1987), *Selections from the Prison Notebooks* (edited and translated by Quintin Hoare and Geoffrey Nowell Smith) International Publishers, New York.

Grewal, J.S. and Indu Banga (eds) (1998), *Punjab in Prosperity and Violence—Administration, Politics and Social Change 1947–1997*, Institute of Punjab Studies, Chandigarh.

Guigon, Charles B. (ed.) (1993), *The Cambridge Companion to Heidegger*, Cambridge University Press, Cambridge.

Gupta, Dipankar (1997), *The Context of Ethnicity—Sikh Identity in a Comparative Perspective*, Oxford University Press, New Delhi.

Guru, Gopal and Geetha V. (2000), 'New Phase of Dalit–Bahujan Intellectual Activity', *Economic and Political Weekly*, January 15, pp. 130–4.

Guru, Gopal (2000a), 'Hindutva's Passive Revolution', *The Hindu Online*, 21 September.

———— (2000b), 'The Left and the Caste Question', The *Hindu*, 20 December.

Habermas, Jurgen (1992), *The Structural Transformation of the Public Sphere*, Polity Press, Cambridge.

———— (1995), *The Philosophical Discourse of Modernity*, Polity Press, UK.

Habib, Mohd (1970), 'Introduction', in Moin Shakir, *Khilafat to Partition: A Survey of Major Muslim Trends among Indian Muslims 1919–1947*, Kalamkar Prakashan, New Delhi.

Hall, Stuart (1996), 'Ethnicity: Identity and Difference', in Geoff Eley and Ronald Grigor Suny, *Becoming National*, Oxford University Press, New York and Oxford.

Hansen, Thomas Blom (1999), *The Saffron Wave—Democracy and Hindu Nationalism in Modern India*, Princeton University Press, Princeton.

———— (2001), *Urban Violence in India: Identity Politics, 'Mumbai' and the Postcolonial City*, Permanent Black, New Delhi.

Hasan, Mushirul (ed.) (1981), *Communal and Pan-Islamic Trends in Colonial India*, Manohar, New Delhi.

———— (1995), 'Muslim Intellectuals, Institutions and the Post-Colonial Predicament', *Economic and Political Weekly*, 25 November, p. 2996.

———— (ed.) (1996), *India's Partition—Process, Strategy and Mobilization*, Oxford University Press, New Delhi.

———— (ed.) (2000), *Inventing Boundaries—Gender, Politics and the Partition of India*, Oxford University Press, New Delhi.

Hasan, Zoya, S.N. Jha, and Rasheeduddin Khan (eds) (1989), *State, Political Processes and Identity: Reflections on Modern India*, Sage Publications, New Delhi.

Heater, Derek (1999), *What is Citizenship?*, Polity Press, Cambridge.

Hegel, G.W.F. (1956), *The Philosophy of History*, Dover Publications Inc., New York.

Heidegger, Martin (1983), *Being and Time*, translated by John Macquarrie and Edward Robinson, Basil Blackwell, Southampton, Great Britain.

———— (1982), *The Question Concerning Technology and Other Essays*, Harper and Row, New York.

Hitler, Adolf (1936), *My Struggle*, Number II The Paternoster Library, Great Britain.

Hobsbawm, E.J. (1990), *Nations and Nationalism Since 1980*, Cambridge University Press, Cambridge, New York, and Sydney.

Holt, Mack P. (1997), *The French Wars of Religion, 1562–1620*, Cambridge University Press, Cambridge.

Horowitz, Donald L. (2001), *The Deadly Ethnic Riot*, Oxford University Press, New Delhi

Howarth, David R. and Norval, Aletta J. (eds) (1998), *South Africa in Transition*, Macmillan Press, Great Britain, and St. Martin Press Inc., USA.

Hughes, H. Stuart (1979), *Consciousness and Society: The Reorientation of European Social Thought 1890–1930*, The Harvester Press, Great Britain.

Ilaiah, Kancha (1998), 'Towards the Dalitization of the Nation' in Partha Chatterjee (ed.), *Wages of Freedom—Fifty years of the Nation-State*, Oxford University Press, New Delhi.

———— (1999), 'Dalitism versus Brahminism: The Epistemological Conflict in History', in Ashish Ghosh (ed.), *Dalits and Peasants—The Emerging Caste-Class Dynamics*, Gyan Sagar Publications, Delhi.

Iqbal, Afzal (1978), *Life and Times of Mohamed Ali*, Idarah-I-Adabiyat-I-Delli, Delhi.

Jacob, T.G. (ed.) (1988), *The National Question in India: CPI Documents*, Odyssey Press, New Delhi.

Jaffrelot, Christophe (1999), *The Hindu Nationalist Movement and Indian Politics—1925 to the 1990s*, Penguin, New Delhi.

———— (2003), *India's Silent Revolution: The Rise of the Low Castes in North Indian Politics*, Permanent Black, New Delhi.

Jain, Girilal (1994), *The Hindu Phenomenon*, UBS Publishers & Distributors Ltd, New Delhi.

Jalal, Ayesha (1985), *The Sole Spokesman: Jinnah, the Muslim League and the Demand for Pakistan*, Cambridge University Press, Cambridge, London, and New York; Orient Longman, and Bombay, Calcutta.

_____ (1998), 'Nation, Reason and Religion: Punjab's Role in the Partition of India', *Economic and Political Weekly*, vol. 33, no. 32, 8 August.

_____ (2001), *Self and Sovereignty—Individual and Community in South Asian Islam since 1850*, Oxford University Press, New Delhi.

Jaszi, Oscar (1929), *The Dissolution of the Habsburg Monarchy*, University of Chicago Press, Chicago.

Katju, Manjari (2003), *Vishva Hindu Parishad and Indian Politics*, Orient Longman, Delhi.

Kaviraj, Nasahari (1982), *Wahabi and Farazi Rebels of Bengal*, People's Publishing House, New Delhi.

Kaviraj, Sudipta (1990), 'On the Discourse of Secularism', in Bidyut Chakravarty (ed.), *Secularism and Indian Polity*, Segment Book Distributors, New Delhi.

_____ (1991), 'State, Society and Discourse in India', in James Manor (ed.) *Re-thinking Third World Politics*, Longman, London and New York.

_____ (1992), 'The Imaginary Institution of India', in *Subaltern Studies*, vol. VII, Partha Chatterjee and Gyanendra Pandey (eds), Oxford University Press, New Delhi.

_____ (1995a), 'Crisis of the Nation-State in India' in John Dunne (ed.), *Contemporary Crisis of the Nation-State*, Blackwell, Oxford and Cambridge.

_____ (1995b), 'Democracy and Development in India' in Amiya Bagchi (ed.), *Democracy and Development*, St Martin Press, London.

_____ (1995c), 'Religion, Politics and Modernity', in Upendra Baxi and Bhikhu Parekh (eds), *Crisis and Change in Contemporary India*, Sage Publications, New Delhi.

_____ (1998), *The Unhappy Consciousness—Bankimchandra Chattopadhyay and the formation of Nationalist Discourse in India*, Oxford University Press, New Delhi.

Kedourie, Elie (1960), *Nationalism*, Hutchinson, London.

_____ (ed.) (1970), *Nationalism in Asia and Africa*, New American Library, New York and Cleveland.

Keer, Dhananjay (1950/1966), *Veer Savarkar*, Popular Prakashan, Bombay.

_____ (1954/1997), *Dr Ambedkar—Life and Mission*, Popular Prakashan, Bombay.

_____ (1973), *Mahatma Gandhi—Political Saint and Unarmed Prophet*, Popular Prakashan, Bombay.

Khan, Mohammed Asghar (1985), *The Pakistan Experience—State and Religion*, Vanguard Books Ltd, Lahore.

Kiernan, Ben (1985), *How Pol Pot Came to Power: A History of Communism in Kampuchea 1930–75*, Verso, London.

King, Robert D. (1997), *Nehru and the Language Politics of India*, Oxford University Press, New Delhi and Calcutta.

Kishwar, Madhu (1994), 'Codified Hindu Law: Myth and Reality', *Economic and Political Weekly*, 13 August, pp. 2145–61.

Kishwar, Madhu and Ruth Vanita (eds) (1984), *In Search of Answers : Indian Women's Voices from Manushi*, Zed Books Ltd, London.

Kohli, Atul (1991), *Democracy and Discontent—India's Growing Crisis of Governability*, Cambridge University Press, Cambridge.

Kohn, Hans (1944/67), *The Idea of Nationalism*, Collier Books, USA.

Kolb, David (1986), *The Critique of Pure Modernity*, University of Chicago Press, Chicago and London.

Koselleck, Reinhart (1985), *Futures Past:On the Semantics of Historical Time*, The MIT Press, Cambridge, Massachusetts and London.

Kothari, Rajni (1986), *Politics In India*, Orient Longman, New Delhi.

———— (1994), 'Rise of Dalits and the Renewed Debate on Caste', *Economic and Political Weekly*, vol. XXIX, no. 26, 26 June.

Kothari, Smitu (1995), 'Development, Dsiplacement and Official Policies: A Critical Review', *Lokayan Bulletin*, vol. 11, no. 5, March–April.

Kumar, Pradeep (2000), *The Uttarakhand Movement – Construction of a Regional Identity*, Kanishka Publishers, New Delhi.

Kumar, Pramod, Manmohan Sharma, Atul Sood, and Ashwani Handa (1984), *Punjab Crisis—Context and Trends*, Centre for Research in Rural and Industrial Development, Chandigarh.

Kumar, Radha (1993), *The History of Doing*, Kali For Women, New Delhi.

Kumar, Ram Narayan and Georg Sieberer (1991), *The Sikh Struggle: Origin, Evolution and Present Phase*, Chanakya Publications, Delhi.

Kymlicka, Will (ed.) (1997), *The Rights of Minority Cultures*, Oxford University Press, Oxford.

Laclau, Ernesto (1990), *New Reflections on the Revolution of Our Time*, Verso, London and New York.

Laqueur, Walter (ed.) (1976), *Fascism: A Reader's Guide*, Wildwood House, London.

Lowy, Michael (1979) *Georg Lukács—From Romanticism to Bolshevism*, New Left Books, London.

Lowy, Michael and Robert Sayre (2001), *Romanticism Against the Tide of Modernity*, Duke University Press, Durham and London.

Ludden, David (1996), *Contesting the Nation—Religion, Community and the Politics of Democracy in India*, University of Pennsylvania Press, Philadelphia.

Lyotard, Jean-Francois (1984/92), *The Postmodern Condition – A Report on Knowledge*, Theory and History of Literature Series, vol. 10, Manchester University Press, Manchester.

Madan, T.N. (1987), 'Secularism in its Place', *Journal of Asian Studies*, vol. 46, No. 4.

———— (1993), 'Whither Indian Secularism', *Modern Asian Studies*, July.

———— (1997), *Modern Myths, Locked Minds*, Oxford University Press, New Delhi.

Mahajan, Gurpreet (1998), *Identities and Rights—Aspects of Liberal Democracy in India*. Oxford University Press, New Delhi.

Mamdani, Mahmood (1996), *Citizen and Subject—Contemporary Africa and the Legacy of Late Colonialism*, Princeton University Press, Princeton.

Manglori, Tufail Ahmad (1994), *Towards a Common Destiny: A Nationalist Manifesto* (English translation of *Mussalmanon Ka Roshan Mustaqbil*), Peoples' Publishing House, Delhi.

Mao Tsetung (1977), *Selected Works of Mao Tsetung*, vols. I–V, Foreign Languages Press, Peking.

Marx, K. and F. Engels (1982), *Selected Works*, Progress Publishers, Moscow.

May, Lini S. (1970), *The Evolution of Indo–Muslim Thought After 1857*, Sh. Muhammad Ashraf, Kashmiri Bazar, Lahore.

Mazumdar, Vina (1999), 'Political Ideology of the Women's Movement's Engagement with the Law', in Amita Dhanda and Archana Parashar (eds), *Engendering Law*, Eastern Book Co., Lucknow.

Mbeki, Thabo (1998), *Africa—The Time Has Come, Selected Speeches of Thabo Mbeki*, Tafelberg, Maube.

Meli, Francis (1989), 'South Africa and the Rise of African Nationalism', in Maria van Diepen (ed.), *The National Question in South Africa*, Zed Books Ltd, London and New Jersey.

Memmi, Albert (1974), *The Colonizer and the Colonized*, Souvenir Press (Educational and Academic) Ltd, London.

Menon, Dilip (1999), 'Being a Brahmin the Marxist Way: EMS Namboodiripad and the Pasts of Kerala', in Daud Ali (ed.), Oxford University Press, New Delhi.

Menon, Nivedita (1998), 'Women and Citizenship', in Partha Chatterjee (ed.), *Wages of Freedom—Fifty years of the Nation-State*, Oxford University Press, New Delhi.

————— (2004), *Recovering Subversion: Feminist Politics Beyond the Law*, Permanent Black, Delhi.

Mies, Maria and Vandana Shiva (1993), *Ecofeminism*, Kali for Women, New Delhi.

Minault, Gail (1982), *The Khilafat Movement—Religious Symbolism and Political Mobilization in India*, Oxford University Press, New Delhi.

Mishra, Vinod (1999), *Selected Works*, CPI(ML) Publication, New Delhi.

Mohanty, Manoranjan, P.N. Mukherjee, and Olle Tornquist (eds) (1998), *Peoples' Rights: Social Movements and the State in the Third World*, Sage Publications, New Delhi.

Mohanty, Manoranjan (1998), 'Social Movement in Creative Society: Of Autonomy and Interconnection', in Manoranjan Mohanty, P.N. Mukherjee, and Olle Tornquist (eds), *Peoples Rights: Social Movements and the State in the Third World*, Sage Publications, New Delhi.

Moon, Vasant (ed) (1990), *Dr Baba Saheb Ambedkar—Writings and Speeches*, Education Department, Government of Maharashtra.

Moore, R.J. (1974), *The Crisis of Indian Unity, 1917–1940*, Oxford University Press, New Delhi.

Mudimbe, V.Y. (1994), *The Idea of Africa*, Indiana University Press, Bloomington and Indianapolis.

Mufti, Aamir R. (1998), 'Auerbach in Istanbul: Edward Said, Secular Criticism and the Question of Minority Culture', *Critical Inquiry*, vol. 25, no. 1, Autumn.

Muhammad, Shan (1979), *Unpublished Letters of Ali Brothers*, Idarah-I-Adabiyat-I-Delli, Delhi.

Mukhopadhyay, Saroj (1985), *Bharater Communist Party O Amra*, vol. I–II, National Book Agency, Calcutta.

Munck, Ronaldo (1986), *The Difficult Dialogue: Marxism and Nationalism*, Zed Books, London; and Oxford University Press, New Delhi.

Munshi, K.M. (1942), *Akhand Hindustan*, New Book Co, Bombay.

Mzala, Comrade (1989), 'Revolutionary Theory on the National Question in South Africa', in Maria van Diepen (ed.), *The National Question in South Africa*, Zed Books Ltd, London and New Jersey.

Nagaraj, D.R.(1993), *The Flaming Feet—A Study of the Dalit Movement*, South Forum Press and Institutue for Cultural Research and Action, Bangalore.

Nairn, Tom (1977/81), *The Break-up of Britain*, Verso, London.

Namboodiripad, E.M.S. (1952), *The National Question in Kerala*, Peoples' Publishing House, Bombay.

———— (1976), *How I Became a Communist*, Chinta Publishers, Trivandrum.

———— (1994), *The Communist Party in Kerala—Six Decades of Struggle and Advance*, National Book Centre, New Delhi

Namboodiripad, E.M.S. and A.K. Gopalan (1976), *In the Cause of the People*, Sangam Books, Madras.

Nandy, Ashis (1983), *The Intimate Enemy*, Oxford University Press, New Delhi.

———— (1985), 'Anti-secularist Manifesto' *Seminar*, 314 October.

———— (1990), 'The Politics of Secularism and the Recovery of Religious Tolerance', in Veena Das (ed.), *Mirrors of Violence: Communities, Riots and Survivors in South Asia*, Oxford University Press, New Delhi.

———— (1998) 'The Twilight of Certitudes: Secularism, Hindu Nationalism and other Masks of Deculturation', in *Postcolonial Studies*, vol. I, no. 3, pp. 283–98.

———— (ed.) (1998), *Science, Hegemony and Violence: A Requiem for Modernity*, Oxford University Press, New Delhi.

———— (2001), *Time Warps—The Insistent Politics of Silent and Evasive Pasts*, Permanent Black, New Delhi.

Nandy, A., Shikha Trivedy, Shail Mayaram, and Achyut Yagnik (1995), *Creating a Nationality: The Ramjanmabhumi Movement and Fear of the Self*, Oxford University Press, New Delhi.

Nayar, Kuldip and Khushwant Singh (1984), *The Tragedy of Punjab—Operation Bluestar and After*, Vision Books, Delhi.

Nehru, Jawaharlal (1936/98), *An Autobiography*, Jawaharlal Nehru Memorial Fund and Oxford University Press, New Delhi.

———— (1946/82), *The Discovery of India*, Jawaharlal Nehru Memorial Fund and Oxford University Press, New Delhi.

Nigam, Aditya (1999), 'Marxism and the Postcolonial World: Footnotes to a Long March', *Economic and Political Weekly*, 9 January, vol. 34, nos. 1 and 2.

———— (2004a), 'Imagining the Global Nation: Time and Hegemony', *Economic and Political Weekly*, January 3–9, vol. 39, no.1

———— (2004b), 'A Text Without Author: Locating the Constituent Assembly as Event', *Economic and Political Weekly*, May 22–28, vol. 39, no. 21

———— (2005), 'Civil Society and Its "Underground": Explorations in the Notion of Political Society', in Helmut Reifeld and Rajeev Bhargava (eds), *Civil Society, Public Sphere and Citizenship*, Sage Publications, New Delhi.

Noorani, A.G. (1990), *Indian Affairs—The Political Dimension*, Konark Publishers, Delhi.

Nugent, Nicholas (1991), *Rajiv Gandhi—Son of a Dynasty*, Universal Book Stall, New Delhi.

Omvedt, Gail (1993), *Reinventing Revolution*, M.E Sharpe, New York and London.

———— (1994), *Dalits and the Democratic Revolution: Dr Ambedkar and the Dalit Movement in Colonial India*, Sage Publications, New Delhi and London.

Pandey, Gyanendra (1992), *The Construction of Communalism in Colonial North India*, Oxford University Press, New Delhi.

———— (ed.) (1993), *Hindus and Others—The Question of Identity in India Today*, Viking, New Delhi.

———— (2001), *Remembering Partition*, Cambridge University Press, Cambridge.

Pandian, M.S.S. (1995), 'Beyond Colonial Crumbs: Cambridge School, Identity Politics and Dravidian Movement(s)', *Economic and Political Weekly*, 18–25 February, p. 387.

———— (1994), 'Notes on the Transformation of 'Dravidian' Ideology: Tamil Nadu, c. 1900–1940', *Social Scientist*, vol. 22, nos. 5–6 May–June 1994.

———— (1993), 'Denationalizing the Past: "Nation" in E.V. Ramasamy's Political Discourse', *Economic and Political Weekly*, 16 October.

Panikkar, K.N. (1992), *Against Lord and State: Religion and Peasant Uprisings in Malabar, 1836–1921*, Oxford University Press, New Delhi.

Paranjape, Makarand (ed.) (1999), *The Penguin Aurobindo Reader*, Penguin Books, New Delhi.

Poduval, Satish (1999), 'The Possible Histories of Indian Television', *Journal of Arts and Ideas*, nos. 32–3, April, pp. 107–18.

Prakash, Gyan (1999), *Another Reason: Science and the Imagination of Modern India*, Oxford University Press, New Delhi.

Prasad, Chandra Bhan (1999), 'Social Fascism is Real, "Communal Fascism" a Mischievous Construct', serialized in the *Pioneer*, 5–11 September.

Prasad, M. Madhava (1999), 'Television and the National Culture', *Journal of Arts and Ideas*, nos. 32–3, April, pp. 119–29.

Ranadive, B.T. (1983), 'Marxism and the Nationality Question in India', *The Marxist*, vol. I, no. 2, October–December.

Ranjan Ray, Nitish (ed.) (1984), *Challenge: A Saga of India's Struggle for Freedom*, People's Publishing House, New Delhi.

Rathor, Renu, Ashish Rathor, and Aviram (n.d.), 'Dakkhin Toley Ka Saval', in Kanwal Bharati *et al.* (eds), *Dalit Jan-Ubhar*, B.M. Prakashan, Lucknow.

Rawat, Ramnarayan S. (2001), 'Partition Politics and Achhut Identity: A Study of the Scheduled Castes Federation and Dalit Politics in UP, 1946–48', in Suvir Kaul (ed.), *The Partitions of Memory—The Afterlife of the Division of India*, Permanent Black, New Delhi.

Renan, Ernest (1996), 'What is a Nation?' in Geoff Eley and Ronald Grigor Suny (eds), *Becoming National*, Oxford University Press, New York and Oxford.

Ricouer, Paul (1990), *Time and Narrative*, vol. 3, The University of Chicago Press, Chicago and London.

Robb, Peter (ed.) (1993), *Dalit Movements and the Meanings of Labour in India*, Oxford University Press, New Delhi.

Robinson, Francis (2001), *The Ulama of Farangi Mahal and Islamic Culture in South Asia*, Permanent Black, New Delhi.

Rodinson, Maxime (1980), *Marxism and the Muslim World*, Orient Longman Ltd, New Delhi.

Rodrigues, Valerian (1993), 'Making a Tradition Critical—Ambedkar's Reading of Buddhism' in Peter Robb (ed.), *Dalit Movements and the Meanings of Labour in India*, Oxford University Press, New Delhi.

Roy, M.N. (1981), *The Historical Role of Islam*, Ajanta Publications, New Delhi.

————— (1984), *Memoirs*, Ajanta Publications, New Delhi.

Roy, Tapti (1994), *The Politics of a Popular Uprising: Bundelkhand in 1857*, Oxford University Press, New Delhi, Calcutta etc.

Rudolph, Lloyd I. and Susanne Hoeber Rudolph (1967), *The Modernity of Tradition—Political Development in India*, University of Chicago Press, Chicago and London.

Said, Edward (1991), *The World, The Text and The Critic*, Vintage, London.

————— (1994), *Culture and Imperialism*, Vintage, London

Samaddar, Ranabir (1999), *The Marginal Nation—Transborder Migration from Bangladesh to West Bengal*, Sage Publications, New Delhi.

————— (2001), *Biography of the Indian Nation 1947–1997*, Sage Publications, New Delhi.

Sarkar, Sumit (1993), 'Fascism of the Sangh Parivar', *Economic and Political Weekly*, vol. 28, no. 5, 30 January.

————— (1994), 'The Anti-Secularist Critique of Hindutva: Problems of a Shared Discursive Space', *Germinal*, vol. 1.

————— (1996), 'Indian Nationalism and the Politics of Hindutva', in David Ludden (ed.), *Contesting the Nation—Religion, Community and the Politics of Democracy in India*, University of Pennsylvania Press, Philadelphia.

Sarkar, Sumit (1997), *Writing Social History*, Oxford University Press, New Delhi.

Schmitt, Carl (1992), *The Crisis of Parliamentary Democracy*, translated by Ellen Kennedy, MIT Press, Massachusetts and London.

Sengupta, Bhabani (1996), *India—Problems of Governance*, Konark Publishers Pvt. Ltd, Delhi.

Seth, Sanjay (1995), *Marxist Theory and Nationalist Politics—The Case of Colonial India*, Sage Publications, New Delhi.

Sethi, Harsh and Smitu Kothari (1983), *The Non-Party Political Process—Uncertain Alternatives*, Mimeograph, UNRISD/Lokayan, Delhi.

Sethi, Harsh (1993), 'Survival and Democracy: Ecological Struggles in India', in Ponna Wignaraja (ed.), *New Social Movements in the South: Empowering the People*, Vistaar Publications, New Delhi.

Seton-Watson, Hugh (1977), *Nations and States*, Methuen and Co., London.

Sheth, D.L. (1999), 'Secularization of Caste and Making of New Middle Class', *Economic and Political Weekly*, 21–28 August, vol. 34, nos 34 and 35.

Sircar, Ajanta (1999), 'Love in the Time of Liberalization: Qayamat Se Qayamat Tak', *Journal of Arts and Ideas*, nos. 32–3, April, pp. 35–59.

Shakir, Moin (1970), *Khilafat to Partition: A Survey of Major Muslim Trends among Indian Muslims 1919–1947*, Kalamkar Prakashan, New Delhi.

Sharma, K.M. (1980), 'The Assam Question—A Historical Perspective' *Economic and Political Weekly*, vol. XV, no. 31, 2 August 2.

Sheth, D.L. (1999), 'Secularisation of Caste and Making of New Middle Class', *Economic and Political Weekly*, vol. 34, nos. 34 and 35, 21–28 August. Special No. on 'Electoral Politics in India, 1989–99', pp. 2502–10.

Shiva, Vandana (1989), *Staying Alive: Women, Ecology and Survival in India*, Kali for Women, New Delhi.

Singh, Jagpal (1998), 'Ambedkarisation and Assertion of Dalit Identity', *Economic and Political Weekly*, vol. XXXIII, no. 40, 3 October.

Smith, Anthony (1986), *The Ethnic Origins of Nations*, Blackwell, Oxford.

Srilata, K. (1999), 'The Story of the 'Up-Market' Reader' *Femina's* 'New Woman' and the Normative Feminist Subject', *Journal of Arts and Ideas*, nos. 32–3, April, pp. 61–72.

Sternhell, Zeev (1976), 'Fascist Ideology' in Walter Laqueur (ed.), *Fascism: A Reader's Guide*, Wildwood House, London.

Talmon, J.L. (1981), *The Myth of the Nation and the Vision of Revolution*, Seeker and Warburg, London; and University of California Press, Berkeley.

Taussig, Michael (1993), *Mimesis and Alterity*, Routledge, New York and London.

Taylor, Charles (1975), *Hegel*, Cambridge University Press, Great Britain.

——— (1989), *Sources of the Self: The Making of Modern Identity*, Cambridge University Press, Melbourne.

——— (1993), 'Engaged Agency and Background in Heidegger', in Charles B. Guigon (ed.), *The Cambridge Companion to Heidegger*, Cambridge University Press, Cambridge.

Thompson, E.P. (1991), *The Making of the English Working Class*, Penguin Books, England.

Titus, Murray T. (1936), *Islam in India and Pakistan*, YMCA Publishing House, Calcutta.

Training For Development Scholarship Society (TDSS) (1987), *Nationality Question in India*, Pune.

U.M., (1974), 'Assam Set for Confrontation', *Economic and Political Weekly*, vol. XIV, no. 49, 8 December.

Vanaik, Achin (1990), *The Painful Transition—Bourgeois Democracy in India*, Verso, London and New York.

_____ (1997), *Communalism Contested: Religion, Modernity and Secularization*, Vistaar Publications, New Delhi.

van Diepen, Maria (ed.) (1989), *The National Question in South Africa*, Zed Books Ltd, London and New Jersey.

Visvanathan, Shiv (1997), *A Carnival for Science*, Oxford University Press, New Delhi.

Weiner, Myron (1967), 'Segmentation and Political Participation: Kaira District', in *Party Building in a New Nation*, University of Chicago Press, Chicago.

_____ (1978), *Sons of the Soil— Migration and Ethnic Conflict in India*, Princeton University Press, New Jersey.

_____ (1989), *The Indian Paradox—Essays in Indian Politics*, Ashutosh Varshney (ed.), Sage Publications, New Delhi and London.

Wignaraja, Ponna (ed.) (1993), *New Social Movements in the South: Empowering the People*, Vistaar Publications, New Delhi.

Wolpert, Stanley (1996) *Nehru—A Tryst With Destiny*, Oxford University Press, New York.

Yadav, Yogendra (1996), 'Reconfiguration of Indian Politics: State Assembly Elections, 1993–95' *Economic and Political Weekly*, vol XXXI, nos 2 and 3, 13–20 January.

_____ (2000), 'Understanding the Second Democratic Upsurge', in Francine Frankel, Zoya Hasan, Rajeev Bhargava, and Balveer Arora (eds), *Transforming India—Social and Political Dynamics of Democracy*, Oxford University Press, New Delhi.

Zizek, Slavoj (1993) *Tarrying with the Negative*, Duke University Press, Durham.

Index